CLUB at SALTHILL.

Published June 1st 18

ENTITLED

www.penguin.co.uk

Also by Chris Bryant

STAFFORD CRIPPS:
THE FIRST MODERN CHANCELLOR

GLENDA JACKSON:
THE BIOGRAPHY

POSSIBLE DREAMS:
A PERSONAL HISTORY OF THE BRITISH
CHRISTIAN SOCIALISTS

PARLIAMENT: THE BIOGRAPHY
VOLUME I: ANCESTRAL VOICES

PARLIAMENT: THE BIOGRAPHY
VOLUME II: REFORM

ENTITLED

A Critical History of the British Aristocracy

Chris Bryant

Doubleday

LONDON · TORONTO · SYDNEY · AUCKLAND · JOHANNESBURG

TRANSWORLD PUBLISHERS
61–63 Uxbridge Road, London W5 5SA
www.penguin.co.uk

Transworld is part of the Penguin Random House group of companies
whose addresses can be found at global.penguinrandomhouse.com

Penguin
Random House
UK

First published in Great Britain in 2017 by Doubleday
an imprint of Transworld Publishers

ISBN 9780857523167

Typeset in 10.75/15 pt Sabon LT Std by Jouve (UK), Milton Keynes
Printed and bound in Great Britain by Clays Ltd, Bungay, Suffolk

Endpaper illustration: Dinner of the Four in Hand Club at Salthill,
George Cruikshank, 1811. © The Trustees of the British Museum

Penguin Random House is committed to a sustainable
future for our business, our readers and our planet. This book
is made from Forest Stewardship Council® certified paper.

MIX
Paper from
responsible sources
FSC® C018179

1 3 5 7 9 10 8 6 4 2

JACOB

Show the people that our Old Nobility is not noble, that its lands are stolen lands – stolen either by force or fraud; show people that the title-deeds are rapine, murder, massacre, cheating, or court harlotry; dissolve the halo of divinity that surrounds the hereditary title; let the people clearly understand that our present House of Lords is composed largely of descendants of successful pirates and rogues; do these things and you shatter the Romance that keeps the nation numb and spellbound while privilege picks its pocket.

Tom Johnston, *Our Scots Noble Families*, 1909

Contents

ACKNOWLEDGEMENTS

I AM INDEBTED TO many people for their assistance and advice in bringing this book to fruition. My agent Jim Gill has regularly steered me in a wiser direction; my editor, Doug Young, was supportive from the beginning, was patient when nothing seemed to be forthcoming and made excellent suggestions when I submitted my first draft; Gillian Somerscales tidied up my typos and my prose with elegant fastidiousness; and Amanda Russell has researched the illustrations.

It has only been possible to cover such a large period thanks to the scholarship of many others who have gone before. I would particularly like to mention the work of David Cannadine, David Crouch, Peter Mandler, Helen Cam and Rosemary Baird, who in their specialist periods have dug deep in the archives to haul out gems, and who have inspired many of the ideas behind this book. I am grateful to them, although any mistakes in this book are entirely my own.

I am especially grateful to the libraries and manuscript collections I have consulted, including the British Library, the Bodleian, the Lambeth Palace library and the collections at King's College London and Southampton University. The staff at the House of Commons Library have always been immensely helpful, especially Phillip Arnold and Greg Howard.

I am very grateful to my friends, family, colleagues and staff who have listened to me while I have attempted to regale them with tales of ancient aristocratic misdemeanours or noble derring-do – and have put up with me when I have disappeared into a library or a book for whole weekends, and when I have stayed up far too late or got up far too early to try to hone another chapter.

ACKNOWLEDGEMENTS

Above all, the people of the Rhondda, which was mined, developed and exploited by the marquess of Bute, whose title lives on in street names in Treorchy and in Treherbert, have shown me the greatest forbearance. I have endeavoured faithfully to be their voice since 2001 and will ever be in their debt. I hope they will find an echo of their own distrust of aristocratic privilege and entitlement in these pages.

Porth, the Rhondda, June 2017

Henry de la Poer Beresford inherited the estates and title of 3rd marquess of Waterford in 1826. Spurred on by his sense of entitlement and large amounts of alcohol, he was a persistent prankster, sportsman and vandal whose antics acquired him a reputation as 'that turbulent piece of aristocracy' and 'the mad marquess'. In 1841 Punch satirized him as the leader of the 'Knocker Boys', who has spent a drunken evening stealing door-knockers in one of many bouts of aristocratic 'disorderism' of which the Bullingdon Club would have been proud.

INTRODUCTION

IT WAS THREE O'CLOCK in the morning of Thursday, 6 April 1837 when Henry Beresford, the 3rd marquess of Waterford (25), and John Cust, Viscount Alford (24), turned up with a band of aristocratic friends at the Thorpe End tollgate in Melton Mowbray after a heavy night's wining and dining at Croxton Park races. They were in a boisterous, disdainful mood. Having first boarded up the tollgate with the keeper locked inside, they stormed through the town, overturning a caravan in which people were sleeping, vandalizing the post office, demolishing flowerpots, threatening the police with murder, and daubing doors, shutters, signs and police constables with red paint. The event gave us the phrase 'painting the town red'.

Plenty of contemporaries were not impressed. The *Stamford Mercury* voiced its contempt for the marauders in pointed sarcasm:

> On being obstructed in their career of mischief by the watchmen, the blood of the Beresfords rises, and the Noble Marquis as *nobly* offers to fight them all! and then (oh *Most Noble*, most magnanimous deed!) knocks down and tramples upon a poor *old* man of 60! vows he'll murder the bridewell-keeper for refusing to set at liberty a prisoner, one of his fellow-rioters; and at length succeeds in releasing him and carrying him away in triumph on his back – a feat we have no doubt it would be his highest ambition to have recorded in the history of the Noble House of Beresford, and emblazoned on its shield.[1]

True, Beresford – a regular duellist, prankster and gambler – paid for the damage, and he and his roistering friends were fined a hundred pounds each for common assault, But such was their sense of entitlement that they imperiously demanded local editors expunge the story from their newspapers; and such was the misplaced sense of deference to the nobility that several editors did as they were asked.

Beresford's antics were by no means the worst aristocratic misdemeanours in British history – other members of the nobility got away with rape, fraud, deception and murder – but his arrogance has been the default attitude of countless numbers of the well-bred and well-heeled through the ages, right up to the members of the Bullingdon Club who did ten thousand pounds' worth of damage to an Oxfordshire pub in 2004. At the heart of their self-indulgent destructiveness lay their sense of entitlement. They knew they could wreak mayhem because nobody would dare question them – and anyway, they could easily afford to pay for the damage.

This book is an attempt to expose and explain that sense of entitlement; that conviction, running through the ages, held by a tiny proportion of society that they have an inherent right to rule, to do what they will, to lord it over others and to receive special treatment and privileges.

When I started my research I, perhaps in common with the many thousands who visit Chatsworth House and Blenheim Palace every year, found the aristocracy of past centuries fascinating. I was intrigued by their luxurious and eventful lives – they were, after all, the celebrities and political leaders of their day – and I appreciated the stately homes they built and the art they collected. I admired several of them, too, for their wit, their bravery and their political courage. Yet as I delved into the archives and history books I found a very different aspect to Britain's noble families. Behind the architraves and pilasters lay a legacy of theft, violence and unrepentant greed. Four key themes emerged.

1. An insatiable craving for wealth and property

In every generation the aristocracy sought to enrich themselves way beyond their personal needs. Anglo-Saxon warriors and Norman invaders demanded vast tracts of lands in reward for their valour in battle. Tudor and Stuart lords sought royal monopolies and exclusive patents to enable them to exploit trade and commerce, enclosed common land for their personal use, and gorged themselves on the profits of land stolen from the church. Eighteenth-century magnates grew wealthy on sinecures, pensions and ministerial office, and their successors ruthlessly exploited their broad acres with little consideration for those who tenanted their land or worked in their mines. When their British estates did not bring in enough profit, they turned their acquisitive eyes abroad, creating and investing heavily in the bloody triangular trade of goods and slaves between Britain, west Africa and the Caribbean, the proceeds of which helped found many of Britain's proudest houses. Today's aristocrats still figure prominently in every list of Britain's richest people, possessing some of the largest estates and the most profitable real estate in the world, and employing the most expensive lawyers to create complex legal arrangements to enable them to avoid inheritance and other taxes while raking in millions of pounds in agricultural subsidies.

The result of all these centuries of self-seeking endeavour has been a phenomenal accretion of land and money in the hands of a tiny number of families. In 1872 twelve peers owned more than four million acres, twenty-nine luxuriated in an annual income from land of more than £75,000, the dukes of Westminster, Buccleuch, Bedford, Devonshire and Northumberland all had incomes of more than £175,000, and the duke and duchess of Sutherland headed the list of landowners, their 1,358,545 acres earning them the nickname 'leviathans of wealth'. Remarkably, despite a century of stories of ducal poverty and stately-home demolitions, a third of Britain's land still belongs to the aristocracy and the Country Land and Business Association's 36,000 members own half the rural land in the country; nearly half of Scotland remains in the hands of 432 private individuals and companies, and more than a quarter of all Scottish estates larger than 5,000 acres are held by aristocratic families.

2. The politics of jealousy

While envy proved a potent force in establishing and endowing many noble houses, jealousy played an equally powerful role in preserving and sustaining them, as a small cadre of families desperately clung to their riches, position and power and took great umbrage when anyone attempted to scale the walls of the peerage to gain admittance. Those in possession of rank and status argued endlessly about rules of precedence – who sat or processed closest to the king – and guarded their rights and privileges with a self-protective ferocity. Medieval exactions such as the relief payable on inheriting a title – an ancient form of death duty – infuriated them. So did the habit of the Stuart kings of awarding new titles to royal favourites and political supporters. Whenever their private interests were affected, they claimed the constitution was at stake, and were quite prepared to bring the nation to civil war in their defence. Well into the twentieth century they, their families and their clients dominated both houses of parliament, drafting laws that defended their financial interests and opposing every step in the long and uneven march towards democracy and equality.

The aristocratic politics of jealousy also directed internal family affairs. Lest the great households' inheritances be frittered away or atomized, they insisted that each pass in its entirety to the eldest son, thereby constantly concentrating more and more wealth in the hands of a few. And lest their bloodlines be tainted by commoners, they arranged matches so that nobody should marry outside their tight circle – unless snobbery was trumped by greed, in a peculiar form of aristocratic pragmatism that saw impecunious noble households happily admitting wealthy but common heiresses to their ranks when their stocks were running low. So when the news broke that Lord Lincoln, the heir to the duke of Newcastle, was to marry Henrietta Hope, the heiress to a banking fortune, in 1866, Lord Stanley commented that while Henrietta was 'illegitimate but pretty' and her father was 'ugly', since the latter was paying off Lincoln's debts and 'starting him fresh on the Turf', and she came with a big house in Piccadilly and all her father's fortune, 'it [was] a great thing for the Dukedom of Newcastle and will put it on its legs again'.[2] William, 6th Baron Monson, was even more open about marital ambitions, repeatedly urging his son 'to find a girl with a fortune to rescue the house of Monson from its predicaments' and admitting: 'I should be very sorry for you to marry for money but a nice rich wife would not be bad.'[3]

3. Pride

At the very heart of the idea of 'aristocracy', which directly translated from its Greek origins means 'rule by the best', lies an assertion that true quality is inherited only through the male bloodline, and that power and prestige should be passed down from father to son in perpetuity. It was an argument that was still being articulated by the supremely arrogant and irrationally vain David Freeman-Mitford, 2nd Baron Redesdale, who told the House of Lords in 1934 that

> a man who has spent all his life in politics and public affairs is more likely to have a son capable of following in his footsteps in that particular line, than a man who has never paid any attention to either, especially when that son has been brought up in the atmosphere of public work, and has always been aware that the day would come when he would have to bear his part as a duty.[4]

That the British aristocracy lasted as the dominant political force in the country well into the twentieth century – and that ninety-two hereditary peers still sit in our legislature – is in no small measure thanks to the fierce determination with which successive generations of the nobility have fenced themselves off. From the very earliest times, families who thought themselves above the common cry sought means of asserting their exclusivity. They spoke of noble blood. They sent their sons to the same schools and colleges, joined the same regiments and whiled away the hours gambling at the same clubs, chasing foxes in the same hunts and racing at the same courses. They established rituals that celebrated their distinctiveness and drew up family trees that 'proved' (often falsely) their ancient honour. They claimed to live by a special code of noble honour, based on ancient chivalry, that led to endless unnecessary duels – and when their central role in the political life of the nation was challenged, they attempted to buff up their credentials with an appeal to the age of chivalry and *noblesse oblige*.

Above all, established families with long pedigrees haughtily disdained anything that smacked of new money. When Robert Spencer, whose peerage dated from 1603, was addressing the Lords in 1621, Thomas Howard, who was immensely proud of being the 21st earl of Arundel (a title that went back to 1267), cut Spencer short, saying: 'My Lord, when these things you speak of were doing, your ancestors were keeping sheep.' Not to be outdone, Spencer instantly replied: 'When my ancestors, as you say, were keeping sheep, your ancestors were plotting treason!'[5] It was a fair riposte, as Howard's father had been attainted and executed in 1589; but it did nothing to puncture this attitude of disdain for people with newer titles or no title, which persisted through the centuries. The incongruity of such arrogance is striking. As the *Spectator* put it in 1831: 'It is remarkable, that so many of the highest rank of nobility, in so moral a country as England, should be the produce [*sic*] of concubinage.'[6] Even so, the fact that the dukes of Beaufort, Grafton, Richmond and St Albans all stem from illegitimate births never hindered the holders of those titles from proudly affirming their own ancient nobility. Nor did they observe the laws on sexual morality that they were so keen to enforce for commoners. Among many other high-born philanderers, the 3rd marquess of Winchester had four natural sons and secured knighthoods for them all; the 5th duke of Devonshire had two children by his wife Georgiana's confidante Elizabeth Foster, the daughter of the earl of Bristol, and another child by another mistress; the said Georgiana, daughter of the Earl Spencer, had a natural daughter by Charles, later Earl Grey; and the twice Prime Minister the 3rd duke of Grafton had a very public affair with the courtesan Nancy Parsons while his duchess became pregnant by the earl of Upper Ossory.

4. Ostentatious display

For the aristocracy, it was never enough to be wealthy; there was a constant pressing need to be *seen* to be wealthy. The earl of Suffolk built Audley End on a prodigious scale before being sacked as Lord Treasurer for embezzlement in 1619, while the earl of Arundel and the duke of Buckingham competed to amass the greatest collection of art in their respective palaces on the Strand. The duke of Beaufort had twelve resplendent residences in the 1670s; the duke of Chandos spent so much building Cannons near Little Stanmore in Middlesex and filling it with expensive bric-a-brac that his son had to sell it in a twelve-day demolition sale in 1747; and later in the eighteenth century the marquess of

Rockingham deliberately reconstructed his family home at Wentworth-Woodhouse so that its façade was the longest in Europe. Nor was this preoccupation confined to their lifetimes: so concerned were they about their legacy that they paid artists to portray them in their best finery, they spent inordinate sums creating vast family mausolea, and they littered the parish churches and cathedrals of the land with their individual funerary monuments.

Celebrations for the coming of age of a son and heir could be especially grand and designed to impress. When the earl of Berkeley's first son was born in 1786, a vast cask of ale was brewed; it was duly drunk twenty-one years later, along with two twenty-gallon bowls of punch. The 5th duke of Rutland's coming of age was celebrated in 1799 at a cost of ten thousand pounds (roughly a million in 2017), including 120 guineas for sixty pineapples. Even in August 1939, with Europe on the verge of war, the duke of Devonshire held an extravagant two-day party at Chatsworth for his son and heir, the marquess of Hartington, who had turned twenty-one the previous December; thousands of people came, and by the end of the evening it was said that the duchess's arm was in a sling from too much hand-shaking.

Not all such ostentatious expenditure had the desired effect. When Archibald Montgomerie, the 13th earl of Eglinton, 14th Lord Montgomerie, Baron Ardrossan and chief of the clan Montgomery, organized a medieval tournament at his castle in Ayrshire in 1839, tens of thousands of spectators turned up to see dozens of his noble friends joust as part of his attempt to revitalize the art of chivalry, but the event was a disaster: heavy rain turned the tiltyard into a pond, most of the public were stranded in the grounds, and although the cast list was impressive, with twenty-four British peers in attendance, spectators were disappointed that the jousting was not violent enough. Indeed, the only hint of danger came with the contest between the Knight of the Black Lion (the Viscount Alford) and the Knight of the Dragon (the marquess of Waterford), as the two men set to with abandon as if settling a personal score and had to be dragged apart. The would-be chivalric hero Eglinton had spent most of his family fortune on a ludicrous washout.

In the middle ages, the aristocratic obsession with displays of wealth and status led them to prohibit the lower orders from wearing rich fabrics such as ermine, satin and silk, while drawing up complex and beautiful coats of arms for themselves and requiring their retainers and servants to wear their special colours. Even in the twentieth century their descendants continued to assert their privileged place at the pinnacle of society, proudly having their photographs taken in robes of state, coronets, tiaras and jewels for Edward VII's coronation in 1902. The occasion brought forth some notably tortuous special pleading. Just weeks before the coronation, *Tatler* had defended the fact that the members of the Goldsmiths' Company had been openly advertising their wares on the grounds that 'now that some of our oldest and best families are very poor, while millionaires are running up the prices of everything, the Goldsmiths have every justification for announcing that they can manufacture the necessary coronets at moderate prices'.[7] On the day itself, the holder of one of the oldest English titles, Daisy Brooke, countess of Warwick, appeared without any diamonds; so *Tatler* generously laid emphasis on 'the absolute perfection of her beauty'.* There must have been much sniggering at this, for Daisy had inherited a fortune from her grandfather and lost it thanks to an extravagant lifestyle. Yet on coronation day in 1902 she made all the peeresses in their diamonds and pearls feel 'as if we were a lot of American or South African millionairesses vying with each other in the weight of our money-bags'.[8] In the ultimate irony, people who had only escaped vulgarity by virtue of an ancestor's acquisition of a fortune sneered at new money.

✠

Two comments about terms are necessary. First, British aristocratic titles provide many challenges. One person can hold several titles simultaneously. Edward Fitzalan-Howard, for instance, is primarily known as the 18th duke of Norfolk, but he is also the 36th earl of Arundel, the 19th earl of Surrey and the 26th Baron Maltravers, and he holds six other titles. One person can also rise through the ranks, holding

*Daisy (she of the song 'Daisy, Daisy, give me your answer do') was one of Edward's former lovers, and so indiscreet in her several affairs that she was nicknamed 'the babbling Brooke'.

several titles in succession. Thus, in the seventeenth century, George Villiers became in turn (and in very short order) Baron Whaddon, Viscount Villiers, earl of Coventry and duke of Buckingham. I have done my best to make such preferments clear, without overloading the text with too many titles. A further complication relates to so-called 'courtesy titles', which come into play through the provision that the heir apparent to a higher title such as duke, marquess or earl may use one of the incumbent's lesser or subsidiary titles 'by courtesy'. Thus the duke of Norfolk's eldest son and heir, Henry, is styled the earl of Arundel, the duke of Devonshire's heir is referred to as the marquess of Hartington and the marquess of Salisbury's heir is known as Viscount Cranborne. None of these entitles the user to a seat in the House of Lords, although several sons and heirs have been summoned to the Lords by a 'writ of acceleration' in the name of the family's original peerage.* In addition, the younger sons of dukes and marquesses are granted the courtesy title of 'the Lord', as in the Lord Randolph Churchill, younger son of the duke of Marlborough; the daughters of dukes, marquesses and earls are titled 'the Lady', as in the Lady Diana Spencer, daughter of the Earl Spencer; and the younger children of earls and the children of viscounts and barons are styled 'the Honourable'. And of course the term 'lord' is often used generically for any member of the peerage. So it is easy to get confused. I have attempted throughout to make these distinctions as clear as possible, occasionally omitting courtesy titles to this end. In addition, several historic titles have become extinct when the family line has died out and have then been re-created or granted to a new family. The dukedom of Bedford, for example, was created six times, and as a result, formally speaking, William Russell was the first duke of Bedford 'in the sixth creation'; but I have omitted such references as unnecessarily complex. In most cases, however, I have included the number of the title (e.g. Andrew Russell, 15th duke of Bedford) except where the individual is the first to hold the title (e.g. William Russell, duke of Bedford). I have not resorted to the practice common among some modern aristocrats of

*This and other specialist terms are explained in more detail in the glossary at the end of the book.

referring to a man by his Christian name and toponymic (e.g. Andrew Bedford).

Second, although many members of the landed gentry were also wealthy and powerful, I have defined the 'aristocracy' as those families with hereditary titles conferring a seat in the House of Lords. This means that although knights and baronets (a hereditary form of knight) were often wealthy and had lengthy landowning pedigrees, I have not included them in the purview of this book except where they acquired peerages.

✠

Narcissism and inbreeding led British aristocrats to believe themselves entitled to their wealth, status and power. Their nobility was not earned, but intrinsic, inherited, in their blood.

Yet their defining feature was not a noble aspiration to serve the common weal but a desperate desire for self-advancement. They stole land under the pretence of piety in the early middle ages, they seized it by conquest, they expropriated it from the monasteries and they enclosed it for their private use under the pretence of efficiency. They grasped wealth, corruptly carved out their niche at the pinnacle of society and held on to it with a vice-like grip. They endlessly reinforced their own status and enforced deference on others through ostentatiously exorbitant expenditure on palaces, clothing and jewellery. They laid down a strict set of rules for the rest of society, but lived by a different standard. Obsessed with precedence and hierarchy, they granted themselves special privileges, they sneered at those without money or title and they established a complete dominance of the political system, which they used to perpetuate their mining, sporting and financial interests. For much of their history they were a perpetual grievance machine, standing on their dignity, asserting their private rights and privileges, and instigating unnecessary wars at home and abroad.

Such was their sense of entitlement that they believed – and persuaded others to believe – that a hierarchical society with them placed firmly and unassailably at the top was the natural order of things. Even to suggest otherwise, they implied, was to shake the foundations of morality.

They were shocked and angered when others sought to deprive or degrade them. They clung tenaciously to their position. They developed ever more specious arguments to defend their privileges. They eulogized themselves and built great temples to their greatness. They jealously guarded access to their hallowed halls. And when democracy finally and rudely shunted them aside, they found new means of preserving their extravagant riches without the tedium of pretending they sought the common interest. Far from dying away, they remain very much alive.

The early aristocracy was forged in battle, as successive waves of invading warriors sought to conquer the native kings and princes. Here Edmund Ironside (left) does battle with the Danish King Cnut at the battle of Assandun in 1016. For a warrior aspiring to serve royalty, guile and rapacious greed were personal traits just as important as valour or military prowess.

CHAPTER 1

NOT OF SOME MEANER SORT, BUT OF SOME QUALITY

C OULD YOU SPOT AN ARISTOCRAT even if he were pretending to be of humble stock?

The Venerable Bede thought so, sitting in his monk's cell in Jarrow in 731. He told the story of the bloody battle of the Trent, in which King Æthelred of Mercia took on the might of Northumbria under King Ecgfrith in 679. Æthelred won the day but was persuaded to pay compensation for the death in battle of Ecgfrith's young brother Ælfwine, in order to prevent a bout of mutual noble blood-letting. One of Ælfwine's warriors, an unmarried noble called Imma, was seriously wounded, and lay unconscious amid the bodies of his dead comrades through the night. Regaining consciousness the next morning, he fled the field. The Mercians caught him and took him before one of Æthelred's noble commanders, who demanded to know his name. Afraid to own up to his noble status, which would almost certainly mean he would be killed in revenge for the many Mercian nobles who had been slain, Imma lied, claiming that he was a poor, married peasant. Taking him at his word, the Mercian commander had Imma's wounds dressed and kept him as a prisoner. His captors soon had doubts, though. As Bede put it: 'Those who attentively observed him, by his countenance, habit, and discourse, took notice that he was not of the meaner sort as he had said but of some quality.'[1] Imma was summoned back before the commander, who promised that he would come to no harm if he confessed. When Imma revealed his real identity, the Mercian honoured his pledge and, instead of putting him to the sword, sold him into slavery.

Bede's purpose in telling the story was to show the power of prayer: for, he said, no matter how many times the Mercians bound Imma, his chains miraculously fell off at the precise moment when, unbeknown to him, his brother Tunna was saying mass on his behalf. Yet the true essence of the tale is even more extraordinary: that, as early as the seventh century, there was a concept abroad in Britain of indelible nobility, which would always shine through any attempt at disguise. It brought privileges and responsibilities, and it could never be hidden. Quality will show. Blood will out.

This early aristocracy was a warrior class, because Britain in the first millennium was a scene of constant conflict. For much of the period the land was divided between the warring kingdoms of Northumbria, Mercia, Kent, East Anglia, Wessex, Sussex and Essex. In the north, the Gaelic-speakers of the Dal Riata, the Britons of Alt Clut and the lowland kingdom of Bernicia did battle for centuries before the kingdoms of Alba and Scotia were formed. In the west, a myriad Brythonic-speaking kingdoms came and went. Some of these found their way into the history books but the majority disappeared from view, their kings slain, their people subjugated, their history forgotten.

A warrior class was needed to repel marauders, too, as Britain was highly susceptible to invasion. First came the Romans, whose reign dwindled into nothingness in the fifth century; soon thereafter the Germanic Angles and Saxons used Britain's wide, navigable estuaries and rivers to steal deep into the hinterland. Viking raiders from Norway, Sweden and Denmark made the same trip, seizing control of swathes of Britain, establishing their cultures and exacting heavy compensation in the form of Danegeld.

With kingdoms and lands under constant threat of seizure by force, invaded, invaders and settlers alike were on near-constant war footing. In these conditions, the people looked for their leaders to successful military commanders who could protect them. Martial prowess was prized above all other qualities of leadership, weaponry was counted as a man's most valued possession, and the ability to inspire troops, master a horse, trick an opponent and/or deal a mortal blow to the enemy was seen as central to a man's quality. As one poet put it: 'Power goes with pride, bold men with brave ones: both must be quick to make war.'[2] Kings and provincial leaders trained loyal retainers in warfare and did battle in their midst, creating a bond of mutual assurance between the leader and his chosen followers, who travelled with him, slept in his hall, ate and drank at his expense and were prepared to die with him on the battlefield. Bede gives a glimpse of such a band of noble warriors in a poetic passage that compares the mutability of life to the swift flight of a sparrow 'through the house wherein you sit at supper in winter, with your ealdormen and thegns, while the fire blazes in the midst, and the hall is warmed, but the wintry storms of rain or snow are raging abroad'.[3]

The harsh reality of this warfare comes into focus in the fragment of historical poem known as *The Battle of Maldon*. It tells of the death in 991 of the nobleman Byrhtnoth of Essex, who stood in the midst of his 'hearth troop, who had all his trust', and prepared them for battle with stirring words. When the Danish invader, Olaf, offered the English their lives in exchange for gold, Byrhtnoth was defiant, shouting that his men 'will give you spears for their tribute, / Poisoned points and ancient swords'.[4] Inexplicably, either out of pride or from an excess of magnanimity, Byrhtnoth then allowed Olaf to cross a narrow causeway so as to have enough room for a battle. This proved a disastrous mistake: Olaf seized the initiative, Byrhtnoth's nephew, Wulfmær, was hacked down in a single full shoulder force blow and some of Byrhtnoth's troops fled. When Byrhtnoth himself was hit, he laughed and gave thanks to God, but when a second soldier charged at him, determined to steal his gold trappings and ornamental sword, his arm suddenly collapsed by his side and he was hacked to death. All was lost; but such was the bond of honour that his retainer Ælfwine encouraged the troops to continue fighting, reminding them of all the bold things they had said when they were drinking mead in Byrhtnoth's hall. Two more of Byrhtnoth's followers spoke up. Leofsunu declared that he would not go 'lordless' on a homeward journey, and Byrhtnoth's old retainer Byrhtwold thrust his shield into the air and proudly bellowed out: 'I am advanced in years. I do not desire to be taken away. / By that favourite of men I intend to lie.'[5]

Such faithfulness unto death was central to this military code and to a man's understanding of his self-worth. According to one of the earliest historical works on the history of Scotland, the *Chronicle of the Kings of Alba*, the battle of Brunanburh (*c.*937) against the English King Æthelstan saw similar loyalty unto death as Dubacan, son of Indrechtach, mormaer of Angus, died alongside his lord, the son of his vanquished King Constantine II. The king was bound to his men because, in words from another poem *Beowulf*, death was 'better for every earl than an existence of disgrace'.[6] The bond was mutual. When Byrhtnoth was told by the monks of Ramsey Abbey that they could feed only him and seven of his men, not his whole entourage, he said that as he had no desire to fight without them all he would not dine without them all either – and passed on to the abbey at Ely. So acutely felt was this bond that from the time of King Æthelstan (924–39) it was considered inconceivable that any freeman should live without a lord, and lordlessness itself was outlawed.

When victory came or peace was negotiated, these warriors returned to their homelands, their wives and their families, but the honour of having been a military companion to the king gave them a special cachet – and with that came a much-coveted formal title. In Old English, especially between about 650 and 750, they were called 'gesiths', meaning companions. According to the laws of Ine, king of Wessex (688–726), for instance, gesiths were responsible for the good conduct of their households; they had to attend the call to arms to gather the king's militia (the fyrd) or forfeit their land and pay a fine of 120 shillings; they had to keep a reeve (a form of early magistrate), a smith and a child's nurse, and protect foreigners who had no family. Although many were single and in almost permanent attendance on the king or some other great person, they could marry, hold lands, build churches, keep attendants and provide sanctuary. There was a hierarchy among them, too. The killing of a gesith who held land incurred a wergild (or man-price) of 1,200 shillings, while a gesith with no land was worth 600 shillings and the family of a mere ceorl or freeman was entitled to just 200 shillings. Fashions in rank and terminology, as in much else, changed, and between the eighth and eleventh centuries such men were more commonly referred to as 'thegns' (a title also later adopted in Scotland with the alternative spelling 'thane', although there it carried different status and responsibilities). Yet the law of wergild continued to set them apart from freemen as 'twelve hundred men' rather than 'two hundred men', and an early form of death duty required a thegn to surrender a heriot, his 'war gear', to his lord or to the king on his death. Under the Danish invader King Cnut, this consisted in Wessex of a horse, its trappings and the thegn's personal weapons – a clear indication that above all else a thegn, like a gesith, was a warrior.

In these early days, the noble rank of thegn was open to newcomers who proved their worth or wormed their way into royal affections. It was assumed that military companions would be rewarded for their bravery, loyalty and prowess – and ambition was to be praised. So, in the Old English epic *Beowulf*, when the eponymous hero returned to his lord and kinsman, Hygelac, he received large estates, a princely stool in Hygelac's hall and a sword as a symbol of his new authority. Another warrior, Shield Sheafson, is described as progressing as far as the throne, thanks entirely to his military worth:

> *A foundling to start with, he would flourish later on*
> *As his powers waxed and his worth was proved*
> *In the end each clan on the outlying coast*
> *Beyond the whale-road had to yield to him*
> *And begin to pay tribute. That was one good king.*

The early eleventh-century author of the *Geþyncđo* (Gethinktho or 'Dignities'), who was probably Wulfstan II, Æthelred's archbishop of York, emphasized another key characteristic of this early nobility. The concept of thegnhood was intrinsically linked with landed wealth. In his words, 'if a ceorl thrived, that he possessed fully five hides* of his own land, church and kitchen, bell-house and "burh"-gate-seat† and special duty in the king's hall, then was he henceforth of thegn-right worthy'.[7] Land and title were indivisible, and noble jealousy ensured that the social divide thus created was well policed. Clause 10 of the ninth-century list of wergilds, the *Nordleoda Laga*, made it clear that even if a

---

*A hide was the amount of land considered necessary to provision a free family – roughly 120 acres.

†A seat at the town gate where a court was held to try cases between tenants.

man had a burnie (shirt of mail), a helmet and a gold-adorned sword, he was still a ceorl if he did not possess five hides of land. What was more, once attained, the status of thegnhood would endure for the life of the king who conferred it: an early ordinance of King Edgar the Peaceful (959–75) guaranteed that his thegns would keep their rank as long as he lived, just as they had done in his father Edmund's lifetime,[8] and successor kings, including the conquerors Cnut and William, reaffirmed the guarantee. The title could even last beyond the death of the holder, for if the son of a thegn held the same lands as his father then he too would be a thegn – and after a couple of generations thegnhood would be a permanent feature of the family tree, even if, as the Domesday Book suggests, the property qualification were no longer met. In other words, a warrior who had been awarded land as the spoils of war would be officially recognized as a noble and his nobility would pass to his sons and his grandsons. The landed hereditary nobility was born.

Not all thegns were equal, though. Most owed their immediate allegiance to a local lord rather than a king, so the 'king's thegns' were a class apart, enjoying special privileges. According to the laws of King Wihtraed of Kent (c.690–725), a king's thegn could acquit himself of an allegation on the basis of his own oath alone; conversely, under the peace treaty of 878 between Alfred of Wessex and the Viking Guthrum, a king's thegn required the support of twelve other king's thegns to clear himself of 'man-slaying', while a lesser man could do so with eleven of his equals and just one thegn. Under King Æthelred (968–1016), the twelve 'senior thegns' in the local hundred or wapentake* played a role in criminal prosecutions, and under Cnut the family of a king's thegn was expected to render a heriot or duty on his death of four horses (two of them saddled), two swords, four spears, four shields, a helmet, a coat of mail and a large payment in gold – considerably more than that expected of a simple thegn.

There was another distinction. As kingdoms grew and amalgamated, the geography of the realm required another rank of men charged with

---

*Several different titles of unknown etymology were used to denote military and judicial subdivisions of shires. In many shires they were 'hundreds', in Sussex they were 'rapes', in Kent 'lathes', in the north and the midlands 'wapentakes'.

substantial regional powers. These vicegerents, variously entitled eorl, ealdorman or earl, might have authority in a single shire or a whole region; but while their geographical scope varied, their role was consistent. They were the highest secular authority below the king in the shire or region to which they were appointed. They had responsibility for raising troops for the fyrd or royal expeditionary army, for maintaining defensive fortifications and for collecting taxes and duties; and, alongside the local bishop, they presided over the twice-yearly shire courts. In exchange they took a cut from fines collected within their territory, keeping every third penny as their very lucrative legal due (a perquisite that was to last for centuries).

The north of Britain had a similar system. No books of early medieval Scottish laws survive, but the twelfth-century additions to the tenth-century Latin Gospel Book known as the *Book of Deer* suggest that when St Columba came from Iona to Aberdour in the sixth century he was greeted by Bede the Pict, the 'mormaer of Buchan', who granted him the monastery 'in freedom till Doomsday'.[9] This title of 'mormaer' (meaning great steward) may be an anachronism, as Bede seems to have been an under-king,* but by the eleventh century several hereditary Scottish mormaerdoms had been established and the kingdom of Alba, which lasted from 900 to 1286, was said to have seven mormaerdoms for seven brothers, the earliest being Oengus (Angus). At various times Scottish kings appointed mormaers of Atholl, Buchan, Carrick, Lennox, Mar, Menteith, Ross and Moray; the last of these proved particularly bloody during the two centuries or so during which Moray was ruled by a Gaelic-speaking dynasty. In 1020 Findlaech, the son of Mormaer Ruaidri of Moray, was killed by his nephews. Twelve years later Macbeth killed his cousin, Mormaer Gilla Comgain, slaughtered fifty of his men, assumed the mormaerdom, married his opponent's widow Gruoch – and in 1040 defeated Duncan I to seize the Scottish crown. Macbeth was killed in 1057 and was briefly succeeded by his stepson Lulach, who lasted a single year before being killed and succeeded by his own son as Mormaer Mael Snechtai. In 1130 the last mormaer of Moray, Lulach's

---

*Also known as 'sub-king' (*subregulus*).

grandson Angus, was killed in battle by Robert the Bruce. In an indirect line the mormaers of Moray would become the earls of Sutherland and of Atholl. Like English ealdormen, mormaers derived their provincial authority, which included the third penny, from the king, but they also held land in their own right – as did Scottish thanes such as Macbeth, thane of Glamis.

An English king's primary purpose in appointing ealdormen was to protect national security. Sometimes this meant appointing a newly subjugated king as ealdorman of his former realm, as when King Sigered of Essex (798–812), who had previously acted as a witness for charters for King Cenewuf of Mercia as *rex* or *subregulus* (king or under-king), was downgraded to *dux*. Elsewhere it meant deploying loyal acolytes as regional commanders and viceroys. So, when Alfred of Wessex saw off the Danish invaders in the mid-ninth century, he appointed one ealdorman for each shire in Wessex, and two for the easily invaded shire of Kent. When his ealdorman for Wiltshire, Wulfhere, 'deserted without permission . . . in spite of the oath that he had sworn to the king and all his leading men',[10] Alfred replaced him with a more reliable ally, Æthelstan, and in the vulnerable shires of Devon and Somerset he appointed two proven military compatriots. The strategy worked. The Devon ealdorman Odda proved his worth by fighting off the Viking siege of Cynwit in 878, and in Somerset Æthelnoth led the Anglo-Saxon army at Buttington in 893 and on the mission to Northumbria the following year.

Far from receiving an honour they could be sure of passing on, ealdormen were appointed at the king's pleasure, and if the king changed or if he changed his mind, the noble could be removed and the post abolished. The poem 'The Death of Edgar', for instance, which forms part of the *Anglo-Saxon Chronicle*, relates that in 975 Ealdorman Oslac, who was probably the first ealdorman for York, 'was driven from the country [by the king], over the tossing waves, the gannets' bath, the tumult of the waters, the homeland of the whale; a grey-haired man, wise and skilled in speech, he was bereft of his lands'.[11] So too in 1002 Leofsige, ealdorman of the East Saxons, was banished for killing a royal high-reeve or senior magistrate called Ælfric in his own house and without warning, and his sister Æthelflæd forfeited her land at Fen

Stanton and Hilton in Huntingdonshire for harbouring him as a fugitive. A fall from royal favour could bring harsh retribution. In 993 King Æthelred ordered that Ealdorman Ælfric's son Ælfgar be blinded, in 1001 Cnut had all his noble hostages blinded when he was forced out of England, and in 1005 it was the turn of Ealdorman Ælfhelm's sons Wulfheah and Ufegeat to be mutilated, again on the orders of Æthelred.

The post of ealdorman may have been insecure, but once elevated, incumbents fought jealously to protect their status and authority. This was particularly difficult when there was a contested royal succession or a hostile invasion. Then the wealthy ealdormen, each with a host of loyal retainers at his disposal, elbowed their way into the dispute, picking sides and changing their allegiance as they saw which way the wind was blowing. These contests were frequent, as there was no assumption in Anglo-Saxon law or custom that the eldest son would inherit. A younger son by a second or third wife might have a doughty dowager queen to fight his cause. An elder son might have his legitimacy or his ability questioned. Collateral wings of the royal family might lay rival claims. And in the whirl of indecision the ealdormen and thegns regularly threw their weight about.

Just such a situation arose when King Eadred died in 946, leaving two nephews, Eadwig and the infant Edgar, as potential heirs. The former was initially made king, but a pro-Edgar faction developed around disaffected aristocrats and churchmen that led to a conclave of thegns from the old kingdoms of Mercia and Northumbria; and in 957 the kingdom was divided, with Edgar taking all his elder brother's lands north of the Thames before reuniting the kingdom on Eadwig's death two years later. Much the same thing happened when Edgar died in 975, leaving two sons: one aged six or seven called Æthelred, who was the undisputed son of the dowager Queen Ælfgifu; and his elder half-brother Edward, whose mother Æthelflæd's marital status was hotly disputed. Edward became king, but the nobles and churchmen were divided and resentments about the old king resurfaced. In the ensuing rows several ealdormen were ranged against one another and civil war was only narrowly avoided. Recognizing the threat posed by these overmighty lords, Edward removed several rebellious ealdormen, but ultimately to no avail: in 978 he was murdered at Corfe Castle, quite probably at the instigation of his stepmother the dowager queen, who was busily rooting for her own son Æthelred.

Invasion posed the same questions. Whom to support? Whether to keep one's counsel, bide one's time or offer early support for the invader in the hope of rich rewards? The early years of the eleventh century showed how important the loyalty or perfidy of individual ealdormen could be. Northumbria, always vulnerable to invasion by either the Scots or the Danes, had been divided between two ealdormen: Waltheof, who governed the north from his castle at Bamburgh, and Ælfhelm, based in York. When the Scottish King Malcolm II mounted an invasion in 1006, Waltheof was too old to fight, but his son Uhtred the Bold raised an army and repelled the invaders so successfully that he paid the women of Durham to wash the severed heads of captured Scots before hoisting them on the city walls. The English king Æthelred rewarded Uhtred by having Ælfhelm murdered and making Uhtred ealdorman of both Bamburgh and York, thereby uniting the whole of Northumbria under one very wealthy Anglo-Saxon ealdorman. Æthelred doubtless thought this a crafty move, but it proved a mistake. When Sweyn Forkbeard launched a Danish invasion in 1013, he stormed up the Trent to Gainsborough to secure Uhtred's support, knowing that once he had such a powerful figure on his side, the thegns of Wessex and the leading men of London would follow. Sweyn's strategy worked. Uhtred submitted with the whole of Northumbria, Æthelred fled to Normandy and Sweyn was proclaimed king of England on Christmas Day. His reign lasted just five weeks, as he died on 2 February and Æthelred resumed his throne; but when Sweyn's son Cnut returned in force in 1015 he wrought a harsh revenge on the whole class of ealdormen. Like his father, he first secured the support of a single powerful ealdorman – in this case Eadric of Mercia. This was a significant piece of treachery, as Eadric was Æthelred's son-in-law and his brutal enforcer. It was he who, at the king's bidding, had arranged Ælfhelm's ambush and murder while out hunting in 1006, and he had murdered two thegns at a council in Oxford in early 1015 so that the king could seize their lands. But by the end of that year Eadric had defected to Cnut, taking forty ships with him. Uhtred, meanwhile, who was by now married to another of Æthelred's daughters, remained loyal to his father-in-law and started harrying Eadric's lands alongside his brother-in-law Edmund Ironside until his absence from his own homelands saw them fall to the Danes. At this point Uhtred had little choice but to submit to Cnut, who proved utterly ruthless. He sent Thurbrand the Hold to slaughter Uhtred and his retinue on their journey to do homage to him, and at the decisive battle of Ashingdon in October 1016 he not only had the bishop of Dorchester killed while he was saying mass but also refused to spare the lives of three captured ealdormen and the son of another. Enough noble blood was spilt to prompt the *Anglo-Saxon Chronicle* to claim that 'all the nobility of England was there destroyed'.[12] With an eye to maintaining his grip on the whole nation, Cnut split the country into regions, each with a territorial commander. Keeping Wessex for himself, he handed control of Northumbria to Eric of Norway, East Anglia to Thorkell the Tall and the western provinces to Æthelweard, his only initial innovation being to abandon the term 'ealdorman' in favour of 'earl'.

As for Eadric, who had feigned a return to the English fold prior to the battle so as to lull Edmund into a false confidence, he was initially rewarded for his double-dealing with control of the whole of Mercia; but within a year Cnut sickened of him. As the annalist John of Worcester put it, on Christmas Day in 1017 he

> ordered the treacherous Ealdorman Eadric to be killed in the palace because he feared that some day he would be entrapped by Eadric's treachery, just as Eadric's former lords Æthelred and Edmund, that is Ironside, were frequently deceived, and he ordered his body to be thrown over the city wall, and left unburied.[13]

Few English chroniclers blamed Cnut for despatching Eadric, whom Roger of Wendover scathingly described in the thirteenth century as 'the very scum of mankind, the disgrace of England, double tongued, crafty, a betrayer of secrets, a practiced dissembler, ready in inventing falsehood'.[14] William of Malmesbury laid it on with a trowel, too:

> This fellow was the refuse of mankind, the reproach of the English; an abandoned glutton, a cunning miscreant; who had become opulent,

not by nobility, by specious language and impudence. This artful dissembler, capable of feigning anything, was accustomed, by pretended fidelity, to scent out the King's designs, that he might treacherously divulge them.[15]

His sins were many. The very fact that he married the king's daughter Eadgyth and was appointed ealdorman of Mercia in 1007 despite his father Æthelric being no more than a simple thegn, was seen as proof of unnatural ambition. He was brutal, too. He harried St David's in Wales and used the Danish invasion of 1016 as an excuse to ravage his opponents' lands and put them to the sword. At one battle he cut off the head of a man who unfortunately looked like King Edmund solely so as to hold it aloft to trick the English into fleeing the field in the belief that their lord was dead. It is said that the English were indeed terror-struck at this, but more by the atrocity of the act than by Eadric's threatening words. All Eadric's personal traits were summed up in his nickname 'streona', meaning 'grasper' in Anglo-Saxon. Rapacious greed was his driving instinct.

His contemporaries poured scorn on Eadric, but he was not exceptional. Early eleventh-century England was dominated by such guileful, grasping and opportunistic Anglo-Saxon nobles. Their epitome was Godwine, the father of the last native king, Harold. He had expert tutors in double-dealing. Eadric was his great-uncle and his father, Wulfnoth, a thegn from Sussex, deserted the royal fleet in 1009, taking twenty royal ships on a piratical spree along the south coast and putting eighty ships commanded by his then loyal uncle to the torch, effectively surrendering the key harbour of Sandwich to a new Danish invasion fleet. Despite this dubious heritage, Godwine prospered under Æthelred, but he too was light in his loyalty and when Cnut came to power he wheedled himself into the conqueror's affections so successfully that the king found him 'the most cautious in counsel and the most active in war',[16] took him to Denmark and gave him his sister-in-law Gytha as wife. So assiduously did Godwine assimilate himself into the Danish conquest that within two years he became earl of the eastern provinces of Wessex and five or so years later he was the first earl of all Wessex, Cnut's right-hand man. With power came riches in the shape of huge former royal manors in Kent,

Sussex and Hampshire. In 1035 Cnut died and Godwine had to take sides in an uncertain succession. On the one hand stood Harold Harefoot, Cnut's son by his first wife Ælfgifu. On the other stood the dowager Queen Emma defending the rights of her son Harthacnut. An assembly was gathered in Oxford at which the thegns of Mercia and the north backed Harold and, as the *Anglo-Saxon Chronicle* put it, 'Godwine and all the chief men in Wessex opposed it as long as they could, but they could not contrive anything against it'.[17] Since his own candidate Harthacnut was absent fighting off a Norwegian invasion of Denmark, Godwine agreed a compromise whereby Harold would hold the north in his own right and act as regent for his brother in the south. Behind this, though, his guile was still at work. When Alfred, the eldest of Queen Emma's two sons by old King Æthelred, returned out of exile in Normandy in 1036 as another putative heir to the throne, Godwine enticed him to his great hall in Guildford by pretending that he would declare his undying loyalty. Alfred fell for it, dining with Godwine and accepting his homage. Then suddenly the trap snapped shut. Godwine clapped him in chains and sent him to Harold, whose men blinded and mutilated him before taking him to Ely where he died of his wounds.

Even this was not the end of Godwine's perfidy. The following year he switched his allegiance again and accepted the sole rule of Harold. It was a premature and unwise move, as in 1040 Harold died and Harthacnut returned to England full of fury. The vengeful king had Harold exhumed and his cadaver thrown in the Thames marshes, and Godwine himself escaped Harthacnut's wrath only by abjectly throwing himself on the king's mercy and swearing that he had never wanted Alfred blinded, 'but that his lord King Harold had ordered him to do what he did'.[18] It was a lie, but it saved his life. Harthacnut was childless, so when he suddenly convulsed and died at a wedding party in 1042, Godwine performed yet another opportunistic volte-face. Despite his self-confessed involvement in Alfred's death, he proposed at the gathering of nobles that Alfred's unmarried 37-year-old Saxon brother Edward be king. On Easter Day Edward was crowned at Winchester, deep in the heart of Godwine's province of Wessex.

Despite – or because of – the immense distrust with which Edward must have looked at Godwine, he swaddled his sponsor with further wealth. He also promoted Godwine's sons Sweyn, Harold and Gyrth as the earls of Hereford, East Anglia and Wessex respectively, and himself married Godwine's eldest daughter Edith – although he seems to have deliberately kept himself from consummating the marriage lest a Godwine family heir ensue. Godwine's wealth multiplied through his own efforts, too, as he accrued lands through gift, purchase, bribery and extortion at Plumstead, Bosham, Fritton, Woodchester, Berkeley, Sandford-on-Thames, Richborough, Sundridge, Saltwood and Langport. Even the third penny in Kent, which had once gone to the archbishop of Canterbury, came to Godwine. Eventually his and his family's lands began to outstrip those of the king.

Nobody can be certain what turned Edward's wary distrust of Godwine and his family into open enmity, but in 1051 Godwine and family found themselves ranged at Beverstone in Gloucestershire against the might of the king and three other earls. For fear of an aristocratic bloodbath leaving the realm defenceless to overseas invaders, battle was averted. Godwine opted to quit the country in search of allies, and a year later returned in greater force with the backing of Diarmait, king of Leinster, and Baldwin, count of Flanders. This time Edward was forced to capitulate, the family lands were restored and Godwine's enemies were dismissed. He was not to enjoy his power for long. In one account he swore to the king that God would ensure that the piece of bread in his hand would not pass his throat if he had ever thought of betraying the king. It was a daring falsehood, and true enough, he choked and died. The *Anglo-Saxon Chronicle* is kinder: according to this version, he was sitting at dinner with the king on Easter Monday in 1053 when 'he suddenly sank against the footstool, deprived of speech and of all his strength; he was carried into the king's chamber, and it was thought it would pass over, but it was not so; but he remained thus unspeaking and helpless, through until the Thursday and then gave up his life.'[19]

✠

Godwine, Eadric, Uhtred and all these warrior lords were capable of considerable deception and violence. They won their places through guile, determination, martial prowess and a sense of their own worth. Their swords and their shields were the emblems of their nobility. They were required to fight as and when the fyrd was raised to defend the realm. If the battle went badly for them they would expect to be slain rather than be taken hostage, so they avoided pitched encounters if they could; yet in many cases their death in action is virtually the only thing we know of them. Æthelmund, ealdorman of the Hwicce, and his opponent Wulfstan, ealdorman of Wiltshire, died at the battle of Kempsford in 802; Ealdorman Hereberht at the battle of Romney Marsh in 841, Ealdorman Ealhhere at the battle of Thanet in 855, Ealdorman Æthelwulf at the battle of Reading in 870. Like all warriors they expected, indeed demanded to be handsomely rewarded – and the one reward they sought more than anything else was land. Land on which to build a fortified homestead with a great hall and a church. Land on which to graze sheep. Land to till, sow and harvest. Land for fuel and food. Land on which to establish a dynasty. Land on which to get rich. Always more land.

This was not as simple as it might seem. The old English system of land tenure dictated that with land ownership (or, more properly speaking, with the right to *use* land) came a set of duties, including food-rent and other tributes payable to the king. These could be onerous. To give just one instance, the sixty hides of Westbury on Trym near Bristol were expected in the late eighth century to supply the king every year with two tuns of clear ale, one cumb of mild ale, one cumb of British ale, seven oxen, six wethers (castrated rams), forty cheeses, thirty ambers of rye corn and four ambers of meal.* How the resident population provided this was up to them, but provide it they must. And the quantities were set not as a proportion of the annual local produce, which might vary according to the harvest, but as predetermined amounts, so in a bad year meeting the obligation could leave the local population hungry. In addition to this food-rent, there was a universal threefold duty of mending bridges, providing defensive fortifications and supplying troops

---

*Measures like cumbs (or coombs) and ambers were not yet standardized, although Magna Carta attempted to do so in 1215. The two tuns of clear ale probably equated to 432 gallons.

in case of war. By the time all these duties had been met, there was little left for personal enrichment.

What was more, most grants of land were temporary, either for the period of the individual's life or, in some cases, for three lives (those of the grantee, his widow and his heir), after which the land would revert to the king. For example, the lease by which the late ninth-century Bishop Ealhferth granted eight hides at Easton near Winchester to Earl Cuthred and his wife Wulfthryth was for three lives only, after which it would revert to the church at Winchester. By definition, such time-limited leases effectively prevented a nobleman from establishing a landed dynasty in perpetuity.

The solution came courtesy of the newly adopted religion, which enjoined charity and personal devotion on Christian kings. Anxious to attain the everlasting life promised to the munificent – or at least to avoid the threatened torments of eternal damnation – successive monarchs and nobles founded churches and monasteries. These required land, both to be built upon and to provide long-term sustenance for the growing numbers of bishops, priests and religious communities. If the traditional royal dues were to be insisted upon, the church would be poorly endowed. So kings began to formalize royal grants of land to the church via charters which expressly exempted land from duties and tributes. When, for instance, King Cuthred of Kent gave some land in Ruckinge to his minister Ealdberht and to Abbess Seleryth, his charter specified that it was to be held 'free from all royal tribute ... in return for their money and for the salvation of my soul, by which I acknowledge the iniquity I have done'.[20]

At first these charters were drawn up solely to benefit the church. But acquisitive laymen saw the attraction of such arrangements, and started demanding similar duty-free 'book-land' grants for themselves, whereby land was expressly granted free of the customary food-rent, which now stayed with the secular lord.

Not everyone agreed with book-land grants. The Venerable Bede complained to his bishop in 734 that Northumbrian nobles had bribed kings to give them estates in perpetuity in the pretence that they would establish devout new monasteries. In fact, he argued, these plush family establishments were monasteries in name alone, and in consequence there was not enough land to endow the church properly or to reward faithful warriors who could reliably defend the realm. Bede's view did not prevail: the pretence of a religious basis for book-land grants was maintained, and by the Norman Conquest more than two hundred such duty-free 'family monasteries' had been endowed.

No matter how piously these grants were dressed up, the end game was clear. Warriors and commanders reckoned they were entitled to hefty rewards for their service, and royal munificence bought their continued support. By the tenth century royal grants of book-land to demanding nobles were increasingly commonplace. Edmund I of England made book-land grants to people he described as *minister* or *comes* amounting to 349 hides in just six years, and King Edgar made similar grants of 351 hides between 958 and 972. Sometimes the grant was an expressly political act, as when the weakened King Æthelwulf of Kent granted land near Rochester to his thegn Dunn in a charter of 855, 'on account of the tithing of the lands ... which I have decided to do for some of my thegns'.[21] By this 'tithing' – releasing a tenth of all the lands already in secular hands from any legal burden – and by allowing nobles to sell or bequeath book-land unencumbered, he bought their gratitude and enabled them to enrich themselves or to prove their piety by endowing monasteries – or, for that matter, to mask the one with a semblance of the other. It was a pattern that was repeated time and again, extending the tendrils of royal patronage and enhancing aristocrats' opportunities for self-enrichment. Ironically, all this industrious activity was conducted not only in the name of devotion but in direct contravention of the parable of the rich fool in Luke's gospel, who built himself bigger barns to store all his grain and goods, and told his soul: 'You have many goods laid up for many years; take your ease; eat, drink and be merry' – only for God to require of him his soul that very night. England's new Christian aristocrats were deaf to their Saviour's conclusion: 'So is he who lays up treasure for himself, and is not rich toward God.'

The annals and historical documents are full of the noble rapaciousness with which aristocrats determinedly set about accumulating and protecting their possessions and influence. The church's very extensive lands were particularly valuable and vulnerable. When King Edgar promoted the rapid endowment of reformed Benedictine monasteries and allowed Bishop Oswald of Worcester summarily to declare estates that had long been held in the hands of one family as loan-land held only at the pleasure of the bishop, many of the nobles affected took exception to this appropriation as soon as the old king was dead. Ealdorman Ælfhere of Mercia despoiled several monastic houses in west Mercia as well as the abbey at Ramsey, which owed its allegiance to Oswald's friend Ealdorman of East Anglia; Æthelwine in turn seized the manor of Hatfield from the monks at Ely, which was under the patronage of Æthelwine's rival, another reforming bishop, Ætholwold of Winchester. So vicious were the attacks on Glastonbury Abbey by Ealdorman Ælfric that Pope John wrote to complain – and when the attacks on the monasteries continued in the reign of Æthelred, it was reckoned that Ealdorman Eadwine of Sussex had combined with the 'section of the public which was the enemy of God'.[22] Surpassing all others in their territorial ambitions were the Godwine family. According to Walter Map's twelfth-century collection of anecdotes *De Nugis Curialium*, Godwine cheated the abbey of Berkeley out of its lands by getting a handsome young nephew to seduce all the nuns, then swooping in and closing the abbey for being dissolute and seizing the lands for himself. The strategically important manor of Bosham also fell into his hands by trickery. The archbishop, asked by Godwine 'Do you give me Bosham?', replied with the quizzical rhetorical question, 'I give you Bosham?' Godwine deliberately mistook his words as an affirmation, and the archbishop was powerless to resist. Godwine's son Sweyn followed in his father's footsteps. So keen was he as earl of Mercia to control the impressive estates of Leominster Abbey that he abducted the abbess.

By the time Edward the Confessor became king in 1042 England was a patchwork of large estates in the hands of a tiny number of violent and opportunistic noble families (as was Scotland, where powerful lords, thanes and mormaers held sway). Edward's nephew Ralph was earl of the east midlands, Godwine's rival Earl Leofric of Mercia held sway in the west midlands and Earl Siward had Northumbria sewn up. Each of this small group of nobles held vast estates in his own right. One thegn, Eadric of Laxfield, held lands in Norfolk valued in the Domesday Book at more than four hundred pounds; another named Ælfstan held manors in Somerset, Dorset, Hampshire, Berkshire, Gloucestershire, Herefordshire and Bedfordshire in addition to his manorial home at Boscombe in Wiltshire; and Asgeir the 'staller' held estates in eleven shires valued at £447 13s. One noble family predominated, though: the Godwines, who among them held the whole of the country south of the Thames, plus East Anglia. Godwine himself was lord of Kent, Sussex, Hampshire and Cornwall; his son Sweyn was in charge of the shires of Hereford, Gloucester, Oxford and Somerset; his younger brother Harold was in command of all East Anglia including Cambridgeshire; and their cousin Bjorn Estrithson filled in the gaps with an earldom covering Bedfordshire, Huntingdonshire, Hertfordshire and (probably) Middlesex. The total value of their privately held heritable lands came to roughly £5,000, which fell not far short of the king's own holdings and was more than double the worth of those held by Earl Leofric and his family. They held the strategically vital manors of Southwark, Sandwich, Bosham and Dover in their own right, and had pulled off the impressive trick of turning high office as earl (with the 'third penny') into a hereditary position, as five of Godwine's sons and a cousin became earls. True, when it came to the standoff of 1051, the Godwines were matched by the combined forces of Leofric, Siward and the king – but that combination in itself reflected the phenomenal power of the Godwine dynasty. No wonder Edward feared them. Even when the old earl died, his sons remained a wealthy, powerful aristocratic force.

✠

If one takes the annals at their word, this was a man's world; most women barely registered in the legal system. Yet women were not yet entirely disenfranchised, and many wives and daughters of kings and nobles were wealthy and influential in their own right. Æthelgyth, 'Thurstan's wife', for instance, held manors in Essex, Norfolk and Suffolk in the early eleventh century. A woman called Wynnflæd, who owned several estates across Wessex in the mid-tenth century, bequeathed two silver cups to the church, and her engraved bracelet and brooch and the estates at Ebbesborne and Charlton to her daughter Ætthelflæd 'as a perpetual inheritance to dispose of as she pleased'. Wynnflæd's will even specifies that she 'grants to her [Ætthelflæd] all the men and the stock' on the two estates and sets free nearly three dozen of her slaves.[23] Both Godwine's wife Gytha and his son Harold's longstanding lover Eadgifu the Fair were major landowners in England in the time of Edward the Confessor. Earl Leofric's wife, 'the noble countess Godgifu' (Godiva), was expressly credited with her husband's generosity in endowing a Benedictine monastery at Coventry, being 'a worshipper of God and devout lover of St Mary ever-virgin'.[24] Often noblewomen were pawns in strategically important marriages. Æthelred married his three daughters to ealdormen in the vain hope of ensuring their loyalty; Cnut married Æthelred's impressive widow Emma of Normandy to buttress his position on the throne; and, despite his many years with Eadgifu the Fair, Godwine's son Harold probably married the widow of his Welsh opponent Ealdgyth in the spring of 1066 in an attempt to end the conflict with her father, Leofric's son Earl Ælfgar, and her brothers Eadwine and Morcar (though it was Eadgifu who identified Harold's body after the battle of Hastings by marks that only she would know). Some of these strategic marriages saw women treated with rude indifference. Edward the Elder seems to have abandoned both his first wife or consort, Ecgwynn, and his second, Ælfflæd. Earl Uhtred of Northumbria adopted a particularly mercenary attitude. Having first married Ecgfrida, the daughter of Bishop Aldhun of Durham, in exchange for a major gift of church land, he then abandoned her in favour of Sige, the daughter of a wealthy York merchant, and when Æthelred returned to power turfed her out to marry the king's daughter Ælfgifu.

Yet many noblewomen carved out distinctive roles for themselves. They were particularly prominent for their piety. All four daughters of King Onna of East Anglia (d. 654) were canonized, including Æthelthryth, the founding abbess of Ely Abbey, who remained a virgin despite two noble marriages. Æthelburh, the founding abbess of Barking in the seventh century, also became a saint (for her miraculous posthumous curing of the deaf and the blind), as did the three daughters of King Merewalh, who were respectively abbesses at Thanet and

Wenlock and a celebrated Northumbrian nun. In 802 King Egbert's sister earned her sainthood by turning the house of secular priests at Wilton into a Benedictine nunnery – an institution subsequently joined by King Æthelstan's half-sisters, led and endowed as abbess by King Edgar's wife, and rebuilt in stone by Edward the Confessor's wife Edith of Wessex. Likewise Edmund I's first wife (or, as one charter calls her, concubine) Ælfgifu helped endow the nunnery at Shaftesbury that had been founded by King Alfred – and when she was buried there a cult grew up around her tomb.

Noblewomen could also be power-brokers. King Onna's eldest daughter Seaxburh ruled Kent when her husband died in 664 until her son came of age, whereupon she succeeded her sister as abbess of Ely. When Æthelred, the ealdorman of western Mercia, died in 911 he was succeeded by his widow Æthelflæd, the daughter of Alfred of Wessex – and she in turn was succeeded for a few months in 918 by her daughter Ælfwynn. Neither woman was termed ealdorman, but they seem to have held the same lands and much of the same authority. A century later, Emma of Normandy and Ælfgifu did battle on behalf of their respective sons, Harthacnut and Harold, after Cnut's death. Emma propagated the slur that Harold was not really Ælfgifu's child but a changeling, and complained to her daughter that Ælfgifu 'your wretched and wicked stepmother, wishing to deprive your brother Harthacnut of the kingdom by fraud, organised a great party for all our leading men and, eager to corrupt them at times with entreaty and at times with money, tried to subordinate them with oaths to herself and to her son'.[25]

What these noble men and women shared was a ruthless passion for self-preservation. The constant round of invasion and civil war elevated guile, opportunism, double-dealing and brute force as noble attributes, while the quest for security entrenched the habit of seeking perpetual dominion over extensive landholdings. In his translation of the sixth-century Latin text *Consolation of Philosophy* by Boethius, Alfred of Wessex nobly asserted that reason ruled the heart of every thegn and that every thegn asked himself at some point why the stars shine in the night sky; and Byrhtferth of Ramsey praised ealdormen for being slow to anger and not insisting on revenge. But those claims fade into hypocritical posturing in the face of the contemporary accounts, which display men of worldly preoccupations and immense brutality. Alfred's own ealdorman Odda of Devonshire was praised for rushing out early one morning against the invading forces of Ubbe from Dyfed and slaughtering Ubbe and 840 of his men. Blood feuds abounded. Thurbrand killed Earl Uhtred in 1016, and was himself murdered by Uhtred's son Ealdred, who was in turn killed in 1039 by Thurbrand's son Carl, two years before Ealdred's younger brother Eadwulf, who had succeeded as earl of Bernicia, was murdered on the orders of Harthacnut. Two generations later Ealdred's grandson Earl Walheof of Northumbria slew two of Carl's sons.

These early aristocrats bowed the knee to Christian piety. They founded and endowed monasteries; they built churches and cathedrals. Several retired to religious houses in their later years or sent their widows and unmarried daughters to such places. Yet in many instances their religiosity was yet another aspect of their desire for wealth and power. A well-endowed abbey or a well-appointed church was a manifestation of the local lord's importance in this world and in the next. It was even better if the lord had direct control over the local religious house and could appoint aristocratic relatives and allies to all the key posts. Many magnates jealously guarded this right and rebelled when King Edgar and St Dunstan, the archbishop of Canterbury and abbot of Glastonbury, attempted to reform the English church at the end of the tenth century by centralizing the administration of all religious houses and insisting on appointing celibate contemplative monks rather than married secular clergy. Dunstan was supported by the East Anglian ealdormen Byrhtnoth and Æthelwine, but the nobility of Wessex, including Ealdorman Æthelmær the Stout and the family of Ealdorman Ordgar, went to war, murdered Edgar's son the young King Edward the Martyr, replaced him with his half-brother Æthelred and forced Dunstan into virtual retirement. Despite the violence, all these men undoubtedly thought of themselves as good, pious Christians. Æthelwine founded Ramsey Abbey. Byrhtnoth gave Ely Abbey thirty mancuses of gold, twenty pounds of silver, two gold crosses and a string of villages. Æthelmær the Stout founded abbeys at Cerne and Eynsham.

Yet these were rarely if ever acts of unalloyed altruism. Æthelwine forcibly seized land belonging to his rivals' religious houses, Æthelmær appointed his allies as abbots, and when Byrhtnoth died his wife insisted that a large tapestry celebrating his achievements hang prominently in Ely Abbey. Vanity, greed and personal rivalry were always more important than the gospel virtues to the Anglo-Saxon nobility. They felt fully entitled to the trappings of immense wealth – gold arm-rings and clasps, elaborate clothing woven and encrusted with gold, intricate ornamental swords and horse-gear, a great hall with a roaring fire and food and drink aplenty. And they were perfectly content to use force to seize land and defend their privileges.

Warriors sought rich rewards for their military service to the king. Above all they demanded land free of any form of duty or taxation, which they could hold in perpetuity and leave to their descendants. The Norman Conquest saw land redistribution on a phenomenal scale, as William (here seen granting Richmondshire to Alan Rufus, the count of Brittany) seized many thousands of acres and gave it to his foreign supporters.

CHAPTER 2

GET IT THEY MUST

THE ONLY EXISTING ORIGINAL text of the Old English poem *The Ruin* lies in a book of manuscripts in Exeter Cathedral. The copy itself is in a bad state, consisting of no more than a scrap; parts of it have been burnt and many of the lines are illegible. But the gist is clear. A castle raised by a great man has been toppled. The fortifications are a pile of rubble. The troops who should have repaired them lie beneath the earth. The hall, 'where of old many a warrior, joyous-hearted and radiant with gold, shone resplendent in the harness of battle, proud and flushed with wine',[1] lies roofless, open to the skies. The message was a favourite Anglo-Saxon one. Our fate, our 'wyrd', is unavoidable. Ruin may be just around the corner. What will be, will be.

It was a difficult message to hear when victory was still ringing in one's ears, though, and Earl Godwine's son Harold might have allowed himself a smile as he surveyed the battlefield at Stamford Bridge at the end of the day on 25 September 1066. He had triumphed against the odds – and not for the first time that year. When King Edward had died on 5 January, Harold had not been the only claimant to the throne, but he had been the swiftest to act. He had himself crowned the very next day and cemented the loyalty of the powerful brothers Eadwin and Morcar, the earls of Mercia and Northumbria, by marrying their sister Edith. Troubles had rapidly accrued, though, and by the autumn he was under serious threat. His exiled brother Tostig, whom Morcar had ousted as earl of Northumbria, had landed in England on 18 September with a Norse invasion fleet led by Harald Hardrada, who two days later defeated the earl-brothers at the battle of Fulford and took York. When the news reached Harold, he was stationed in the south; but he had stormed up north as fast as he could, covering the 190 miles in just four days and nights, so his force had fallen upon the invaders at Stamford Bridge before they even knew he was coming. The battle was especially bloody. So many were slain, including Tostig and Hardrada, that fifty years later people would still avoid the field, which was said to be white with sun-bleached bones.

Harold had no time to enjoy the victory. From across the Channel came disturbing news. William, the duke of Normandy, also had a claim to the English throne. It was a tenuous one, as he was only Edward's first cousin once removed and the bastard son of the old duke. Yet he maintained that Edward had promised him the English throne and that Harold had sworn to uphold his claim. Since Harold had therefore perjured himself in accepting the crown, William had gathered an invasion force and had been sitting awaiting an opportunity to set sail since the start of August. That came on the morning of 28 September, when Harold was still in the north. William landed unchallenged at Pevensey and moved inland to build fortifications at Hastings from which to ravage the locality. Harold hastened back south, but William was better prepared than the Norsemen had been. On 14 October the contenders did battle. Their forces were roughly equal in number, but by the end of the day Harold and his two brothers, Earl Leofwine and Earl Gyrth, were dead.

William was the victor, but not yet the Conqueror. A swiftly convened assembly of nobles threw their weight behind Edward the Confessor's one remaining blood relative, his great-nephew, the teenage princeling Ætheling Edgar, whom they elected king. Undeterred, William advanced through Kent to Southwark, where he narrowly failed to storm London's bridges, and thence on to the Thames valley. Edgar's supporters faltered. First Stigand, the archbishop of Canterbury, marched out to Wallingford to submit to William; then, after another great assembly, the whole aristocracy swore their fealty to the Norman at Berkhamsted in Hertfordshire. What changed their minds? Maybe Edgar was too young and weak to inspire confidence. Perhaps the pope's support for William weighed on the minds of the archbishops, or the earls were persuaded that William would only retain the English hierarchy in post if they didn't dawdle. Whatever their motives, when they gathered in Westminster Abbey on Christmas Day to witness Ealdred, the archbishop of York, crown William king of England, each of the surviving earls had been confirmed in place – and even Edgar had been bought off with additional lands. English noble consciences had their price.

This was an uneasy peace. William knew that English loyalty was no more than skin-deep, so he set about littering the land with strategically placed castles, built in the forbidding Norman style with motte and bailey. When he visited Normandy in triumph in March 1067 he took Morcar, Eadwin, Edgar, Stigand and Waltheof with him as hostages, and left his half-brother Odo, the bishop of Bayeux, with strict commands to quell any uprising. Resistance was never far away. William antagonized Eadwin by failing to deliver on the promise of his daughter's hand in marriage and by appointing a Norman as the earl of Shrewsbury, a city in the heart of Eadwin's Mercia. He provoked Morcar by supporting one of his declared Northumbrian rivals, Copsi, in his bid to seize the northern earldom and then forcing one of Morcar's relatives, Gospatric, to pay for the earldom when Copsi was murdered after just a few weeks. In 1068 the two riled earls launched a full-on assault on Norman rule. It was a desperate and brutal last throw of the dice. They 'sent envoys into every corner of Albion, to incite men to recover their former liberty and bind themselves by weighty oaths against the Normans'; their men disdained to sleep in houses 'lest they should become soft'.[2] The insurgency failed. William forced Eadwin and Morcar to surrender and replaced Gospatric as earl with a vicious Norman, Robert de Comines, who, it was said, was 'one of those men who paid the wages of their followers by licensing their ravagings and murders'.[3] The English matched Comines blow for blow. In January 1069 they cut down nine hundred of his men in the streets of Durham and set fire to the local bishop's palace, with Comines inside. That summer Waltheof and Gospatric returned to the fray. Having recruited Danes and Scots to their cause, they seized York in a battle in which it is said that Waltheof 'singly killed many of the Normans ... cutting off their heads one by one as they entered the gate'.[4] William retaliated with a bloody war of attrition against the northern provinces, burning crops and herds, homes and food, putting thousands to the sword and forcing many more to flee to the hills. Even his staunch defender the twelfth-century historian and Benedictine monk Orderic Vitalis reckoned that God would punish him because he 'made no effort to control his fury, punishing the innocent with the guilty'.[5] By the end of this 'harrying' through the winter of 1069–70, the north from the Humber to the Tees was a scene of devastation.

The troublesome English earls were also dispatched. In 1071 Eadwin was betrayed by three of his servants and killed on a riverbank, along with twenty of his men. In 1072 Gospatric, stripped of his earldom by William, fled back into exile. Morcar soldiered on with the help of Bishop Æthelwine of Durham and another major landholder, Siward Barn, but eventually they were routed at Ely and incarcerated. As for Waltheof, though he was reputed to be devout and 'muscular in the arms, brawny in the chest, tall and robust in his whole person',[6] he proved to be a man of weak will. He attempted yet another revolt in 1075, but almost immediately ran to the archbishop of Canterbury to confess. On 31 May 1076 he was executed in the English manner, his head sliced off with a sword on St Giles's Hill near Winchester, thereby further angering the faithful English, who maintained his innocence, opened his coffin, discovered that his head had been miraculously reunited with his body and founded an insurgent English cult in his honour. It was little solace. In the words of the monk Ælnoth of Canterbury, the English had been 'killed, scattered or reduced to servitude',[7] and William, who had reputedly declared at Hastings that the English were nothing but a people 'accustomed to be conquered', was indisputably their Conqueror.

✠

The Conquest enabled a massive redistribution of landed wealth and the complete restructuring of the aristocracy, as thegns and earls were deprived of their lands and the spoils were parcelled out to loyal Normans. It started straight after Hastings. As William put it in a writ to the abbot of Bury St Edmunds, the abbey was to surrender 'all the land which those men held . . . who stood in battle against me and there were slain'.[8] Since the three Godwine-sons and a host of thegns had perished, this forfeiture alone represented rich pickings. But Harold's surviving supporters were also dispossessed. Thegns were given the option of redeeming their lands for hard cash – a levy that few could afford – and successive defeated rebellions brought more forfeit lands into the royal grasp.

William had scores of Norman allies crying out for what they considered their just reward, but at the head of the queue were his own relatives and those who had fought at Hastings. For them, the payback was dramatic. Back in Normandy he had promoted his two half-brothers, Odo and Robert, as bishop of Bayeux and count of Mortagne; in England he granted Odo the lucrative earldom of Kent along with estates in twenty-three shires, and loaded Robert up with 797 manors, incorporating nearly all of Cornwall, a swathe of Sussex and tranches of twenty other shires. Another of his relatives, Roger de Montgomerie (Montgomery), who had stayed behind during the invasion as regent of Normandy, got nearly all of Shropshire and West Sussex, along with seventy-six valuable manors in nine other shires.

Eight other Norman aristocrats were stacked up with booty. William fitz Osbern was made William's steward and right-hand man in England, and was invested with much of the wealth and honour of Harold Godwineson's old earldom of Wessex. William de Varenne (Warenne), who had already earned himself the Mortemer and Bellencombre estates in Normandy for his previous military service, received the manors of Castle Acre in Norfolk and Conisborough in Yorkshire. Richard fitz Gilbert, the son of William's childhood guardian the comte de Brionne, had already been granted the Norman lordships of Bienfaite and Orbec and now received 176 English lordships and the castle rights to Clare in Suffolk and Tonbridge in Kent.* Even the especially snobbish and corrupt Geoffrey de Montbrai thrived. His brother Mauger, the archbishop of Rouen, had bought him the bishopric of Coutances in 1049, but to his disappointment the diocese turned out to be impecunious; so he was

---

*The right to build a castle or crenellate a mansion was keenly coveted and consequently strictly regulated by the king, who feared the threat posed to his security by impregnable castles.

now mightily relieved to be granted 280 manors in England, seventy-seven of them in Somerset alone.

Many of these land grants were made in direct reward for long service in Normandy. 'Those wise and eloquent men,' wrote Orderic Vitalis, 'who for many years lived at King William's court, observed his deeds and all the great activities there, were privy to his deepest and most secret counsels and were endowed by him with wealth that raised them above the condition to which they were born.'[9] Behind the courtly language lay the hard fact that William had also recruited mercenary allies, and these too had to be rewarded. Alan 'the red', who arrived with his brother Brian and a large contingent of fellow Bretons, did particularly well, initially receiving substantial manorial rights in Suffolk and Cornwall and then gaining the lordship and castle of Richmond in Yorkshire, a holding which in total made him the fourth wealthiest man in the realm. Eustace II, the comte de Boulogne, nicknamed *aux gernons* ('whiskers'), who had been exiled owing to a dispute with Earl Godwine, almost certainly participated in the invasion in the expectation of winning back the lands of his late wife, Edward the Confessor's sister Goda. An excitable and fickle ally, Eustace appears in the Bayeux tapestry gesticulating fiercely at William at Hastings, and one account of the battle tells of his attempted retreat before being struck between the shoulders with such force that blood gushed out from his mouth and nose. Yet having survived, he too was rewarded with extensive acres in Kent and Essex.

As a result of this wholesale reallocation of land, by 1086 a little over half the kingdom was in the hands of about 180 nobles. Of these, eleven held land worth more than £750 a year and three – Bayeux, Mortain and Montgomery – were each worth more than £2,000 a year. The combined lands of the eleven richest men barely amounted to 80 per cent of the land formerly held by the Godwinesons, but this was still a very significant concentration of landholding in a few foreign hands. It involved the virtual extinction of the old order – as one man's new fortune shows. William's cousin Walter Giffard, the lord of Longueville in Normandy, was long in the tooth by the time he fought at Hastings. He had helped see off the attempted French invasion of Normandy at the battle of Mortemer, he had done service against the Saracens in Spain, and in 1066 he volunteered thirty ships for the duke's invasion force. His rewards – and those that came to his son, also Walter – were substantial, with manors spread across Buckinghamshire. Some of these were straight transfers from the English aristocracy. But much of Giffard's package had been purloined from middling folk. Under the Confessor, the nine hides that comprised the hamlet of Bow Brickhill just off Watling Street had been held between one of the bishop of Lincoln's men, Godwin, and eight thegns. Three brothers had held the 2,000-acre manor of Ashendon, but with Giffard as the new tenant-in-chief, just one man, Richard, acted as sub-tenant. Many other Giffard manors suffered the same fate. Chearsley had previously been split among six thegns, Loughton among five, Edgcott among four, and the ten hides of Moulsoe among eight. Almost certainly these had been resident Englishmen, now dead, gone or dispossessed, their lands passed to a single absentee tenant-in-chief who sought to make a killing out of rents and the profits of local office. Giffard was not an exception. Orderic Vitalis noted that 'foreigners grew wealthy with the spoils of England while her own sons were either shamefully slain or driven as exiles to wander hopelessly through foreign kingdoms'.[10]

This agglomeration of land into single vast estates was common and deliberate, compact territorial units reflecting a real Norman aristocratic dominance of the landscape. The wealthy and vulnerable shire of Sussex, which had been in the hands of countless lesser thegns, was split into five strips running down to the coast, each with a castle and a single foreigner acting as castellan or castle governor, territorial commander and lord. The Conqueror's cousin, Robert, comte d'Eu, was lord at Hastings, as were Mortain at Pevensey, Warenne at Lewes, Montgomery at Arundel and William de Briouze at Bramber. It was a formidable phalanx – and William repeated the pattern in key defensive areas around the country. Some of these castle-based lordships were held by the great beneficiaries, such as Mortain, who built Montacute Castle in his new manor of Bishopstone, and William fitz Osbern, who built at least six castles including Carisbrooke on the Isle of Wight, Chepstow, Monmouth and Berkeley. But lesser figures on the victorious side were also entrusted with strategic lordships. Richard fitz Gilbert's brother Baldwin de Meulles held the new castle of Rougemont at Exeter along with much of Devon; the elderly William de Mohun built a castle on the site of an old West Saxon fortress at Dunster in the middle of his 55-manor holding in Somerset; and Ralph Bainard was granted a compact lordship centred on a new castle at Stansted. Ranged across the country like so many pieces on a chess set, these encastled lords were the visible embodiment of Norman domination.

All had fought and all must have prizes, but this was not just about rewarding the faithful. William sought domination, something the old system of regional earldoms had never achieved. Derbyshire is a case in point. Henri de Ferrières (later Anglicized as Henry Ferrers) fought at Hastings, where his older brother William, the heir to the family barony of Ferrières-Sainte-Hilaire in upper Normandy, was slain; but it was not just the Norman title that came to Henry, who accumulated English territories and titles at each stage of the Conquest. First came the estates of an English casualty at Hastings, Godric of Fyfield, sheriff of Berkshire; these were followed by the castellanship at Stafford and the wapentake of Appletree, including much of south Derbyshire. When Siward Barn's rebellion was suppressed in 1071, all his Derbyshire lands also went to Ferrers, so that by 1086 he held 210 manors and lordships – 114 of them in or near Derbyshire. This was a powerful, compact lordship, with imposing castles at Tutbury, Pilsbury and Duffield, enabling Ferrers and the three client families he had brought over from Normandy to dominate the land from the Derwent to the Dove, from the Trent to High Peak.

Land was at the core of the Conquest, but it was not the whole story. The Normans came with their own way of doing things and looked down on English manners. As one early annalist put it, William 'implanted the customs of the French throughout England and began to change those of the English'.[11] The Normans spoke a language that was incomprehensible to the conquered populace, who looked after sheep, swine and cows while their lords ate *moton*, *porc* and *boef*. Instead of Godwin, Siward and Harding, Norman sons were called Robert or Henri, and Eadgifu and Ælfgiva gave way to Emma and Matilde. Many towns had a mixed English and Norman population, as shown by the names of the 276 burgesses recorded in the Domesday Book as living in Colchester, which include the thoroughly Anglo-Saxon Ælfric, Grimwulf, Sæwulf and Leofsexe alongside men called Peche, Demiblanc and Pinel. It was not an easy coexistence, though, and the story of an English parish priest called Brictric being laughed at because he could not speak French cannot have been unique. There were other differences. The English preferred a beard, and the Bayeux Tapestry shows them sporting long curly locks; but the conquerors arrived clean-shaven or with just a moustache and caustically dismissed Harold II's companions as 'champions with combed, anointed hair, effeminate young men'.[12]

The new Norman aristocracy was undeniably pious, their devotion ostentatiously displayed in the glorious abbeys and churches of their homeland. But the English church was among those who felt the full blast of Norman greed in William's purge. Anything movable of any worth was considered the spoils of war and carted off to religious houses in Normandy. Harold's college of secular canons at Waltham Holy Cross was plundered for the Conqueror's St-Etienne in Caen; William fitz Osbern expropriated tithes to support his monastic foundations at Lire and Cormeilles. Peterborough Abbey protested that the Benedictine monk Remigius de Fécamp had unjustly taken its manor of Dunsby, and Ramsey Abbey complained that the king had wrongly awarded its two manors of Yelling and Hemingford to another favoured Norman, Aubrey de Vere. The abbeys at Canterbury, Abingdon, Worcester and Shaftesbury all saw the lands they had leased to thegns redistributed to Normans. Nowhere was this emptying of the church's coffers more complete than in Wales, where the bishoprics of Llandaff and St David's lost most of their endowments to lay aristocrats. So deeply felt were the conflicts between English monks and their newly appointed Norman abbots that when Abbot Turstin wanted to impose the plainsong chant in use at Fécamp Abbey at Glastonbury, three monks were killed by Norman archers in the ensuing liturgical rebellion, 'although they clung to the altar; and eighteen others were wounded, so that the blood ran down the steps of the sanctuary on the floor of the church'.[13]

Only rarely did the morality of all this avarice trouble the new aristocracy. Gilbert de Heugleville, for instance, was happy to fight for

William, but refused to stick around after the Conquest, maintaining that it was wrong to expropriate other people's land. Some noble wives took exception to their husbands' prolonged absence and forced them home under threat of marital desertion. Yet even when the Normans attempted pious regret they failed. As Nigel d'Aubigny, the Anglo-Norman lord of Thirsk and of Mowbray, lay ill on what he thought was his deathbed around 1110 he laid bare his soul to his brother and heir William. He had appropriated lands from the church, he had 'disinherited' laymen, and as the gates of hell beckoned he wanted to make recompense for his sins. Although he hoped his brother would approve of 'the restorations of the lands which I have made to my men whom I have disinherited',[14] he required him to make further recompense after his death. Well he might. Nigel's 'restorations' had involved taking back lands from his new men as summarily as he had seized them in the first place. True, he had returned one man's land just as he had 'found him seised'; but he had snatched the lands of another man called Anseis, given them to Hugh of Rampon, then taken them back and restored them to Anseis' sons on the condition that they did homage to Hugh. It was reparation of sorts, but hardly an act of unalloyed magnanimity. Anseis and Hugh could understandably conclude that what the Norman lord giveth, the Norman lord taketh away.

A few lesser English thegns survived as sub-tenants to new Norman overlords, but only thirteen Englishmen remained as tenants-in-chief to the king, and only three of these had lands worth more than £100. The English nobility vanished, swallowed by the grave or chased into exile, leaving their sisters and daughters to make what accommodation they might. Later chroniclers were clear that it was a hateful humiliation. As Henry, the early twelfth-century archdeacon of Huntingdon, put it, 'there was now no prince of the ancient royal race living in England, and all the English were brought to a reluctant submission, so that it was a disgrace to be called an Englishman'.[15]

✠

The Conquest was total, but it was not tidy – certainly not as tidy as later historians supposed when they claimed that the Norman kings imported an alien system of 'feudalism' into England. It was an attractively comprehensive theory. Anglo-Saxon book-land and laen-land (leased land), so it went, were done away with. Now only the king held land in his own right, which he granted as 'fiefs' or 'fees' to his great men in exclusive return for their fealty and service in battle. That service could be rendered in person, by household members or by men 'enfeoffed' as sub-tenants, and was set at a fixed quota of knight's fees for each secular or ecclesiastical landholding, each knight's fee being the amount of land reckoned sufficient to support a knight – anywhere between 1,000 and 5,000 acres, depending on the richness of the soil and its location. Any holding of twenty knights' fees or more was termed an 'honour' or 'barony' (*per baroniam*), entitling and requiring attendance at the royal court and granting the right to hold one's own honorial court. Fees could be commuted and rendered in cash or in kind – in the form of horses, weapons and supplies as 'scutage' ('shield money') – and the king could exact other monies in proportion to the knight's fees in order to pay for 'feudal incidents' such as a royal wedding. Thus the king, his tenants-in-chief and their vassals were held together in a perfect pyramid of homage paid and protection afforded.

Except it wasn't really like that. When William arrived in 1066 he had no baronial blueprint in his tunic, and although the personnel changed, the structure of the new aristocracy in England was an amalgam of Anglo-Saxon and Norman traditions. Many of the old manorial holdings remained intact as baronies under new landlords, and new aristocrats enjoyed the same ill-defined but potentially lucrative juris-dictional rights of sake and soke* as their predecessors. In deference to local custom William appointed earls instead of using the Norman titles of *comte* and *vicomte*, so Odo of Bayeux, Roger de Montgomery and Hugh d'Avranches became earls respectively in Kent, Shropshire and Cheshire, and William fitz Osbern struck a very Harold-like pose across much of Godwineson's old territory. Their number grew under William's successors, as William Rufus made William de Warenne,

---

*The alliterative term was used to denote a variety of jurisdictional rights, including that of holding court and receiving fines.

Henry de Beaumont and Walter Giffard earls of Warwick, Surrey and Buckingham; Henry I created the earldoms of Gloucester and Leicester for his illegitimate son Robert and for Robert de Beaumont; and by the time King Stephen had finished rewarding his friends and relations in 1138, there were fourteen earls, including another Beaumont and another illegitimate son of Henry I. In two key respects, these new earldoms were different. William gave much of the legal authority the Anglo-Saxon earls had enjoyed to the 'shire-reeves' or sheriffs; and he made earldoms unambiguously hereditary.

Nor was the concept of military service rendered in exchange for manorial rights exactly new to England. True, the duty to serve in the Anglo-Saxon fyrd was set universally as one man's service for every five hides of land, but the new quota system of knight's fees amounted to much the same obligation. According to the Domesday Book, by 1086 the little village of Bishampton on the lands of the bishop of Worcester had passed from four unnamed Englishmen to one Norman, Roger de Lacy, but he had exactly the same rights and duties as his predecessors, namely 'all soke and sake and churchscot, burial, military expeditions, naval expeditions and pleas'.[16] So too, the borough of Bedford was assessed at fifty hides for service by land and by sea before the Conquest and at ten knights' fees afterwards.

It was one thing to seize land, quite another to hold it in perpetuity. The Anglo-Saxons had dabbled in dynastic ambition, but the Normans bought it wholesale and found it pulled them in two directions at once. On the one hand, it was good to have many sons, who could fight shoulder to shoulder. If the eldest should die, a younger brother could pick up his sword and shield. On the other hand, younger sons had to be provided for, and a family estate that was split between sons could atomize and vanish in just a couple of generations. Even the highest family in the land knew that. The Conqueror had three sons who survived into adulthood, and when he fell ill on another military campaign in July 1087, he settled his affairs in the priory of St Gervase in Rouen. The duchy of Normandy would go to his eldest son Robert, despite the fact that Robert had quarrelled with his father and brothers, allied himself with the count of Flanders, plundered the county of the Vexin, humiliated his father in a jousting tournament and sired a few illegitimate children. Nevertheless, he was his father's eldest son and the duchy was the patrimonial inheritance, and therefore his by expectation if not by absolute right. England, though, was a different matter. William had conquered it, not inherited it, and he reckoned himself at liberty to dispose of it separately. So on 7 or 8 September he dispatched his second (and much preferred) son William Rufus to Archbishop Lanfranc of Canterbury, nominating him as his successor as English king. As for Henry, he was to have money with which to purchase lands, and the two elder brothers agreed that they would each be the other's heir. On 9 September the Conqueror died.

So far, so sensible. All three surviving sons of the king had been accommodated. But the aristocrats were in turmoil. Many held lands in both England and Normandy. They now owed divided loyalties to the eldest son, a duke, and to a younger, who was king. It was unsustainable, they argued. 'If we serve Robert, Duke of Normandy, worthily, we will offend his brother, William, and we will be stripped by him of our great revenues and large estates in England. On the other hand, if we obey King William fittingly, Duke Robert will deprive us of all our inherited lands in Normandy.'[17] The first to rebel was the Conqueror's half-brother Odo, who sought to reunite England and Normandy under Robert; he was backed by most of the Hastings victors, but when Robert failed to cross over to England and William Rufus promised the nobles advantageous terms, the rebellion crumbled and the red-headed king was secure enough to deprive Odo of his lands and send him back to Normandy. The chaos continued. Another rebellion was put down in 1095; Mowbray, the earl of Northumbria, was dispossessed of all his holdings; William of Eu was mutilated after losing a trial by battle. When William Rufus was killed in suspicious circumstances in a hunting accident in 1100, the third brother, Henry, sped to Winchester to secure the royal treasure house and have himself crowned King Henry I; from 1106, he ruled as both king of England and duke of Normandy, with Robert under lock and key. Since his only legitimate son William Adelin was drowned along with 300 or so drunken crew and noble passengers aboard the White Ship in 1120, another bout of noble infighting ensued when he died in 1135, as his daughter Matilda, the widow of the Holy Roman Emperor and wife of Geoffrey V, comte d'Anjou, battled out the succession with his sister Adela in favour of their respective sons, Henry and Stephen of Blois. This civil war ended with Stephen's death in 1154, when Matilda's son took the throne as Henry II, but the vast Angevin empire remained in tumult as Henry's eight children impatiently quarrelled over the succession. His first son died aged three, his second in 1183 of a fever (while leading an empire-wide revolt with the earls of Norfolk, Leicester, Huntingdon and Derby) and his fourth (another rebel) in a jousting tournament. This left the spoils to the lion-hearted Richard, who defeated his father in battle in 1189 and succeeded him when he went away to die of a perforated ulcer – and after him to John, the last of the brothers, who on the largely absentee crusader king's death in France in 1199, replaced him on the throne of England.

All this royal turbulence had a marked effect on the aristocracy. The concept of the *allodium*, a family's historic patrimony, was strong in Normandy. Families were reluctant to see it split up. It was safer and simpler for a single son to inherit the whole of his father's holding. Yet ambition, impatience and misfortune often complicated matters. Few younger sons wanted to live in poverty or under the heel of an elder brother. Sometimes a younger son was more competent. A minor could fall victim to an uncle's ambition, and untimely death carried away many an heir. Often there was no legitimate son and it was difficult to know who should come first – a bastard, a daughter, a brother, a nephew or a cousin? If a daughter was to be included, should she hold a lordship in her own right or should her husband hold it for her – and if there was more than one, should the estate be divided equally among all the daughters or remain impartible? Following the royal example, it became common practice in the decades after the Conquest for noble households to give the patrimonial inheritance to the eldest son and any acquisitions to a younger. The early twelfth-century volume known as the *Leges Henrici Primi*, which brings together some of the customs of the period, states as much. 'The ancestral fee of the father,' it suggests, 'is to go to the first-born son; but he may give his purchases or later acquisitions to whomsoever he prefers.'[18] As with the Conqueror's sons, this meant that Norman territories stayed with the eldest son, and English ones tended to go to the second son. Thus, thanks to his service at Hastings, Hugh de Grandmesnil held a hundred-manor fief in England, most of it in Leicestershire, but the lands he had inherited from his father Robert lay in the valley of the River Ouche in Normandy. These were the family patrimony, so when Hugh took a monk's habit and retired exhausted to die in his bed in Leicester in February 1094, they went to his eldest son Robert, while the English honour of Leicester, with its castle and manor, went to the next son, Ivo. Others followed suit. William fitz Osbern was succeeded by his eldest son William as lord of Breteuil, but by his second son Roger as earl of Hereford. Roger de Montgomery's Norman estates went to his eldest son Robert de Bellême: the English acquisitions, including much of Sussex and Shropshire and the earldom of Shrewsbury, went to the next son, Hugh. The irony that all three families opposed William Rufus' right to rule England because he was only the younger son clearly passed them by.

Such partition was by no means a fixed law, and many families made ad hoc arrangements, but its regular practice had a pernicious effect. At first there was plenty of land to parcel out from the dead and dispossessed English. But once one generation had passed on, those original acquisitions became part of the patrimony; so if all the children of later generations were to be provided for, the family had to acquire more land, whether by gift, by purchase or by force. A younger son could marry an heiress. Plenty did. Roger of Poitevin, the third son of the earl of Shrewsbury, came into an impressive manorial holding stretching from the river Mersey to the Ribble through his marriage to an heiress from Poitou. The family could ingratiate itself with the king. That was how Roger's younger brother Arnulf of Montgomery ended up with the honour of Holderness and Henry I's butler William d'Aubigny attained the barony of Old Buckenham in Norfolk (and the earldom of Lincoln and Arundel for his son). Or a family could back a challenger for the throne in the hope of forfeit land falling into its lap. That was how the manors of Skelton, Skipton, Thirsk, Cottingham and Warter in Yorkshire became baronies. It was how Richard de Redvers acquired the two honours of Plympton and the Isle of Wight (which had been held respectively by William fitz Osbern and his son the disgraced 2nd earl of Hereford), and was made earl of Devon by the Empress Matilda when he rebelled against Stephen. Thus, as each rebellion waxed and waned, there was new scope for ambition, and as each new generation brought forth progeny and the aristocracy burgeoned, every noble family had to make new acquisitions just to maintain younger brothers. Belligerence acquired the sheen of piety when a younger son took the cross and soldiered his way to Jerusalem, but back in England this acquisitive imperative was a recipe for endless internecine strife.

The ambiguity about inheritance added spice to this cauldron whenever there was a complicated family succession. The Beaumont twins, Waleran and Robert, for instance, were particularly close to King Stephen and had a younger brother, Hugh, whose exclusion from the Beaumont inheritance in 1118 had earned him the nickname 'the Poer' or 'the Pauper'. When the castellan of Bedford, Simon de Beauchamp, died in 1137 it seemed like a golden opportunity to sort out Hugh's finances, as Simon held the honour of Eaton and had left as heir only a young daughter, who was promptly affianced to Hugh. The king ordered that the castle be handed over to Hugh, who was to be made earl of Bedford (despite being 'a lax and effeminate man',[19] according to the contemporary *Gesta Stephani*) – but Simon's nephew, Miles de Beauchamp, refused to comply, leading to an unsuccessful attack on the castle by the king followed by a lengthy siege by Hugh. This was raised when the king's brother, the bishop of Winchester, negotiated a settlement; Miles retired humiliated, but soon returned to oust the Beaumont intruders and retained possession of the castle up until his death, when it passed to his brother. Evidently, where the law was unclear and land was up for grabs, it was best to resort to violence.

One might have expected this acquisitive tradition to have been consigned to disuse by the law of diminishing returns (if not by a desire for a peaceful life), but dynastic ambition and a lust for wealth helped it survive up to the end of the twelfth century. It gets an honourable mention in Ranulph de Glanville's tract of 1188,[20] and is reasserted uncompromisingly in the *Très Ancient Coutumier*, a treatise of 1200 on customary law: 'The first-born knight shall have the knight's fee complete, and it shall not be divided. The rest shall share the acquisitions equally.'[21] The first part of the statement was just as important as the second, because the hundred or so compact baronies that William created after the Conquest – and the small number of earldoms awarded by him and his successors – survived in large measure thanks to the growing assumption that the whole package should pass to the eldest son intact. This presumption of primogeniture was to prove the cement that held the British aristocracy in place for centuries.

Considering the perils of pestilence, famine, infertility and war, the resilience of the Anglo-Norman aristocracy was remarkable, as even a cursory glance at the *Cartae Baronum*, the fee certificates returned by the bishops, barons and earls in 1166, shows. Many of the names are identical to those of 1066. Here is another Walter Giffard ensconced in Nutley, another William de Beaumont, the 3rd earl of Warwick, and another William Ferrers, the 3rd earl of Derby, who listed sixty men, including three Baskervilles and two Curzons. Great honours including Stafford, Totnes, Clare in Suffolk and Richmond in Yorkshire were still held by the direct lineal descendants of the conquerors. Even when the direct line had died, the old Norman name had been kept alive, as on the death of William de Warenne, the 3rd earl of Surrey: his only child Isabel invested her first husband, William de Blois, with the earldom, and when he died childless she married Hamelin, the illegitimate half-brother of Henry II, who took the name of Warenne with all its honours and passed it on to his heirs and successors.

This resilience and adaptability had another significant consequence. Over time these Norman aristocrats acquired immense power and privilege and became accustomed to exercise authority as territorial magnates. The law gave the king undoubted rights over his nobles. He could raise up his protégés from the dust – witness the obscure knight Simon of Senlis, whom William Rufus made earl of Huntingdon and Northampton – and he could dispossess his opponents, as when

William Rufus removed Dolfin as lord of Carlisle and handed the town over to Ranulf, vicomte de Bayeux. Yet as landed generation succeeded landed generation, the nobles of England increasingly became a rule unto themselves. They held court, they meted out justice (of a sort), they exacted rents and fines. Ensconced in their castles, the great men felt they had the upper hand and enjoyed a considerable degree of impunity. Lustrous with the patina of established use, their authority felt so assured that retribution barely seems to have concerned them as they plotted rebellion. They learned by experience. When the plot to replace William Rufus with Stephen of Aumale crumbled in 1095, the king was reluctant to deprive the rebel barons. Orderic Vitalis wrote that 'he shrewdly spared the older barons . . . out of love of his father', and added that 'in any event he knew that illness and speedy death would soon put an end to their activities'.[22] But this was a mistake. Throughout the twelfth century the barons and earls became steadily more powerful. Lucrative royal offices became permanently attached to specific families. The Beaumonts, earls of Leicester, for instance, became hereditary stewards, and the earls of Hereford hereditary constables, of England. They started to develop their own liveries, displaying their quality with personal emblems emblazoned on shields and surcoats, so that although it was still difficult to identify an individual combatant at the siege of Exeter in 1136, by the end of the century no self-regarding aristocrat would step into the field or the lists without his own costly and elaborate identifying emblems. Geometric shapes such as lozenges, crosses, saltires, annulets and chevrons were combined with symbolic representations of birds, animals and flowers in red (gules), blue (azure), white (argent), black (sable) and gold (or) to create a unique and often beautiful shield or coat of arms. So proud were aristocrats of these devices – and so complex did they become – that a whole art of heraldry was developed with its own language, a college of arms was set up to award coats of arms, and the Earl Marshal was given the authority to adjudicate disputes in his Court of Chivalry. Crests, mottoes and supporters were added to the basic design to form an impressive and exclusive personal emblem. By the end of the thirteenth century lengthy rolls of arms were being produced, often displaying the shields of those who had fought in a particular battle. One of these, known as the Dering Roll, which now sits in the British Library, includes the coats of 324 knights and another, the Camden Roll, bears 270 shields, including those of the earls of Gloucester, Hereford, Oxford, Cornwall and Richmond.

Heraldry was bound by strict rules. Only those with a true claim to nobility were entitled to a shield. Those who disparaged their honour could have it removed. Through its quartering, a man's shield would make clear his precise relationship to the original holder of the coat of arms. Certain animals betokened specific virtues. An antelope was a sign of purity, a donkey a sign of patience and a bee a symbol of industry. A pelican piercing her own breast (known as 'in her piety') was a reference to Christ's sacrifice. The shield of the Talbots, earls of Shrewsbury, had (and still has) two 'talbots' or dogs as supporters, and the present duke of Northumberland retains the five gold fusils (or spindles) on a blue background of the first Baron Percy, much as the royal arms of England still display the three gold lions with blue claws and tongues on a red background ('gules three lions passant in pale or armed and langued azure') of Richard the Lionheart. Clearly it was not enough to *be* noble; one had also to be *seen* to be noble.

One can see the development of this self-aggrandizing tendency in the history of Robert of Bellême, who was mythologized in Normandy long after his death as Robert the Devil. He had come from mixed stock. His father, Roger de Montgomery, was one of the Conqueror's shrewdest allies, whose acquisitions put him in the first rank of Anglo-Norman lords, but who died in 1094 having taken a monastic habit at the abbey he had founded at Shrewsbury, where he was earl. By contrast, Robert's mother Mabel, heiress of Bellême, was said to have poisoned two men (one accidentally) and to have killed an infant by forcing it to suck on her diseased nipple. So rapaciously had she disinherited others that a band of knights burst into her castle and chopped off her head as she lay in her bed in 1077. An early supporter of Duke Robert against William Rufus, Robert of Bellême was a military man through and through, with a genius for building castles at speed and a propulsive energy that won him many a tough battle. Countless tales are related of his iniquity. When news reached him that the Conqueror had died he seized several of the king's castles, encouraging his men to pillage them. Instead of putting prisoners up for ransom, he tortured them, put out their eyes and cut off their hands and feet. So feared was he that prisoners begged not to be handed over to him, and so abusive was he to his wife Agnes of Ponthieu that she fled for her safety. Orderic Vitalis thought him grasping, cruel, vindictive to the church and to the poor, and inspired by indecent fury, 'a slave to gluttony, a mountain of fat given over to carnal lusts';[23] but another twelfth-century chronicler, Geoffrey Gaimar, appears to have been besotted with him, devoting fourteen lines of his verse history of England to praising his prowess, his magnificence and his vast retinue of a thousand men. 'For war he was the best knight that man could ever have known,'[24] he wrote. As was customary, Robert inherited the Norman patrimony of Bellême on his father's death, while the English acquisitions, including the rape of Arundel and the earldom of Shrewsbury, went to Robert's younger brother Hugh; but when Hugh died these, together with the countship of Ponthieu (from Agnes) and the important Yorkshire honour of Tickhill, all came to Robert, making him the richest noble in either kingdom. Either a grossly inflated sense of his own importance or an addiction to violence – or both – saw him constantly at war, supporting Duke Robert's attempts to depose William II, then turning against the duke before again backing his invasion of England to oust Henry I in 1101. Barely recognizing the customary religious sentiments of his era – he stole from religious houses rather than endowing them – he devoted his life to military conquests. Bellême's constant search for advantage eventually caught up with him when Henry I laid a string of charges against him, declared all his estates forfeit and had him placed in close confinement for the rest of his life. But Robert was an exception in being routed: in this era of acquisitive adventurism, determined conquerors prospered. Rapacity and violence were their hallmarks. Robert's grandfather precipitated a longstanding family feud when he blinded and mutilated William fitz Giroie; and when Robert rebelled against Duke Robert in 1089, the duke ordered that Robert's castellan at Saint-Céneri in Normandy, Robert Quarrel, be blinded, that his soldiers be mutilated and that the castle be handed to the Giroie family. Such violence was intrinsic to the Anglo-Norman nobility. As Henry of Huntingdon put it: 'All the great lords were so blinded by an inordinate desire of amassing wealth, that it might truly be said of them, "Whence it was got no one asked, but get it they must."'[25]

Early Anglo-Norman aristocrats thought highly of themselves and constantly sought to assert the rights to which they thought they were entitled. This seal-die, belonging to one of the rebellious barons at Runneymede, Robert fitz-Walter, seeks to proclaim its owner's bravery, prowess and intrinsic nobility.

CHAPTER 3

Give me my father's inheritance

I N THE LATE SEVENTEENTH century a 450-year-old circular seal-die was
found in Stamford in Lincolnshire. Sitting today in the British Museum,
it weighs in at 227 grams and measures seven centimetres in diameter:
a hefty piece of silver. The documents that it sealed would have impressed
everyone with the wealth and status of the man for whom it was made,
Robert fitz-Walter. It shows him astride a great horse, holding a shield
and brandishing a mighty two-edged sword at a coiled dragon that
cowers at his feet. More than that, though, the die tells the story of an
early thirteenth-century aristocratic friendship, for while the shield and
the horse's trappings carry Robert's coat of arms (a double chevron), on
the left of the die stands a second shield with very different armorial
bearings: the empty lozenges of Robert's cousin, Saer de Quincy. The
chivalrous compliment was mutual; a battered seal of Saer's in the British
Library also carries Robert's coat of arms on its shield.

Such heightened male camaraderie infused much medieval aristocratic literature. One song from just after the Conquest tells of two
noble friends, Lantfrid and Cobbo, who 'were so sharing that neither of
them possessed anything solely his own, neither treasure nor servants
nor any sort of furnishing'.[1] In similar fashion the two knights in the
French romance *Ami et Amile* share all their possessions, including
military booty, and their bond is so tight that Amile kills his own sons in
the belief that the only way Ami will be cured of leprosy is to bathe in
their blood. It all turns out miraculously, as Ami is cured and the sons
are brought back to life, but the central message was that for great men

of noble valour friendship transcends all else – a message that was as true for Robert and Saer as it was for their fictional counterparts.

The two men had much in common. Robert fitz-Walter came from an established Anglo-Norman family. Four generations back his ancestor Richard fitz Gilbert had been rewarded for his part in the Conquest with the lordship of Clare in Suffolk. The cadet or junior branch of the family, which Robert now led, had also prospered. Robert fitz Richard,* younger son of the first Norman lord of Clare, had been granted the barony of Little Dunmow in Essex in 1110 with the important hereditary posts of constable of Baynard's Castle and chief banneret† of London, charged with raising the London fyrd. Thence the Dunmow barony had descended via son Walter to grandson Robert in 1198. As for de Quincy, his grandfather, Saer I, had arrived from Cuinchy in Béthune in northern France after the Conquest; he too had secured a lordship, that of Long Buckby in Northamptonshire, which he passed on to his first son Saer II. Saer I's second son Robert made for Scotland, where he married Orabilis, the heiress of the extensive lordship of Leuchars. Their son Saer III inherited both Long Buckby and Leuchars. The two men wived wealthily, de Quincy making a match with Margaret de Beaumont, whose two brothers Robert and Roger were the 4th earl of Leicester and the bishop of St Andrews respectively, and fitz-Walter with Gunnora, heiress to the 58-fief lordship of Benington in Hertfordshire. Here the family connections came full circle, as Gunnora's cousin William married Saer III's daughter Lora.

Fitz-Walter and de Quincy were typical of the nobility of their time. Trained for warfare, they held substantial estates in more than one area, wherein they wielded complete authority over their retainers, freemen and serfs. They travelled extensively, including to other kingdoms, and they consorted with princes and kings. Above all, they had a prickly sense of their own rights, privileges, status and entitlements, which they reinforced through displays of wealth and heraldic symbolism. They were not shy of taking up arms against a neighbour or taking legal issue

* The prefix 'fitz', a version of the French word *fils*, meant 'son of'.
† A knight banneret fought under his own square-shaped banner, unlike an ordinary knight, who carried a tapering standard.

with their own relatives. In the normal course of things they expected to take their most serious grievances to the king and get swift redress, but when that failed they were not averse to violence.

This sense of entitlement was, in essence, what led to the two barons' wars of 1215–17 and 1264–7. The nobility – and their later apologists – dressed their actions up as righteous constitutionalism. Some even detected an early belief in democracy in the baronial cause, Franklin D. Roosevelt arguing in his third inauguration address of 1941 that: 'The democratic aspiration is no mere recent phase in human history. It is human history. It permeated the ancient life of early peoples. It blazed anew in the Middle Ages. It was written in Magna Charta [*sic*].'[2] Yet the real impulse behind both wars was not a concern for England's freemen, let alone the serfs, but a pent-up anger about a series of personal affronts to the country's barons and earls.

Noble dissatisfaction began to build up steam not long after King Stephen's death in 1154 and the subsequent incorporation of England into the dominion of the Empress Matilda's son Henry II, count of Anjou and duke of Normandy. After so many years of anarchy, the arrival of Henry II and peace of a kind must have come as something of a relief – but there was a downside to being part of his Angevin empire. Henry needed all the money he could get to defend his vulnerable lands on the continent, and England, with its tight, centrally controlled administration, was a ready milch cow. All that stood in the way of his raking in the country's profits was the self-assured English aristocracy; so the Angevin kings systematically and deliberately set about degrading their social status, military might and inherited wealth. Henry summarily suppressed the earldoms of York, Hereford, Northampton, Somerset and Worcester, and put a stop to the proliferation of earldoms doled out with competitive generosity by Stephen and Matilda, thereafter reserving the title for members of the royal family. This was a severe blow both to the self-esteem of the families directly affected and to the ambitions of the wider nobility, as the title had become highly valued as a sign of 'the generosity of kings, in consideration of ... distinguished service or extraordinary merit',[3] and its importance had been reinforced by a new investiture ceremony in which the king girded a new earl with an unsheathed sword as a symbol of his authority.* The earls were not necessarily the wealthiest or the most powerful people in the land, but every lay lord credited with more than a hundred knights' fees in the scutage list of 1166 was an earl, and every significantly endowed family expected to be at the front of the queue for the creation of a new earldom as of right.

Henry had the nobility's strength, as well as its status, in his sights. Many a leading man who could afford it had transformed his manor into an impregnable castle during the anarchy, often without royal permission. William le Gros, for instance, enlarged an old fort at Scarborough with a curtain wall, a dry moat and a gate tower when Stephen made him earl of York; Aubrey de Vere, whom Matilda made earl of Oxford, strengthened Hedingham Castle; the earls of Pembroke rebuilt Goodrich Castle on the borders of the Welsh marches in stone; and Stephen himself built a ring of castles at intervals of a few miles around Cambridge in the hope of defeating Geoffrey de Mandeville, who was based at Ely. As the *Peterborough Chronicle* put it,

> they filled the land full of castles. They greatly oppressed the wretched people by making them work on the castles; and when the castles were finished, they filled them with devils and evil men. Then they took those whom they suspected to have any goods, by night and by day seizing both men or women; and they put them in prison for their gold and silver, and tortured them with pains unspeakable.[4]

Seeing these castles as an affront to his royal authority and a threat to his military control, Henry II seized and demolished many of them, including Goodrich and Scarborough, which he then rebuilt in stone for his own defence.

Since the nobility had come to see their titles as theirs by rightful descent rather than royal gift, they also resented the king's interference when a noble died, a minor inherited or a woman sought to marry, even though to do so was a traditional royal prerogative. Glanville records that 'upon the death of a baron holding of him in chief, the king immediately retains the barony in his own hands until the heir has given

---

*It is difficult to say with any certainty when, and by which king, this ceremony was introduced, but it became conventional in the twelfth century.

security for the relief, although the heir be of full age'.[5] This security, paid in cash, could be substantial enough to leave a family in financial difficulties. Likewise, when a minor inherited a barony, the king became his guardian with complete power over his affairs. There was a good reason for this. As the anonymous author of the legal treatise *Le Grand Coutumier de Normandie* put it, 'A fatherless heir must be in ward to someone. Who shall be his guardian? His mother? No. Why not? She will take another husband and have sons by him, and they, greedy for the heritage, will slay their first-born brother, or the father will slay his stepson.'[6] Likewise, in his Charter of Liberties of 1100 Henry I claimed the right to be consulted before the marriages of any of his barons and of widowed or orphaned noblewomen; and although he promised that he would not withhold his consent unless any planned to marry an enemy, he regularly withheld consent unless and until a substantial fee was offered and received. These prerogatives were as lucrative for the monarchy as they were unwelcome to the aristocracy, as fewer than a fifth of noble estates passed exclusively from father to son, and between 1200 and 1327 one lordship a year passed to a daughter. The Angevins increasingly milked these historic dues for all they were worth. While Henry II's average annual receipts from widows' fines amounted to £117, the figure rose to £770 under Richard and under John to more than £2,000. In 1198 alone, Richard received £1,125 from thirty-nine heiresses. The fine roll of 1199 makes clear quite how infuriating these extractions must have been. Nichola, the widow of William le Rous, whose estates at Hemingford had come to her through her father, had to pay £100 not to be remarried. Alice, the heiress to her father Robert de Hastings' lordship of Little Easton in Essex, was so keen to keep her own lands when her husband Ralph de Cornhill died that she begged not to marry the duke of Lorraine's second son Geoffrey (who had a smart title as count of Louvain but little else). Despite a counter-offer from Geoffrey, the king relented when Alice surrendered 200 marks,* three palfreys and two goshawks.

---

*Payments at this time were sometimes made in marks (1 mark being equivalent to approximately two-thirds of a pound), sometimes in pounds.

The antagonism was exacerbated by the Angevins' administrative innovations. Henry II's initial changes to the common law, introduced between 1166 and 1170, enabled lesser folk to secure proper legal redress for grievances by transferring the arbitration of many property rights from baronial courts to royal tribunals. This flew in the face of Henry I's assurance that 'cases concerning the demarcation or seizure of land ... between the vassals of any baron ... should be heard in the court of their lord'.[7] In 1179 the establishment of the Grand Assize further shifted the balance of power by allowing a defendant in a civil case over property rights to refuse arbitration through trial by combat (which always benefited the fully trained noble) and request a trial by a jury of knights. By 1189 virtually all criminal cases were the preserve of a royal court. This was self-evidently more equitable, but the aforementioned degradation of baronial courts caused such resentment that a new avenue of financial exaction opened up, as the king started to sell barons a double exemption (from being sued in the courts and from paying the land tax known as the sheriff's aid, which was paid to the Treasury). By the end of the century barons regularly paid anything between fifty and a hundred marks for this exemption – and they did so about as willingly as a modern-day duke pays death duties.

All of this meant that even before Richard died in April 1199, there was a sense of baronial grievance abroad. Then came King John, who had neither the military prowess, nor the strategic vision, nor the simple common sense of his predecessors. He lost Normandy to the French through his own ineptitude, and his English nobles refused him support for a new naval expedition unless he subjected himself to their counsel. He picked a fight with the pope over the appointment of a new archbishop of Canterbury, and that led to his own excommunication and a papal interdict banning all religious services in England. The ensuing mayhem was compounded by the petulant, wayward and vindictive way he dealt with his English lords, the most notorious example of which related to his treatment of William de Briouze (or Braose) and his wife Matilda. De Briouze's family was as brutal as any medieval aristocratic house. His father, also William, was the 3rd lord of the valuable Sussex rape of Bramber, with additional lands in Wales, and his mother Bertha of

Hereford inherited Abergavenny and Brecon from her father, the earl of Hereford. There was bad blood between them and the neighbouring lord in Wales, Seisyll ap Dyfnwal of Castell Arnalt, who had reputedly murdered one of Bertha's brothers at an Easter feast. On the pretext of cementing a peaceful end to the hostilities, William summoned Seisyll and his son Geoffrey to Abergavenny at Christmas 1175. It was a trap. William had Seisyll, Geoffrey and several of their men massacred in the great hall of the castle, and he hunted down and murdered Seisyll's seven-year-old son Cadwalader. Even in a savage era, this duplicity was considered indefensible. The king exceptionally deprived William of his titles and gave them to his son William as 4th lord of Bramber; and in 1182 Hywel ap Iorwerth, lord of Caerleon, had Abergavenny Castle burnt to the ground in retaliation.

The 4th lord prospered, though. From 1192 to 1199 he was sheriff of Herefordshire, he fought alongside Richard in Normandy and at Chalus, where Richard died, and in reward he was given further Welsh possessions, including the castles of Glamorgan, Skenfrith, Grosmont and White, and four more lordships. Yet in 1208 John inexplicably turned against him and demanded immediate repayment of a string of invented debts. When William refused to pay up, John removed him from office, seized his lands in Sussex and Devon, and tried to take the Welsh possessions. William fled at first to Ireland, where he was granted shelter by William Marshal, the great military commander of the Angevin kings' campaigns in France, who was also taking refuge from John's anger. When John led an expedition into Ireland, de Briouze had to make a second escape to France (dressed as a beggar), leaving his wife Matilda to deal with the king. She was a brave, independently minded woman who managed large herds of cattle and apparently produced fine cheese. She was in no mind to capitulate. When John demanded 40,000 marks, a sum that no one could possibly raise (or consider just), 'she told [him] curtly that she would pay [him] nothing and she had no more money to pay towards the fine than twenty-four marks of silver, twenty-four gold coins and fifteen ounces of gold'.[8] Furious, John incarcerated her and her eldest son William in the grim dungeons of Corfe Castle in Dorset, where they were left to die. It is said that when they were found, William was sitting against a wall, his mother lying between his legs with her head on his chest, having eaten her son's cheeks out of starvation. One can only imagine the effect such news had on her husband and his father, who died in Corbeil near Paris on 4 September 1211. In John's own account of the Briouze case, to which he forced seven barons and seven earls to attest, he claimed that he had shown enormous forbearance; but in truth he had arbitrarily and summarily called in factitious debts, and the very fact that he felt obliged to explain himself betrayed his guilty conscience.

If the fate of the de Briouze family had been an exception, the nobility might have averted their gaze, but so many other lords were scarred by John's violent mood swings that an individual complaint became a common grievance. Even William Marshal felt the royal whiplash. Torn between his loyalty to John and the need to pay homage to the French King Philip II for his lands in Normandy, he found himself arraigned for treason by John in a court of his English peers. The speech attributed to Marshal at this point was probably invented later by his infatuated anonymous biographer, but it captures the sense of foreboding that many felt whenever they witnessed another fall from John's good favour. 'My lords, look at me,' he said, 'for, by the faith I owe you, I am for you all this day an exemplar and model. Be on your alert against the king: what he thinks to do with me he will do to each and every one of you, or even more, if he gets the upper hand over you.'[9]

Within this vortex of arbitrary rule stood the two cousins fitz-Walter and de Quincy. The former was distantly related to the de Briouzes, and de Quincy's cousin Isabel, countess of Pembroke, was married to William Marshal. Both fitz-Walter and de Quincy had initially been loyal to the Angevin crown, but the allegiance had become strained. Saer had a particular grievance. In 1204 his brother-in-law the earl of Leicester died without issue, precipitating a long inheritance battle with another brother-in-law, Simon de Montfort (the elder). For three years Saer was given custody of the earldom and the concomitant hereditary post of steward of England, but in 1207 John split the estate, granting the stewardship, the earldom and Mountsorrel Castle in Leicestershire to de Montfort, while Saer was made earl of Winchester and awarded some lesser lands. This loss of Mountsorrel was particularly irksome. How could an earl *not* have a castle? And Saer was litigious by nature – he waged another lengthy war of words with St Andrews Cathedral over the parish church of Leuchars. Yet for now he remained a loyal supporter of John.

As for fitz-Walter, he was one of the barons who attested to John's account of the dispute with de Briouze, but during the papal interdict John had intervened in a legal dispute between him and St Albans Abbey over the priory of Binham, which fitz-Walter believed to be part of his family inheritance. When a new prior was appointed against his wishes, he took Binham by force, whereupon the king sent his own troops against him, declaring, according to St Albans' own chronicler Matthew Paris, 'by the feet of God (for that was his customary oath) that either he or Robert should be king of England'.[10] The king's decision to find in the abbey's favour resolved the case, but the mutual distrust festered. So too did the matter of fitz-Walter's long-held claim to the castle of Hertford, which John granted and then withdrew in 1209. Three years later, the pustule burst, as Robert was implicated with a northern lord, Eustace de Vescy, in a plot to assassinate the king. John caught wind of the plans and unleashed his fury at the ringleaders. Fitz-Walter's castles were laid waste, his estates were seized, and he and his close family fled to France. In time, other stories of his visceral hostility towards King John surfaced. When his son-in-law Geoffrey de Mandeville killed one of William Brewer's men, the king threatened to have Geoffrey hanged. 'You would hang my son-in-law!' bellowed fitz-Walter. 'By God's body you will not. You will see 2,000 laced helm[et]s in your land before you hang him.'[11] And while in exile he claimed that John had tried to seduce Geoffrey's wife, Matilda – a claim lent credence by Vescy's similar allegation that John had also seduced *his* wife.

John ruled by alternating fear and favour and by addressing just enough specific individual grievances to keep the victims from uniting. In the words of the anonymous writer of Béthune, he 'set his barons against one another whenever he could ... [he] lusted after beautiful women and because of this he shamed the high men of the land for which he was much hated'.[12] In 1213 this strategy started to unravel. Fearful that his excommunication absolved the English lords from their oaths of allegiance and granted Philip sanction to invade England, he tried to strike a deal, whereby he would restore Marshal, Vescy and fitz-Walter and pay a fine of 100,000 marks, and in return the pope would lift the interdict and excommunication. And then he ruined it. It seemed he couldn't help himself. He ordered the much-despised foreign bishop of Winchester, Pierre des Roches, his new justiciar, to levy the highest ever scutage on the English barons to pay for a new military expedition in Poitou. They were incandescent. Roger Bigod had already paid King Richard the exorbitant sum of 1,000 marks to inherit the earldom of Norfolk and now he was being asked for 2,000 marks in scutage. Roger de Lacy faced a demand for 6,000 marks to inherit the lordship of Tickhill; Giles de Briouze (to add financial insult to the injury already done to his family) was expected to find 9,000 marks; and Geoffrey de Mandeville was forced to marry John's ex-wife Isabel, countess of Gloucester, and to pay an exorbitant relief of 20,000 marks in return for estates that could only possibly bring in 800 marks a year. Predictably enough, the nobles refused to pay the scutage or serve in Poitou, so with little support or provision, John's ill-considered campaign foundered on a searingly hot Sunday afternoon in July 1214 at the battle of Bouvines, where his illegitimate half-brother William Longespée, the earl of Salisbury, was taken prisoner.

In late November John summoned a Great Council* to meet at the London headquarters of the Knights Templar, the New Temple, at which he placated the church by issuing several charters granting it extensive lands and favours and guaranteeing that he would no longer interfere in the election of bishops and abbots. Several barons were present, including not only Geoffrey de Mandeville, Saer de Quincy and Robert fitz-Walter, but also the earls of Chester, Pembroke, Arundel, Warenne and Ferrers, and they started angling for a royal charter of their own along the lines of one granted by Henry I at his coronation in 1100. It is not difficult to see the attraction, as Henry's charter had included promises that he

---

*At this time the king held two types of council: a large, specially convened assembly of all the king's tenants-in-chief and officers of his court, known as the Great Council; and a lesser council, which was in more or less permanent session and consisted only of the officers of state and key members of the nobility in attendance at the court.

would not marry off a widow against her wishes or a daughter against those of her family, and that reliefs would be levied at a rate that was 'just and lawful'. These were promises that John had never honoured – and now he played for time by suggesting he would consider their request in due course.

At some point before Christmas the disgruntled barons gathered at the abbey church of St Edmund King and Martyr, ostensibly for unspecified religious duties, but in truth to forge a plan to secure similar freedoms for themselves as had just been granted to the church. If the king refused, so they swore on the altar, they would 'make war on him, till he should, by a charter under his own seal, confirm to them every thing they required'.[13] On 6 January 1215 they met the king again at the New Temple and produced a draft charter. When John stalled, abruptly announcing that he was taking the cross and promising a full answer at a meeting at Easter in Northampton, some of the barons, including de Quincy, joined him in swearing the crusader's oath, but many more began to arm themselves for war and mustered at Stamford before marching on Northampton, where they were confronted with the news that John had fled to Corfe Castle and that they all stood condemned by the pope. Their reaction was to elect fitz-Walter as 'Marshal of the Army of God', to lay siege to Northampton (unsuccessfully) and Bedford (successfully), and surreptitiously to take London on Sunday 17 May while the city was at mass. John agreed to meet them on the meadow at Runnymede west of London on 10 June, where they presented a draft charter. Its forty-nine articles were haggled over, but the key provisions all reflected quintessentially baronial concerns. Reliefs were set at £100 for an earl or baron, no more, no less. Scutage had to be assented to by common counsel. The church would be free. The body of a freeman would not be 'arrested or imprisoned or disseized or outlawed or exiled or in any way ruined . . . except by the judgement of his peers or by the law of the land'. And the king's adherence to the deal would be overseen by a council of twenty-five men: seven earls, three sons of earls, fourteen barons and the mayor of London. Some private matters were also resolved – fitz-Walter and Richard de Clare had their castles of Hertford and Buckingham restored, John de Lacy's brother Roger was released and Pierre des Roches was removed from his post as justiciar. John sealed the Great Charter on 15 June, and four days later the barons reaffirmed their fealty to him.

The settlement did not last. The pope sided with the king, who recruited a mercenary army from the continent and unleashed it on a vicious new harrying of the north, razing castles, burning towns and chasing rebel lords into Scotland. Fitz-Walter and de Quincy sailed for France to beg Philip to send his dauphin Louis to be the new English king and returned in January 1216 with forty-two ships laden with French soldiers. When Louis landed on 21 May he met no opposition, so he stormed through Kent to London, where he was hailed as king in St Paul's Cathedral on 2 June and received homage from fitz-Walter and the other barons the following day, swearing to restore their good laws and their lost inheritances.

John had still not lost all hope. The royal garrisons at Dover and Windsor remained firm and William Marshal and the earl of Chester remained loyal, so John made one more venture north from his foxhole at Corfe. New disasters befell him. Hastily crossing the Wash, he lost much of his baggage train in the mud, including his treasure, his relics and his regalia. He contracted dysentery. By the time he made it to the bishop of Lincoln's castle at Sleaford he was near the end of his tether, and when he pushed on to Newark he was preparing himself for death, which came on 18 October as a gale howled around the town. Roger of Wendover claimed poetically that it was a dish of peaches and new cider that carried him off, but in all probability it was sheer exhaustion.

John's death led to a swift reassessment by some of the rebels. True, they were Norman by descent, but a French King Louis of England now seemed less attractive than before – and besides, there was a more malleable candidate for the throne, John's nine-year-old son Henry. With London under Louis' control, Marshal and des Roches wasted no time in having the boy crowned at Gloucester Abbey as Henry III on 28 October. Others remained unconvinced, though, among them de Quincy and fitz-Walter. The final confrontation came with the battle of Lincoln in 1217. The earl of Chester had laid siege to de Quincy's long-coveted castle at Mountsorrel, but when fitz-Walter's army arrived to raise the siege, Chester retreated to Nottingham Castle to await reinforcements. With Mountsorrel secure, fitz-Walter turned to Lincoln, where the rebels had taken the city and were laying siege to the castle, which was being defended by the doughty châtelaine, Nicolaa de la Haye, who had inherited her post from her father, Richard, another Lincolnshire lord. Marshal, meanwhile, also had his eye on Lincoln, and had commanded all the castellans loyal to Henry to meet at Newark at Whitsun to raise the siege. When Marshal's army appeared on the horizon on 19 May the rebel camp was divided. De Quincy and fitz-Walter reckoned their troops outnumbered the king's men, so preferred to go out and take Marshal's forces head-on, but the French commanders were less optimistic and opted for a defensive strategy of closing the gates of the city behind them and concentrating on attacking the castle. It was a mistake. Thanks to intelligence from inside the castle (and a blocked-up postern gate that opened outside the city walls), Marshal breached the defences and the city fell – and was ransacked with such abandon that the day's work was known as the 'Lincoln Fair'. Had the battle been in open country, many of the rebels might have escaped, but hemmed in by the city walls dozens of them were captured, including de Quincy, fitz-Walter, the earls of Hereford and Lincoln, and forty-five other lords. The rebellion was over.

With the realm in the hands of the immensely competent William Marshal as regent, a degree of national unity was achieved. Rebels, loyalists and switchers all joined the Fifth Crusade. The boon companions de Quincy and fitz-Walter sailed for Egypt together and arrived in July 1219 in time to take part in the crusaders' siege of the city of Damietta. De Quincy died – whether in battle, of sickness or of wounds we don't know – and was buried at Acre on 3 November, three days before the city fell, but the campaign as a whole was no more successful than its predecessors: the crusaders were trapped on their march to Cairo by an unexpected flood and Sultan Al-Kamil retook Damietta in 1221. By then fitz-Walter was already back in England. He was to last sixteen years longer than his friend, witnessing the re-issue of the Great Charter in 1225 and dying in 1235 to be buried in Little Dunmow Priory (now the parish church).

✠

History has tended to blame John's financial demands and capricious behaviour for this first barons' war, but the barons were every bit as acquisitive as the king. They hated parting with their money, even for scutage, the traditional means of funding and equipping the defence of the realm. They objected to the historic form of baronial death duty, the relief. They insisted on their heritable rights, even when these were in legal dispute, and they jealously guarded their possessions and status. The depth of this sense of baronial entitlement became apparent when the young Henry III shrugged off his minority and married the twelve-year-old Eleanor of Provence, who came with no dowry to speak of but a considerable entourage of relatives who expected royal favour. Henry obliged. He appointed one of Eleanor's uncles, William of Savoy, as his leading counsellor and tried (unsuccessfully) to have him elected as bishop of Winchester. He persuaded the monks at Canterbury to elect another uncle, Boniface, as their archbishop, and he handed a third uncle, Peter of Savoy, the extensive earldom of Richmond in Yorkshire, topped up with the estates of the recently deceased earl of Surrey, the wardship of the Vescy family, and all the land between the Strand and the Thames in London, where he built himself the Savoy Palace on the site of the present hotel and chapel. When four of Henry's half-brothers made their importunate way across the Channel in 1247, Henry again obliged. He granted the youngest two, Geoffrey and Guy, large incomes straight from the exchequer, he levered Aymer de Valence into the bishop's throne in Winchester, and he gave William de Valence the hand of Joan Marshal, the fourth daughter and co-heiress of the great warrior William, with which came the lordship of Wexford and the earldom of Pembroke.

The English lords were not intrinsically xenophobic – many had lands and relatives in France and Scotland – but Henry's nepotistic munificence set in motion a repeat performance of the baronial rebellion against John, fuelled by envy of these freeloading foreigners and jealous protectiveness of their own possessions. It all came to a head when Henry accepted Pope Innocent IV's offer of the wealthy throne of Sicily for his son Edmund Crouchback in March 1254, in exchange for an English contribution of £90,000 for the military campaign required to seize it. Not surprisingly, the barons balked at this, and made their feelings clear at assemblies held in 1255 and 1257.

Aristocratic tempers were running high when a third meeting was summoned in April 1258. By this time Aymer de Valence had murdered one of the retainers of John fitz Geoffrey, the son-in-law of the earl of Norfolk, in a dispute over the right to appoint a priest to the church in Shere; William de Valence had antagonized Roger Bigod, the 4th earl of Norfolk, and his brother Hugh, over their mother Maud's share of the Marshal inheritance; King Henry's younger brother Richard of Cornwall had married another Marshal heiress, Isabel, the widow of the earl of Gloucester, thereby infuriating her son Richard de Clare, the 6th earl; and Henry himself was refusing to hand over monies owing to his sister Eleanor, who was married to Simon de Montfort (the younger), earl of Leicester. On 12 April, these aggrieved barons secretly swore allegiance to one another, and on 30 April they marched into the Great Hall at Westminster and confronted Henry in full armour. At first he thought he had been taken prisoner, and when Hugh Bigod laid out their central demands – that Henry's half-brothers the Lusignans be banished and that the king agree to convene a council of twenty-four barons to meet at Oxford – Henry realized that he had little choice but to comply.

The next six years saw a series of startling constitutional innovations. The council of twenty-four, assented to by the king under duress as part of a set of provisions presented to him at the Oxford meeting, would effectively rule in his stead. Writs, grants, payments and appointments would all have to be authorized by the council, and the king would be little more than a figurehead. The council would meet with a parliament including representatives of all the shires three times a year to review the state of the realm. And for the first time the justiciar, the senior minister with sway over the courts and the exchequer, would be entirely independent of the king and would seek out grievances against royal agents, including baronial complaints.

There were disputes within the confederate ranks. De Clare thought de Montfort was obsessed with his own finances, and de Montfort was so infuriated by de Clare's moderation that he stormed out of one meeting, declaring: 'I do not want to live or have dealings with men so fickle and deceitful. For we have promised and sworn together to do what we are discussing.'[14] Yet when Richard de Clare died in 1262, his son Gilbert was so infuriated by Henry's delaying his inheritance and awarding some of his lands to William de Valence that the young earl became a more determined reformer than his father and joined de Montfort in openly defiant rebellion. Battle was finally joined in 1264 when Henry and his son Edward marched north and seized the rebel city of Northampton, followed by Nottingham and Leicester, before turning south again to take Rochester, the Cinque Ports and Clare's castle at Tonbridge. De Montfort was still minded to negotiate. He even offered terms. But Henry's heart was set on victory, not on compromise. Edward proceeded to destroy the Ferrers castles at Chartley and Tutbury, and when the king refused further talks, the rebels renounced their allegiance to him. On 14 May, with crusaders' white crosses over their surcoats and de Montfort's religious zeal in their hearts, they marched against the king's forces at Lewes. The rebels were young – Gilbert de Clare was just twenty-one, Robert de Ferrers was twenty-five and several others were still under thirty – and they were significantly outnumbered; yet they won the day, and that night Henry agreed to pardon the rebels, restore their lands and uphold the Provisions of Oxford. Henry was king in title only; the land was ruled by his barons.

De Montfort spent the next fifteen months in full control of the kingdom and enjoyed substantial support while he saw off threats of a French invasion led by Henry's queen, Eleanor of Provence. He summoned two parliaments, and in order to bolster the reformers' numbers hit upon the innovative idea of assembling not just knights from every shire but burgesses from the main towns of England as well, and inviting only allies among the lords. Even so, his popularity did not last. De Clare, who had significant interests on the Welsh borders, was so horrified when de Montfort did a deal with the Welsh prince Llewellyn ap Gruffudd and enriched his own sons with lands seized from Richard of Cornwall that he switched sides and plotted with his younger brother to enable Prince Edward, imprisoned after the battle of Lewes, to escape on 28 May. This proved to be a decisive moment, as Edward, who was more charismatic and able than his father, rapidly gathered a new royalist army. On 4 August de Montfort was forced to face Edward at Evesham with a much-diminished army. This time it was the royalists who wore crosses, red ones, and Montfort exclaimed: 'they have not learned that for themselves, but were taught it by me!'[15]

The result was an exact reversal of the battle of Lewes, except for one fact. Instead of capturing their opponents and imprisoning them, the royalists slaughtered de Montfort's aristocratic followers in unprecedented numbers. John de Beauchamp, the young lord of Bedford, was butchered in cold blood on his very first day in action, along with Ralph Basset, lord of Drayton; Hugh Despenser and his brother-in-law Roger, lord of Stanton St John; Robert, lord of Hartshill; Thomas, lord of Astley, and his son-in-law William of Birmingham; and the two young brothers John and William de Mandeville. When the body of the Scottish lord of Cavers, Guy de Balliol, was found it was so mangled that nobody could bring himself to strip it for burial. The royalists had put together a special team to search out de Montfort on the battlefield, but it was his son Henry who was killed first. Moments later Roger Mortimer fell on Henry's father, slaying his horse under him and hacking him to death as he reportedly shouted 'Thank God!'[16] Matthew Paris claimed that 'at the time of his death, a storm of thunder and lightning occurred and darkness prevailed to such an extent, that all were struck with amazement',[17] and Mortimer was so pleased with his triumph that he claimed de Montfort's mutilated appendages as a prize and sent the head home to his wife, who paraded it on a lance at dinner. By common consent it was a barbarous day's work, and it stood in stark contrast to the experience of the first barons' war, when only one of the twenty-five barons who stood surety for the charter died in rebel action – Eustace de Vescy, who was shot in the head during the siege of Barnard Castle in August 1216. The other twenty-four recovered their lands and witnessed re-issues of the charter. Death came to them on crusade, on overseas campaigns alongside the king or peacefully at home. Eight of them survived into the 1230s and one, Richard de Montfichet, the lord of Stansted Montfichet in Essex, even outlasted the second barons' war, dying in 1267.

✠

The survival of some historical documents rather than others is often misleading. That is certainly the case with the two thirteenth-century barons' wars, which are often presented in grand constitutional terms as battles over the Great Charter or the Provisions of Oxford and their limits on the powers of the king. In fact, it was not idealism that drove the baronial cause; it was a heartfelt sense of entitlement. Never mind the historic right of the lord king to insist that his tenants-in-chief provide military service or financial assistance to pay for the security of the realm or a royal dowry. These were now matters to be haggled over by a self-assured class who reckoned they too had rights. The heir to a lordship was entitled to his inheritance, so they thought, without arbitrary royal impediment or unfair 'relief'. The heiress and the dowager were entitled, if not to choose their spouses, at least to consent or refuse to marry, especially when they had the support of their families. The lord was entitled to his castle, to free justice and to judgment by his equals. The earl was entitled to the third penny. Where an inheritance was complex, it should be adjudicated fairly, not on the basis of bribery. So when Hugh Bigod, earl of Norfolk, died in 1177 and his second wife Gundreda 'offered the king many great gifts that he should grant to her son [Hugh] the earl's purchases and acquisitions'[18] – property that should rightfully have gone to the earl's son by his first marriage, Roger – the young earl considered he had every right to feel aggrieved. As did any one of the rebel lords when their due inheritance was denied.

This is particularly striking in the case of the second barons' war, when the list of rebel lords consisted of the slighted and the aggrieved. Henry of Hastings and William de Mountchesny, lord of Swanscombe, both had plenty to resent about the Lusignans, for instance, having been made wards respectively to Guy of Lusignan and William de Valence when their important inheritances were in the balance. Hastings could count the earls of Huntingdon and Chester among his forebears and both men had links to the great contested estate of William Marshal, as Mountchesny's mother was Joan Marshal and Hastings' wife was granddaughter to Eva Marshal, one of the five daughters of William, earl of Pembroke. The pattern is repeated time and again. Another rebel, Nicholas de Segrave, had been forced to pay £300 for his father Gilbert's lands in 1258, as had John fitz John for the lordships of Aylesbury, Whaddon and Steeple Claydon on the death of his father, John fitz Geoffrey. In Gilbert de Clare's case, the affront was even more manifest. When his father died in 1262 King Henry prevaricated about his inheriting the earldom of Gloucester, eventually settling vast swathes of it, including the castles of Usk, Trelleck and Clare and the third penny of the county of Hertford, on his widowed mother Maud rather than on him, and requiring a £1,000 relief for the rest. Gilbert's marriage to Henry's half-niece Alice de Lusignan was so unhappy that it gave him a lifelong hatred of foreigners – yet another reason for him and his younger brother Thomas to support the rebel cause. Ironically enough, it was a very similar cavil that returned him to the royal fold when de Montfort enriched his own sons at the expense of other barons.

So accustomed are we to believe that ownership of property is an intrinsic and inalienable right that our modern sympathies mostly lie with the rebels, who seem to us to have been hard done by; but in the thirteenth century this sense of personal entitlement was an innovation. It was not how things had always been – nor indeed was it how things were then, formally. Each of these lords still held his land as a tenant of the king, whose vassal he was and to whom he owed due obeisance. Yet increasingly English lords felt they held their land, their manors, their castles and their titles by right, not by gift. Some overtly asserted this independence from royal patronage. As early as the twelfth century Alan of Brittany, for instance, referred to himself as earl of Cornwall by virtue of having inherited the title from his uncle Brian and by the grace of God (rather than by the grant of King Stephen), and by the thirteenth century this belief in ownership by inheritance was so deeply ingrained that lords were prepared to go to war with their liege lord the king to assert it.

These men had a high opinion of themselves and of their lineage, which they were keen to display. Armorial bearings had a utilitarian purpose in identifying friend and foe in battle, but they also reinforced the close-knit nature of noble families and manifested their ancient history. Geoffrey de Mandeville, the earl of Essex who died in 1144, fashioned himself a simple escutcheon of red and gold quarters, which was subsequently used by his and his in-laws' descendants. Likewise the several branches of the Clare family stuck to variants of the gold field with three red chevrons to show their ancient affinity. Like de Quincy and fitz-Walter, they fashioned hefty and impressive seals as a means of displaying their authority. Both the elder and the younger Simon de Montfort had seals that displayed them on horseback, and when Ela Longespée, who married Thomas de Beaumont, earl of Warwick, and then Philip Bassett, justiciar of England, handed the manor of Thorncroft in Surrey to Walter de Merton in 1266, she sealed the document with a wax image that showed her clasping the knot of her expensive long cloak and standing between the shields of her husband and her father.

The nobility commissioned great memorials for themselves, too: memorials that proclaimed their wealth, their status and their piety as well as a self-confident belief in themselves belied by many of their lives. An early example, the tomb of Ela's father William Longespée, an illegitimate son of Henry II who had become 3rd earl of Salisbury on his marriage to the nine-year-old sole heiress to the 2nd earl (also named Ela), is in Salisbury Cathedral. Bishops had started the fashion for carved effigies of themselves early in the twelfth century, but it was still an innovation when Longespée's likeness in Tournai marble was placed on top of this painted oak chest. His large pointed shield with its six lions rampant covers most of his left side, and his chain-mail covers him from head to toe, his surcoat flowing luxuriously over the side. The effect is graceful and impressive; the earl looks surprisingly relaxed and comfortable, with his head turned gently to one side as if he is thinking of getting up. A similar tomb in the church at Belton in Leicestershire shows the wealthy heiress Roesia de Verdun with one hand on her waist, another on her chest and a book under her left arm. Her robes, too, cascade over the side of the catafalque and she looks at peace; priests and nuns pray around her and angels hold her soul in a napkin. In both cases the effigies are exceptional works of art, but they are also statements of noble self-belief. The Temple Church in the City of London houses five such early effigies and it is striking how many of their originals were inconstant in their loyalties to the crown. Geoffrey de Mandeville, earl of Essex, swapped sides between Stephen and Matilda so often that he was under a writ of excommunication when he died in 1144 and had to be wrapped in lead to be buried by the Knights Templar lest his presence offend the sanctity of others. Likewise Robert de Roos, whose great-great-grandfather Walter Espec had built the castles at Helmsley and Wark and founded Kirkham Priory and Rievaulx Abbey, flitted in and out of royal favour under Richard and John and was one of the twenty-five nobles who appointed themselves guarantors of the Great Charter of 1215. His effigy shows him praying, with his legs casually crossed and his feet resting on a tamed lion, yet he was so anxious about his security that he rebuilt Helmsley Castle in stone. Even William Marshal, earl of Pembroke and another subject of a Temple effigy, who acted as a wise royal counsellor and defender in the first barons' war, was exiled for several years to his Irish estates, and his son Gilbert, the 4th earl of Pembroke, took part in the rebellion against Henry III. Yet all four look devout, faithful and comfortable, their heads resting on gentle pillows, symbols of wealthy nobility.

Another innovation was the creation of family mausolea. The de Clares, for instance, turned Tewskesbury Abbey into a family resting-place, interring full corpses or partial remains around the altar through the twelfth and thirteenth centuries. With so many widows and widowers remarrying, complex family ties could lead to strange compromises when it came to interments. For example Isabel, the widow of Earl Gilbert de Clare, insisted that her heart be buried next to him even though her second husband the earl of Cornwall, who outlived her, demanded that the rest of her be buried in *his* family's resting place, Beaulieu. Nor was the tradition of family memorials confined to actual burials. When Eleanor de Clare, one of three daughters of the 7th earl of Gloucester, married Hugh Despenser the Younger in 1306 and inherited the lordship of Glamorgan and Tewkesbury on the death of her brother the 8th earl at Bannockburn, she installed a series of family portraits and shields in the abbey's stained-glass clerestory windows, covering the generations from Robert fitz Haimon, who died in 1107, to her own husband Hugh.

These monuments sought to proclaim the permanence of a family lineage, but try as they might, few noble families of this era survived the vicissitudes of war, rebellion and infant mortality intact. The trajectory through the twelfth and thirteenth centuries of the Comyn family, descendants of Robert de Commines, is a good example of these fluctuations of fortune. Robert was brutally killed in Durham in 1069, but by 1136 his descendant William Comyn was both archdeacon of Worcester and chancellor to the Scottish king, David I, whose kingdom then included Comyn family lands in Northallerton. Two years later William joined David's invasion of England in support of his niece, the Empress Matilda, and fought at the battle of the Standard where the Scots were routed, twelve thousand were killed and William was captured. William was no mild-mannered cleric. In 1142 he attempted to foist himself on the chapter at Durham by forging a letter from the pope supporting his bid to be bishop – a piece of trickery for which he was excommunicated – and it was said that his soldiers incessantly foraged around the city, hung opponents from the walls of their own houses and drowned them in the river. Yet when he settled his claim to the see of Durham peaceably, the Scottish king granted him the valuable honour of Richmond, which he passed to his nephew Richard along with Northallerton. This Richard made his way in Scotland, where he became justiciar of Lothian and a loyal minister to Malcolm IV and his brother William the Lion, and where his oldest surviving son, another William Comyn, was born in 1163. Thus far the Comyns had held lands and important positions, but no hereditary aristocratic title. The younger William changed all that. Having served the king loyally as sheriff of Forfar and justiciar of Scotia, he was temporarily made warden of Moray in 1211 and charged with repressing the rebellion of Godfrey MacWilliam. So successful was he in this that in 1212 the now elderly king gave him Marjorie, the only child and heiress of Fergus, earl of Buchan, for his second wife. With Marjorie and the earldom came enormous tracts of north-eastern Scotland, to which he added the neighbouring lordship of Badenoch and Lochaber (when he finally saw off the MacWilliams and beheaded Godfrey) and other grants of land in Lenzie and Kirkintilloch. This was now a great dynasty. William's sons by his two wives became earl of Buchan, earl of Angus (through marriage) and lords of Badenoch, Inverallochy and Kilbride; his daughters married the earls of Ross and of Mar, respectively the marischal of Scotland and the justiciar of Scotia. The Comyn family thus became one of the most powerful in Scotland, with a caput or main residence at Ellon, a market town at Kelly, a religious centre at the abbey of Deer, strong castles ranged across the territory, and relatives at the castles of Inverlochy, Blair Atholl, Ruthven and Urquhart. Their Scottish lands crossed from the North Sea to the Irish Sea and included chunks of Dumbartonshire, and thanks to the marriage of Alexander, the 2nd earl of Buchan, to Elizabeth de Quincy, they acquired yet more land, including holdings in fourteen English shires (most of which he never visited). The Comyns' cross-border landholding was eventually their undoing, though, when at the turn of the century the two kingdoms went to war over the disputed succession. The English king forced Alexander's son, John, the 3rd earl, to side with him, and his Scottish opponent, Robert the Bruce, retaliated by killing John Comyn of Badenoch. In the ensuing civil war, Earl John fled to England while Robert the Bruce set about harrying Buchan, demolishing the castles at Rattray and Dundarg, torching the Comyns' homes, farms and crops, and putting their retainers to their sword. When Earl John died in 1308 he had no son to inherit his devastated dominion.

✠

The epitome of aristocratic self-assertion was Simon de Montfort the younger. He confessed as much in a fragment of autobiography he wrote in the early 1260s, where he relates how he left his home in France as an impecunious young man. 'I went to England,' he wrote, 'and asked my lord the king to give me my father's inheritance.'[19] Despite his subsequent reputation as a proto-democrat, that one sentence summed up his life's work. His father and elder brother had been prevented from taking up the earldom of Leicester by their status as vassals of the French king. Simon expressly came to England to claim it, together with every acre, manor and advowson that he believed was his by right. And after his clandestine marriage to the king's sister Eleanor he had another battle, for her rightful dowry. Justice denied inspired a reforming zeal in him, but what spurred him on was a desire to take and hold in perpetuity what he considered his.

This was the politics of jealousy. When you got up close you could smell the sweat of aristocratic entitlement.

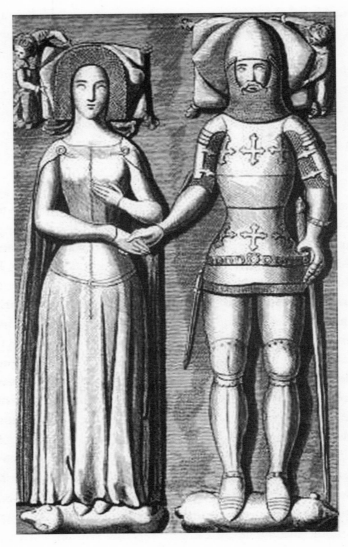

Waging war was a lucrative means of making a living for the medieval English aristocracy. Thomas Beauchamp, 11th earl of Warwick, seen here in effigy holding hands with his wife, Katherine Mortimer, ransomed the archbishop of Sens after the battle of Poitiers for £8,000 in 1356.

CHAPTER 4

They could not transport
all the spoils

WHEN HENRY III'S SON Edward I died in the arms of his servants as they tried to get their normally formidable king to sit up and take breakfast at Burgh by Sands near the Scottish border on the morning of 7 July 1307, he left behind him a degraded English aristocracy. A myriad families held a jigsaw of manors, lordships and baronies across the land. Edward had invited some of these manorial lords to successive parliaments. But the only aristocratic title in England was that of earl, of whom there were just ten; and no tenant-in-chief who held land directly from the king – whether an earl, a baron or a lord of the manor – was guaranteed a seat at the king's council table, other than those who held hereditary household posts like the Earl Marshal. The diminution of the aristocracy seems to have been a deliberate royal policy: Edward let the earldom of Cornwall lapse when Edmund, the 2nd earl, died childless in 1300, and by the time Roger Bigod, 5th earl of Norfolk, died in December 1306, Edward had permitted him to disinherit his only possible heir, his brother John, thereby allowing that great earldom also to wither. Yet the next two centuries saw the steady rise of the nobility and the brutal concentration of ever more land, money, prestige and power in the hands of a small number of greedy, jealous and ambitious aristocrats.

The resurgence started with Edward III. His father Edward II's habit of surrounding himself with favourites had incensed the established nobility. They rebelled when Edward II awarded the vacant earldom of Cornwall to his friend and confidant Piers Gaveston, a Gascon and a commoner who treated them with disdain. They took up arms against him when he embraced two new upstarts, Hugh Despenser and his father, and they supported his wife Isabella and her lover Roger Mortimer, the earl of March, in having him deposed in 1327. Yet ten years later Edward III created six new earls, granting them the traditional third penny (in the now standard form of £20 a year) and explicitly stating that he wanted to revitalize the aristocracy. 'Among the marks of royalty,' he argued, 'we consider it to be chief that, through a due distribution of positions, dignities and offices, it is buttressed by wise counsels and fortified by mighty powers. Yet . . . this realm has long suffered a serious decline in names, honours and ranks of dignity.'[1] In other words, he thought that far from diminishing or challenging his authority, additional aristocratic titles added to his status; and, as one of the patents put it, he wanted to increase the number of men 'by whose counsels the kingdom should be governed'.[2] He had another idea, too. Thus far the only duke in England was the king, who held the title of duc d'Aquitaine; Edward set about establishing the rank more widely. First he appointed his seven-year-old eldest son Edward of Woodstock, later known as the Black Prince, duke of Cornwall. Fourteen years later he made his companion-in-arms Henry of Grosmont, who was already an earl, duke of Lancaster, and in 1362 he made his own second son Lionel duke of Clarence. By the end of the century three more of Edward III's sons ('phials full of Edward's sacred blood', as the duchess of Gloucester puts it in Shakespeare's *Richard II*), two of his grandsons and two of his grandson Richard II's half-brothers were the dukes of Lancaster, York, Gloucester, Hereford, Aumale, Exeter and Surrey. England's aristocracy now had a hierarchy of titles, and the sons and heirs of dukes and earls came to be styled by their fathers' subsidiary titles. This deliberate increase in the distribution of dignities continued under Richard II, who created five new earls on his coronation day in July 1377, fashioned a new title of marquess (set above an earl) for his favourite Robert de Vere, whom he made marquess of Dublin in 1385 and then duke of Ireland in 1386 (the first non-royal duke), and granted the earldom of Suffolk to Michael de la Pole. Despite his own manifold airs and graces (he plastered his palaces, his courts and his men with his personal emblem, the white hart), Richard seemed blind to aristocratic pretensions. The established nobility superciliously complained that he was degrading these dignities, as de Vere was Richard's lover and de la Pole a mere financier, yet when the Lords Appellant wrested control from him and impeached the two upstarts for treason in the Merciless Parliament of 1386, he learned nothing. When he regained the upper hand he created five dukes and four earls on one day in September 1397 and then provoked a new rebellion by banishing Thomas Mowbray, duke of Norfolk, and Henry Bolingbroke, son of the duke of Lancaster, and attempting to seize all the Norfolk and Lancaster estates. After a successful rebellion, on 30 September 1399 Bolingbroke persuaded parliament to depose Richard in his favour. Richard had sought to exalt the aristocracy and reward his adherents with titles and lands, yet he had reckoned without the jealous sensitivities of the established leading families of the land.

Nor did the ardour with which aristocratic pretensions were promoted necessarily reflect their basis in history, as a book of charters belonging to the de Norwich family in the Bodleian Library in Oxford proves. The family's actual origins were rather humdrum: they started out as Norfolk townsfolk with a small manorial holding at Mettingham. But as of 1314 Walter de Norwich became successively a member of the Privy Council, chief baron of the exchequer and treasurer to Edward II, in which capacity he was summoned to parliament. His wily son John, also summoned to parliament – in his case as 'Baron de Norwich' – seems to have been embarrassed by his relatively parvenu status, as he rebuilt Mettingham as a baronial castle and hired an antiquarian to invent an entirely bogus ancestry, 'proving' that de Norwiches went all the way back to the Conquest – hence the cartulary. It was a nugatory exercise, as John's son predeceased him and when his grandson died childless in 1373 the barony died with him, but it goes to show how keen men were to assert their historic ancestry.

Kings were keen to foster these pretensions and to establish a pseudo-ancestry of their own. Edward III portrayed himself as a latter-day King Arthur. He named his son after Sir Lancelot's Arthurian cousin Lionel, he jousted in Lionel's coat of arms, and at a tournament at Windsor in January 1344 he declared that he wanted to found 'a Round Table of the same manner and standing as that which the Lord Arthur formerly King of England had relinquished'.[3] When he heard four years later that the French king – with whom he was about to go to war – was thinking of creating a college of knights in honour of St George, he snapped into action to pre-empt him, creating the Order of the Garter and dedicating it to – St George. The order was wrapped in high-minded religiosity and a fair degree of ritualistic flummery, but its real purpose was far from moral. Binding together by oath twenty-four knights as companions-in-arms, it promoted an aristocratic code of honour that gave a veneer of respectability to constant warmongering: for aristocrats were not only essential to the conduct of war, they were addicted to it. They supported the king's ludicrously tenuous claims on foreign lands. They said they fought for a just cause with God on their side. They trained their young in warfare, and with jousting and tournaments they made war into an aristocratic sport. Yet the real reason for the ceaseless round of foreign wars was that war was a remarkably lucrative business, even if you were on the losing side. Take just one of Edward III's great military commanders, Richard Fitzalan, 10th earl of Arundel. He accumulated such wealth as a commander in Scotland, in France and at Crécy, and as Admiral of the Western Fleet, that between 1336 and his death in 1376 he was able to spend £4,000 buying up manors in Surrey and Sussex. The spoils of war came in many forms. For a start there was military pay. A duke was paid a mark a day to go to war, garrison commanders were well rewarded, dukes and earls were awarded significant amounts for their large retinues (including, after the 1340s, a 'regard' or bonus for new recruits), and it was expected that they would siphon off large sums for themselves. Thus, when Thomas of Woodstock, duke of Gloucester, was sent to Ireland as lieutenant in 1392, nearly £4,500 of parliament's military grant disappeared, used by Thomas to pay off his private debts and buy himself a new manor. When (under arrest for treason) he was murdered in 1397, an inventory of his opulent residence at Pleshey in Essex listed fifteen large tapestries, sixteen beds hung with gold and silk, gold vestments and a large and expensive library. It is not surprising, then, that he had told parliament in 1391 that he was opposed to the very idea of a peace treaty with France: the livelihood of the aristocracy of England depended on war.

There was booty, too. When the English sacked Caen in 1346 they took only 'jewels, clothing and precious stones because of the abundance', and sent so much of it to their ships 'that they could not transport all the spoils'.[4] And the best booty was human: for there were noble ransoms to be exacted. At Poitiers in 1356 it was said that 'you might see many an archer, many a knight, many an esquire running in every direction to take prisoners'.[5] The reason for the frenzy was simple – prisoners meant prizes. In all, the English captured at that one battle the French king, his youngest son, the duke of Bourbon, the marshal of France, eight counts, the archbishop of Sens, the bishop of le Mans and a string of lesser men. The rewards were vast. Thomas Beauchamp, earl of Warwick and knight of the Garter, ransomed the archbishop for £8,000 and received three-quarters of the ransom paid for the bishop; King Edward himself paid the Black Prince £20,000 for three of his noble prisoners from Poitiers and Sir Bartholomew Burghersh, another knight of the Garter, £6,666 for the count of Ventadour. In 1375 Ralph Basset, 4th (and last) baron of Drayton, received £2,000 for a French prisoner, and the antiquarian John Leyland reckoned that following Agincourt in 1415 the former Speaker, Walter, Baron Hungerford, built his castle at Farleigh in Somerset entirely on the back of the money he secured for the freedom of the duc d'Orléans, just as the Botelers built Sudeley Castle in Gloucestershire, and the Stourton family built their castle in Wiltshire, out of the spoils of war.

Being captured, of course, was commensurately costly. When John Hastings, 2nd earl of Pembroke, was seized at La Rochelle in 1372, it took three years to put together a ransom of 130,000 francs secured by his fellow earls of March, Warwick, Stafford, Salisbury and Suffolk and four other lords – and by then he had died in captivity in Picardy. And when John Holand, earl of Huntingdon, was caught at Baugé in 1421 his ransom was 20,000 marks, exactly the same as his ancestor had received for the comte d'Eu in 1346 after the sacking of Caen. The effect of meeting such demands on a family's fortunes can be seen most clearly from the case of Lady Margaret Hungerford's son and heir Robert, Lord Moleyns, who was taken prisoner in Gascony in July 1453. The ransom demand was substantial – £6,000 – but what really weighed on the family estate for years to come was a series of additional charges. Lady Margaret had to pay an extra 10 per cent to the ransom negotiators, plus the costs of her son's lodgings and attire for six years until he was freed, plus fees charged on the £1,100 she borrowed to pay the ransom itself. Most of the family lands were put in hock by her husband to raise £2,000 of the charge, and even after her son was later captured again at the battle of Hexham and executed as a prominent Lancastrian in Newcastle in 1464, her will in 1476 showed that there remained outstanding debts from the ransom to be paid off. She fretted that 'mine heirs have no occasions to grudge for that I leave not to them so great an inheritance as I might and would have done, if fortune had not been so sore against me.'[6] She went on to insist that the erosion of her fortune had come about 'not . . . by folly, nor because of any excess or undiscrete liberality, but only I have been arted and caused by necessity of fortune and misadventure, that hath happened in this season of trouble time late past'.[7]

It wasn't all about money. The nobility had another ambition: full local power such as the church enjoyed. Within his county the bishop of Durham had total control of taxation, justice and administration over not just the church and clergy but the whole territory, and appointed his own justices, jailers, exchequer and chancellor. Likewise the bishop of Ely was entitled to hold his own court, and the abbeys of Bury St Edmunds, St Albans, Ramsey and Glastonbury managed their own affairs without the interference of royal officials. But most lay lords could only gaze on these ecclesiastical powers with envy. True, the earldom of Chester had long held similar palatinate powers to the prince-bishopric of Durham, but Henry III granted it in 1254 to the future Edward I on the grounds that it 'should never be separated from the crown but should remain entirely to the kings of England for ever'.[8] As earls of Pembroke, Aymer de Valence (1307–24) and Lawrence Hastings (1339–48) were granted very extensive jurisdictional rights in the Welsh marches; and dozens of minor marcher lords claimed that since they held their lands by virtue of ancient conquest, they too had special rights of extra-regal jurisdiction. The same was true in the north. The king's sheriff in Cumberland had no authority over Allerdale, Egremont and Copeland, the lords Clifford were hereditary sheriffs of Westmorland,

and the king's writ did not extend to much of the land between the Tyne and the Tees, as the 'liberties' of Redesdale, Hexhamshire and Tynemouthshire were held respectively by the de Umfraville family, the archbishop of York and the prior of Tynemouth. The powers enjoyed by these franchise-holders amounted to nothing less than 'jurisdiction and power over the people', as the chief justice of the King's Bench, Geoffrey le Scrope, put it in 1329.[9] They enforced their own peace, they held their own courts and they issued their own writs. Their territories felt like little kingdoms, with bureaucracies to match. In the 1370s, for instance, the earl of Richmond's semi-regal administration for the 'liberty' of Richmondshire, based at his castle, included a steward or seneschal, a receiver heading the earl's treasury, a constable, an auditor, a clerk, a lord's adviser who ran the half-yearly court or leet, a keeper of the castle, a watchman, several foresters, a warden of the castle orchard, a master miner of lead, a warrener to keep the lord's rabbit warrens, collectors and bailiffs for each of the manors in the liberty – and a recluse in the castle chapel. These semi-regal powers reached their apogee with the palatinate of Lancaster, which was first created in 1351 for Henry of Grosmont, duke of Lancaster. It gave him full regal powers over the whole of Lancashire, powers that eventually passed to his son-in-law, Edward III's son John of Gaunt, in 1377. The duchy encompassed a large administration extending across the former estates of the earls of Leicester and of Derby, and Gaunt's records show that he took his authority seriously, ensuring close scrutiny of his accounts and creating his own chancery. The duchy of Lancaster still operates today, for when Gaunt's son and heir Henry Bolingbroke usurped the crown in 1399 he determined that the duchy be retained as a royal entity; the present duke of Lancaster is the monarch, and the chancellor of the duchy is a Cabinet member. With Chester and Lancaster both subsumed into the crown, one might have expected the other non-ecclesiastical liberties to have fallen away; but as late as 1414 Northumbrians were complaining to parliament that these privileges meant that in Tynedale, Redesdale and Hexhamshire you could get away with murder, treason or robbery.

Local power was one thing, but the greater prize lay in exercising power across the whole realm. Successive monarchs had long gathered a selection of senior lay and clerical magnates and advisers as the king's great council, but by the middle of the fourteenth century the body that really mattered was parliament, for which two forms of summons were sent. To the county sheriffs went a general writ asking them to ensure the election of knights for each shire and burgesses for each town, and to each lord, bishop and mitred abbot went an individual writ of summons. There was no question about which bishops and mitred abbots to invite. Unless a particular cleric was in bad odour with the king, they were all expected to attend or send a proxy. In the case of the lay lords, though, the matter was not so simple. All the titled lords – the earls, dukes and marquesses – would be summoned, but it was still uncertain whether the holder of a particular lower 'lordship' or 'barony' would be called to parliament.* Apart from anything else, the full list of such lordships ran to several hundred, so although there was a clear assumption that only such landholders could be summoned, many were excluded. Even if a landholder had once been summoned, there was no guarantee that he or his son and heir would be summoned again. Minors were automatically excluded until they came of age, and when a baron left a single heiress it was customary for her husband to take the seat in his wife's name. But when there were two or three co-heiresses, the king could decide either to summon one of the heiresses' husbands, or to let the summons fall into abeyance. Thus the parliaments in August and November 1295, November 1296 and February 1297 each had a different cast of barons in attendance, numbering fifty-three, forty-one, thirty-six and seventy-five respectively in addition to the titled lords. The number continued to fluctuate wildly (eighty-nine in 1314, thirty-eight in 1325, forty-six in 1327) and several men were summoned once, never to be invited again.

This fluidity left considerable power in the hands of the king, as the 1459 list of writs issued by Henry VI shows. Successive Lords Dacre had attended parliament since 1321, and when Thomas, Lord Dacre, died in 1458 he left two potential heirs: Joan, a granddaughter by his deceased

---

*There was a similar distinction in Scotland, as titled nobles were automatically summoned to assemblies of the three estates, along with other 'lords of parliament', while many others were excluded.

elder son, and Randolph, his second son. The family lands passed directly to Randolph, who was duly summoned to parliament and told to take his father's place as Lord Dacre. Joan, though, had married Richard Fenys, a favourite of the queen, Margaret of Anjou; so he too was summoned 'as Lord Dacre and one of the barons of our realm'.[10] Thereafter the descendants of both men were summoned, as the king had effectively split a title in two. So too in 1483 Edward IV found another means of adding to the list when he summoned Thomas Fitzalan, the son and heir of the 16th earl of Arundel, while his father was still alive, using one of Arundel's subsidiary titles, Baron Maltravers. Such 'writs of acceleration' were to prove convenient over the centuries, allowing ninety-eight men to take seats alongside their fathers until 1999, when the practice was abolished.

The list of guaranteed summonses was not ultimately fixed until Tudor times, but well before then those summoned came to have a very clear understanding of their exalted status. From early in the fourteenth century they began to refer to themselves as 'peers', a term that was first used in 1312 and became an accepted part of the aristocratic lexicon by 1317 when Thomas, the overbearing 2nd earl of Lancaster, wrote to the king denouncing him for taking the question of whether to muster against the Scots, which he thought should have been discussed 'in parliament and in the presence of the *peers of the land*', to a mere council meeting.[11] By 1325 it was standard practice to talk of those summoned by individual writ as 'peers', with the implication that these men were equal to one another and a class apart from anyone else. This latter point was made manifest at the parliament in York in 1333, when the prelates and lay magnates deliberated on their own, without the knights and burgesses.

In 1341 the peers went a step further, albeit almost by accident. The king, Edward III, had returned from an expensive but disastrous military campaign in Flanders determined to lay the blame on John Stratford, the archbishop of Canterbury, his brother Robert, the bishop of Chichester, and their nephew Ralph Hatton, the bishop of London. John had resigned his longstanding post as Lord Chancellor and had briefly been replaced by Robert, but Edward now replaced him too and threatened them both with imprisonment, prompting the archbishop to hole up in his cathedral claiming that the king could not imprison a cleric. Edward included the three bishops in the writs of summons for a parliament to meet in Westminster on Monday, 23 April, and when they appeared on the Tuesday the king's henchmen barred their entry to the Great Hall and told them to attend the exchequer to answer a series of charges. This they did, before joining the other bishops in the Painted Chamber, the peers' normal meeting place. The following day the Stratfords returned – only to be told again that they were not welcome. But, they pointed out, they had been summoned by the king's writ, and had more right to attend than some of the scoundrels before them. Again they made their way to the Painted Chamber, although no serious business was done until the Thursday. Initially Stratford had few allies beyond his immediate family, but within a week, having cast a general archiepiscopal curse on the king's new ministers, having proclaimed himself a new Becket and the king a new Rehoboam, and having engaged in several bouts of high melodrama, he won the lay peers round to his way of thinking. The earl of Warenne even proclaimed that 'all is topsy-turvy and new-fangled. Those who should be the chief here are excluded, and other lowly people are here in parliament who should have no place in such a council, but only the peers of the land.'[12] By offending the collective *amour propre* of the assembled peers, Edward had inadvertently created a powerful and hostile coalition of interest against himself. Central to Stratford's case was his willingness to answer any charges against him as long as he did so before his peers – an offer that chimed with the peers' growing belief that they should enjoy an exemption from the king's common courts. When Stratford eventually gained the right to put his case, the peers demanded that the king assent to a statute guaranteeing that 'no peer of the land . . . shall be brought in judgment to lose his temporalities, lands, tenements, goods and chattels, nor to be arrested, imprisoned, outlawed, exiled, nor forejudged, nor put to answer, nor be judged, but *by award of the said peers in Parliament*'.[13] This, they thought, only accorded with their dignity. After all, how could a peer be tried by his social inferiors? Surprisingly, the Commons supported the statute, and Edward and his successors had little choice but to honour it. A hundred years later parliament returned to the matter. So indignant were its members in 1442 when an ecclesiastical court convicted the duke of Gloucester's second wife, Eleanor Cobham, of witchcraft and banished her to the Isle of Man that at the Commons' request, parliament thereafter extended the privilege of trial by peers to their wives. The privilege was to remain in law until 1949.

While the majority of the lords attending parliament were there by virtue of their longstanding landholdings, ratified by summons, others gained entry by express royal creation. Initially this merely took the form of the writ of summons, but in 1387 Richard II issued letters patent in which he 'preferred' John Beauchamp of Holt, whom he had appointed steward of the royal household earlier that year, 'to be one of the peers and barons of our realm of England, willing that the said John and the heirs male of his body issuing shall possess the estate of baron, and shall be called lords Beauchamp and barons of Kidderminster'.[14] This was a significant departure on three fronts. For the first time the status of baron was being created without an endowment of land (the award of Kidderminster was a fiction as he was granted no lands in the town), it was being conferred as a title, and it was limited through the 'remainder' to heirs male of the body, meaning that only direct male descendants, rather than the husbands of heiresses, could inherit the title. A similar change affected earldoms. All those in existence in 1272 were held in fee simple, that is to say, they passed down according to the same rules that governed land. Edward I broke with that convention, changing the three earldoms of Norfolk, Hereford and Essex from fee simple to fee tail male (that is to say, the title would descend through male heirs rather than under common law), thereby excluding collateral heirs who were not directly descended from the deceased, whether they be brothers or nephews, and all females including daughters. Other earldoms, including those of Oxford, Warwick, Arundel and Surrey, went the same way in the fourteenth century, and virtually all new dukedoms, marquessates, earldoms and viscountcies* thereafter were created in fee tail male. The

---

*The title of viscount was created in 1440 for John Beaumont and awarded for the second time in 1478 for Robert Peston, who was made Viscount Gormanston, the premier viscount in Ireland.

invention of baronies created by letters patent with clearly determined lines of descent, rather than by writ of summons to parliament, lasted, too. Four more were created by patent in tail male in 1447, and in 1461 Henry VI issued a patent to his new chamberlain, Ralph Boteler, creating him baron of Sudeley and adding that he should enjoy 'the status of a baron of our realm of England, both in sitting in our parliaments and councils . . . and . . . be called a noble of our realm; to have and to hold the name . . . to himself and the heirs male of his body lawfully begotten in perpetuity'.[15] Like Beauchamp, Boteler was endowed with an annuity rather than with land, and Lord Herbert of Herbert was also ennobled that same year despite having no estate to speak of. Thus the automatic link between land and a parliamentary summons was broken. There would be exceptions – George Neville was deprived of the dukedom of Bedford in 1477 primarily on the grounds that he was not landed enough – but increasingly a man was a lord, a peer and a 'noble' by virtue of the royal writ or patent issued to him or his ancestor rather than the baronies or lordships that he held.

When Henry VI used the word 'noble' in Boteler's patent, he was speaking to two other aristocratic obsessions – exclusivity and seniority. It was not enough to be wealthy; one had to be seen to be wealthy. That meant ostentatious expenditure on the latest fashion in fine clothing, which the peerage regularly attempted to restrict to themselves. One of Piers Gaveston's first mistakes was to reject the cloth of gold worn by other lords at Edward II's coronation in favour of royal purple decked with pearls, thereby apparently infuriating the earls so much that they wanted to kill him there and then. Edward II himself condemned the 'outrageous consumption of meats and fine dishes' by the aristocracy, but such was their sense of their own importance that statutes were passed in 1336, 1337 and 1363 limiting the wearing of miniver,* ermine, letus,† silk, cloth of gold, pearls and embroidered material to the upper echelons of society. The 1336 statute stated that anyone ranking lower than a lord or gentleman who was found wearing shoes or boots with

*Fur from the white winter coat of an ermine or a red squirrel.
†Fur from the winter coat of a weasel.

spikes (pointed toes) measuring two inches or more would be fined forty pence. These statutes – known as sumptuary laws – were motivated in part by a protectionist opposition to foreign imports, but even more important was the sense that expensive clothing should be reserved for people of a certain quality.

Peers came to wear robes denoting their rank. When Robert de Vere was 'invested' as duke of Ireland in 1386 he was given special deep red ducal robes, and the contemporary French historian Jean Froissart records that although all the lay peers wore scarlet ceremonial robes for Henry IV's coronation in 1399 the dukes and earls were differentiated from the barons by having three bars of ermine on the left arm rather than two.

The pecking order had always been a noble obsession. From the early Anglo-Saxon era on, the order in which men attested royal charters intimated their closeness to the king. Earls came first, and an earl whose name was listed ahead of another might subsequently slip down the list or disappear entirely. Courtiers agonized about such promotions and demotions. Then, as parliament came to the fore, rows about who should sit where – especially on those days when the lay peers were formally arranged in the Painted Chamber in strict order on the king's left-hand side – became frequent. When Richard II made John of Gaunt's legitimized son John Beaufort the earl of Somerset in 1397, he not only vested him with a velvet cloak and a sword, but 'he caused him to be seated in his place in parliament, between the earl marshal and the earl of Warwick'.[16] Likewise, in March 1405, King Henry IV and his council resolved after lengthy debate that Richard de Beauchamp, 13th earl of Warwick, should sit above the Earl Marshal, Ralph Neville, earl of Westmorland, and that Lord Grey of Codnor should sit above Lord Beaumont.[17] The ruling did not put an end to the matter, as the successor Earl Marshal, John de Mowbray, returned to it twenty years later and was not satisfied until he was able to assume his father's confiscated dukedom of Norfolk, thereby indubitably outranking a mere earl. As for the contest between the two barons, Grey and Beaumont, the decision was perhaps not so difficult. Edward I had summoned the first Lord Grey to parliament in 1299, and although Lord Beaumont could claim an earl as a distant ancestor and a droplet or two of royal blood by virtue of his descent from Henry III, his title had only been created by Edward II in 1309. As long as it was unblemished, the older the title, the greater the honour.

To the nobility, these were matters of life and death. On the last day of parliament in 1410 the Court of Chivalry delivered its verdict in the dispute between Reginald Grey, 3rd Baron Grey of Ruthyn, and Edward Hastings, both of whom claimed the right to bear the Hastings coat of arms ('or, a maunch gules') by virtue of their descent from John, 2nd Baron Hastings, respectively by his first and his second wife. The court found against Edward. He appealed, but owing to the war in France the trial was delayed until 1417, at which point he adamantly refused to pay his legal costs of £987 from the first trial or to relinquish his claim. Grey had him thrown in the debtors' prison at Marshalsea, where he spent at least sixteen years, much of it 'bound in fetters of iron . . . liker to a thief or traitor than like a gentleman of birth'.[18] Such was his pride that he held out even when his first wife and several of his children died. It seems he never capitulated.

Having clawed their way into parliament, peers sought to dominate it by also getting sons, brothers and uncles into the lower house. The Commons could prove meddlesome, as one aristocratic practice particularly rankled with them. Many peers had built a personal affinity or entourage of tenants, supporters and others who were retained in consideration for a fee. In time of war, these retainers would be a peer's loyal army. In peace, they enjoyed a bond of mutual support, whereby the lord would 'maintain' or defend the cause of his retainer to the utmost of the law (and indeed beyond) and the retainer would wear his lord's uniform, livery or badge. In many cases this led to anarchy, as men of different affinities engaged in violent feuds and aristocrats interfered in the fair prosecution of justice. The Commons repeatedly attempted to deal with the problem, securing increasingly aggressive statutes in 1275, 1285, 1305 and 1327, and in 1346 condemned livery and maintenance on the grounds that 'many bearers and maintainers of quarrels and parties in the country be maintained and borne by Lords, whereby they be more encouraged to offend'. So many people had been disinherited, 'delayed and disturbed of their right' or convicted when they were innocent that parliament required the peers to 'void [any such people] from their retinue, fees and robes'.[19] The statute was ignored, as there was no means of enforcing the measure and peers argued that the king, who had no standing army, could not go to war without their readily identifiable retinues. Still the matter rankled, and from 1377 the Commons returned to the matter repeatedly. An ordinance was granted in 1390 – and ignored. A statute was promulgated in 1393 – and ignored. It was only in the reigns of Henry IV and V that any prosecutions for pernicious livery and maintenance were brought.

The Commons was also central to another innovation with a direct impact on the peerage: bills of attainder, whereby parliament (rather than a court of law) declared a person guilty of treason or another felony. The first to suffer such a fate were Edward II's favourites, Gaveston and the Despensers, whom parliament banished and declared tainted men in 1308 and 1321 respectively. In Gaveston's case parliament decided, at the instigation of Henry de Lacy, 3rd earl of Lincoln, that the people 'regard[ed] him as a man already attainted and adjudged'.[20] He was condemned to death by the earls of Warwick, Lancaster, Arundel and Hereford, and murdered in 1312. As for the Despensers, a specially convened Court of Chivalry tried the father as earl of Winchester and condemned him to be hanged, drawn and decapitated; and when his son was similarly condemned, he was dressed with his arms reversed, crowned with stinging nettles, dragged to the gallows on a hurdle, hanged and presented with his entrails and his heart before being finally beheaded. The physical process of execution was gruesome enough; but the key aspect of attainder was that if a man's blood were declared tainted, his lands, his titles and his rights in common law were automatically forfeit. This was to prove a useful tool in times of civil war, as a triumphant faction in the court or in parliament could declare defeated rebels attainted and permanently exclude them and their families from the political scene; and a rebel could be attainted posthumously. Hence parliament itself became a means of continuing civil war.

Yet by far the biggest threat to a family's dynastic ambitions lay in the lack of male heirs. Neither the plague, nor the scaffold, nor the battlefield brought so many noble families to a full stop. The figures are striking. In all, 102 barons were summoned to parliament in 1299, and thirty-four more either had been summoned or were the heirs of those who had been. Of those 136 families, just forty-seven survived to 1400, and a mere sixteen of those to 1500; and although successive monarchs issued 221 summonses to new men between 1300 and 1499, only forty-five of them survived, leaving a much-diminished baronage in 1500 of just sixty-one. It was the same in the higher echelons. Between 1300 and 1309 seventeen men held the rank of earl. Four of them were executed or defeated as rebels, but six others died without legitimate male issue, ending the Warenne, Lacy, Bigod and Clare earldoms. The pattern was repeated in the latter half of the fifteenth century. Thirty-eight aristocratic families failed in these years, but only twelve of them met a violent end – and that included Lord Scales, who was lynched by boatmen in 1460, William Neville, earl of Kent, who died on campaign in 1463, John, Lord Wenlock, who died at the battle of Tewkesbury in 1471 and Edward Plantagenet, 17th earl of Warwick, who was executed in 1499. None of them had a legitimate male heir.

The nobility cared deeply about this extinction of lineages. In 1419 old Sir Thomas Erpingham, one of the great Lancastrian knights, who had fought at Agincourt, paid for a new chancel window for the church of the Austin Friars in Norwich. Disappointed still to be without children, despite having married twice, he devoted each of the eight panes to the names and coats of arms of the 'lords, barons, bannerets and knights that have died without issue male in the counties of Norwich and Suffolk since the coronation of the noble King Edward the IIId'.[21] The window is now long gone, but two antiquarians made notes from older documents.* Their lists differ, but they make the same elegiac point. Both, for instance, mention the Ufford family, commemorated in the first pane. Sir Robert de Ufford was first summoned to parliament as a baron in 1332 and five years later was made earl of Suffolk. When he died in 1369 his amiable second son William succeeded him; but all Earl William's children had

---

*They were the seventeenth-century MP Henry Spelman and the eighteenth-century rector of Fersfield, Francis Blomefield.

already died when he suddenly collapsed and died on the stairs leading into the Lords' chamber in 1382. So the Uffords arrived on the aristocratic scene and departed it in just fifty years.

The threat of extinction pulled peers' heartstrings in two different directions. On the one hand, an ambitious patriarch sought to leave everything to one son and exclude younger brothers, sisters and daughters from the succession lest endless subdivision atomize the estate. On the other hand, parents had a natural desire to provide for all their children. They had a choice. The law allowed gifts between the living (*inter vivos*), so they could endow as many younger sons as they wanted in their lifetime, just so long as they didn't deprive themselves of the wherewithal to maintain their dignity and didn't disparage the eldest son's inheritance. When they died, though, the common law of inheritance took effect. The eldest son would inherit, and other sons would get a look-in only if the son and heir were to die. If sons, brothers and uncles were to run out, the lands would 'fall among the spindles' (that is, be divided between married sisters and daughters and their husbands). Land, though, was not normally granted outright, as the king, who remained the ultimate owner of the whole of England, merely granted an 'estate in land' (that is, rights over it), which could not be sold or permanently alienated, though it could be sub-enfeoffed or sub-tenanted.

Two statutes of 1285 and 1290 subtly changed the position. The declared aim of the former, known as the *De Donis Condicionalibus* ('concerning conditional gifts') clause of the Statute of Westminster, was to stop heirs from being disinherited by their parents: it allowed the original donor of an estate in land to limit its inheritance to the direct lineal descendants of the recipient and his wife (the 'heirs of their bodies'), and it prevented the recipient from selling or otherwise permanently alienating it or contravening the donor's original wishes.* On the recipient's death, the estate would pass automatically to the heir, and if

---

*Although all land was still in theory owned by the crown and all that was being inherited, sold or alienated was the right to use the land, in practice nobles felt they were the owners of their land and so could alienate it.

the recipient's direct line should die out, the original grantor (or his primogenitary heir) could reclaim it. The statute also meant that lands legitimately granted to a younger son would revert to the head of the family if the cadet branch were to die out. In practice the statute encouraged the development of 'entails' whereby the grantor could impose conditions such as a 'tail male', which meant that the land would remain with the family only through the direct *male* line, or a series of remainders specifying further beneficiaries after his death. By entailing the estate on himself and his declared beneficiaries, he ensured he could enjoy its profits during his lifetime and secure its dynastic future.

The statute of 1290, known as *Quia Emptores* ('because the buyers'), ended the system of sub-enfeoffment and declared that all sales or grants of land were 'in fee simple': that is to say the land was alienated absolutely, without any residual feudal rights remaining with the grantor, allowing the recipient to sell it, mortgage it or bequeath it as he wished. When this was combined with the *De Condicionalibus* provisions it allowed a further innovation akin to a modern discretionary trust – an 'enfeoffment to use' (often referred to as a 'use'). The grantor would 'enfeoff' or entrust his estate in fee simple to friends or relatives (enfeoffees), who would then re-enfeoff the grantor or someone else in accordance with his directions. On the death of the grantor his last will – rather than the common law – would take effect. In other words, you could make provision for your younger son, without either permanently atomizing the family estate or letting it fall to daughters. In order to ensure your widow was not dispossessed, you could settle your estates jointly on yourself and your wife, the only danger being that a dowager countess might outlive her son and become a nuisance to her grandson in her dotage. You could lock male primogeniture into your dynasty, evade feudal obligations such as wardship and – at least theoretically – escape the threat of forfeiture on conviction of treason as the land was held by enfeoffees. It is easy to see why entails and uses became commonplace.

Families took advantage of these provisions with relish. So, for instance, Thomas Beauchamp, 11th earl of Warwick, entailed most of his substantial estates on 24 April 1344 in tail male, putting them in the hands of his enfeoffees, and made his last will on 6 September 1369, two months before he died. His eldest son Guy had died in 1360, leaving a daughter Katherine, who was forced to renounce the world and join the nunnery at Shouldham with £20 and a gold ring, and her younger brother Thomas, who inherited the earldom and the bulk of the estate. The 11th earl also entailed about £5,000 worth of estates in a tail male grant to his only other surviving son William, whose son William and grandson Richard acquired more lands through wealthy marriages to Joan Fitzalan and Isabel le Despenser respectively. Richard became earl of Worcester not long before dying at the siege of Meaux in 1422, leaving a sole daughter, Elizabeth, whereupon Isabel married Richard's namesake and cousin, the 13th earl, bringing with her the original entailed Warwick estates, the Despenser manors of Hanley in Worcestershire and Tewkesbury in Gloucestershire, the lordship of Glamorgan and several other properties, thereby agglomerating one enormous estate. This aristocratic accumulation was both common and intentional.

Women were rarely as feeble as the law implied. Take Joan de Burghersh. She was an astute and entrepreneurial woman. Born to a minor baron who held important posts as warden of Dover and the Cinque Ports, in 1341 she married John, the 2nd Baron Mohun, who was ward to her uncle Henry, bishop of Lincoln and chancellor of England, and held the 55-fee barony of Dunster in Somerset. Mohun fought at Crécy and was a founding knight of the Order of the Garter, along with Joan's brother Bartholomew de Burghersh, but was constantly out of pocket. The couple had no sons, but Joan married her three daughters (Elizabeth, Philippa and Maud) off so well (to an earl and two barons) that in 1374, before her husband died, she arranged to sell off the reversion of his barony* together with the manors of Minehead and Kilton and the hundred of Carhampton, to Elizabeth, wife of Sir Andrew Luttrell, for 5,000 marks. As Mohun had regularly mortgaged Dunster Castle and died with extensive debts, it is easy to see what Joan stood to gain. She lived at court on the proceeds of the sale and, thanks to her close support for Richard II, even managed to acquire the manor of

---

*That is, the right to assume the barony after the death of Mohun and his wife.

Macclesfield and a lease of Leeds Castle during her widowhood. As for Lady Elizabeth Luttrell, as the daughter of the 2nd earl of Devon and widow of Sir John de Vere, who had died before inheriting the earldom of Oxford, she clearly hoped that the barony would fall to her and her husband when Joan died. If so, she was to be disappointed. Mohun died in 1375 and Lady Elizabeth had been mouldering in the grave for nine years by the time Joan was buried under a great stone monument in the crypt of Canterbury Cathedral in 1404. After a prolonged legal battle with Joan's daughters, Lady Elizabeth's son Hugh inherited the lands, but he was never summoned as a baron. Joan de Burghersh's daughter Elizabeth followed her mother's example when her husband, William Montagu, 2nd earl of Salisbury, accidentally killed their only son William in a joust in 1383. With no children to inherit the estates, and knowing that the title of earl would pass to William's nephew John, the couple sold the reversion of their Somerset manors of Martock and Curry Rivell to John of Gaunt for 5,000 marks and the lordship of the Isle of Man to Baron Richard le Scrope of Bolton for his son William for 10,000 marks.

An heiress was a prized possession and could raise even a younger son to great heights of wealth and power. The best example (among many) is that of John of Gaunt, whose marriage at Reading Abbey in 1359 to Blanche, the younger daughter of Henry of Grosmont, duke of Lancaster, was a resplendent and happy affair. Their fathers were companions-in-arms, the bride and groom were third cousins and their alabaster effigies lie side by side in Old St Paul's Cathedral holding hands. But the real point of the marriage was Edward III's desire to make proper provision for his third son by marrying him to an heiress, as Lancaster was already forty-nine and his only children were two daughters. It turned out even better than Edward might have hoped. When the duke died in 1361, his lands were divided between the two daughters and his subsidiary titles of earl of Lancaster and earl of Leicester went to their respective husbands. Gaunt was now one of the greatest landowners in the realm. Then, the very next year, Blanche's sister Maud died; and since her husband was permanently detained as insane, Gaunt then held the whole inheritance, including the earldoms of Lancaster, Lincoln, Leicester, Derby and Richmond. Nor was that the end of Gaunt's successful career in the marriage market. Blanche died in 1369 and two years later he married another heiress, the Infanta Constance, daughter of Pedro I, King of Castile. When Pedro was murdered, Gaunt mounted a brief and wholly unsuccessful attempt to claim his crown, but in 1377 he received the next best thing: the duchy of Lancaster, with full palatinate powers over much of England. In 1376 Gaunt's younger brother Thomas, duke of Gloucester, had married the ten-year-old Eleanor de Bohun, elder daughter and co-heiress to the vast estates of Humphrey, 7th earl of Hereford, in the expectation that her younger sister Mary could be prevailed upon to renounce her share by joining the convent of Poor Clares. Spying yet another inheritance, Gaunt abducted Mary in 1380 and married her to his son Henry Bolingbroke. Greed clearly outranked brotherly love – and these financially advantageous marriages did not preclude infidelity, as during both of his marriages Gaunt sustained an affair with his daughters' governess, Katherine Swynford, who bore him four illegitimate children (given the name Beaufort). At least when Constance died he and Katherine made their relationship and their children legitimate.

Gaunt's estates were so extensive at his death – and his family life so complicated – that his will takes up seventeen pages of Norman French. By far the most extensive such document of its time to survive, it shows a man deeply reluctant to part with his earthly goods. He made the usual genuflections to religion. Masses were to be sung for his and his wife's souls. Ten tapers were to be lit at his funeral for each of the commandments he had broken, seven for the deadly sins he had committed and another seven for the works of charity he had neglected. He made bequests to St Paul's Cathedral, to the monasteries of Bury St Edmunds, Lincoln and Leicester, and to support hermits, lepers and prisoners. But his central obsession was dynastic. He went into minute detail, listing gold and silver hanaps (goblets), plates and saucers, silk mattresses, taffeta curtains and velvet vestments as well as manors, fiefdoms and advowsons. His eldest surviving son, the banished Bolingbroke, would be (so he hoped) heir to the dukedom, and Henry Beaufort was well provided for as bishop of Winchester, but his final entail in a long codicil is tortuous, specifying that the remainder should pass 'to the said Thomas, my son, and to the heirs of his body, and by default of the issue of his body the remainder to the said John his brother and to the heirs of his body, and by default of the issue of the said John, the remainder to Joan their sister and the heirs of her body, and by default of the issue of the said Joan, the remainder to my right heirs, who are the heirs of the heritage of Lancaster'.[22] One can sense a vain, rich old man slowly and reluctantly losing his grip on his possessions.

Gaunt was a younger son of the blood royal and his son would unexpectedly become king, but lesser families relied on precisely the same practice of social climbing through marriage. Over the course of the next century the Lovels of Titchmarsh married rich baronial heiresses three times in five generations, leaving Francis, the 9th Baron Lovel, as 6th Baron Holand, 8th Baron Deincourt, Baron Burnell and Baron Grey of Rotherfield, and in possession of Minster Lovel and Rotherfield Greys in Oxfordshire, Deincourts Manor in Yorkshire, Titchmarsh in Northamptonshire, Holgate Burnell and Acton Burnell in Shropshire and the feudal barony of Bedale. As the wealthiest peer not to be an earl and having become an early follower of Richard, duke of Gloucester, he was rewarded with a viscountcy in 1483; but unlike Gaunt's, his dynasty was not to last. He fought at Bosworth as Richard III's chamberlain and escaped; he fought again at Stoke and fled the field; but after that he and his title disappeared. He had no children, his forfeited estates were given to the countess of Richmond – and he has now no memorial.

That was the fate that every medieval aristocrat hoped to evade: family oblivion. It made them so jealous of their dynastic fortunes that although they did occasionally allow partition, the overwhelming presumption by the end of the fifteenth century was that an estate would pass entailed in its entirety to male heirs. Originally, baronial land and title had gone hand in hand, descending to men first and women when necessary. Then earldoms and dukedoms were entailed to male descendants only. Then land followed suit, through enfeoffment to use; and finally patented baronies were restricted to male descendants. A few old exceptions (the baronies by summons) remained, and even fewer new ones were created, but they were a tiny minority, as the vast bulk of the peerage's titles and landed wealth descended by primogeniture through men to men and for men alone. Some have argued that this strict and almost universal rule of male primogeniture prevented England from developing a caste removed from the rest of society, for it meant that younger sons of peers had to make their way in the professions – the law or the church. But the real effect was to concentrate land, wealth and prestige in the hands of a very small elite. It is only natural to want to establish and maintain a family; but in hedging themselves around with the trappings of wealth and power, the peerage made England a land of closely guarded inherited wealth and gross inequality.

The dissolution of the monasteries provided rich pickings for the aristocracy. Sir Thomas Audley was made Baron Audley of Walden and acquired several wealthy former religious houses, which became the foundation of the modern-day de Walden estates. This engraving shows how large the original mansion of Audley End was before two-thirds of it were pulled down.

CHAPTER 5

TO MAKE MY FAME ENDURE

THOMAS RADCLIFFE HAD BEEN the 3rd earl of Sussex for twenty-six years. He had governed Ireland. He had been the Lord President of the North. And since 1572 he had been Lord Chamberlain, in daily contact with Queen Elizabeth, who had been unusually generous to him, granting him several manors in Essex – including Henry VIII's favourite palace of Beaulieu at Boreham – to add to his grand residences at Woodham Walter and Attleburgh in Norfolk and the magnificent house that had been fashioned out of the dissolved abbey at Bermondsey, where he died on 9 June 1583. Despite debts of £11,000 to the crown on his demise, it was thought only right that such a great man should be treated with reverence in death as in life. He thought as much himself, as is clear from his will. 'I desire', he wrote, 'that my body shall be by mine executors, decently and comely, without unnecessary pomp or charges, but only having respect to my dignity and state, buried in the parish church of Boreham.'[1] The only restriction he made was that no more than £1,500 be spent (nearly £600,000 in 2017 values). Most of his instructions were followed. The renowned Dr Cloves, with three assistant surgeons, disembowelled and embalmed the corpse. The bowels were interred in Bermondsey and the body was sealed in wax, enclosed in a tightly moulded lead coffin and taken to Boreham. There, a host of mourners dressed in black (at the earl's expense) processed in strict order. At a similar funeral in 1524 the 2nd duke of Norfolk was marched to his sepulchre at Thetford by nine hundred mourners and nineteen hundred were invited to the wake afterwards; and for the 3rd earl of Derby's funeral at Ormskirk Church in 1572 the procession included a hundred paupers, forty choristers, eighty gentlemen and fifty knights and esquires. Five hundred yeomen straggled behind and might just have caught a glimpse of the late earl's household officers breaking their staves and throwing them into the grave before the earth was shovelled in. Afterwards money known as 'dole' was handed out to paupers – to the tune of £14 at the funeral of Henry, Lord Hunsdon in 1596.

Earl Thomas had made one more stipulation. His father and grandfather had been buried in the collegiate church of St Laurence Pountney in London, but since Thomas had no son and his title was to pass to his brother, he built a new chapel at Boreham and commissioned the best funerary designer in the land, the Fleming Richard Steevens, to build an altar tomb of alabaster and black and coloured marble to house the bodies of the three directly descended earls. It remains impressive (though Steevens enjoyed some whimsy – there are apes with hats and oxen with crowns among the decorations). The three men lie on rush mattresses wearing encrusted plate armour and peascod breastplates, their swords broken; around the left leg of each is tied the Garter. This monument cost a staggering £292 12s 8d out of a funerary total of £1,629. The earl may have specified that there be no 'unnecessary pomp'; but for the Tudor aristocracy ostentatious grandeur was not just desirable but vital, and never more so than in death.

✠

As individuals they were grand, but as a whole the Tudor nobility was politically supine. The pattern was set when Henry Tudor took the throne. His victory in 1485 over Richard III at Bosworth was unexpected and sweet, but it was a tawdry triumph. The outcome of the battle was determined by Thomas, Lord Stanley, who waited until he saw which way the battle was going before committing his troops and thereby earned himself the earldom of Derby. Such patent opportunism left the new Henry VII in little doubt that a Yorkist rebellion was always a possibility. Writing in the seventeenth century, Algernon Sidney said of Henry that his own meanness inclined him to hate the nobility; and thinking it to be as easy for them to take the crown from him, as to give it to him, he industriously applied himself to glean up the remainders of the House of York, from whence a competitor might arise; and by all means to crush those who were most able to oppose him.[2]

Sidney was exaggerating, but Henry did keep the peerage on a short leash, with particular attention to unreconciled Yorkists. One such was Edmund de la Pole. He was still a minor when his father, the Yorkist 2nd duke of Suffolk, died in 1491, so Henry insisted that Edmund pay the crown £200 a year during his wardship and that sixteen of the Suffolk manors be enfeoffed as a guarantee. Edmund probably thought himself hard done by, especially when Henry insisted that he be styled earl, not duke, of Suffolk. Yet Henry had reason to doubt the de la Poles, for Edmund's elder brother John, the earl of Lincoln, had been Richard III's nominated heir and had died a rebel at the battle of Stoke Field in 1487. Sure enough, in 1501 Edmund left the country, hoping to raise a foreign force to seize the English crown. Henry took swift action. He arrested his family and collaborators and had fifty-one of them attainted while Edmund awaited his chance to strike from across the Channel. That chance never came, and when the Holy Roman Emperor's son Philip of Burgundy was diverted by a freak storm and accidentally landed at Weymouth, the Emperor offered Edmund in exchange for Philip's safe return. The swap was made with a guarantee from Henry that he would not harm Edmund; but he slapped him in prison and set down in his will that his son Henry VIII should execute him, which he did in 1513. Edmund's evident treason proved that it made sense to keep bitter Yorkist nobles in check.

Henry VII's primary means of enforcing the quiescence of the nobility was an imaginative use of financial bonds and 'recognizances'. It was not a new idea. In 1413 Henry V had forced ten peers to sign bonds to the tune of 80,000 marks guaranteeing that they would not engage in any further lawlessness, and in 1479 Edward IV had banned the earl of Pembroke and his younger brother from entering Wales on pain of forfeiting £1,000 each. In like manner Henry VII extracted a bond from George Neville, Lord Abergavenny, guaranteeing that he would not enter Kent, Surrey, Sussex or Hampshire without permission, and he required Thomas Grey, 2nd marquess of Dorset – the queen's very unreliable half-brother – to surrender his lands to twelve enfeoffees who would hold them for the use of the marquess and marchioness in their lifetime and thereafter for their heirs, unless the couple committed treason, in which case the lands would revert to the king. Many reckoned Henry's sole motive was avarice. Yet in fact he was simply holding a financial sword over potentially rebellious heads, as these bonds, recognizances and guarantees meant that at least forty-six out of the sixty-two aristocratic families were bound over for good behaviour. Henry could rightly boast that apart from the pretender rebellions of Perkin Warbeck and Lambert Simnel, his new Tudor monarchy brought an unaccustomed peace to the realm after decades of internecine warfare. Even disconsolate peers were grateful for that.

Henry VIII's reign, though, saw an innovation that undermined the established aristocracy. Peers were jealous of their right to attend the king and give him counsel. The Latin equivalent of earl was after all *comes*, meaning companion. Parliament had become the most important venue for provision of this counsel. But peers still provided separate counsel, either individually or when they were summoned to a Great Council, which was effectively a meeting of parliament without the Commons. Henry VII summoned at least five such council meetings between 1487 and 1502, but his son came to rely instead on a much smaller body of men, primarily selected because they held one of the important offices of state or a post in the royal household. This 'Privy Council' soon became the driving force of Tudor government, and by the end of the century it was meeting nearly every day, with a fixed, invited membership that acted collectively in the name of the monarch. In the words of one Elizabethan, Thomas Norton, it was 'the wheels that hold the chariot of England upright';[3] but in the eyes of the established peers it usurped their former role in government, as although it always included some peers, they were never there by right *as* peers. The make-up of Henry VIII's Privy Council in 1540 makes the point. In addition to three bishops, there were eight lay peers: the dukes of Norfolk and Suffolk, the earls of Southampton, Sussex and Hertford, plus Thomas, Lord Audley, John, Lord Russell, and William, Lord Sandys. That sounds aristocratic enough. The eleven peers outnumbered the seven mere knights. Yet several of those eleven were new creations or promotions, men appointed to the Privy Council for their administrative usefulness or their closeness to the king rather than by virtue of their ancient titles. Suffolk, for instance, was Charles Brandon, whose father had died as Henry Tudor's humble standard-bearer at Bosworth. Granted the most intimate of royal posts as Master of the King's Horse in 1513, he was catapulted through the ranks of the aristocracy as duke of Suffolk in 1514, and after two unsuccessful attempts at profitable marriages (plus being widowed and having another marriage annulled) he settled on Henry's sister Mary in 1515 – without asking the king's permission first, which cost him a lot of grovelling later. Likewise Southampton was Henry's childhood friend William Fitzwilliam, who had served as a naval commander and treasurer of the royal household and was now Lord Privy Seal. Only Thomas Howard, 3rd duke of Norfolk and Lord High Treasurer, could claim a lengthy noble pedigree, stretching back through his father to Thomas Mowbray, duke of Norfolk under Richard II, and through his mother to Edward I's sixth son Thomas, earl of Norfolk. As for the rest, this was a government of experts and intimates.

The same was true of Edward's, Mary's and Elizabeth's Privy Councils. The numbers varied enormously, between a peak of fifty under Mary and a trough of nine under Elizabeth, but all three monarchs stuck to Henry's pattern. Edward VI's council of 1553 had thirty-nine members, only thirteen of whom were lay peers – and eight of them were new creations. Only Edward, Lord Clinton, could claim an unbroken family line back to 1299, and even he owed his place on the council to his position as Lord Admiral, not to his lineage as the 9th Baron Clinton. The trend was even more marked on Elizabeth's council of 1591, just one member of which had started life in a noble family: Charles Howard, 2nd Baron Howard of Effingham, who served as Lord High Admiral for thirty-four years from 1585. The balance was only slightly redressed in 1601, when Howard, newly made earl of Nottingham, was joined by the earls of Shrewsbury and of Worcester, whose titles went back to 1442 and 1514 respectively. It is significant, though, that neither of them held important posts, unlike the nine new men who served as Lord Keeper, Lord High Treasurer, Comptroller of the Household, Principal Secretary, Lord Chamberlain, Lord Privy Seal, Vice-Chamberlain, Chancellor of the Exchequer and Lord Chief Justice. The most impressive regional magnates, like the earls of Northumberland and Westmorland, had been elbowed aside by the talented and ambitious sons of the gentry.

It was not spite or an ideological objection to nobility that prompted this change. If anything, Elizabeth's reluctance to grant new titles sprang from a snobbish desire to retain the ancient nobility undiluted. No, the truth was that modern government in the sixteenth century required an infinitely broader set of talents than could be furnished by the fifty or so old families that remained. The Privy Council's workload was varied. When it met at Greenwich on 8 March 1573, for instance, the six members considered troop deployments in Ireland, the punishment of prisoners in the Tower and the Fleet, a shipwreck in Devon, maritime insurance against piracy, reprisals against Spain, a visa for Lord Kilsyth to go to Scotland, a letter from the bishop of London regarding a complex religious case and a letter from the mayor of Chichester regarding some 'lewd words' spoken by a shoemaker called Penne.[4] Such business would have seemed distinctly stale, flat and unprofitable to a lively aristocrat.

The rise of the Privy Council might have prompted peers to exploit their place in parliament more effectively, but here too they proved inactive. From 1515 to 1529 they allowed Cardinal Wolsey to dominate the upper house, and when he fell they took their lead from Thomas Howard, 3rd duke of Norfolk, who advanced the king's cause in the Lords* while Thomas Cromwell managed parliamentary affairs from the Commons until he was ennobled as earl of Essex in 1540. Admittedly, Henry's parliamentary managers were ruthlessly adept and held many of the trump cards. A difficult peer could find himself out of favour or in the Tower. Moreover, despite the social standing and self-importance of

---

*It was only known as such from 1544, but the distinction is minor.

the peers, it was easier to intimidate the House of Lords than the Commons. The upper house held just 107 members in the Reformation Parliament of 1529–36 – fifty-seven of them lay peers – and whereas voting in the Commons was still by collective acclamation (which meant an individual member could keep his vote secret), peers voted out loud one by one in reverse order of seniority. Any dissent was therefore all too apparent, especially as Henry often attended in person. The bishops and abbots felt relatively protected by their clerical status, but lay peers who mildly disagreed with the king's measures were intimidated into tacit acquiescence and those who felt more strongly were reluctantly granted royal permission to absent themselves. So when it came (on 19 March 1532) to the Lords' consideration of one of Henry's first measures to lay royal hands on ecclesiastical revenue, the Conditional Restraint of Annates Bill, while all the clergy voted against, they were only joined by one lay peer – William Fitzalan, 18th earl of Arundel – while the whole of the rest of the lay peerage voted it through.

Such evident capitulation is difficult to excuse but easy to understand, as Henry's assault on the church offered the tantalizing prospect of phenomenal self-enrichment, especially when it came to the dissolution of the lesser and greater monasteries enacted in 1536 and 1539: every peer in the land had his eye on a well-endowed local priory, convent, college or friary. So, whatever their personal views on religion, peers nodded Henry's legislation through and set about securing the spoils for themselves. The appositely named Sir Richard Rich is a case in point. He had conservative religious tastes, but his capacity for bending morality to the will of the king in his own interests proved limitless. He helped the legislation through as Speaker of the Commons, and then ensured that he profited handsomely as Chancellor of the Court of Augmentations, which was put in charge of disposing of the nine hundred or so monastic properties. In addition to the estates of St Bartholomew the Great in Smithfield, he took for himself the fifth wealthiest religious house in Essex, the abbey of Stratford Langthorne, plus the handsome Augustinian priory of Leighs (or Leez) and the Cluniac priory of Stanesgate. Each came with extensive lands, so he ended up with more than a hundred manors in Essex, and when he was made a baron in

1547, he styled himself after the new home he had built on the foundations of the priory at Leez. So flexible was he that he helped prosecute the Catholic bishops under Lord Protector Somerset, then turned face once under Mary, and back again under Elizabeth. Thus out of rich monastic pickings was born a family that would last in the English peerage – acquiring a couple of earldoms (Warwick and Holland) en route – until 1759, when Edward Rich, 10th Baron Leez, died without an heir.

Other new peers also went profiteering. Sir Thomas Audley, who was Lord Chancellor in 1533 and was ennobled in 1538 as Baron Audley of Walden for assiduously doing the king's bidding, scooped up the sixth wealthiest house in Essex, the Benedictine Abbey at Walden, plus the House of Augustinian Canons of St Botolph, Colchester, the Cluniac priory of Prittlewell, much of the Cistercian Abbey of Tilty and Holy Trinity Priory in Aldgate. The rest of Essex was parcelled out in similar fashion, to the enrichment of the earls of Sussex and Oxford, the marquess of Northampton and the Lord Clinton; the most valuable Essex abbey and the last to succumb, Waltham Holy Cross, went to one of the king's closest intimates and member of his privy chamber, Sir Anthony Denny, who also got his hands on the abbeys of Hertford and St Albans.

Thus, as the dissolution brought a fifth of the total land of England on to the market, the old families extended and concentrated their landholdings and a large number of new men established well-endowed dynasties. The benefits of this wholesale state-sanctioned theft can still be seen today. Although Audley's barony died with him, his daughter Margaret's son Thomas Howard became Baron Howard de Walden in 1597 and earl of Suffolk in 1603; he built the magnificent palace of Audley End on the grounds of the old abbey at Walden, and Charlton Park on the former lands of Malmesbury Abbey in Wiltshire, both of which remain grand family homes. Likewise, the house of Augustinian canons at Longleat passed briefly through the hands of the earl of Hertford before ending up with Sir John Thynne, whose descendants made it their ancestral home as the marquesses of Bath. Sir John Russell, great-grandson of a wine merchant, so impressed Henry as a soldier (he lost his eye at the siege of Morlaix in 1522) and as Lord Privy Seal that, in addition to a peerage, he was awarded the three wealthy abbeys in Devon of Tavistock, Plympton and Dunkeswell, plus Blackfriars in Exeter and seven acres of Westminster Abbey's lands later known as Covent Garden. When he was additionally made earl of Bedford under Edward VI, his old family home at Chenies in Buckinghamshire scarcely seemed adequate for his new status, so he transformed Woburn Abbey in Bedfordshire into an opulent palace, which remains the home of the dukes of Bedford.

A tiny handful of religiously conservative nobles objected. Thomas, Baron Darcy, and John, Baron Hussey (both of whom had been ennobled for their youthful military service), stayed away when Arundel voted against the Annates Bill, but in October 1536, along with John, 4th Baron Lumley and his son George, they joined the Pilgrimage of Grace – a popular insurgency in Yorkshire against Henry's breach with Rome, his dissolution of the monasteries and expropriation of church assets. All of them were attainted and only Lumley was spared execution. One convinced adherent of the old faith was the well-read (and later sainted) Margaret Pole. A sister of Edward IV and Richard III, she was a lady-in-waiting to Catherine of Aragon, and in recognition of her status and service was created countess of Salisbury in her own right and restored to a suite of formerly forfeited family lands which made her the fifth richest peer in England. When Henry's marriage turned sour, she locked horns with the king over his treatment of his daughter Mary, was accused of being involved in a Catholic plot centred on her son Cardinal Reginald Pole, and was executed, along with her son Henry, Baron Montagu, and her cousin the marquess of Exeter. In the main, though, through a combination of fear, greed, dynastic ambition and a sense of entitlement, the nobility quashed any religious scruples they may have had so thoroughly that nearly one in four noble estates was substantially better endowed in 1550 than in 1485, and only one in twenty-five had lost more than ten manors.

Despite the Tudors' bloody reputation, this pragmatism meant that just nine peers were executed in thirty years on religious grounds. As in the previous century, the greatest risk to a noble family lay not in politics but in genetics. The numbers make the point. For his first parliament in

1485 Henry VII sent writs of summons to two dukes, ten earls, two viscounts and twenty barons. Including the six titles held by minors and those not summoned because of their Yorkist sympathies, there were fifty-five lay peers. While Henry had several attainted, he created and promoted a few, too; but by the time he died in 1509 all these new titles had lapsed for want of an heir, along with nine older titles. So at the time of Henry VIII's accession the peerage consisted of one duke, ten earls, thirty barons (three of them minors) and one marquess (Thomas Grey, marquess of Dorset, who was in prison in Calais). That made a total of just forty-two lay peers. There was little recovery across the Tudor era. Despite the rewards in the form of titles offered by Henry VIII to soldiers and administrators after 1529, so that forty-seven titles were created, restored or resumed between 1509 and 1553, family extinctions and attainders meant that the total number of peers was just fifty-seven in 1558.

Elizabeth was particularly sparing in her allocation of titles. She created only two baronies from scratch – those of Burghley and Compton – and the rest of her 'creations' involved the younger sons of peers.* This parsimony left ambitious courtiers and peers feeling frustrated – so much so that her Lord High Treasurer William Cecil, Lord Burghley, tried to get the queen to agree to a set of new creations in the winter of 1588–9, producing a suitably conservative list of six promotions to earldoms and six new barons from established families. To no avail: none of them was ever appointed, and in her last thirty years Elizabeth promoted only two men: Lord Howard of Effingham became an earl, and Peregrine Bertie became Lord Willoughby de Eresby. When the queen's favourite, Robert Devereux, 2nd earl of Essex, importuned her about creating new peers, she prevaricated; and when her household comptroller Sir Edward Wotton offered £1,000 to an intermediary if Essex could sort him out a title, he got nowhere. By the end of her reign in 1603 the peerage was down two to fifty-five.

*Such as Thomas Howard, the second son of the 3rd duke of Norfolk, who was made Viscount Bindon, or royal cousins such as Henry Carey, who was made Baron Hunsdon (both in 1559); or restored family members such as Reginald Grey, (re)instated as 5th earl of Kent in 1572 after his family had spent fifty years in degrading poverty.

Financial ruin, too, was an ever-present danger. In some cases this was an entirely self-inflicted wound. Peers with no son and heir could be particularly reckless. One notable Tudor example was Henry Percy, the 6th earl of Northumberland between 1527 and 1537. His was an illustrious family. They had held important lands in the north since the Conquest and had accumulated others across the realm, bringing in a total annual income of £4,000 in 1489. Henry was unfortunate in his personal relationships: his mean-spirited father treated him appallingly, an early crush on Anne Boleyn was frustrated, and he came to think of his wife, Mary Talbot, daughter of the 4th earl of Shrewsbury, as a spy. His besetting sin seems to have been extravagant generosity, as he doled out vast swathes of his inheritance to childhood friends and household servants. He liquidated assets, he granted leases at knockdown rates and he sought royal favours for those in his service. A childhood friend, Thomas Arundell, received lands in the West Country; one household retainer, Sir Reynold Carnaby, received Hexham Abbey; another, his comptroller Sir Thomas Wharton, received an annuity and lands in Cumberland and Yorkshire; and a third, his treasurer Thomas Johnson, was elevated to the status of gentleman. In total, Percy willingly surrendered all his lands in Somerset, Devon, Dorset, Sussex, Lincolnshire and Wales, plus the manors of Cockermouth, Hackney, Petworth, Heulaugh, Catterton and Craven. His motives are unclear, but family relations soured to such an extent that he determined to disinherit his remaining heirs, his younger brothers Thomas and Ingram, because, so he told Thomas Cromwell, of their 'debility and unnaturalness'.[5] In February 1536 he officially made the king his heir, and that autumn both Thomas and Ingram took part in the Pilgrimage of Grace. The initial rising was bought off with assurances, but when a second rising burst out in February 1537 the ringleaders, including the two Percy brothers, were arrested. Thomas was attainted and executed, Ingram died in the Tower and the earl died of natural causes at Hackney on 29 June. Cromwell's agent wrote from Wressle Castle on 20 August that he had never 'seen a finer inheritance more blemished by the follies of the owner and the untruth of his servants'.[6]

Similarly, Edward de Vere entered into the second oldest earldom in the land as the 17th earl of Oxford at the age of just twelve when his father died in 1562. With the title came lands that brought in £2,500 a year and the hereditary title of Lord Great Chamberlain with an annual stipend of £2,250. Edward was a wealthy young man; but despite spending his teenage years as a ward to Sir William Cecil – whose daughter Anne he married – he never learned prudence. Admittedly, his father died in debt, his mother retained possession of her jointure until her death in 1568 and the queen extracted as much as she could out of Edward's wardship, taking a third of the de Vere lands and charging him £7,000. Even so, by the time he was allowed to take possession of his estates (on payment of another £4,000) he had taken out further expensive bonds totalling £23,000. Unhappy in his marriage and addicted to the theatre, to jousting and to foreign travel, Oxford seemed incapable of tightening his belt, however much the queen lectured him about his 'unthriftiness'. In 1575 he went on an expensive foreign tour, with £9,000 of debt still hanging over him but £6,000 in cash in his pocket thanks to the sale of his estates in Cornwall, Staffordshire and Wiltshire. Having taken out a further £4,000 in loans in Italy, on returning to England he sold at least seven more manors, including all his holdings in Devon. The next year he asked the queen to grant him the manor of Castle Rising, which had reverted to the crown on his relative the duke of Norfolk's attainder. Elizabeth obliged – and he immediately sold it. Then he sold the family home at Wivenhoe in Essex, followed by seven acres near Aldgate and a mansion known as Fisher's Folly in Bishopsgate. The last of the estates – Hedingham Castle and Colne Priory – went when Anne died in 1588. With three daughters but no surviving legitimate son and heir, it seemed that Oxford was wilfully spending his inheritance; but a second marriage to one of the queen's maids of honour, Elizabeth Trentham, finally produced a son, Henry, in 1593. Cecil made provision for Oxford's daughters in his will but wisely made sure that their father, who was still occupied fending off tailors and other creditors, could not touch their inheritance. Oxford was always full of plans. He begged to be appointed governor of Jersey, he wanted to mine for tin in Cornwall, he invested in Frobisher's second voyage in search of the north-west passage. But when he died in 1604 the whole of his patrimony was gone, and his equally dissolute son had to make his fortune anew by buccaneering on land and at sea – and marrying wealthily.

Ambition could destroy a fortune as surely as profligacy: although many prospered as ministers of the crown, the cost of royal service could be crippling. Henry Hastings is a case in point. First summoned to parliament by Elizabeth as Lord Hastings while his father the 2nd earl of Huntingdon was still alive, he was a convinced Protestant, little attracted by the fripperies of life. From his father and uncle he inherited castles, manors and estates across Leicestershire. He might have felt honoured to take over the post of Lord President of the Council of the North in 1572; but it was to be his ruin, as his costs were never fully met by the crown. By 1587 he reckoned that he had spent £20,000 more than the queen's allowance to him, and by the time of his death in 1595 he had been forced to raise £100,000 from the sale of inherited lands. He died so deeply in debt that his brother George, the 4th earl, was reluctant to take up the management of his remaining estates.

These were exceptional cases, but other economic realities wrought havoc with noble fortunes. Depopulation in the late middle ages as a result of successive outbreaks of plague deprived landlords of labourers, tenants and rental income, and made it difficult for them to increase rents to meet soaring inflation. Most agricultural land had always been devoted to arable crops, but ploughing, sowing, planting and harvesting was labour-intensive and unprofitable, whereas grazing flocks and herds could bring in a healthy income on the back of a much smaller workforce. The landowning class made a rapid calculation: sheep were more profitable than crops, and it was better to exploit your own lands than rent them out to others. The result was a mass expropriation by the nobility of lands that had historically been thought of as public commons, and their enclosure as deer parks and grazing for the exclusive use of noble flocks and herds. By 1500 much of the common land in England had been enclosed, in some cases accompanied by the destruction of homesteads and the wholesale incorporation of villages into aristocratic estates. Parliament repeatedly objected that the enclosures had led to some 20,000–30,000 people being rendered homeless and forced to wander the land as vagrants. Anti-enclosure statutes were passed. A new ban on turning arable land into pasture was introduced. Fines were levied on lords who destroyed homes and villages. Yet the nobility continued enclosing common land.

The tensions thus created could burst into open rebellion, as Sir William Cavendish, who pursued the dissolution of the monasteries as a man 'that little feareth the displeasure of any man',[7] found out. In 1540 he obtained the manor of Northaw in Hertfordshire, which had formerly belonged to St Albans Abbey, and in August 1547 he married his third wife Elizabeth ('Bess of Hardwick'), who brought with her a share of her father John Hardwick's estates in Derbyshire and the bulk of her first husband Robert Barlow's. Cavendish was wealthy, yet he claimed that his several ministerial posts left him 5,000 marks out of pocket, and in 1548 he enclosed the common lands at Northaw. The villagers reacted with fury, storming on to his land on Whitsunday and blowing up his warrens, killing over two thousand rabbits. A year later Cavendish sold up and moved to Derbyshire, where he bought the manor of Chatsworth. Sir Thomas Wharton, a protégé of the 6th earl of Northumberland, had a similar experience. When he rebuilt the family manor house in Wharton, destroyed the village to improve the view from the Hall and enclosed the whole of Ravenstonedale as a park, local anger forced him to move to Yorkshire, where he saw out his days in the elegant moated grounds of the former Healaugh Park Priory. So strong was the sense of national anger at these appropriations that hedges were torn down, most notably in Essex and Norfolk, and Lord Protector Somerset set up a commission into illegal enclosures. In the following year, 1549, one dispute took on a national significance when rioters attacked the enclosures at Wymondham in Norfolk, which Robert Kett held from John Dudley, the recently elevated earl of Warwick (later duke of Northumberland). Far from opposing the rebels, Kett sided with them in tearing down his own fences and led them on a march to Norwich, where 16,000 of them tore down the hedge surrounding the town close and set up camp on Mousehold Heath just outside the city. When the city refused them access to the town market to buy food, Kett's army took the city by force. The revolutionary nature of the protest was clear. A set of twenty-nine demands was sent to Protector Somerset, and Alexander Neville, secretary to Matthew Parker, archbishop of Canterbury, wrote at the time that Kett was 'ready not only to restrain but also to subdue the power of the nobility: that, as they were weary of their misery, so he hoped in a little time to make the others sorry for their pride'.[8] Kett took over the ostentatious town palace in Norwich that had recently been built for Henry Howard, earl of Surrey (but in which he never lived: he was executed as a suspected Catholic shortly after its completion in 1547). Whatever Somerset's private sympathies with the anti-enclosure movement, he could not allow England's second city to remain in the hands of the mob, so he sent William Parr, the marquess of Northampton, and Edmund, Lord Sheffield, with a force of 1,500 men to winkle Kett out. In the ensuing battle in the narrow streets of Norwich Kett's supposedly unruly mob sent the royal army packing back to Cambridge without Sheffield, who fell from his horse near Cathedral Close and was struck down by a butcher. A second army was sent, led by the earl of Warwick. This time the royalists took no chances. With Spanish, Italian, German and Welsh mercenaries, their force totalled 14,000 men, so when battle was joined on 27 August outside the city at Dussindale the outcome was hardly in doubt. The insurgents were slaughtered in their thousands; many dozens more were executed. Robert Kett was hanged from the walls of Norwich Castle and his brother William from the west tower of the old Abbey Church at Wymondham. The nobility was clearly determined that nothing would stand in the way of their exploitation of the land.

✠

The root of the nobility's support for the dissolution of the monasteries and their theft of common land was straightforward greed; but it was well watered by a desperate aristocratic competition in conspicuous consumption, fuelled by the moral justification for greed derived from the argument that landed wealth was a sign of God's blessing. As Sir John Cheke put it in 1549, 'riches and inheritance be God's providence, and given to whom of his wisdom he thinks good'. Further, he asked, 'why do we not then being poor bear it wisely, rather than by lust seek riches unjustly, and show ourselves contented with God's ordinance?'[9] This may sound like special pleading, but to a Tudor Protestant it was a potent argument. If riches were God's gift to the good, then conspicuous consumption was a virtue, not a vice. Old and new peers took this message to heart. In 1579 Lord Burghley complimented Sir Christopher Hatton on his new house at Holdenby, with its 'large, long, straight fair way', its 'stately ascent from your hall to your great chamber; and your chambers answerable with largeness and lightsomeness, that truly a Momus could find no fault'. Thinking of his own palaces at Burghley and Theobalds, on which he spent many thousands, he boasted that both he and Hatton 'meant to exceed our purses'.[10] In other words, it was important that a noble's sumptuous expenditure set him apart from the rest by its excess.

Extravagant hospitality remained a means of asserting one's regional prominence, too. Thus between 1504 and 1519 Edward Stafford, 3rd duke of Buckingham, maintained a private household of between 125 and 148 at Thornbury Castle in Gloucestershire, all of whom ate at his expense every day. On Christmas Day in 1507 he hosted 294 guests and the following Epiphany there were 459. His brother-in-law Henry Percy, 5th earl of Northumberland, had 166 servants at Wressle Castle and at Christmas in 1588 George Talbot, 6th earl of Shrewsbury, provided his guests with 441 gallons of beer, twelve sheep, ten capons, twenty-six hens, seven pigs, six geese, seven cygnets, 118 rabbits and a turkey. These families got through large quantities of meat. Buckingham's *daily* provender included twelve rounds of beef (each amounting to the whole of the meaty part of the hind leg), four sheep, half a deer, half a pig, two geese, eight lambs, two sucking pigs, three capons, seven rabbits, three woodcocks, six swans and a mallard; Burghley's household consumed 1,600 rabbits and 2,500 chickens a year, and at his daughter Elizabeth's wedding in 1581 he provided thirteen different kinds of wildfowl.

So too with clothes. In 1501 Edward Stafford, the 3rd duke of Buckingham, wore a gown worth £1,500 (worth roughly £1.4 million in 2017) for the wedding of Prince Arthur and Catherine of Aragon, and his household accounts for 1504 show that he spent £351 2s on textiles,

£62 13s on jewels and £25 2s on furs and skins. Among these totals were sums for silk ribbon, gilt daggers, ivory beads, pearls from Cyprus and gloves from France. At the same wedding Nicholas, Baron Vaux, wore 'a gown of purple velvet with pieces of gold so thick and massy that besides the silk and fur it was valued at a thousand pounds, as also a [Lancastrian] collar of SS* weighing eight hundred pounds in nobles'.[11] The effect could be striking. At Henry VIII's meeting with Emperor Maximilian in 1513 Buckingham wore 'purple satin, his apparel . . . full of antelopes and swans of fine gold bullion and full of spangles, and little bells of gold, marvellously costly and pleasant to behold'.[12] When William Fitzwilliam, earl of Southampton, went to receive Anne of Cleves, he too dressed to impress in 'a coat of purple velvet cut on cloth of gold and tied with great aiglettes and trefoils of gold, to the number of four hundred and baudrickwise he wore a chain, at which did hang a whistle of gold set with rich stones of great value'.[13] The two Henries made attempts at limiting this sumptuary excess, but the Tudor century saw a significant inflation in sartorial extravagance. In 1515 dukes and marquesses were allowed to wear cloth of gold and, along with earls, sable. In 1533 there was a further relaxation. Cloth of gold of tissue costing more than £5 a yard was limited to dukes and marquesses; they and earls could also wear crimson, scarlet or blue velvet, silver or tinselled satin, and gold or silver embroidery. Some objected to such extravagance. Erasmus reported that Sir Thomas More disdained silk or purple or gold chains except where it would be indecent not to wear them; and when Henry Howard, earl of Surrey, was put on trial for treason one of the charges against him was that he wore a doublet and hose of purple silk and gold tissue, materials that were reserved for royalty. Elizabeth issued ten stern proclamations during her reign on who could wear what, all aimed at limiting extravagance and reinforcing class gradations, but they proved of little worth, as her godson Sir John Harington quipped:

---

* The 'collar of esses', a heavy decorative collar formed of a linked series of the letter 'S'. An ornamental collar, akin to a chain of office, was part of the livery denoting adherence to a particular noble household. The Lancastrian collar of entwined esses often carried a white swan pendant.

Our zealous preachers that would pride repress
Complain against Apparell's great excess;
For though the laws against it are express,
Each Lady like a Queen herself doth dress,
A merchant's wife like to be a baroness.[14]

Though some purported to deride 'these strange flies, these fashion-mongers . . . who stand so much on the new form, that they cannot sit at ease on the old bench',[15] the Elizabethan nobility competed in fashionable splendour and demanded elaborate imported brocades, damask, velvet and silk for their quilted peascod doublets, their starched ruffs and their heavily decorated farthingales. The result was an outburst of ostentatious costumery. The countless portraits of Henry Wriothesley, 3rd earl of Southampton, for instance, show him in fashionable high heels, immaculate white silk trunk hose, brocaded doublet worked with silver and gold, and embroidered French gloves. This appetite for finery could be ruinously expensive for a family estate. Ben Jonson made the point in his play *Every Man Out of His Humour*, suggesting that an ambitious courtier would have to turn five hundred acres of his best land into two or three trunks of apparel. When Elizabeth's favourite, Robert Dudley, earl of Leicester, died in 1588 his seven doublets and two cloaks were valued at £543, and he left total debts of £59,006 (£21.7 million in 2017). So too Roger Manners, 5th earl of Rutland, spent £11,000 a year in the 1590s, more than twice his income, £1,000 of it on clothes and at least as much on gambling. It was only the shock of imprisonment for his involvement in the Essex rebellion that forced him to mend his ways.

There were specific sartorial signs of nobility. For state occasions such as a coronation, a royal wedding or christening, and the procession to a new parliament, peers wore 'robes of estate' made from crimson silk velvet, lined with white sarsenet (a particularly soft silk fabric) and decorated with a set number of ermine tails (four for dukes and marquesses, three for earls, two for barons). These too were expensive. John de Vere's set of mantle, tabard, surcoat and hood was valued at £15 at his death, and the separate robes of estate and robes of parliament belonging to George Talbot, 4th earl of Shrewsbury, were valued at £30 and £40 in 1538. Knights of the Garter had additional sartorial privileges. The order's gold collar weighed in at 47oz for a duke and 36oz for an earl. The one made for Henry Howard, 3rd duke of Norfolk, had fifty-four gold garters and knots and from it hung a weighty gold pendant representing St George, which was studded with rubies and diamonds.

Ostentatious expenditure was not the only means of asserting and perpetuating noble exclusivity. The aristocracy developed a separate code of living. Not for them the vulgar sweat of hard labour. A career in the law was acceptable for the son of a nobleman, or even in agriculture, if one were in a supervisory capacity. Trade was just about allowable, as long as one were not selling something oneself. Most strikingly, the nobility deliberately eschewed intellectual endeavour, a fact much decried by a succession of Tudor administrators. While he awaited execution in 1510, Henry VII's agent Edmund Dudley blamed the ignorance of the nobility on the fact that 'the children of poor men and mean folks are promoted to the authority that the children of noble blood should have if they were meet therefore'.[16] So too Henry VIII's secretary of state Richard Pace, who had studied at Winchester, Padua and Oxford, was scandalized that a peer had told him that he would rather his son were hanged than be a scholar or know anything other than how to train a hawk, and the humanist scholar Sir Thomas Elyot complained that 'to a great gentleman it is a notable reproach to be well learned and to be called a great clerk'.[17]

A few did take up intellectual pursuits. John Bourchier, 2nd Baron Berners, published translations of Froissart's *Chronicles* and the *Golden Book of Marcus Aurelius* between 1523 and 1534. Henry Stafford, who was made a baron in 1547 twenty-six years after the execution of his father the 3rd duke of Buckingham, collected a library of more than three hundred books and translated Latin tracts by Erasmus and Bishop Edward Fox. John Lumley, who had the family barony restored in 1553, accumulated a great library, which in time formed the foundations of the British Library, and endowed the Lumleian lectures on anatomy and surgery, which continue today. Henry Parker, 10th Baron Morley, published several works, including a prose essay on the psalms ('a pious lucubration' according to Sir Sidney Lee) and a 'very long-winded' translation in 'uncouth verse' of Petrarch's *Trionfi*, to which he appended a poem of his own entitled 'Vergil in his epigrams of Cupid and drunkenness'. And in translating books 2 and 4 of the *Aeneid*, Henry Howard, earl of Surrey, found a rhythmic form that gave English shape to Vergil's hexameters and became a commonplace of English dramatic poetry as blank verse. None of Surrey's poetry was published in his lifetime, but when his sonnets appeared in the Elizabethan era he and his close friend Thomas Wyatt were reckoned by George Puttenham in 1589 to have 'greatly polished our rude and homely manner of vulgar poesy' and to be the 'first reformers of our English metre and style'.[18]

Notwithstanding these exceptions, the courtly Elizabethan poet Edmund Spenser felt strongly about the corporate intellectual delinquency of the peerage. Writing in *The Tears of the Muses*, he argued that 'the honourable race of mighty peers' should promote learning because 'that is the garland of nobility'. Sadly, though:

> ... *All otherwise they do esteem*
> *Of th'heavenly gift of wisdom's influence,*
> *And to be learned, it a base thing deem* ...[19]

Spenser's complaint was that it was a dereliction of duty to be a mindless, incompetent or foolish peer, because the whole point of a hierarchical society with peers at its apex was that it was well ordered. Elyot's contention that 'where there is any lack of order needs must be perpetual conflict'[20] was such established religious wisdom that throughout Elizabeth's reign every congregation in the land was regularly required to listen to a couple of homilies on obedience. One, probably written by Thomas Cranmer in 1547, states: 'Take away kings, princes, rulers, magistrates, judges and such states of God's order, no man shall ride or go by the highway unrobbed, no man shall sleep in his own bed unkilled, no man shall keep his wife, children and possessions in quietness.'[21] This theocratic assertion was a common Tudor belief.

Spenser also complained that the nobility 'only boast of arms and ancestry'.[22] He was right. Pretensions to martial prowess remained a central part of the Tudor nobility's belief in its own exclusivity. In the early part of the sixteenth century the country had need of courageous commanders. Henry VIII notably promoted several of his commanding officers at Flodden, Tournai and the battle of the Spurs. He bumped Thomas Howard up from earl of Surrey to duke of Norfolk for his efforts at the first of these engagements, and in recognition of Charles Somerset's valour at Tournai he made him earl of Worcester and granted his son Henry his mother Elizabeth's barony of Herbert so that both father and son, unusually, were peers simultaneously. In one case King Henry demonstrated a sense of ironic humour, joking that his gift to the earl of Derby's younger son Sir Edward Stanley of the entirely made-up title of Lord Mounteagle was made on the basis that 'he won the mount against the Scots' at Flodden 'and also in consideration that his ancestors bare in their crest the eagle'.[23] At the other end of the century Elizabeth relied on aristocrats to lead her military campaigns. Robert Dudley, who was the fifth son of the duke of Northumberland but raised by royal favour to earl of Leicester, and Peregrine Bertie, 13th Baron Willoughby de Eresby, led her forces in the Netherlands, as did Robert Devereux, 2nd earl of Essex, and Charles Blount, 8th Lord Mountjoy, in Ireland; and Lord Howard of Effingham was the Lord High Admiral who in his own words successfully plucked the feathers of the Spanish Armada one by one in 1588.

Even though England enjoyed long periods of peace in the Tudor era, the aristocracy maintained a military air, as the houses they built clearly demonstrate. Older castles like the one built by William Clinton, earl of Huntingdon, in 1345 and improved a century later by Humphrey Stafford, duke of Buckingham, at Maxstoke in Warwickshire, were genuine fortifications, with thick curtain walls, embattled parapets, tall angle-towers, an impregnable gatehouse and a wide moat. One of Richard III's allies, William, Lord Hastings, started a similar castle at Kirby Muxloe in Leicestershire in 1480. It too was to have parapets, a portcullis and a moat. Yet this was largely for show, as the heavy artillery gun-ports he installed could only be used if the moat were dry. This *faux* militarism became the Tudor fashion. The residence built for Edward Stafford, 3rd duke of Buckingham, in Thornbury in south Gloucestershire was a grand crenellated castle, but its lofty battlements were little more than a quaint martial affectation, as he installed huge oriel windows in the main living quarters. Chepstow Castle, once the defensive masterpiece of William Marshal and Roger Bigod that glowered stonily across the river Wye, was converted into a comfortable Tudor residence in the hands of Charles Somerset, earl of Worcester, illegitimate son of the 3rd duke of Somerset. The Percy citadels went through the same process of domestication. The family had held the motte-and-bailey castle at Topcliffe, where the River Swale meets Cod Beck, since not long after the Conquest. In time they had built a more accessible adjacent manor house, but by the sixteenth century they had largely moved to their other castles at Alnwick, which benefited from a deep ravine to the south and east, at Warkworth, which was similarly surrounded by a tight loop in the river Coquet, and at Wressle. Each of these they decorated in the latest opulent style – making them more Tudor palaces than Norman castles – so that when John Leland visited Wressle in 1540, he commented that it was 'one of the most proper beyond the Trent, and seemeth as newly made', adding that the extensive gardens and orchards were 'exceedingly fair'.[24] Since these were outside the moat, it seems the fortifications were only really for show.

Others, especially the newly elevated nobles, went further. When Sir William Paulet, who was treasurer to Edward VI, Mary and Elizabeth and rose to be marquess of Winchester, was allowed to fortify the family manor at Old Basing in 1531, it consisted of an old keep surrounded by defensive earthworks; by the time he had finished, it had two main buildings with 360 rooms, part of the old ramparts had been turned into terraced gardens, and most of the new building stood outside the defensive works. Many thought it the greatest private house in England, to rival even the archbishop of Canterbury's mansion at Knole Park with its 365 rooms, 52 staircases, twelve entrances and seven courtyards. As for Castle Ashby in Northamptonshire – which Henry, Lord Compton, probably started around the time of the death of his wife, Frances Hastings, in 1574 – the only vaguely military element about it was its name.

The sums involved in this splurge of house-building were spectacular. Somerset and Syon Houses set the duke of Somerset back £15,000 in 1548–51 (around £7.4 million in 2017), and the marquess of Winchester spent £14,000 on his house at Chelsea, no doubt contributing to the debts of £46,000 (£16.6 million) he left behind him. Robert, earl of Salisbury, went even further, expending £39,000 on Hatfield House with its elaborate garden and a water feature full of artificial shells, fish and snakes. This seems to amount to reckless mania, but that was the whole point: to go beyond what was in any sense necessary and to exceed what others could only dream of. A grand country house was an essential aspect of maintaining the myth of exclusivity. Some nobles might even have been aware of the incongruity of their building works; Leland claimed that Henry Percy, 5th earl of Northumberland, inscribed one of the main apartments in Wressle Castle with a poem:

When it is time of cost and great expense
Beware of waste and spend by measure:
Who that outrageously maketh his dispense
Causeth his goods not long to endure.[25]

Whether Percy was being deliberately ironic, considering the inordinate expense of restoring Wressle, it is difficult to know.

✠

The aim of all this house-building, peacockery and overt wastefulness was to fashion an ideal of a tiny elite set apart from the rest, to justify it to the world and to sustain it into eternity. For a self-consciously noble aristocrat, fake battlements proclaimed his ancient chivalry, luxurious apartments proved his wealth, and a prodigious new house made possible a royal visit, with all the favour and prestige that might bring.

Above all, though, a good marriage ensured the perpetuation of the family line. Many aristocratic Tudor marriages were overt acts of family alliance, as when Henry Clifford, earl of Cumberland, took Margaret Percy, the eldest daughter of the 5th earl of Northumberland, as his second wife in about 1516, cementing relations between two northern families; and when the marriage of Anne Dacre to the 2nd earl of Cumberland in 1553 (also as his second wife) brought a longstanding family feud to an end. One celebration at Holywell in Shoreditch in 1537, which was attended by much of the court, was a particularly notable declaration of noble alliance as it joined three couples simultaneously, thereby binding together the families of the earls of Rutland, Westmorland and Oxford. The fact that the family alliance was generally more important than the personal match is shown by the arrangement between John de Vere, 16th earl of Oxford, and Henry Hastings, 3rd earl of Huntingdon, in 1562, in which the two men agreed that Oxford's son and heir would marry one or other of Huntingdon's daughters within a month of his eighteenth birthday. In the end, he married neither.

A truly successful aristocratic marriage was one that produced offspring, especially a son and heir, so many noble women spent much of their married life bearing children. Given the threat of infant mortality, nobles deliberately produced large families: roughly 40 per cent of aristocratic women between 1450 and 1550 had five or more children, and nearly 30 per cent had six or more. Margaret Percy had seven children, Cecily Neville bore her husband the 3rd duke of York eleven, including Edward IV and Richard III, between 1438 and 1455, and Eleanor Paston bore Thomas Manners, the first earl of Rutland, at least ten children between 1526 and 1539.

Giving birth might have been a noble wife's primary duty (and it was dressed up with considerable ritual), but it was not the only way a wife could assist in the family ambitions. The end of the Wars of the Roses enabled the nobility to spend far more time at court, seeking preferment and enticing favour. Women could play just as significant a role in this as their men, especially if they could secure a place in the separate household of the queen; so, despite her ten pregnancies, the countess of Rutland managed to attend Anne Boleyn's creation as marchioness of Pembroke and Jane Seymour's funeral as a prominent courtier, and to serve as lady-in-waiting to four of Henry VIII's wives.

Considering how important women were in establishing and maintaining aristocratic lineages, it is striking that noble attitudes around women changed so markedly for the worse during the Yorkist and early Tudor era, as the legal concept of 'coverture' became the accepted norm. This meant that a woman's legal existence was entirely 'covered' by her marriage; so once married she had no right to sign a legally binding contract, initiate or defend a suit in a court of law, hold goods and chattels in her own right or write a will without the consent of her husband, who also enjoyed the absolute right to determine where and how she lived and to admonish or punish her. There was considerable misogyny in this new attitude: women were considered morally and intellectually inferior and prone to hysteria. Even when a well-educated noblewoman proved herself forceful and decisive, she would be accused of unnaturally trying to be manly. Hence the countess of Westmorland was not praised for helping to suppress the Pilgrimage of Grace, but instead accused of playing the part of a knight rather than that of a lady; and when the earl of Southampton interrogated Margaret Pole, countess of Salisbury, for treason he found her 'so earnest, vehement and precise' that he despised her for being 'rather a strong constant man than a woman'.[26] So pervasive was this belief that many women absorbed it themselves. When her husband and son stood accused of treason in 1535, Gertrude Blount, the impressively steadfast marchioness of Exeter, claimed that since she was a woman her 'fragility and brittleness [was] such as [was] most facilely, easily, and lightly seduced and brought into abuse and light belief'.[27] Sadly, she probably thought this her best line of defence.

The vast majority of aristocratic women at this time did get married – in one estimate, 95 per cent[28] – so this harsh patriarchy left women entirely at the mercy of their husbands. Thus Henry Percy, 6th earl of Northumberland, virtually incarcerated his wife Mary because he thought she had been spying on him for his political enemies and point-blank refused to allow her father the 4th earl of Shrewsbury to visit or speak with her. When the unhappy and childless couple separated, Northumberland insisted on leaving all his property to the king rather than his wife or his brothers, whom he hated. Mary, who outlived her husband by thirty-five years, never took another husband – perhaps because she was so bruised by her first – but half of all aristocratic widows of her time did marry again. This gave them an influence far in excess of their legal status, as it was accepted that noble households would simultaneously include the children of several different marriages. A noble bridegroom, acknowledging that his bride might outlive him, would commonly enter into prenuptial arrangements that guaranteed his widow's position via a jointure in exchange for the dowry (at the going rate of something around 10 per cent: a 1,100 mark up-front dowry payment would secure a jointure of 100 marks a year). Occasionally wealthy noblewomen were able to secure more favourable arrangements. When the widowed Joan Strangways married the marquess of Berkeley in 1468, for instance, she insisted on being allowed to use the annuity she had inherited from her first husband 'at her pleasure, for the maintenance of herself and her children, and of her women servants'.[29] In at least one case the family avoided providing a dowry at all by keeping the marriage within the confines of the close family: Arthur Plantagenet, Viscount Lisle, married his eldest daughter Frances to his stepson John Bassett, thereby prompting Lady Lisle (who was a baroness in her own right) to consult the Heralds of Arms as to whether the countess of Rutland was right to say that her daughter's status would be degraded by a marriage to a mere Devonshire squire. She was relieved to hear that 'they saith plainly that the woman shall never lose no part of her degree, but shall always be taken as her father's daughter'.[30]

Above all, Tudor nobles were trying to protect themselves from oblivion. They heard Coverdale's translation of Isaiah: 'All flesh is grass, and all the beauty thereof is as the flower of the field.' They authorized Cranmer's burial service, with its reminder that 'we brought nothing into this world, neither may we carry anything out of this world'; but they tried to escape the clutches of everlasting obscurity. The poetic earl of Surrey might have been speaking for every other Tudor peer when he adopted 'Sat superest' (Enough survives) as his personal Latin motto. He was in earnest. After all, Coverdale's accurate translation of Ecclesiastes 2: 4 read: 'I made gorgeous fair works, I builded me houses, and planted vineyards.' But Surrey rendered the same verse very differently:

> To build my houses fair then set I all my cure:
> By princely acts thus strave I still to make my fame endure.[31]

That was what it was all about – making their fame (and their family) endure. That alone explains why Elizabeth's principal secretary Sir Francis Walsingham almost bankrupted himself when his son-in-law, Sir

Philip Sidney, was shot at the battle of Zutphen in the Netherlands in October 1586 and died of a gangrenous wound twenty-six days later. The funeral Walsingham paid for broke all the rules. Sidney's coffin was borne aloft in a specially commissioned black hearse, and seven hundred mourners processed from the Minories to St Paul's Cathedral. The heralds stipulated that 'no man of greater title than the defunct should be permitted to mourn',[32] yet four earls escorted Sidney to his funeral. To all intents and purposes he had been posthumously promoted to an earldom. Yet Sidney made more bequests than his estate could afford, Walsingham had to fork out £6,000 to meet his son-in-law's debts, and no permanent memorial was ever erected to the man who many thought epitomized the noble ideal.

THE
ARRAIGNMENT
AND
CONVICTION
OF
MERVIN Lord *AVDLEY,*
Earle of Castlehaven, (who was by 26. Peers
of the Realm found guilty for committing Rapine
and Sodomy) at Westminster, on Mon-
day, April 25. 1631.

By vertue of a Commission of Oyer and
Terminer, directed to Sir *Thomas Coventry,* Lord
Keeper of the Great Seale of England, Lord
high Steward for that day, accompanied
with the Judges.

As also the beheading of the said Earle shortly after on
Tower Hill.

January 3rd   LONDON,
Printed for *The. Thomas.* 1642.

The true por-
traiture of
the Earle of
Castlehaven.

The Lords that were his Peeres sate on each side of a great Table
covered with greene, whose names are as followeth.

1. *The Lord* Weston, *Lord Treasurer.* 2. *Earle of Manchester,
Lord Privy Seale.* 3. *Earle of Arundel and Surrey, Marshall.* 4. *Earle
of Pembroke and Montgomery, Lord Chamberleyn.* 5. *Earle of Kent.*
6. *Earle of Worcester.* 7. *Earle of Bedford.* 8. *Earle of Essex.* 9. *Earle
of Dorset.* 10. *Earle of Leicester.* 11. *Earle of Salisbury.* 12. *Earle
of Warwicke.* 13. *Earle of Carlisle.* 14. *Earle of Holland.* 15. *Earle
of Danby.* 16 *Viscount Wimbleton.* 17. *Viscount Conway.* 18. *Viscount Wentworth.* 19. *Viscount Dorchester.* 20. *Lord Piercy.* 21. *Lt
Strange.* 22. *Lord Clifford.* 23. *Lord Peter.* 24. *Lord North.* 25. *Lt
Howard.* 26. *Lord Gering.*

The Stuart aristocracy took exception to any affront to their honour,
including any perceived disparagement of the nobility by the monarch's
creation of new titles. Pandering to this sense of slighted honour, King
Charles I ordered severe action against the 2nd earl of Castlehaven, who
was executed for sodomy.

CHAPTER 6

WE WILL NOT THAT PERSONS OF PLACE SHOULD BE SO NEGLECTED

G EORGE VILLIERS LOOKS STRAIGHT out at you, with a tight red-lipped smile on his young, clean-shaven face. A shiny scarlet silk curtain with a gold hem frames him. On a table by his side lies his flamboyant ostrich-feather hat. He wears the insignia of the Garter – the heavy gold chain and emblem of St George round his neck, the pearl-encrusted garter tied below his left knee – with which he has just been invested. His white silk stockings, padded trunk hose and doublet contrast sharply with his crimson velvet robe, the gold tasselled rope from which hangs his sword and his starched filigree lace ruff. The eye is drawn to his legs, one turned at an angle to show his elegant thigh, his calves tightened by his three-inch heels and his ankles glittering with silver pom-pom roses. This portrait of Villiers, attributed to William Larkin and painted around 1616, is clearly aimed at displaying both his status and his personal attractions. Others flaunt his wealth. In one, his doublet is studded with pearls and four long ropes of pearls cascade round his neck. In another, his wife Katherine holds their infant son as the baby reaches out for a basket of fruits. George was never shy or modest. Another portrait displays his supposed military prowess and authority as duke of Buckingham and Lord High Admiral as he gestures with his baton from a rearing thoroughbred; Rubens painted him rising to a marble temple of Abundance and Virtue while Envy tries to hold him back and a lion roars at him; and just before his assassination in 1628 he commissioned another large canvas which was to portray him as Mercury, leading the liberal arts out of the darkness into the wonderful light of royal patronage. He clearly thought of himself as the apotheosis of nobility. Others begged to differ. After all, he was merely the second son of the second wife of a Leicestershire knight, and his elevation to a dukedom was the product not of the steady advance of noble blood but of James VI and I's infatuation.

Most accounts of the tumult that convulsed the three kingdoms of England, Scotland and Ireland in the seventeenth century focus on the political battle between the Commons and the king. They suggest that highly principled disagreements about taxation, religion and the powers of the monarchy were the nub of the issue. Yet the jealousy of the established aristocracy played just as important a part in the forty-year collapse into civil war. The nobility clamoured for titles – and complained when men like Villiers were promoted. They demanded financial favours and denounced the sudden wealth of others. But above all, they wailed that upstart grandees like Buckingham disparaged their nobility.

The trouble was, the new King James was only too happy to dole out favours. From the moment he started on his slow progress from Edinburgh to London in April 1603 he succumbed to the incessant demand for new honours and titles. Whenever he met a half-presentable gentleman he made him a knight, totting up 906 such investitures in four months; and by the end of the year he had created ten new English barons and two new earls. It was the fastest expansion of the aristocracy in decades. At first the ancient aristocracy had little reason to object. Many of the newly ennobled had been sitting on the threshold of the peerage for some time. Few could seriously quibble with Robert Cecil being made a baron in 1603 and Viscount Cranborne in 1604. He had served as an effective principal secretary of state since 1596, he smoothed James's accession, and on the day he was made earl of Salisbury in 1605 the king ensured nobody could feel slighted, as he simultaneously appointed his elder but less talented half-brother Thomas, 2nd Baron Burghley, as earl of Exeter. Nor could people object to Thomas Howard being made earl of Suffolk. His father, the 4th duke of Norfolk, had been attainted and executed in 1572, but Suffolk had captained the *Golden Lion* against the Spanish Armada, he had been vice-admiral in the successful attack on Cadiz in 1596, and Elizabeth had summoned him to parliament as Baron

Howard de Walden and appointed him Lord Chamberlain. With these appointments James was reinforcing the old order, not disturbing it.

Feelings were more mixed, however, regarding the Scots who came in James's wake. Sir John Holles keened that they monopolized the king, 'standing like mountains betwixt the beams of his grace and us',[1] and others questioned the Scottish nobles' cleanliness and their tendency to assassinate their kings. With a few rare exceptions, English peers were reluctant to marry into the Scottish nobility, whom they deprecated. Edward Denny, for instance, was one of the wealthy Elizabethans who finally got a barony in October 1604; but the king had to load him up with perquisites before he would countenance his only daughter Honoria marrying the king's Scottish confidant and gentleman of the bedchamber, Sir James Hay – and then had to pull off the same trick a second time when Honoria died in 1614, inveigling Henry Percy, 9th earl of Northumberland, into allowing his daughter Lucy to marry Hay. James was not insensitive to these English complaints. Instead of immediately granting Hay an English peerage, he created a special category for him as a baron for life, without a seat in the Lords; a proper hereditary English title as Baron Hay of Sawley in Lancashire followed only in 1615. Yet James's manifest reliance on his gentlemen of the bedchamber, all bar one of whom was Scottish, rather than on his English Privy Council, antagonized the English peers, as did his creation of nine earls, two viscounts and fourteen lords for Scottish recipients.

The English peers were on the lookout for signs of being slighted – and found them aplenty, as James promoted a succession of handsome young intimate protégés. One favourite, John Ramsay, had impressed James when, as a mere page in the Scottish court, he stabbed the earl of Gowrie to death in 1600, thereby frustrating an assassination plot; for this bravery he was brought as a gentleman of the bedchamber to London, where he was granted lucrative posts, enough land to provide an annual income of £1,000, and the Scottish titles of Lord Ramsay of Barns, Viscount Haddington and Lord Melrose. When James secured him a wealthy English bride, Elizabeth, the daughter of the 5th earl of Sussex, he gave her away in person at the ceremony in Whitehall Palace and wiped out the groom's £10,000 of debts. After a brief flirtation with

Philip Herbert, the striking and racy younger brother of the 3rd earl of Pembroke whom James made earl of Montgomery, there came another infuriating infatuation, with another obscure Scottish page, Robert Carr, who came to the king's attention when he broke his leg in a tilting accident in 1607. James nursed him to health, knighted him, granted him the manor of Sherborne and made him Viscount Rochester and a privy councillor. Then, in 1612, factional politics took over. When Salisbury, the mainstay of the Privy Council, died, the Catholic-leaning Howard family, which included the earls of Northampton, Suffolk and Nottingham, attempted to fill the power vacuum by promoting Carr. An irritating wrinkle in this plan was that Carr was having an affair with Suffolk's daughter, Frances Howard, countess to the young Robert Devereux, 3rd earl of Essex. The family elders managed to iron this out the following December by securing a sour annulment of the marriage, enabling Frances to marry Carr and James to make them earl and countess of Somerset with lands, fortunes and power to match.

Then came Villiers, with his shapely legs, his ambitious mother Mary, and the active support of the Howards' opponents: a clique of Protestant peers, including the two Herbert brothers, the earls of Pembroke and of Montgomery, who dressed him in expensive new clothes, bought him a position as royal cupbearer and waited for his charms to do the rest. They were lucky. In September 1615 rumours began to circulate that the earl and countess of Somerset had been involved in the murder of Sir Thomas Overbury, who had angrily opposed the annulment of the Essex marriage. Their trial and conviction opened the way for Villiers' blazing trajectory through the ranks. Knighted at the queen's request in 1615, he became Master of the Horse, Knight of the Garter, Baron Whaddon and Viscount Villiers in 1616, earl of Buckingham in 1617, marquess of Buckingham in 1618 and Lord High Admiral in 1619. No commoner had been promoted to a dukedom since John Dudley had effectively made himself duke of Northumberland in 1551, but in 1623 James made Villiers earl of Coventry and duke of Buckingham, the senior noble in the land. The king, who shared a bed with Buckingham at Farnham Castle, told his council that he loved Buckingham 'more than any other man' and that 'Jesus Christ had done the same as he was doing ... for Christ had his John and he had his George'.[2] The young man was now in an extraordinary quasi-royal position, exercising total control over personal access to the king and his heir, leading the Privy Council and governing all royal patronage.

It was this last element that came to irritate the nobility beyond measure, for two reasons. First, he assiduously secured titles and noble matches for his relatives, thereby creating a powerful, many-tentacled Buckingham connection, incorporating the Barons Dunsmore, Boteler of Brantfield and Howard of Escrick, the Viscounts Purbeck and Grandison, the earls of Rutland (his father-in-law), Anglesey (his younger and regularly drunken brother Kit), Denbigh, Northampton, Marlborough and Newport, and the *suo jure* countess of Buckingham (his mother). Second, while James had hit upon the idea of selling a new hereditary title of baronet to assist in the enforced Protestant plantation of Ireland (they went for £1,095 apiece), Buckingham went one further, putting peerages on the open market. John Holles was one of the first in line. He had some noble attributes. He had seen military service in 1586, he had twice been elected knight of the shire for Nottinghamshire, he was considered gentle and affable, he spoke several languages fluently and his maternal grandfather had been Baron Sheffield. But he had been fined £1,000 and sent to the Fleet for four months for defending Somerset over Overbury's murder; so it was only the estate he inherited from his grandfather, a successful London mercer and property speculator, that secured him the title of Baron Haughton within months of leaving prison, along with the £10,000 he handed over to the crown. Four months later, probably thanks to another £10,000 bribe, his nephew Philip Stanhope was made Baron Stanhope of Shelford, despite only recently having been pardoned for murder and twice indicted for sodomy. After further substantial backhanders in 1624 and 1628 the two men were made earls of Clare and of Chesterfield. Over the coming years plenty of others took this greased route to nobility. The earl of Huntingdon sold Sir Richard Wingfield the Irish (and therefore cheaper) title of Viscount Powerscourt for £2,500 in 1619; Sir John Tufton bought a baronetcy; his son Nicholas bought a peerage in 1626 (for £5,000), following up with an earldom in 1628. Edward Noell bought himself a baronetcy and a peerage out of the profits of his marriage to Juliana, the daughter of the wealthy merchant Baptist Hicks – and persuaded his father-in-law to exclude a second daughter from his will and leave his estate and recently acquired title as Viscount Campden to him. William Craven paid £7,000 of his inheritance from his father (who had risen from obscure poverty to obscene wealth as the Lord Mayor of London) to become the first Baron Craven in 1626; Paul Bayning purchased a baronetcy in 1611 and a barony and viscountcy for a 'loan' of £15,000 in 1628; and Richard Robartes, who had made his fortune as a Cornish tin-miner, was persuaded by the threat of prosecution to 'lend' the crown £12,000 and then hand over a further £10,000 to become Baron Robartes of Truro (this combined outlay equating to £5 million in 2017).

It would be impossible to overstate the sense of self-righteous fury this sale of ranks animated in the breasts of the established aristocracy, as the greater liberality in doling out titles that they had so craved under Elizabeth, now espoused with enthusiasm, seemed to dilute their own nobility. The first blisters of disaffection showed themselves in the House of Lords in January 1621. Aristocratic *amour propre* was very much to the fore, as the members fretted about the rules of precedence governing the Scottish and Irish peers, most of whom had no right to a seat in the Lords, though a few now also had English peerages. Should a Scottish earl with a new English barony sit or process ahead of an English baron? Henry Wriothesley, 3rd earl of Southampton, and Richard Sackville, 3rd earl of Dorset, hosted angry meetings at which thirty-three peers drafted and signed a fiercely worded petition to the king claiming that they sought 'to preserve [their] birthrights . . . against the new peers and that they wish to give them not the respect nor place as to noblemen strangers'.[3] That the charge was led by Southampton and Dorset – the former a combative and theatrical wild card, the latter an inveterate womanizer, gambler and general wastrel – itself indicates the root of the protest in aristocratic spleen. So bruised were noble sensitivities that while the Commons debated court corruption and the threat of war, the Lords set up a special committee under another scion of the older nobility, Henry Hastings, 5th earl of Huntingdon, tasked with investigating the historic rights of the English baronage. Its conclusions led to the first set of standing orders for the Lords and the unilateral declaration of their right to act as a court of law – a significant aristocratic land grab.

The nobility had much to defend. London was sprinkled with magnificent aristocratic palaces replete with the latest fashion in luxurious furnishings, as every aristocrat worth his salt had an impressive city residence from which to attend court and lobby for an annuity, a wardship, a title, a place or some other form of preferment. The most elaborate palaces, those of the earls of Salisbury, Exeter, Bedford and Essex, the bishop of Durham and the archbishop of York, were on the Strand, but early in the new reign Henry Howard, earl of Northampton, trumped them all by demolishing an old convent and building a house with a 162-foot frontage at Charing Cross, diagonally across from Whitehall Tilt Yard, which placed him closer to the king than all his rivals. When Northampton died, his nephew Thomas Howard, earl of Suffolk, inherited it and continued spending seemingly infinite sums on it that had been peculated from his post as Lord Treasurer – until he and his countess were convicted of embezzlement. The earl of Arundel had similar pretensions. His father had lost Arundel House, the former palace of the bishop of Bath and Wells further down the Strand, when he was convicted of treason in 1585, but in 1607 Thomas purchased it back from the crown with his wife Alethea Talbot's money. A *soigné* connoisseur of Italian art, Arundel substantially upgraded the mansion with an extension designed by Inigo Jones in which to display his collection of ancient marbles, paintings and porcelain in the hope, so a draft of his will declared, 'that all gentlemen ... or artists which are honest men may always be used with courtesy and humanity when they shall come'.[4] So proud of his new gallery was he that it appeared in the background of fresh portraits he commissioned of himself and his countess. She, the daughter of the earl of Shrewsbury, was equally extravagant, constructing Tart Hall near modern-day Buckingham Palace as a Venetian palazzo with a special 'Pranketing' Room, its floor covered with red and yellow leather druggets, to display her porcelain, Indian textiles, Turkish rugs, and French, Spanish and Italian furniture.

As if that were not enough, Stuart peers constructed additional mansions within striking distance of the city. Arundel purchased and enhanced the grand house at Highgate, Exeter upgraded Wimbledon Palace, the 2nd earl of Salisbury completed Hatfield, Suffolk built Audley End and Charlton Park, Northumberland built Syon House at Richmond to complement his palatial family residences at Alnwick and Petworth, and Sir Walter Cope built a castle on 500 acres in Kensington, which between 1624 and 1635 was elaborately extended by his son-in-law Henry Rich, earl of Holland,* as Holland House. New peers got in on the act, too. Thomas Howard, the second son of the earl of Suffolk, used a £20,000 bribe to finance a Westminster house soon after being made earl of Berkshire; and as Lionel Cranfield rose from being a valued merchant to a well-connected minister, his building projects got ever more ambitious. In 1603 he started on a modest townhouse in Cheapside; in 1611 he bought Pishiobury in Hertfordshire and had it remodelled; in 1621 he took over Sir Thomas More's old property Beaufort House in Chelsea and made expensive improvements, including a gated entrance by Inigo Jones; in 1622, now earl of Middlesex, he acquired Wiston House in Sussex and modishly refashioned it; and in 1623 he bought the 62-room Copt Hall in Essex, where he moved the loggia, added pilasters and gave it a 180-foot façade (60 feet longer than that at Hatfield). When Cranfield fell from grace in 1626, Buckingham took Beaufort off his hands, to add to his own burgeoning collection of properties, already worth £100,000 (£22.5 million in 2017). These included Burley-on-the-Hill near Rutland, New Hall in Essex, Wallingford House overlooking St James's Park and York House on the Strand. York House had once been the London residence of the archbishop of York, but in recent years the lay nobility had continued in the footsteps of Henry VIII by expropriating much church property. Early in James's reign Salisbury forced the bishop of Durham to hand over a valuable sliver of land to enable him to enlarge Salisbury House, and when William Cavendish, the wealthy new earl and then marquess of Newcastle, built Newcastle House in Clerkenwell in the 1630s to complement his four castles of Bothal, Ogle, Slingsby and Bolsover, he did so – as he had with his favourite country home, Welbeck Abbey – on the site of a former monastic house.

*An area of Lincolnshire.

This architectural spree continued unabated. In 1630 Robert Sidney, 2nd earl of Leicester, bought a large chunk of land to the west of Covent Garden which had formerly belonged to Westminster Abbey and built Leicester House as one of the largest properties in London. It was only an outcry from the local parishioners that forced him to leave some of the space open to the public – an area that later became known as Leicester Square. Not even civil war could put the nobles off their building stride. Serving in the second bishops' war in 1640, the 2nd earl of Bridgewater worried that his London neighbours might 'take advantage of my absence to erect their buildings to my annoyance'.[5] Two years later, with full-scale civil war about to erupt, James Hay, 2nd earl of Carlisle, commissioned a grand establishment on the corner of Lincoln's Inn Fields and John Tufton, 2nd earl of Thanet, built a new Inigo Jones mansion with Ionic pillars opposite Peter House, the equally palatial home of the marquess of Dorchester in Aldersgate. The 10th earl of Northumberland spent more than £15,000 on refurbishments in 1644, and even in 1648, with the nation in tumult and parliament in session, the earl of Pembroke chose to oversee personally the elaborate reconstruction of Wilton after a fire, installing the beautiful 'double cube' room in which to display portraits of himself and his family, his brother, the king and the queen.

These noble houses were more than just architectural statements. In much the same way as a medieval baron created a retinue of fellow warriors with whom he shared his castle and his hearth, Tudor and Stuart lords sought to maintain a bustling household of family members, servants, clients and political allies that proclaimed their prestige. By exercising the power of patronage, they both extended the tendrils of their personal influence and impressed others with their bounty. They fiercely defended the right to appoint clergy to local livings as an essential aspect of enforcing moral discipline, and enjoyed giving musicians and writers board and lodging in exchange for entertainment and suitably laudatory verses. These accoutrements of a humanist education added lustre to a great man's household, without his having to go to the trouble of acquiring the skills himself.

Where the British aristocracy were to prove spectacularly mean, though, was in their patronage of home-produced fine art. Throughout the centuries the Spanish, French and Italian nobility commissioned great works of art and cultivated native painters as their protégés, whereas the British almost exclusively collected the works of continental artists, whose reputation and value were already well established. These did not come cheap. Buckingham's collection at York House, which supposedly included nineteen canvases by Titian, seventeen by Tintoretto, thirteen by Veronese and by Rubens, and three by Leonardo,[6] was so impressive that the architect Sir Balthasar Gerbier told him that 'out of all the amateurs and princes and kings there is not one who has collected in forty years as many pictures as your excellency has collected in five',[7] and his son the 2nd duke managed to sustain himself through several years of exile in the civil war by selling it off in Antwerp. Thanks to a very active London art market, aristocrats continued to splash out vast sums on major works by Raphael or Correggio well into the eighteenth and nineteenth centuries – so much so that one commentator complained in 1749 that sums were being given for a single work by an ancient master that equalled the annual revenue of a gentleman's estate.

But it was the depth of their pockets, not the keenness of their eye or the generosity of their heart, that created these collections of antiquities from around the world. These competitive collectors congratulated themselves on their taste and reinforced their sense of ancient title by hanging another Old Master on their palace wall, but their interest in art was parasitic and vainglorious: for the only contemporary painters they regularly commissioned were portraitists, whom they engaged to create works that proclaimed their wealth, power, dignity and/or martial prowess. Hence the countless pictures of British nobles in the finery of the Order of the Garter, the looming equestrian figures, the allegorical canvasses that hint at heavenly glory, the beguiling images of beautiful wives and daughters dressed exquisitely in the fashion of the day, that adorn so many British stately homes. The only way that Thomas Gainsborough, Joshua Reynolds and Thomas Lawrence could flourish in Britain was by painting narcissistic lords and ladies. Yet British aristocrats even preferred imported portraitists: just as the Tudor nobility favoured Hans Holbein from Augsburg in Bavaria, so their Stuart successors turned to the Flemish painters Peter Paul Rubens and Anthony Van Dyck, Peter Lely from Westphalia and Godfrey Kneller from the Hanseatic city of Lübeck, all four of whom were knighted in England for their efforts. It was said that when the Frenchman Jean Baptiste van Loo opened up shop in London in 1737 the carriages were stacked up at his door and the nobility offered bribes to jump the queue – an honour that never came the way of a British painter.

The result was that while a few nobles amassed admirable collections thanks to a real interest in art – the most notable connoisseur was probably the 3rd Earl Cowper, who acquired a couple of exceptional Raphaels, some Titians, a Van Dyck and the usual set of portraits for his home at Panshanger – British art languished unloved by the landowning classes, and the likes of William Hogarth had to exercise considerable entrepreneurial flair by appealing to the masses with controversial prints. As the noted engraver John Pye, who helped found the Artists' Annuity Fund, put it in 1845:

> The various sources of patronage, through which the talent of a country is usually called forth, and cherished when it appears, were estranged from the British artists; and the enormous sums which continually flowed for the formation of collections of foreign works ... being inimical to the advancement of modern art, of course greatly prejudiced the claims of native talent.[8]

There were other repercussions, too. All this building and fine furnishing required up-front expenditure far in excess of aristocratic income from traditional sources, chiefly land rental, so peers relied increasingly on a more lucrative alternative – the corrupt farming of monopolies and duties, a practice indulged in by the early Stuart nobility with considerable entrepreneurial invention. Some monopolies made perfect sense – it would have been difficult to object to the 21-year licence granted to composers Thomas Tallis and William Byrd to print music and ruled paper – they seem not to have exploited it to prevent other musicians from making a living – but others were decidedly corrupt, and their proliferation fostered deep unhappiness. In 1621 Sir Edward Coke estimated that two thousand such monopolies had been awarded, netting the beneficiaries £400,000. Many went to the nobility. Robert Dudley, earl of Leicester under Elizabeth I, held a string of exclusive licences over sweet wines, oils, currants, silks and velvets. He paid the queen £6,000 a year for the sweet wine patent alone, but the profits he extracted from it and from the patent on currants were reckoned to be 'inestimable', prompting one contemporary to complain that 'Edmund Dudley's brood have learned . . . to be more cunning gatherers than ever their progenitor was'.[9] A later Elizabethan favourite, the 2nd earl of Essex, was the subsequent licensee for sweet wine; Sir Walter Raleigh had the monopoly on playing cards; the earls of Suffolk and of Salisbury farmed the import duties on currants and silk; the earl of Northampton and then Lord Hay held an exclusive licence to produce starch; the earl of Montgomery was involved in the glass patent; the duke of Lennox held the valuable right of 'alnage', the official supervision of the shape and quality of woollen cloth; George Hume, earl of Dunbar, was awarded the monopoly on logwood and blockwood for forty-one years; and the 3rd earl of Southampton had licences for tin-plate production, for sweet wine import duties and for an iron foundry at Titchfield. When profits from the patent for making glass with coal were threatened by Staffordshire glassmakers burning wood, the peers concerned, including the earl of Berkshire, successfully lobbied the king to ban any glass manufacture other than with coal.

All the most extortionate monopolists had noble connections. One of the most lucrative monopolies, for licensing inns and taverns, was granted to Charles Howard, earl of Nottingham (who also conveniently held a wine monopoly). He sub-let the former to Sir Giles Mompesson, who in 1621 was arraigned by parliament and exiled for corrupt practices. Likewise Arthur Ingram, who was considered so corrupt that in 1625 he was forced to surrender all his patents and pay £20,000 in compensation, owed his patents for starch and dyewood (species such as Brazilwood that can be used for dyeing), for wines and for alum production in Yorkshire and Dorset to Sir Thomas Wentworth (later earl of Strafford) and his relatives by marriage Lord Henry Clifford, the son of the earl of Cumberland, and William Cecil, 2nd earl of Salisbury. A series of peers battled for the valuable alum patent, including the very same Lord Sheffield (as of 1626, the earl of Mulgrave) who attacked Bacon and Buckingham for corruption in the Lords in 1621. The most successful patent farmer of them all, though, was George Goring, who made a fortune out of his patents for the export of butter, the manufacture of gold and silver thread, and the import and sale of tobacco. The sums involved were startling. He sold one licence outright for £18,000 (about £4 million in 2017) and the reversion of another for £2,000, and was reckoned to have exploited his patents to the tune of £9,000 per annum. Despite all this, Goring acquired a peerage in 1628 and an earldom in 1644.

Yet other means of enrichment were available to an acquisitive courtier. James and his successor Charles both paid generous 'benevolences' direct to their favourites – in 1611 alone James awarded £29,000 to the earls of Montgomery and Essex, the Viscounts Fenton and Rochester and Lord Hay – and in case the exchequer should plead poverty, these payments were often termed 'assignments' or first charges against the revenues of the infallibly solvent Court of Wards or the duchy of Lancaster. The navy might have to go without, but not a favoured peer. Peers sold ministerial posts, too. The earl of Nottingham was eighty-three and had been an incompetent Lord High Admiral for thirty-four years by 1619, yet Buckingham still had to furnish him with a lump sum and a pension to purchase the post. Sir Albertus Morton paid Sir George Calvert £3,000 to succeed him as secretary of state in 1625 (and then died before the end of the year); and Sir Henry Montagu paid £20,000 for the post of Lord Treasurer and the concomitant peerage (which was later boosted to the earldom of Manchester).

The court was soaked in corruption, but the peers' anger with the royal favourite was focused on their own privileges, as became apparent again in parliament in 1626. The matter in hand this time was the use of proxy votes, whereby an absent peer could nominate another to vote on his behalf. Many had hoped that Buckingham's power might have waned on the death of King James the preceding year, but already it was clear that he was ensconced in every nook and cranny of the new King Charles's affections; so, with several rows brewing, everyone expected a rumbustious session in which there might be tight votes. Of the forty lay peers with absence slips, twenty-nine had nominated proxies. Buckingham held thirteen, Arundel and Pembroke (no longer a Buckingham ally) five each. The peers saw an opportunity to swing the pendulum back in their favour, and on 25 February Arundel and another proud scion of the old nobility, William Fiennes, 8th Baron Saye and Sele, pushed through a reform that limited the number of proxies any one peer could hold to two. Everyone knew what this meant. As John Chamberlain wrote to Dudley Carleton: 'Last week the duke [of Buckingham] had one feather plucked from his wing in the upper house in the matter of proxies.'[10]

The crown then made a fatal mistake. In 1621 it had arrested Southampton, the following year it threw Saye and Sele in the Tower, and this time the king seized Arundel and prevented him from attending the Lords, supposedly on the grounds that his eldest surviving son Henry had just eloped with the daughter of the 3rd duke of Lennox, thereby thwarting a royal plan to marry her to the son of the 7th earl of Argyll. James could not have chosen a worse person to arrest. Arundel had done well for himself, considering his father's long imprisonment for his Catholic faith (he was sainted for his efforts) and the poverty into which the family had consequently slipped. He had restored the family fortunes by marrying wealthily, and by the 1620s he was on such good terms with Buckingham that he was made a privy councillor. He eschewed the contemporary fashion for flashy colours and dressed entirely in black, and so dedicated was he to the ancient nobility to which he most assuredly belonged (he regularly clamoured for the restoration of the family dukedom of Norfolk) that in 1621 he persuaded James to make him Earl Marshal with responsibility for the Court of Chivalry and the adjudication of all matters of aristocratic precedent, precedence and privilege. He threw himself into this work, getting his protégé Sir Robert Cotton to research ancient precedents for punishing corrupt ministers of the crown and campaigning against any disparagement of the ancient nobility. His plaints fell on deaf ears under James, but at the first Privy Council of the new reign in April 1625 he told Charles as forcefully as he could that it was 'honourable and necessary to limit honours; that titles should not be distributed broadcast as in the past, but only to

The Anglo-Saxon nobility was forged in blood-thirsty war against rivals and invaders, as at the battle of Stamford Bridge in 1066 (*above*). The rich rewards for doing battle alongside the king included sharing his bounty and his companionship, as in the powerful myth of King Arthur, seen below presiding over a banquet with his barons.

La bataille de Caen

War was a lucrative business for medieval lords. When the English violently sacked Caen in 1346 (*above*) it was said that they could not transport all the spoils. To wrap this warmongering elite in an aura of noble piety, Edward III established the Order of the Garter (*below*) and dedicated it to St George.

Funerary monuments were a means of displaying both prestige and piety. A wealthy and warlike widow, Roesia de Verdun (**above**), was buried at the abbey in Leicestershire she had endowed. Eleanor de Clare, one of three daughters of the earl of Gloucester, filled the clerestory windows of Tewkesbury Abbey with family portraits and emblems (**below**).

Peers in every age have jealously guarded their exclusivity, constantly disputing matters of precedence and complaining about the creation of new honours. They developed complex coats of arms and liveries, and insisted that fabrics such as silk, damask and satin be reserved exclusively for them. Here a duke (**far left**) and seven earls process in order of seniority in their crimson and ermine robes of state for the opening of Henry VIII's parliament.

The dissolution of the monasteries provided rich pickings for avaricious would-be Tudor peers. Sir Richard Rich (**above**) held conservative views on religion, but profited handsomely from helping the legislation through parliament, acquiring several monastic houses including the priory of Leighs (**below**), where he founded a baronial dynasty that later acquired two earldoms.

Few commoners rose through the ranks of the nobility as fast as King James I's favourite George Villiers. This portrait of him, dressed to impress as duke of Buckingham, typifies the aristocratic fascination with peacock display.

Many aristocratic fortunes were based on corrupt, and ferociously guarded, monopolies. In this satirical print the duke of Newcastle, dressed as an old woman, shovels gold coins into a pickled salmon tub assisted by the earl of Hardwicke, Viscount Barrington and Lord Holland.

Few noblewomen were more determined to secure advantageous marriages for their children than the duchess of Gordon, here seen chasing the duke of Bedford in the shape of a Bedfordshire Bull. She snared three dukes, a marquess and a baronet.

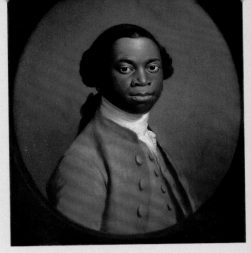

Aristocrats were involved in every aspect of the slave trade, running slave colonies such as Willoughbyland (later Suriname, **left**). Some noble families had black servants: the duchess of Montagu employed Ignatius Sancho (**above**) as her butler.

Many of Britain's finest stately homes were built on the proceeds of slavery, including Harewood House (**below**), the home of the Lascelles family, who made their fortune out of slave plantations and were lavishly compensated by the taxpayer when their slaves were eventually emancipated.

persons of quality and of noble birth'.[11] His advice hit home – briefly – as Charles announced that he would make no new awards without Arundel's prior knowledge; but when Buckingham whispered in the royal ear that the coffers were still empty, the favourite was allowed to open up shop again, selling another eighty-five baronetcies and taking the English peerage to 126, double what it had been in 1615.

Arundel, then, was the one man in the realm upon whose noble bunions Charles should have known not to tread. The reaction to his arrest was predictable. When the Lords reconvened, Saye and Sele weighed in with a complaint about Arundel's arrest, which he argued offended the principle that a peer had a right to attend parliament. This direct attack on the king was supported by the earls of Essex, Mulgrave, Hertford and Pembroke and the Lord Russell. In this grouping was hatched what would become a fledgling noble opposition, all of it drawn from the ancient aristocratic furniture. Ironically, both Saye and Sele and Mulgrave had only recently been promoted, to a viscountcy and an earldom respectively, during a brief attempt by Buckingham to reach out to disaffected peers; but their inherited baronies dated from 1447 and 1547. Essex's father had been executed for his armed rebellion in 1601; but he had imbibed a deep respect for the ancient nobility from the elder earl, and would have applauded his declaration as Earl Marshal in 1599 that England was 'most mighty when the nobility led and commanded in war and were great housekeepers at home', and that 'the upholding of the nobility [was] a most necessary and religious care' for the king.[12] Essex's brother-in-law Hertford was a great-grandson of Lord Protector Somerset and held a distant claim to the throne, while the 4th earl of Pembroke was heir to the ancient Herbert family. As for Russell, although the barony had been created for his father as recently as 1603, he was a grandson of the magnificently wealthy 2nd earl of Bedford, whose earldom he stood to inherit when his cousin Edward died. This was a band of indignantly affronted nobles keen to defend their historic honour – and they were intransigent, persuading the Lords not to consider any other business until Arundel was permitted to take his seat. Their allies in the Commons, meanwhile, laid charges against Buckingham, making clear that the inflation of honours was one of their chief gripes.

The high offices of the kingdom had been 'engrossed, bought and sold'. So too had honours, which should be a 'treasure inestimable'. Divers of the duke's 'poor kindred' had been raised to great honours, and the duke himself had misled the late king and exercised 'this exorbitancy of will, this transcendency of power' in a way never heard of before.[13] As one member put it, 'the sale of honour is an offence unnatural against the law of nature ... it extremely deflowers the flowers of the crown; for it makes them cheap to all beholders [and] it takes from the crown the most fair and frugal reward of deserving servants'.[14] Buckingham had been busy packing the Lords for years, but without the proxies, and unable to rely on the loyalty even of those he had elevated, he was now clearly in danger; so Charles swiftly appointed two more allies as English peers and helped him survive by just four votes.

Charles kept that small majority in the Lords over the next two years, but the cadre of opposition-minded peers used every delaying tactic they could think of to wear the king and his supporters down until he capitulated. The storm swirled around Buckingham, but in 1628 he was dead, murdered in a public house in Portsmouth. Charles threw himself on his bed and wept, but it was said that the public celebrated – and they were joined by plenty of peers whose noses Buckingham had put out of joint. Arundel suddenly found himself in a key position, as the king resolved to improve his relationship with the peerage. Charles put an end to the sale of honours. He reinstated traditional rituals of peers dining or attending chapel with the king. And he ferociously attacked anything that might possibly impugn the nobility. When James, Lord Audley, petitioned him in 1630 against his father Mervyn Tuchet, 2nd earl of Castlehaven, alleging that the earl was unnaturally close to his servant Henry Skipworth, Charles took immediate action, appointing a commission of inquiry, which rapidly found that Castlehaven had restrained his wife while encouraging Skipwith to rape her, had arranged for Skipwith to sleep with his daughter-in-law and had buggered two of his own servants. On 25 April 1631 Castlehaven was tried in Westminster Hall before twenty-five of his peers presided over by Lord Keeper Thomas Coventry as Lord High Steward. The earl always maintained his innocence, and his wife's evidence was suspect since she stood to gain substantially by her husband's death, but he was executed on Tower Hill, the only mercy granted him being a beheading rather than a hanging. Throughout, the king thought he was acting to protect the nobility as a whole from being brought into disrepute.

The Star Chamber court, which had originally been designed to mete out justice to those who might otherwise be thought to be above the law by virtue of their title or position, also became more assertive in defending the peerage. Edward Eure might have had a point in 1632 when he alleged that Henry Danvers, the elderly earl of Danby, was 'a base cozening lord, a cheating lord and a base fellow', as Danvers and his elder brother had got away with murdering a local rival in 1594 and his younger brother was reckoned to have feathered his own nest corruptly. The court, though, had become an arbitrary plaything subject to the whim of the king and was not interested in such niceties. Danvers was a peer, so Eure was pilloried and forced to pay £2,500 in damages and £1,000 in fines.[15] Similarly, in 1637 Thomas Bennett was told to pay the earl of Marlborough £1,000 because he had taxed the earl with baseness and base dealing; and when Peter Apsley, the son of the Keeper of the Tower, challenged the earl of Northumberland to a duel he was fined £5,000, forced to make formal apologies to the earl and to the Privy Council, and forbidden from ever wearing a sword. On occasion, the king himself got directly involved. When John Burges brought a case to the Star Chamber against Francis, 5th Baron Willoughby of Parham, Charles demanded that it be dropped, writing that:

> although we be willing that all our subjects should find our courts of justice open to all men alike, yet when a man of mean quality shall prosecute against a nobleman for an offence of passion or heat only, and that provoked by ill words and saucy carriage as we hear this was, it is not reasonable to give way to every man's will in such a case. Therefore we will not that persons of place should be so neglected.[16]

Even the Privy Council itself took the peers' side without fail: so although two London draymen were cleared by the courts when they accidentally collided with the earl of Exeter's coach in July 1637, the council insisted that the men be 'presently whipped publicly through the town, as well for their bold and insolent carriage towards the said earl as also for an example to deter others from the like insolencies and misdemeanours'.[17]

The flip side of this obsession with insolence was that peers were over-eager to take offence; and when the offence emanated from an equal, that meant a challenge to a duel. Duelling was illegal, and James made several determined efforts to put a stop to it, urging Francis Bacon as Attorney-General to prosecute offenders and issuing a royal proclamation against 'private challenges and combats'. But the practice continued. In the 1610s there had been thirty-three such challenges a year, the most notorious of which involved Edward Sackville, younger brother of Richard, the dissolute 3rd earl of Dorset, who killed Edward Bruce, 2nd Lord Kinloss, in August 1613 in a duel arranged in the Netherlands so as to avoid the wrath of the king. The precise details of the quarrel are uncertain. In one version of events the two men fought over the great society beauty Venetia Stanley. In another Sackville returned home drunk one night and struck Bruce for declaring his love for Sackville's sister Clementina. Bruce initially ignored the blow, but when news of it reached the public he reckoned the noble code of honour required that he seek satisfaction. Sackville repeated the blow, the challenge was issued and the duel went ahead. Sackville was run through and lost a finger but eventually prevailed. The king had regularly inveighed against duelling, but the episode did Sackville's reputation no harm as contemporaries reckoned that his 'fair carriage and equal hazard maketh even his adversaries speak favourably',[18] and he went on to succeed his brother as earl, becoming an active member of the Privy Council and the Lords.

The real problem was that the quaint system of noble honour had at its heart the belief that a nobleman who let an injury pass unpunished showed 'himself worthy of contempt, and consequently unjust and wicked; for only the wicked man is worthy to be ignominious'.[19] This was patently absurd; but the feuds continued until another notorious incident in April 1633 when Henry Rich, earl of Holland, demanded satisfaction of the earl of Portland's son Jerome Weston, who had intercepted letters from Holland to one of the French king Louis XIII's councillors and had presented them to Charles, with the imputation that Holland was up to no good. So as to sidestep the royal prohibition on intentional duelling, the two men arranged that they would start a swordfight as if by accident; but Portland told the king, upon which Charles had Holland confined to his house. Others started taking sides. George Goring suggested that Weston had been a coward, which prompted Weston's soon-to-be-brother-in-law Lord Feilding to challenge Goring to a duel in Hyde Park, which ended prematurely when some passing workmen dragged them apart. This scrap closely affected the court, for Portland was Lord Treasurer and Holland was Master of the King's Horse. So, in an attempt to put an end to these disputes for good, the following March the king charged Arundel's Court of Chivalry with resolving all matters of noble honour, including contested peerage cases and allegations of 'saucy', 'scandalous' or 'libellous' words against a peer or gentleman. Over the next six years the court met roughly once every ten days and dealt with 738 cases.

One of those cases gives an insight into the mindset of the time. Thomas West was already fifty when he became the 9th Baron de la Ware in 1525. He had no children and his eldest half-brother Owen had only daughters, so he initially settled the title on his younger half-brother George's son William. This nephew proved an impatient heir, however, and was caught attempting to poison him, leading to a spell in the Tower and an Act of parliament disinheriting him. The two were reconciled by the time of Thomas's death in 1554, but when William was tried for his treasonable involvement in the Dudley conspiracy in 1556 he was denied trial by peers on the grounds that the Act was still in place. Pardoned by Queen Mary, he was granted the barony as a new creation in 1570 and was succeeded in the direct line in turn by his son, grandson and great-grandson. The last of these, Henry, 4th Baron de la Ware, died in 1625, aged twenty-four, leaving a widow, Isabella, and a young son, Charles, who became a ward of court. Isabella went to considerable legal lengths to protect her son's status. In both 1632 and 1635 she brought Court of Chivalry suits against one George West, denying his claim that he was related to the 9th Baron – and asserting for good measure that he was neither a real West nor a true gentleman. This was not just an aristocrat being pernickety. Isabella feared that if her son were to die childless this George West would stand to inherit the title and estates and she would be left in penury. Unfortunately for her, the Garter King at Arms, William Segar, furnished George West with a pedigree proving that he was indeed related to the 9th Baron, which he presented to the court in 1632. In 1635, though, Lady de la Ware returned to the fray, claiming that George West's real name was Crutchman and that his grandfather John Crutchman had been a professional wrestler who had changed his surname in reference to his ring-name as 'Jack of the West'. This Jack had subsequently made his way in Basingstoke as an innkeeper and his son had prospered as a draper, but Isabella's witnesses maintained that George West was no gentleman. There were plenty who stated otherwise and alleged that witnesses had been threatened, bribed and suborned, but the court came down firmly in favour of Lady de la Ware. In addition to being ordered never to style himself as a gentleman, West was issued with a staggering fine of £500.

Other cases heard before the court show how pompous and precious the nobility could be. In March 1637 Robert Pierrepont, earl of Kingston, sought damages from a Yorkshire gentleman, Christopher Copley, for insulting him by suggesting that he was better born than the earl or his wife. The court, presided over by two fellow earls, duly forced Copley formally to submit to the earl and pay him a massive fine of £500. So too in November 1638 another prickly peer, Henry Carey, earl of Dover, sued a London merchant called Humphrey Fox for insulting his noble livery by referring to the insignia emblazoned on the livery coat of one of the earl's servants – a noble swan – as a mere goose. Fox had instantly apologized, but the vainglorious earl was not satisfied until the court awarded him 200 marks. Such biased decisions inevitably brought the court into disrepute and incensed many otherwise law-abiding gentlemen to such a degree that they were prepared, as was Copley, to join the parliamentary army in the civil wars against the corrupt and arbitrary system.

This obsession with rank, title and reputation was so transparent that it even irritated and amused the monarch on occasion. When James VI of Scotland travelled south to assume the English throne in 1603 he stopped en route at Lumley Castle, a bright yellow freestone quadrangular castle that overlooks the sharp ravine where the Lumley Beck joins the River Wear. In the hands of John, Lord Lumley, the original castle had been transformed into an overblown tribute to his family's ancestry, which he maintained stretched back to the Saxon era. He installed a large painted wooden equestrian monument to Edward III in the main courtyard and dotted the walls with a series of heraldic shields for each of his ancestors. King James was shown round by William James, the bishop of Durham, who was apparently so gushing about Lumley's ancient progenitors that the king stopped him short, saying that he hadn't known that Adam's other name was Lumley.

The aristocracy acted as a persistent grievance machine in the run-up to civil war, but when war came they largely sided with the monarch. Parliament retaliated by fining royalist peers, imprisoning them and destroying their mansions – among them Basing House, the enormous palace where the marquess of Winchester was besieged.

CHAPTER 7

STONE-DEAD HATH NO FELLOW

F EW EVENTS ARE INEVITABLE and the death, aged nineteen, of Sir
Francis Villiers, the third son of the duke of Buckingham, was not
one of them. Had he not sent his company ahead of him so as to spend
the night with his lover Mary Kirke, he would not have been surprised
alone by parliamentary soldiers near Kingston-upon-Thames on 7 July
1648. Had he not insulted them when they shot his horse from under
him, and had he not refused to give quarter to a rebel, they might not
have dashed off his helmet, run him through from behind, cut off his
nose and mangled his body 'in a most barbarous and inhumane manner'.[1]
Andrew Marvell's epitaph to the young aristocrat made his death seem
a moment of transcendent fate:

> *Scorning without a sepulchre to die*
> *And with his steel which did whole troops divide*
> *He cut his epitaph on either side.*
> *Till finding nothing to his courage fit*
> *He rid up last to death and conquered it.*

But for many contemporaries Sir Francis's death was a potent symbol of
the futility of the royalist cause in the civil war. Even the ardent
parliamentarian John Hall recognized that Sir Francis's wounds 'had
been brave enough', but only, he added caustically, 'had they been
received in another cause'.[2]

Civil war was not inevitable, either. Henry Carey, the bookish 2nd
earl of Monmouth, thought the nobility had a particular role to play in

157

preventing discord, and argued as much in 1640, in his only known speech in the Lords: 'God hath placed us (my Lords) in the medium betwixt the King and his people . . . Let us play our parts, let us do our duties and discharge our consciences; let us really prove what we are by name, Noblemen; let us endeavour to work a perfect and a true understanding between the King and his people.'[3] Monmouth was right. They were the one body of people who could have steered the country away from war. They had a privileged place in parliament, they considered themselves the king's natural counsellors, they held sway over the landscape of public opinion and they expected deference in their localities. Yet in the two decades of turmoil from 1638 they effected no understanding between the king and his people and, in Monmouth's terms, they manifestly failed to prove their nobility.

The primary reason for their failure was the automatic and unwavering support most of them gave to the hereditary monarchy and to the king. Many owed a debt of gratitude to the crown, having received great favours from James or Charles. Eighty-one of the 124 English peerages in 1640 had been created since 1603, including 44 out of 64 earldoms, 6 out of 7 viscountcies and the sole dukedom, that of Buckingham, which had passed to his son George. It was the same in Scotland, where only 39 out of the 116 titles predated James VI's reign. Royal generosity had enriched these men with land, pensions and monopolies to match their titles, and it would have been churlish not to return the favour with loyal support.

There was another factor. The default position of the peerage in time of war was to support the king in battle. In the normal course of things this was not a matter of choice. The peers' oath of allegiance enjoined this military duty on the nobility. So, when the General Assembly of the Church of Scotland flouted Charles's authority by agreeing a Covenant abolishing bishops and banning his new prayer book in 1638, the king looked to his nobles to put together a 16,000-strong force against the Scots. It was something of a gamble, though. Most Stuart aristocrats had little or no experience of war. Prolonged peace had slackened their martial instincts so that, just like the *faux* battlements on their palaces, the swords that hung at their sides were mostly for decorative effect.

Some had a refresher course in the 1620s and 1630s as nobles and their sons fought in the Thirty Years War, the Dutch Revolt, the raid on Cadiz, the attempt to regain the Palatinate, and the sieges of Breda and the Île de Ré. Horace de Vere was one such. Born with few prospects in 1565 as the fourth son of a younger son of the 15th earl of Oxford, he served as a soldier on the continent almost continuously for more than four decades from 1590 and saw fierce action in a long series of battles, including the siege of Ostend in 1602, where he was badly wounded in the leg, the unsuccessful Palatinate expedition in 1620, where he led the 3rd earl of Essex and his kinsman the 18th earl of Oxford, the attempted relief of Breda in 1625, at which Oxford was mortally wounded, and the capture of Maastricht in 1632, at which the next earl of Oxford was killed. Horace was well rewarded. James gave him the lucrative post of Muster-Master-General of the Ordnance, and Charles made him Baron Vere of Tilbury in 1625. Essex claimed that these campaigns were 'the school of honour for the nobility of England in their exercise of arms',[4] and the poets and dramatists eulogized de Vere's martial prowess and his equable temperament alike as clear signs of his nobility. Ben Jonson ended his epigram to Horace de Vere by praising his:

> *Humanity, and piety, which are*
> *As noble in great chiefs, as they are rare.*
> *And best become the valiant man to wear,*
> *Who more should seek men's reverence, than fear.*[5]

In other words, even though the closest many Stuart peers got to warfare before 1639 was their childhood fencing lessons and a ceremonial joust at the tiltyard, battle-worthiness was the quintessence of noble honour, and it was incumbent on nobles to follow their lord.

The summons came on 26 January 1639, when Charles required every member of the English peerage to attend 'our royal person and standard at our city of York by the first day of April next ensuing in such equipage and with such forces of horse as your birth, your honour and your interest in the public safety do oblige you unto and as we do have reason to expect from you'.[6] The initial response to this raising of a royal host was ambivalent. Some of the opposition-minded clique of peers demurred. Viscount Saye and Sele and Robert Greville, 2nd Baron Brooke, argued that since Charles had not summoned a parliament since 1628, and no king had gone to war without a parliament since 1323, he had no mandate for making war, let alone raising money to pay for it. Such objections soon melted away, though. Edward Montagu, Viscount Mandeville, was persuaded when his father the earl of Manchester threatened to disinherit him, and the two Rich brothers, the earls of Warwick and of Holland, signed up even though they had been critics of the king and their sum of military experience was a bout of piratical plundering in the Caribbean and a brief visit to the Netherlands. Even Manchester's 76-year-old brother Edward, Baron Montagu, wrote to say he was prepared to lay down his life despite being 'riven' with infirmities. He was excused on health grounds, and several lords provided money or troops rather than attend in person, but among others Saye and Sele and Brooke turned up, the wealthy earl of Newcastle sent a regiment of his neighbours, and Lord Clifford appeared in the gilded armour of his buccaneering uncle the 3rd earl of Cumberland. The muster proved that the ancient tie of allegiance between the monarch and his nobles was still strong, no matter how deep the misgivings of individual peers.

The same applied in parliament, as Charles maintained a healthy majority in the Lords even without the cushion of support he was guaranteed by the bishops (whom he appointed and could dismiss). He did have aristocratic critics, of course, with several peers finding themselves pushed to the edge of loyalty – and beyond. The earl of Essex is a case in point. Having served on the continent throughout the 1620s, he was by far the best qualified of the senior nobles to command the royal force in the first bishops' war. But Charles chose instead to appoint Arundel, who had never commanded troops before, and gave the second-in-command post to the queen's favourite, the earl of Holland, leaving Essex to nurse his grievances as mere lieutenant-general in command of the cavalry. Essex's first marriage had ended in a notorious show trial in which he had had to defend himself from the charge of impotence by saying that he had 'found an ability of body to know any other woman, and hath oftentimes felt motions and provocations of the flesh ... but that he hath lain by the lady Frances two or three years last past, and hath no motion to know her, and he believes never shall'.[7] That had been humiliation enough; now he was left in the equally humiliating position of having to request supplies through the treasurer at war, Sir William Uvedale, who had conducted a much-publicized affair with his second wife. A child of uncertain fatherhood had died and Essex was now reconciled to the fact that he would have no heir. He had sponsored at least fifteen opposition-minded MPs in Charles's first turbulent parliaments, he had voted with the opposition since 1628, and by 1640 he was reckoned to be 'the most popular man of the kingdom and a darling of the swordsmen'.[8] His being passed over for command only added to his existing disenchantment with the king.

Essex was not alone in his disgruntlement. Although Charles won the first major vote in the Lords in the Short Parliament of 1640, a vocal minority of twenty-five peers voted against him including the Lords Essex, Bedford, Hertford, Lincoln, Warwick, Saye and Sele, Brooke, Mandeville and Wharton. This was a closely intertwined group: Hertford was Essex's brother-in-law, Lincoln had married Saye and Sele's daughter, Brooke was Bedford's son-in-law and Warwick was Essex's cousin. They had other things in common besides family links. Several were Puritans and had invested in colonial development schemes in America, and most boasted lineages that stretched back for centuries. They had supported the House of Commons' statement of liberties, the Petition of Right, in 1628 and opposed Charles's illegitimate attempts at raising cash without parliamentary approval through the forced loan and ship money. Now they stuck together when Charles dissolved parliament after three weeks and mounted yet another under-resourced and failed expedition against the Scots. Eleven of them met at Bedford's London home and sent a petition to Charles demanding a new parliament; the king responded by summoning a Great Council in York, at which he was forced to succumb to their demand.

Charles presumed that he would maintain his majority in the Lords, and sure enough, when the Commons agreed to impeach the king's right-hand man and brutal Lord Deputy of Ireland, Thomas Wentworth, the earl of Strafford, on the grounds that he had told the king that he could use his army in Ireland to 'reduce this kingdom' (which MPs chose to interpret as referring to England), the Lords refused to convict him. Round one to the king. Three days later, though, the infuriated Commons carried a Bill for Strafford's attainder by 204 votes to 59 and sent it up to the Lords. At this point Charles tried to bolster his support in the Lords by making Essex and Warwick privy councillors, Essex's brother-in-law Hertford a marquess and his younger brother Francis Seymour a peer, Saye and Sele Master of the Wards and Essex's Irish half-brother Ulick de Burgh earl of St Albans. But just as the Lords were getting to the meaty clauses of the attainder Bill the first news broke of a government plot 'to discontent the Army with the proceedings of parliament'.[9] At this threat of force Strafford's support dissolved; Henry Grey, the earl of Stamford, who had thus far been a keen supporter of king and court, reckoned that the plot was an even greater danger than 'the Gunpowder Treason. For by this time had this not been discovered ... we had all been made slaves.'[10] There were angry scenes in the Lords as supporters of the attainder argued that the novice Lord Seymour be barred from voting on the grounds that he had not been a peer when the charges were originally introduced, and the earl of Pembroke struck Lord Maltravers with a cane (for which affront Pembroke was removed as Lord Chamberlain, to be replaced in July by Essex despite the latter's assertion that Strafford should be executed, for 'stone-dead hath no fellow').[11] Against this fractious background, the Catholic peers stayed away, as did the royalist earl of Bristol and Strafford's brother-in-law, the earl of Cumberland, and John Williams of Lincoln persuaded his fellow bishops to sit on their lawn sleeves. We do not know the precise voting figures on each of the clauses, as they were later expunged from the *Lords Journal*, but the upper house voted the Bill through and on 12 May 1641 Charles reluctantly allowed Strafford to be executed.

From this moment on, a concatenation of events saw the law of equal and opposite forces applied unremittingly. Bedford, one of the most moderate royal critics, died, Arundel unaccountably vacated the scene, and the rebels adopted increasingly zealous positions as Essex and Warwick spoke openly of creating a Venetian-style commonwealth with tight restrictions on the monarch. In retaliation, Charles brought hard-line defenders of the royal prerogative into the Privy Council and thereby managed to keep rebel initiatives at bay. The royal strategy was a catastrophic misreading of the Lords, though, as the house thought it more dignified to proceed by consensus than by division. Even controversial matters should be handled with a degree of sensitivity to opposing views. This preference for keeping an even keel meant that a small group could delay business, but it also meant that the king would alienate wavering peers if he disturbed the unanimity through impatience or intransigence. The core group of dissidents might not agree on everything, and since they were in a minority they could not control the Lords, but they were better-tempered than the king, who regularly overplayed his hand, lapsed into authoritarianism and resorted to violence. First came the rumour of an attempted assassination of two peers who were close to the Covenanters. Then, when most of the bishops were kept out of the Lords by angry stone-throwing London apprentices at the end of December 1641, Charles responded by trying to get the Lords' proceedings that had gone ahead without the bishops declared 'null and of no effect'. The Lords huffily claimed their dignity was affronted and had ten of the bishops imprisoned, whereupon Charles forced the Attorney-General to charge Mandeville and five MPs with treason. When the earl of Bristol's royalist son, George, Lord Digby, attempted to argue the case for Mandeville's arrest in the Lords, he was so distressed by the manifest anger that he skulked off, apologetically whispering to Mandeville that the king was very mischievously advised. He forgot to mention that he himself had tendered the advice. This attempt at hardballing was not only bathetic but completely counterproductive: the Lords refused to investigate the six supposed traitors and instead launched an inquiry into the actions of the Attorney-General. Within days the king had fled London for Windsor, and when the duke of Richmond and the earl of Bristol tabled a motion to adjourn parliament for six months while everyone calmed down, this was so comprehensively defeated in the Lords that the royalist peers joined Charles, leaving a skeleton House of Lords who voted to entrust the militia not to the king but to such hands as parliament might confide in, and to exclude the bishops permanently.

Charles had squandered his majority in the Lords, but when it came to war the majority of peers took to the field as active royalists with gusto, much as they had done in the first bishops' war. Most of them never questioned their allegiance. Why would they *not* support the hereditary monarch, especially when there was honour to be won, and money and land to be seized from conquered rebels? Nevertheless, in order to entice as many peers as possible up to York, Charles announced a feast for the Order of the Garter and demanded that individual peers join him on their 'allegiance'. By June 1642 around forty nobles had done so, each of them signing an 'engagement . . . not to obey any rule, order or ordinance whatsoever concerning any militia that hath not the royal assent',[12] and promising to fund a 2,000-strong cavalry force for three months. (Two of the wealthiest men in the land, Henry Somerset and William Cavendish, between them contributed more than £1,500,000, worth £325 million in 2017, and were rewarded with new titles as marquess of Worcester and duke of Newcastle.) Not everyone found this easy. Lucius Cary, the 2nd Viscount Falkland, a gentle, rational man who gathered a circle of clerics, poets and men of letters at his house at Great Tew and attempted to hammer out a middle way between hard-line Calvinism and Catholic-seeming Anglicanism, had voted for Strafford's attainder in the Commons (from which his Scottish title did not bar him) and had sought an accommodation in the Long Parliament. His friend and ally Edward Hyde, who became earl of Clarendon and Lord Chancellor to Charles II, penned a portrait of Falkland:

> Sitting amongst his friends, often, after a deep silence and frequent sighs (he) would with a shrill and sad accent ingeminate the word 'Peace, Peace,' and would passionately profess that the very agony of the war, and the view of the calamities and desolation the kingdom did and must endure, took his sleep from him and would shortly break his heart.[13]

Yet despite his hope for peace and his love of compromise, even Falkland joined the king; and yet again it felt as if a medieval monarch had mustered the ancient royal expeditionary force, the fyrd.

This was a role that the aristocracy understood. Most royalist commanders were peers. At major battle and minor skirmish alike, peers took the royalist lead. When Charles unfurled his standard at the highest point of Nottingham Castle in August 1642, he set off from Thurland Hall, the Nottingham seat of John Holles, 2nd earl of Clare (though the earl refused to attend in person), and was accompanied by John Tufton, 2nd earl of Thanet, who had inherited the titles his wealthy father had purchased and arrived with a hundred horse. Several peers were present at Edgehill in October, including Patrick Ruthven, the Scottish earl of Forth, who ousted the earl of Lindsey in a row over tactics, leading Lindsey to pronounce that 'since he was not fit to be a general, he would die a colonel in the head of his regiment'[14] – a prophecy he fulfilled that same day, bleeding to death from a wound in the thigh. In 1643, Sir Ralph (later Lord) Hopton secured Cornwall; the earl of Chesterfield seized Lichfield and defended its Cathedral Close until it and he were captured; the earl of Northampton was killed by a halberd blow to the head while leading the cavalry at Hopton Heath; Lord Wilmot, the earl of Crawford, Sir John Byron and the marquess of Hertford comprehensively defeated the parliamentarians at Roundway Down; and the tender-hearted Viscount Falkland and the earl of Carnarvon were killed at the first battle of Newbury, at which Byron won a peerage. So too in 1645 Chesterfield's son Philip died in the defence of the family home Shelford Manor in Nottinghamshire, and after the battle of Naseby Charles rewarded Bernard Stuart, the youngest son of the duke of Lennox, and Henry Bard with the titles of earl of Lichfield and Viscount Bellomont, though the former was killed in a brave sortie at the battle of Rowton Heath before the patent came into force (and the latter died in a windstorm on an abortive mission to the Shah of Persia).

Some found it all too difficult. Arundel left for Padua, where he died in 1646; Monmouth sat out the wars translating classical works; Henry Danvers, the normally belligerent earl of Danby, was too old and ill to leave his Oxfordshire estate at Cornbury; Anthony Grey, who unexpectedly became 9th earl of Kent on the death of his childless second cousin once removed in 1639 aged eighty-two, preferred to remain at his altar as the rector of Burbage in Leicestershire; and William Russell, 5th earl of Bedford, switched sides and, having earned everyone's distrust, spent most of the war in retreat at Woburn. Others were dragged in reluctantly. William Cecil, 2nd earl of Salisbury, was persuaded to support the Commonwealth by his two parliamentarian sons (and by an attack on his Dorset home, Cranborne House) and retired to Hatfield House under the protectorate. Edward Sackville, 4th earl of Dorset, pledged sixty horse, but was distressed when Charles actually called on them. 'Behold', he wrote, 'into what a sad condition blind zeal, pride, ambition, envy, malice and avarice . . . hath plunged the honour, quiet, safety, peace, plenty, prosperity, piety of this late, very late, most happy kingdom . . . All is lost, all is lost: so lost as I would I were quiet in my grave.'[15] John Paulet, the Catholic 5th marquess of Winchester, tried to retire to Basing House, along with some of the men of letters to whom he was patron, including Inigo Jones and Wenceslaus Hollar. It was a vain hope, though, as Basing House lay at a key junction on the road west from London and the parliamentarians reckoned it to be a nest of papists. A two-year siege ensued. When William Waller offered the marchioness Honora free passage, she defiantly declared that she was 'resolved to run the same fortune as her Lord, knowing that there was a just and all-seeing Judge above, who she hoped would have an especial hand in the business, from whom Sir William Waller could pretend no commission. Whatever befell she was not unprepared to bear it.'[16] This dismissal was delivered with the patrician disdain that one might have expected of a daughter of the earl of St Albans and granddaughter of Sir Francis Walsingham, but in the end her husband was imprisoned in the Tower for treason and deprived of all his estates, and the Commons resolved that Basing should be 'totally slighted and demolished' and anyone who wanted to fetch away any of its stones and bricks should feel free to do so.

Honora was not the only noblewoman to take an active part in the war. As peers sallied forth with the king, their wives and daughters found themselves in the front line defending their houses and castles. When Wardour Castle, the fortified home of Thomas, 2nd Baron Arundell, was besieged in 1643, his sixty-year-old wife Blanche, daughter of the 4th earl of Worcester, held out for six days. The terms offered her were generous, but were immediately ignored by the parliamentary troops, who looted Wardour so thoroughly that when her husband died a week later she had to rely on the marquess of Hertford to find her lodgings as she 'had not a bed to lie on, nor means to provide herself a house or furniture'.[17] The doughtiest of the royalist noblewomen, though, was Charlotte de la Trémouille, daughter of the duc de Thouars in Poitou, who had married James Stanley, later the 7th earl of Derby, in The Hague in 1626. With her husband serving the king, she was left in 1644 defending Lathom House in Lancashire against Sir Thomas Fairfax, who demanded vacant possession. As commander-in-chief of three hundred trained defenders, she organized sorties and refused to budge, even when her own room was hit in the bombardment. When a 'last' demand was sent, she tore it up in front of the messenger and scornfully told him:

> Thou art but a foolish instrument of traytors pride . . . Tell that insolent rebell, hee shall have neither persons, goods, nor house; when our strength and provision is spent, we shall find a fire more mercyfull . . . and if the providence of God prevent it not, my goods and house shall burne in his sight; myself, children and soldiers, rather than fall into his hands, will seale our religion and loyalty in the same flame.[18]

Charlotte's defiance paid off: Prince Rupert raised the siege four days later.

Although most peers were ready royalists, twenty-two remained in London and declared that any peer who failed to appear in parliament was an enemy of the state. Parliament's first Committee of Safety included five peers – Essex; Saye and Sele; Henry Rich, 1st earl of Holland; Algernon Percy, 10th earl of Northumberland; and King James's one-time favourite Philip Herbert, now 4th earl of Pembroke – and when it voted to raise its own militia it appointed Essex as its commander and required the members of both houses to swear 'to live and die with the earl of Essex'. In the first burst of war several more peers became parliamentary commanders: these included Northumberland, Wharton, Saye and Sele, Mandeville (now having succeeded his father as 2nd earl of Manchester) and Brooke, who was the first peer to lose his life in parliament's cause, shot by a sniper during the siege of Lichfield.

All was not plain sailing for the parliamentarian peers. Saye and Sele fell out with Essex; he and Manchester were accused of being half-measures men and in 1645 were deprived of their military commands by a Self-Denying Ordinance which put the army on a more professional footing by banning members of either house (apart from Oliver Cromwell and Thomas Fairfax) from holding military posts. The Committee of Both Kingdoms included three Scottish and seven English peers, but parliamentary hostility to the peerage grew. One rabble-rouser, Richard Overton, called for the abolition of the Lords, and the author of *The Just Man in Bonds* cast the peers as 'sons of conquest . . . and usurpation . . . not made by the people, from whom all power, place and office that is just in this kingdom ought only to arise'.[19] When Charles was captured in 1648 and the army purged parliament of Presbyterians, attendance in the Lords sank to between three and fifteen. Four – Pembroke, Salisbury, Denbigh and North – told Fairfax that they no longer desired 'to maintain peerage or any other any privilege whatsoever that might be perceived prejudicial to the public interest'.[20] When Fairfax laughed at them, North decided to retire to Kirtling Tower in Cambridgeshire; he need not have bothered, as when the Lords refused to put Charles on trial for treason, the rump of MPs went ahead anyway and abolished the Lords days after Charles's execution. During the ensuing eleven-year interregnum the Council of State included six peers, a string of peers resurfaced as MPs in the Protectorate and Barebones parliaments, and when Oliver Cromwell created his Other House in 1657 he included Manchester, Wharton, Saye and Sele (and his son); the Lords Eure and Broghill; Thomas Balasyse, 2nd Viscount Fauconberg; the 2nd earl of Mulgrave; the earl of Leicester's son, Philip Sidney, Viscount Lisle; and Charles Howard, whom he created a peer. Only one nominee, Robert Rich, who had recently succeeded his father as 3rd earl of Warwick, imperiously refused to attend – on the grounds that the other members included a drayman and a cobbler.

✠

Ostensibly concerned with matters of high principle, the aristocracy spent much of their time and energy during the civil wars and protectorate indulging in a rearguard action to protect their wealth. Parliament was well aware of this. In pursuit of hard cash to fund its campaigns, and hoping that the threat of financial destitution might act as a deterrent, it resolved in October 1642 that the estates of 'delinquents' who had taken up arms against parliament should be sequestered 'for the use and service of the commonwealth';[21] and the following spring it agreed another resolution 'sequestering and seizing the estates, real and personal, of all such persons as have been, are or shall be in actual war or arms against the parliament'.[22] Soon a national committee for 'compounding' with delinquents started meeting at Goldsmiths' Hall, to which anyone worth more than £200 a year could apply for restoration of their estates on payment of a fine. It rapidly acquired a reputation for ruthlessness. William, 2nd Baron Brereton in the Irish peerage from 1631, for instance, turned his father's elegant prodigy house at Brereton in Cheshire into a royalist garrison, but was captured by Cromwell when he fled to his cousin Francis Biddulph's house in Staffordshire. His estates were then valued at £1,400 per annum, for which he was forced to compound for such a large sum (£2,538 18s) that he had to sell much of his land, and five of his daughters died without dowry or husband. So too Robert Cholmondeley, who had been made an Irish viscount and earl of Leinster as well as an English baron by the time he was captured by parliament at Oxford in June 1646, had his Cheshire mansion sequestered and converted 'to a hogsty and render[ed] ... unfit for a place of residence for a person of such quality'.[23] He compounded that September for £7,742 and had to sell lands at Kentish Town to meet the fine; similarly, another Irish peer, Robert Needham, 2nd Viscount Kilmorey, escaped the siege at Chester but was also captured at Oxford and was fined £3,560. When the earl of Thanet returned from exile in 1644 he compounded for £9,000, reckoning that he had lost the best part of £17,000 on his estates, including £1,600 of silver plate stolen from Wiston House, which he was forced to sell, along with Bodiam Castle.

Thanet was hardly impoverished. He still held the former priory of Lewes in Kent, which the Sackville family had transformed into the sprawling mansion known as Lord's Place, and Thanet House in London. But others did suffer. When John Savage, 2nd Earl Rivers, and his mother the dowager countess Elizabeth (who had inherited considerable property, including Frodsham, Halton and Rocksavage in Cheshire,

Melford Hall in Suffolk and St Osyth Priory in Essex), took an uncompromising royalist position, parliamentary forces destroyed Rocksavage and Halton, the mob sacked St Osyth and Melford, and parliament sequestered the family lands in Cheshire and Essex. Elizabeth compounded for £16,979 9s 10d and her son had to sell off Long Melford, as well as goods and personal effects including the family linen. So impoverished was the family thereafter that both mother and son were imprisoned in the 1650s for debt, and although Elizabeth claimed privilege of peerage, this was denied her and she died a pauper in 1651; she was followed four years later by her son, whose body was awaiting burial at Frodsham when a fire took hold of the castle and burned it to the ground.

Canny nobles became ingenious in dealing with this threat to their wealth, as shown by the Pierrepont family. Robert Pierrepont had been wealthy enough to marry a Talbot and acquire Thoresby Park, and loyal enough to be made earl of Kingston-upon-Hull in 1628, yet his allegiance at the start of the war was uncertain and two of his five sons, Henry and William, took diametrically opposed views. In July 1643, Robert himself was captured by parliamentarian forces at Gainsborough, and while he was being transported to Hull the royalists fired at his boat, accidentally cutting him in two with a cannon-ball. The new earl, Henry, was less ambivalent in his support for the royalist cause, attended Charles at Oxford, negotiated on his behalf at Uxbridge and was made marquess of Dorchester for his pains; but on 4 September 1646 he compounded as a delinquent and the following March was fined £7,467. This was a large sum, but it was paid directly to his younger brother William, an MP in the Short and Long Parliaments, who was an active member of the Committee of Both Kingdoms. Thus the family astutely guarded its own back. James Hay, 2nd earl of Carlisle, found another way out. His father, another of James's former favourites, died in 1636, leaving him with extensive estates and expensive debts. He might have hoped that these would be alleviated when his wealthy maternal grandfather, Edward Denny, earl of Norwich, died the following year, but his creditors were still pursuing him for £11,000 in 1641. Having served as a colonel in Germany, he was a natural recruit to the royalist cause in the first civil war, but with debt still hanging over him and only the Denny estates in Essex to keep him in the manner to which he had grown accustomed, he made his peace with parliament and left for the Carlisle Islands (later known as Barbados), which he eventually had to mortgage to Lord Willoughby of Parham.

When Prince Charles allied himself with the Scottish Covenanters who proclaimed him king of Scotland and marched south in 1650, royalists who had compounded and sworn an oath that they would not take up arms again were put in a difficult position. Parliament had captured four recidivist royalist peers back in 1648 – the duke of Hamilton, the earl of Holland, George Goring (now earl of Norwich) and Lord Capell – and put them on trial for treason. Capell had managed to escape the Tower by scaling the walls and wading the moat, but when he was recaptured all four men were convicted on 6 March 1649. Three days later petitions for mercy were heard by the Commons and voted on. Hamilton and Capell were both ordered to be executed; required to resolve tied votes on Norwich and Holland, the Speaker excused the former and condemned the latter, despite the support of his parliamentarian brother, the earl of Warwick. On their way to execution Hamilton, Capell and Holland claimed that they had only surrendered on condition that their lives would be spared, so many royalists were very chary of returning to the fray. In the end it was a tiny coterie of peers that joined Charles at the battle of Worcester – and they were routed. George Villiers, 2nd duke of Buckingham (who had escaped from St Neots), fled with Lord Wilmot and the king, and the 2nd duke of Hamilton died of a musket-ball wound that shattered his leg. The fate of James Stanley, 7th earl of Derby, proved the caution of many peers well-founded. Derby had fought relentlessly and ruthlessly at Preston, at Lancaster, at Bolton and at Marston Moor in the first civil war, and in 1646 had retreated to the safety of the Isle of Man. In 1651, however, his countess, Charlotte, who as described above had shown considerable bravery in defending the family seat Lathom House when it was twice besieged, persuaded him to join Charles. Although Derby escaped at Worcester, he was captured near Nantwich and court-martialled. His plea for mercy on the grounds that he had surrendered on the promise of mercy was ignored and he was hauled back to the marketplace in Bolton, where he was beheaded.

In such unpropitious circumstances, royalist peers became even craftier in their determination to reclaim their estates. The younger George Villiers, 2nd duke of Buckingham, is the best example. As soon as he was old enough, he and his brother Francis joined the earl of Holland in Surrey in 1648. George saw action at Kingston, narrowly escaped at St Neots and escaped again after the battle of Worcester. A close friend of Prince Charles, with whom he had been brought up in the royal household following his father's assassination, he joined him in exile and was made a privy councillor. In 1657, though, he returned to England and managed to persuade Mary, the daughter of parliament's commander-in-chief Lord Fairfax, to whom parliament had awarded the sequestered Buckingham estates, to jilt Philip Stanhope, 2nd earl of Chesterfield, even though their banns of marriage had already been read twice. It was a crafty move. Fairfax defended Buckingham from Cromwell's wrath, and after the Restoration the duke was perfectly placed to have his own estates restored. Mary might also have thought luck was on her side, as Chesterfield proved to be a negligent husband and was imprisoned for wounding one man and killing another in duels. But Buckingham was little better. A dilettante and a philandering rake, he had a spell as a senior figure in the Cabal administration and was a leading figure in the Country Party, but was forced out of office over an adulterous affair with the countess of Shrewsbury, with whom he lived for some time in a loose *ménage à trois* with his wife.

Buckingham was an exception in returning early; there remained some thirty royalist peers in long-term exile on the continent, including courtiers such as the earls of Norwich and Bristol, wealthy magnates such as Newcastle, and newly ennobled cavalier commanders such as Wentworth, Byron, Hopton and Widdrington. What is particularly striking is that not one of these émigrés had a title that preceded 1603. Some of them had achieved a settlement of sorts, with their wives or daughters managing their estates and sending them much-needed subventions, but their hope was always to return, and when Cromwell died and his son 'tumbledown Dick' proved unable to hold the country together, moves were made to bring about a restoration of the monarchy. The Long Parliament was reconvened with the formerly excluded Presbyterians (but without the Lords) and voted to dissolve itself and summon a Convention Parliament. Manchester, who had spoken against the trial and execution of Charles I and had spent the intervening years in rural retirement, returned to act as Speaker of the Lords, and Saye and Sele, now seventy-eight, who had also been in quiet seclusion on Lundy Island, appeared with just eight others for the first meeting of the Lords on 25 April. At first there was a row about which peers should be invited, as fifty-two English titles had changed hands between August 1642 and 1660, twenty of the sixty-four earls had died in the 1650s, and Manchester wanted to exclude any of the younger peers who might vote for an unfettered monarchy. Eventually, on Thursday, 3 May 1660, forty-two peers gathered in the Lords to welcome Charles's conciliatory letter from Breda, in which he promised religious freedom. 'The Peers', they wrote back, 'have a just Ground to own a more particular Dependance and Subservience to the Throne of Majesty, not only by the Prescriptions of Law, but by that Affection and Duty which is fixed in their Hearts upon the Foundation of Loyalty, which gives them the Privilege to style themselves.'[24] It was weighty rhetoric; but as if to underline the fact that the matter at hand was every bit as much about their personal dignity as about the welfare of the nation, that same day they referred yet another battle for precedence between the Lords de la Warr and Berkeley to the committee on privileges.

The Creation Robe, of a Duke.
Duke of Buckingham

The Creation Robe of a Baron.

One of the perennial narcissistic obsessions of aristocracy was each individual's place in the hierarchy. Barons, earls, marquesses and dukes all had distinct robes, and processed and were seated in the House of Lords in strict order of precedence. The Lords and the Court of Chivalry regularly adjudicated cases of disputed precedence.

CHAPTER 8

THERE IS RESPECT DUE TO A LORD

WHEN THE LORDS MET on Tuesday, 25 April 1660 they adopted a pious attitude, ordering that the following Monday be kept as 'a day of fasting and humiliation' in the prayerful hope of 'a settlement of this Nation';[1] but it rapidly became clear that their real priority was the settlement of their own private finances, as they pronounced that the duke of Buckingham, the earl of Derby and Lord Craven were to be restored to their lands *forthwith* along with 'all other Lords that are in the like Condition'. This was a phenomenally self-serving move. Many lesser royalists had had their lands sequestrated for equally valiant service to the king and had spent years racking up debts in impecunious exile – but they would have to wrangle their cases through the courts at great expense, while peers, and peers alone, could secure immediate restitution for themselves via parliament.

This parliamentary brand of justice was evidently partisan, as the case of William, Baron Craven, shows. The son of a successful City financier, he inherited such substantial estates that when he bought himself a peerage for £7,000 in 1627 he was one of the nine wealthiest peers in England. Although he did not fight in the civil wars, he contributed £50,000 to the royalist cause, for which parliament seized and sold his estates in 1652. Craven objected that these had been 'damnified above £200,000 besides the total loss of all his real estates',[2] so in 1660 he sought the return of all his estates by Act of parliament, plus rent arrears. This hardly seemed fair to Dorothy, Lady Grey of Groby, who petitioned the Lords that her late husband had bought some of Craven's lands using her jointure. Was she not to be compensated? Since Lord Grey had signed Charles I's death warrant, her plaint was doomed, and on 6 June the Lords petitions committee declared that Craven should have all his personal and real goods restored 'in whose hands so ever the same is'.[3] Craven moaned that Charlton Park was in ruins; but he was restored to his exorbitant wealth, he built a new house at Hamstead Mansell and added a wing to Coombe Abbey – and in 1665 he was made an earl. Other peers reaped the same swift rewards through the Lords. The 2nd duke of Buckingham wanted to stop people felling timber on 'his' estates. The Lords obliged. The marquess of Winchester's records had been destroyed by fire, so he needed an Act of parliament to prove possession. He got it, as did the marquesses of Newcastle and Worcester, the earls of Huntingdon, Northumberland, Derby, Suffolk and Lichfield, and the Barons Colepeper and Arundell. Rarely had there been such a flurry of *ad hominem* legislation.

Not every peer's thirst was slaked. The 8th earl of Derby and his mother the dowager countess were certainly not satisfied. The family owned large tracts of Lancashire, Cheshire, north Wales and the Isle of Man; after the 7th earl was executed at Bolton in 1651, the question became whether he had *voluntarily* sold some of his estates during the interregnum, had been hoodwinked into doing so or had been coerced by parliament. Three Bills asserting the earl's right to repossession foundered in the Commons, and a fourth was considered so generous to him that although it was carried in the Lords, twenty-five peers entered a formal protest against its third reading and when the Commons surprisingly let it through, Charles vetoed it. The family never forgot. In 1732 the 10th earl had the following inscribed over the south front of the family seat, Knowsley Park: 'James, earl of Derby . . . was beheaded at Bolton . . . for strenuously adhering to Charles II, who refused a bill passed unanimously by both Houses of Parliament for restoring to the family the estate lost by his loyalty to that King.' Bitterness had clouded the memory, as Charles had granted the 8th earl the lucrative office of chamberlain of the county of Chester, which many would have thought recompense enough.

The individual demands were endless. The earl of Winchester wanted

£19,000, the earl of Bristol £6,500 and Lord Lexington £2,860. Edward Hyde, the earl of Clarendon, received £20,000, plus Cornbury House in Oxfordshire, the manors of Langley, Leefields and Ramsden, and valuable slices of Westminster and Lambeth. George Monck, the soldier who had been instrumental in bringing about the Restoration, was given three baronies, an earldom and the duchy of Albemarle, along with Enfield Old Park, the royal palace at Theobalds, the parks at Hampton Court, swathes of the province of Carolina and other lands worth £7,000 a year. Even John Mordaunt, whom many royalists distrusted, was made a viscount and constable of Windsor Castle, and in addition was awarded the old priory of Reigate on a peppercorn rent, the manors of Currey and Shepton Mallet, and a third of a shilling for every chaldron* of coal unloaded on the River Tyne.

As well as their various personal claims, the avaricious peers also had a communal demand, namely the restitution of 'creation money', which had been paid twice yearly prior to 1642 to peers for each of the titles they held above baron. Since a viscount got £13 6s 8d, an earl £20, a marquess £26 13s 4d and a duke £40, this was a significant sum. Just days into the Restoration, the earl of Lincoln demanded its reinstatement – with arrears. The Treasury initially balked at the arrears, but on 5 January 1661 the 2nd earl of Denbigh was the first to get his warrant for payment, and the Treasury books show a steady stream of disbursements thereafter. The earl of Bedford was awarded £40, as was the earl of Salisbury. The earl of Rutland was given a warrant for back payment for two and a half years 'and of the said creation money in future',[4] and even Katherine, dowager countess of Chesterfield, was paid her dues for 'the dignity of a countess'.[5]

☩

The abundant financial fruits of the Restoration were easily harvested, but the self-regarding peers sought an even greater prize as well: power, so that their status and privileges should not be slighted again by the

---

*A measure of coal that was used from medieval times until 1835. A Newcastle chaldron was fixed in 1678 at 5,880lb and increased to 5,940lb in 1694.

monarch, nor their authority overthrown by the populace, and that they might retain and enhance their property without let or hindrance. Amazingly, it took just fifty-five years for them to achieve an adamantine ascendancy that survived for nearly three centuries.

The foundation stone of this edifice was religious conformity to the rites and teachings of the Church of England. At first this had Charles II's support: the bishops were re-admitted to the Lords, corporation members were required to take Church of England communion, and office-holders, including MPs, had to swear an oath against transubstantiation. But this smooth progress was derailed in 1678 by one of those quirks of history – a national panic engendered by a pack of lies – in the shape of the Popish Plot, which supposedly implicated five Catholic peers in an attempt to assassinate the king. Only one of them was executed – William Howard, Viscount Stafford – and that was in large measure because he alienated the eight members of his own family who participated in his trial by peers. Yet in the midst of the moral panic the Commons pushed for 'papists', including the king's younger brother and heir to the throne, James, the openly Catholic duke of York, to be barred from office on the grounds that 'the king's person is at this time in danger from popish conspiracies'.[6] When the Bill came to the Lords, the king secured an exemption for his brother, but this merely led to a protracted battle over York's exclusion from the succession, which was played out in successive elections and parliaments, as Buckingham and his more serious-minded colleague Anthony Ashley Cooper, earl of Shaftesbury, successfully campaigned for exclusionist MPs to be elected and unsuccessfully presented three Exclusion Bills in successive parliaments. Their campaign foundered when the Rye House Plot in favour of Charles's illegitimate but Protestant son the duke of Monmouth was discovered. Shaftesbury, the earls of Melville and Leven, and the Lords Marchmont, Lovelace and Grey of Werke fled to the continent, the earls of Argyll, Macclesfield, Warrington and Stamford had a spell in the Tower, and nine of their allies were hanged, drawn and quartered as common traitors. Again, just one aristocrat – William Russell, the son and heir of the duke of Bedford – was executed, by the cack-handed executioner Jack Ketch, who would later take five blows to remove Monmouth's head after an abortive rebellion in 1685.

Once king, James II's attempt to reintroduce Catholicism through his prerogative powers was met with fury. The bishops rebelled, the courts refused to convict them and the peers increasingly cohered as a 'Country party' (as opposed to the 'Court party') with a defined set of beliefs: arbitrary and absolute royal power was to be abhorred, the divine right of kings was a dangerous myth, the Protestant succession must be asserted even over the normal rules of heredity, the individual had a right to dissent, the monarch must rule by consent, the people and the monarch should be held in balance by the nobility, and the right to property was absolute. Thus far the term 'Whig' had been a catch-all term of abuse for Scottish Covenanters, Presbyterians, radicals and Shaftesbury's Exclusionists, but under James the fissiparous grouping who called themselves Whigs had a uniting doctrine in the explicit belief that a Catholic monarch would threaten life, liberty and property. So when James's wife finally bore him a Catholic son in June 1688, a group of peers[7] staged a quiet and bloodless coup and asked William, the stadtholder* of the Dutch United Provinces, and his wife, James II's daughter Mary, to take the throne.

The Whigs called the co-regents' arrival and James's involuntary departure a 'Glorious Revolution', but this was no radical republican upheaval. As if to make the point that the transfer of power was about protecting not dismantling the established order, the Whig peers insisted on a Bill of Rights, a legal requirement that parliaments be summoned and elected regularly (but not too regularly), and a guaranteed Protestant succession. When Mary and William died without issue in 1694 and 1702, and Mary's Protestant sister Queen Anne failed to produce an heir, the Whigs, who dominated both houses of parliament, settled the succession on the Protestant descendants of the Electress Sophia of Hanover through an Act of Settlement. Anne's personal preference for the 'Tories' (in origin, a term every bit as pejorative as 'Whig'), who held

*Formally, the 'steward' or chief magistrate, but by this stage national leader.

the hereditary right of the Stuarts to the throne as sacrosanct and supported a more Catholic-style Anglican Church, brought them briefly to power, but when she died in 1714 and the Hanoverian George I arrived with 'strong prepossessions against the Tories',[8] they were excluded from every vestige of patronage. Some went into exile with James and took part in the 1715 rebellion with his son James Stuart, the Old Pretender, thereby ceding both the realm and the moral high ground to the Whig aristocracy. The upshot was that by 1715 every pillar of the Whigs' aristocratic ascendancy was in place – religious conformity, government by consent, regular parliaments, aristocratic pre-eminence in royal counsels, and the right to property.

The nobility proved extremely assiduous, cohesive and adept at preserving this position throughout the eighteenth century. Their most obvious advantage lay in their ability to dominate parliament. In the Lords this meant a very jealous attitude towards the granting of new titles. Although many peers were the beneficiaries of the early Stuarts' honours inflation, they attacked any attempt to increase their number almost as frequently as they sought promotions for themselves and new titles for their relations. The issue came to a head early in the century under Queen Anne, whose desire to keep her Tory friends in office made her a serial inflationist. In 1703 she appointed five new peers and promoted two more – all of them Tories. In 1707 the Act of Union provided for the election of sixteen Scottish 'representative peers' by the Scottish lords at the start of every parliament to sit in the House of Lords – a group of poorer peers who proved readily amenable to financial inducements in return for support for the ministry of the day. And when the Treaty of Utrecht was in danger in the Lords in the winter of 1711–12, Anne acceded to a request from her leading minister, Robert Harley (who had very recently been made earl of Oxford and Earl Mortimer), for a dozen more peers. All of them had proved their Tory loyalty as MPs, and five either held an Irish title or were the sons of Scottish or English peers, yet there was outrage at both their number and their quality: people superciliously commented that Samuel, the new Baron Masham, was a mere equerry married to one of the queen's household servants. The following year the nobility had a further complaint to make when the Chancellor of the Exchequer, Robert Benson, was made Baron Bingley. Benson's entrepreneurial father had left him land worth £3,000 a year and £120,000 in ready money, and Benson himself was already building a suitably baronial mansion at Bramham Park near Leeds; but William, 4th Baron Berkeley of Stratton, who struttingly prided himself on his pre-Conquest noble antecedents and his ancestral house at Bruton Abbey, was furious, arguing that this proved that every year the Lords received 'some great blow'.[9] A Tory ally, Dr William Stratford, snootily wrote to Harley that although it was alleged that all the new peers were of ancient families, 'no one I have met with is much acquainted with the new Lord [Bingley]'s pedigree'.[10] So sorely were these promotions resented that the moment Anne died, the Commons impeached Harley before the Lords, their final charge being that he had 'most wickedly determined at one fatal blow, as far as in him lay, to destroy the freedom and independency of the House of Lords'.[11] The impeachment proceedings saw an exceptional turnout of 142 peers, and although Harley was acquitted, his health had largely drained away in the Tower.

The Whigs were equally exasperated by George I, who appointed fifteen new peers and promoted another twenty-two in his first three years, and under whom it was rumoured (accurately) that Christopher Vane and Robert Marsham had bought their titles as the Barons Barnard and Marsham. What with the Scots, the Irish and a handful of Dutch and German appointments, the peerage felt invaded by impecunious foreigners. On top of this, the Whig administration led by Charles Spencer, 3rd earl of Sunderland, and James, the new earl of Stanhope, feared that when the king's son succeeded to the throne, he might create yet another wave of potentially hostile peers. At the heart of this noble hysteria was the ancient grumble that a 'vast glut of creations' had 'overflowed us like the torrent'.[12] In 1719 the ministry accordingly drafted a Peerage Bill, which would fix the peerage forever at 209. This was the most explicit attempt yet made to protect the titled elite, and it was presented in the Lords on 28 February 1719 by the embodiment of patrician elitism, Charles Seymour, 6th duke of Somerset. Contemporaries referred to him as 'a man of vast pride',[13] and as 'humoursome, proud and capricious',[14] while the Victorian historian Macaulay reckoned him 'a man in whom the pride of birth and rank amounted almost to a disease'.[15] Stories of his haughtiness abounded. He gestured imperiously at servants rather than address them, he refused to let his children sit in his presence, and when his second (much younger) wife tapped him familiarly on the shoulder with her fan, he is said to have cried out with great indignation: 'Madam, my first wife was a Percy and she never took such a liberty.'[16] Yet his family history might have suggested to him that nobility was often a child of chance. He had himself only become duke thanks to the death of his father's cousin without an heir and the murder of his elder brother outside an inn in Italy – and much of his wealth had come from the afore-mentioned Percy, Elizabeth, the sole heiress to the 11th earl of Northumberland. Somerset's Bill was abandoned before its third reading in the Lords, but an identical one presented later that year by another proud peer, Edmund Sheffield, 2nd duke of Buckingham and Normanby, sailed through the upper house. It ran aground, however, in the lower, where Sir Robert Walpole lampooned the attempt to 'over-preponderate' the finely balanced British constitution and appealed to MPs' personal ambitions by asking whether they really intended to 'consent to the shutting the door upon [their] family ever coming to the House of Lords'.[17]

It is ironic that MPs' envy thus trumped peers' jealousy. Other countries had strict limits on the number of noble families. France had its laws of *dérogeance* and Venice its *Libro d'Oro*, but the British peerage remained uncapped. Still, the rate of creations slowed after 1719 and did not accelerate again until William Pitt needed to bolster his support in the 1780s. Yet aristocrats continued to complain. Horace Walpole (son of the earl of Orford, the Whig Prime Minister Robert Walpole, who himself later became the 4th earl) moaned about each new 'cargo of peers', claimed that the list of new Irish peers in 1756 contained nothing but 'brewers and poulterers',[18] and said the list in 1776 was so long that half of them could only have been gentlemen for less than a generation or two – indeed, he argued, 'their very number makes them a mob'.[19] Walpole's friend Lady Townshend jested that she expected at any minute to get a bill from her fishmonger signed Lord MountShrimp, and in

1797 Thomas Noel, 10th Baron Wentworth, lamented to Basil Feilding, 6th earl of Denbigh, that soon 'Lords will be as cheap as stinking mackerel'.[20] This pretentious outrage was ludicrously over-egged. For most of the century, the number of new titles barely kept up with extinctions, as aristocratic jealousy acted as a very effective drag on further royal patronage and the vast majority of new peers came from the same aristocratic circle as the old. Of the 113 peers in 1800 whose titles had been created since 1780, 106 were promotions within the English peerage, Scottish or Irish additions, or relatives of existing peers. Four of the remaining seven had risen to prominence as lawyers and Charles Anderson-Pelham (Lord Yarborough as of 1794) was one of the richest MPs in the land. So the Peerage Bill had never been necessary. There were other ironies. Buckingham's dukedom died with him in 1735; and when Somerset and his son died in 1748 and 1750 the dukedom went to an impecunious distant cousin – a mere baronet – and the vast estates were split up between two other commoners who were made the earls of Northumberland and Egremont.

The system was soaked in corruption, for the political dominance of the Whig aristocracy depended on the regular greasing of their lordships' palms through ministerial salaries, pensions and sinecures. In the 1750s, for instance, there were 172 peers, including twelve Catholics and eleven minors. Of the remaining 153, eleven were lords of the royal bedchamber, twenty-six were bishops, sixteen were impoverished and dependent Scots, thirteen were ministers and in all ninety were in the direct pay of the crown. Ministerial office could be spectacularly profitable, so peers who in a previous generation might have remained in their regional power-bases in the countryside now spent large parts of the year in London seeking and monopolizing the best-paid national posts. As the Cabinet became more important than its parent, the Privy Council, peers successfully sought to keep it almost exclusively to themselves. In 1744 the Cabinet had fifteen members, six of whom were dukes (seven after a November reshuffle), one a marquess, two earls and two barons. Just one was an MP, and he was the younger brother of a duke. This became the norm. The duke of Newcastle's ministry of 1754 had five dukes, one marquess, four earls, three barons and three MPs. Lord North's administration in 1770 was stuffed with nobility – six earls, two sons of earls and two viscounts – and contained just a single commoner, Edward Hawke, a naval officer who took the post of First Lord of the Admiralty. Of the sixty-five Cabinet ministers between 1782 and 1820, forty-three were peers and fourteen more were sons of peers.

The key offices of state were kept in the manicured hands of the landed elite. There were fourteen eighteenth-century prime ministers. Nine were peers and four were sons of peers; the sole commoner was Sir Robert Walpole, and he put his son in the Lords in 1723 and was made earl of Orford in 1742 after twenty-one years of corrupt lubricity. Twelve out of fourteen lord chancellors and all nineteen masters-general of the ordnance (one of the posts most open to peculation as it was easy to siphon off funds from large-scale military procurements) were either British or Irish peers, and below them a myriad noble friends and relations were accommodated in comfortable sinecures. For the poorer peers even lesser bribes sufficed. When Richard Fiennes, 6th Viscount Saye and Sele, dropped a subtle hint in the ear of the duke of Newcastle in 1752 that he could not afford to attend the Lords, he was awarded an annual pension of £600 and became an assiduous supporter of the government. To the aristocratic mind, this was a virtuous circle. The landed elite governed the country and used their power to extract yet greater wealth. This did not absolutely preclude the government's losing a vote in the Lords – the marquess of Rockingham's administration was twice overturned in 1766, and in December 1783 the India Bill was defeated by 87 to 79 – but since the Lords regularly saw attendances of just thirty, it was never difficult to buy the loyalty of the assembled nobility and render it the unquestioning, uneventful, tedious and moribund body that it proved to be throughout the century.

Even so, it was not enough to dominate the Lords alone. The Commons had substantial powers, especially over taxation and expenditure, which were particularly important to the class of landlords in an era of almost constant war. Here too the aristocracy extended its tentacles. Irish peers could sit in the Commons, and it became standard practice for English peers to encourage their sons, brothers, nephews and grandsons to take seats in the lower house. Between 1690 and 1715 nearly half of all MPs were relatives of peers, baronets or knights; and the numbers rose significantly through the century and into the next. In 1708 just 70 out of 558 MPs were sons of peers, but in 1754 there were 113 of them, in 1794 there were 120, and in 1820 one MP in four was the son of a British or an Irish peer. If you include all the male relatives of peers and baronets, the figure stood at 271 in 1784, not far off half the membership.

Parliamentary seats were treated as another form of aristocratic property, to be bought and sold for profit and advantage. Most famously, the ancient constituency of Old Sarum had two MPs but just three houses with five votes, which Thomas 'Diamond' Pitt bought in 1691, thereby enabling him, his sons Robert and John, his grandsons William Pitt the Elder and Thomas Pitt (later Baron Camelford) and his great-grandson William Pitt the Younger to sit as MPs. In 1802 Camelford sold the seat for £60,000 to the Irishman James Alexander, who also bought the parliamentary borough of Newtownlands and Caledon in Ireland from which he took his name when given an earldom. Significant sums changed hands in these transactions. George Wyndham, 3rd earl of Egremont, bought Midhurst near his home at Petworth in Sussex for 40,000 guineas in 1787 from the trustees of the impoverished 7th Viscount Montagu – and sold it in 1795 to the banker and MP Robert Smith, who 'used it for the purchase of his [Irish] peerage'.[21] When the Prime Minister Lord North, son of the earl of Guilford, came hunting for supporters in Cornwall in 1774, the 3rd Baron Edgcumb demanded £15,000 for the five seats he controlled, but had to settle for £12,500, while the infamously greedy 2nd Viscount Falmouth insisted that he be paid for his six seats in guineas rather than pounds. The corrupt nature of this exchange was shameless. On another occasion Falmouth openly warned Pitt the Elder: 'I bring in five votes, who go with the ministry in the House of Commons; and if my application [to be made a knight of the Garter] is disregarded, you must take the consequence.'[22] In 1812 the 6th duke of Bedford sold the two seats at Camelford for £22,000, and in 1815 William Vane, 3rd earl of Darlington, paid a staggering £51,000 (around £4.2 million in 2017) for them, having outbid Francis Basset, Baron de Dunstanville, and the 3rd Viscount Falmouth. Pocket boroughs (so named because they were in the pocket of a grandee) often had to be corruptly cultivated, too. Thomas Pelham-Holles, duke of Newcastle-upon-Tyne (and -under-Lyme) could count on East Retford and Newark in Nottinghamshire and Aldborough and Boroughbridge in Yorkshire (as could the 2nd and 3rd dukes, and even the intransigent and unpopular 4th) – but the voters at Newark expected half a ton of coal each at Christmas, those at East Retford wanted twenty guineas a year, and in order to get his men returned in London in 1754 the duke poured £2,285 of booze down the voters' throats.

✠

The whole point of all this corruption was to keep the aristocratic bandwagon in self-perpetuating motion, in service of the nobility's convenient and frequently re-asserted twin beliefs that a property-based elite was the natural or God-given order of things, and that government should be exclusively in the hands of those with property in the form of land because only they had a permanent investment in the nation's future. The Irish peer, Robert, Earl Nugent, boasted of it, telling the Commons in 1780 that 'five-sixths of the borough [of St Mawes] was his own property, his constituents were his tenants, and he was sure of his election'.[23] The land qualification, indeed, was written into law. From 1711, MPs for county seats had to possess land with an annual income of at least £600 – a provision mirrored in a sudden increase in the property qualification for magistrates introduced in 1732 on the grounds that they could not be people of mean estate. The aim was to exclude the 'monied interest' – men mired in commerce, trade or finance – but it had another effect, as both houses of parliament constantly legislated to protect the rights of property-holders and magistrates backed them up. They drove through laws on turnpikes, forests, docks and canals. They extended the death penalty to property crimes relating to everything from cattle rustling and poaching to any interference with a landowner's hedges, fruit, grain, wood, horses, dogs or game. Further parliamentary enclosures transformed the agricultural landscape, too. Between 1730 and 1780 there were 1,257 such enclosure Acts reallocating and enclosing fields, meadowland, and common and waste ground. True, there were benefits, as farmland was made more efficient and productive; but the negative effects on the poor and those who held no land were terrible. Small farmers found their farms unviable, and those who had always relied on common pasture were forced to give up work on the land and seek employment in the burgeoning towns and cities. More than half the land parliament reallocated in this way went to landowners who already held more than 500 acres. For the landed aristocracy this was a double victory – power was being used to protect wealth, and wealth to protect power. As the radical Thomas Spence put it in 1800: 'Are not our legislators all landlords? ... It is childish to expect ever to see small farms again, or ever to see anything else than the utmost screwing and grinding of the poor, till you quite overturn the present system of landed property.'[24]

Nor was it just what happened *on* the land that was of interest; the exploitation of mineral rights underneath it became one of the most significant new sources of aristocratic income. Landowners had mined coal for centuries, but as shallow shafts and adits were exhausted and engineers developed means of extracting much deeper sea-coal, aristocrats stood in a uniquely privileged position. They could lease their land and harvest the royalties, or make direct investments of their own. Wealth bred wealth, as the appetite for coal increased exponentially. Right across the country, peers became prominent mine-owners. In Scotland the dukes of Buccleuch, Hamilton and Portland dominated the landscape, while in Wales it was the marquess of Bute and the Lord Windsor. The Earls Manvers and the Pierrepont family of Thoresby Hall, who were earls and dukes of Kingston-upon-Hull, owned mines in Derbyshire and Yorkshire; the dukes of Norfolk, Rutland and Devonshire had mines in Sheffield, Ilkeston and Goyte Moss; and much of the Great Northern Coalfield in the counties of Durham and Northumberland belonged to a small cadre of nobles. Near Chester-le-Street lay Harraton, where John Lambton significantly extended his family's historic operations and transformed the family hall into a castle on the back of the profits. Lambton's radical grandson John became earl of Durham and Lord Privy Seal thanks to his marriage to the Prime Minister Earl Grey's daughter, and he and successive earls of Durham owned, ran or licensed pits, earning him the nickname 'His Carbonic Majesty'. Nearby lay Lumley Castle, home to Richard, 2nd Viscount Lumley, who was made earl of Scarborough in 1690 and became a significant mine-owner. Further north, the Percy family's long local dominance paid double dividends when Lady Elizabeth Percy opened Whitley colliery at Cullercoats in 1677 and helped pay to dredge the harbour and build a new pier.

The profits from mining were significant. At the start of the nineteenth century the Viscounts Dudley were raking in £17,500 a year, the earls of Lonsdale £30,000, and Frances Vane (who inherited rich-seamed pits at Renshaw and Rainton in 1813 at the age of thirteen and married the 3rd marquess of Londonderry in 1822) £60,000 (roughly £3.8 million in 2017). Some owners also invested heavily at considerable risk to themselves, and brought about vital innovations. The earl of Dover boasted in 1638 that he had brought a Coventry coal mine 'to perfection' at great expense to himself, the first Newcomen steam engine was installed in 1712 at the Coneygree colliery belonging to Edward Ward, 9th Baron Dudley, and although the Molyneux family had held the manor of Sefton from the start of the twelfth century, it was only when Richard, 5th Viscount Molyneux, started to use boring to sink his pit at Sefton in 1720 that the profits climbed. Without their greed-inspired innovation the industrial revolution could never have progressed, especially as the demand for coal required both its extraction and its transport, spawning an era of mass infrastructure development. Thus Francis Egerton's worldly endowments when he succeeded his brother as 3rd duke of Bridgewater at the age of twelve included extensive mining estates at Worsley, but it was his innovative inland waterways, the Bridgewater and Liverpool-to-Manchester canals, designed to carry his coal to market, that dramatically transformed his fortunes and made him the richest noble in the land with an annual income of more than £80,000, just as Frances Vane's new harbour at Seaham, along with a railway to carry the coal to the ships, brought yet more of the concealed seam into profitable play.

Deep mining was a harsh industry, though, built on hard labour. Many men (and in some coalfields women) died young because of the grinding work and the slum conditions in which they had to live. By far the greatest fear was the accumulation of gas – either toxic fumes or highly flammable firedamp – from which their overlords provided little protection. An explosion at Stoney Flatt in Gateshead in 1705 killed thirty people, including a woman. The Lambtons' Fatfield colliery saw three major explosions in 1708, 1763 and 1767, killing 147 colliers. Sixty people died in a single accident in 1727 in Lumley Colliery, where a further thirty-one lost their lives in 1797 and thirty-nine in 1799. In 1766 an explosion at Lambton colliery threw 'men, horses and all in its passage' up through the shaft 'like balls out of the mouth of a cannon', scattering heads, arms and legs all around the mouth of the pit. Fortunately, on that occasion most of the men had already finished for the day; but still six were killed, including two men whose names, unusually, survive: Coxon and Gardiner, both burned to death. It is a sad fact that many of those who died in the mines were buried without inquest or memorial, but the even greater scandal is that the owners consistently prevented any examination of the working conditions in their pits. Following one disaster in 1767 the *Newcastle Journal* wrote:

> It certainly claims the attention of coal owners to make provision for distressed widows and fatherless children occasioned by these mines, as the catastrophes from foul air become more common than ever; yet as we are persuaded to take no particular notice of these things, which, in fact, could have very little good tendency, we drop further mentioning of it.[25]

✠

Political power and influence were vital in preserving the privileges of the aristocracy – their aim was, after all, to rule – but their enduring obsession was with property and the rules that governed its inheritance. Unlike their continental cousins, the British stuck (with rare exceptions) to the principle that the whole shooting match went to the eldest legitimate son and his sons after him *ad infinitum*. So absolute was this rule that the strict settlements entered into at (normally) the heir's marriage could only be undone by a private Act of parliament. This meant that most aristocrats were effectively life tenants of a family patrimony; it also meant that the patrimonial estate was inalienable and the family's succession secure, just so long as the production line continued to produce male heirs.

This is not to say that families found the rules simple. Hours and small treasuries were spent with lawyers and accountants. There were often unexpected intricacies, as the rules governing titles differed from the common law governing estates, and some estates were not entailed. These variations could lead to a complex tapestry of inheritance, as the several titles held by one peer might not descend collectively on his death. Francis Hastings, 10th earl of Huntingdon, for instance, had not married when he died in 1789, and his only child was the fruit of a dalliance with a Parisian dancer. His younger sister Elizabeth, the recently widowed countess of Moira (in the Irish peerage), inherited all the 10th earl's estates and his subsidiary titles, becoming 16th Baroness Botreaux, 15th Baroness Hungerford and de Moleyns, and 13th Baroness Hastings. The earldom of Huntingdon, however, was entailed to heirs male, which meant trawling back through six generations to a great-great-great-grandson of the 2nd earl, Theophilus Hastings. He was an ordained priest and chose never to exercise his rights, but after his death in 1804, his worldlier nephew Hans Hastings went to considerable pains to claim the title of 12th earl, which was eventually granted in 1819.

The fear of extinction prompted many aspirant peers to insist on exceptional conditions for their new titles. The title of Baron Lucas of Shenfield was created for John Lucas in 1645 with a special remainder to his *younger* brother Sir Charles followed by his *elder* brother Sir Thomas, who had been born before their parents married (and was therefore, in English law, illegitimate and ineligible). Sir Charles had two daughters but no son and died in 1648, while Sir Thomas had two sons, Charles and Robert, one of whom had two daughters but no son and the other of whom never married. This left the first Baron Lucas with no male heir; so in 1663 Charles II created an extra barony for Lucas's daughter Mary, who had recently married the 11th earl of Kent. This title of Baroness Lucas of Crudwell had a special remainder, too. It would descend to the heirs male of her husband or to her heirs general, without division, meaning that, unlike most peerages which would fall into abeyance if there were two or more co-heiresses, the title would be held by the senior heiress. The family secured a couple of further favours. Mary's son was promoted to duke, and *his* son was summoned to the Lords by a writ of acceleration as the 3rd Baron Lucas; and when he died and the duke could see his family line heading for extinction, he secured a brand-new marquessate with yet another special remainder, this time to his heirs male and failing that to his granddaughter Jemima, who subsequently became 2nd Marchioness Grey and 4th Baroness Lucas of Crudwell. Since then there have been four more Baronesses Lucas. There were other such privately engineered arrangements. William III was so grateful to the Anglo-German general Friedrich von Schomberg for his support in the Glorious Revolution that he let his peerage descend to his youngest son Charles *followed* by his eldest, Meinhardt. The barony Walpole secured for his son in 1723 had a bizarre remainder to his father. And since Admiral Horatio Nelson had no sons or younger brothers, his title of Baron Nelson of the Nile was allowed to pass to his elder brother followed by his sister Susannah's sons. Nelson's friend and second-in-command at Trafalgar, Cuthbert, Baron Collingwood, was not impressed when the admiral's heir was made an earl in 1806, suggesting that 'nature never intended him for anything superior to a village curate and here has fortune, in one of her frisks, raised him, without his body and mind having anything to do with it, to the highest dignity'.[26]

✠

Here was the rub. The eighteenth-century nobility prided themselves on their dignity and their quality. They believed in their intrinsic right to rule. Yet time after time they proved their short-sightedness and incompetence – most notably in their fatuously arrogant mishandling of the American colonists. Moreover, the whole system was soaked in corruption and over-vaunting ambition and propped up by hypocrisy.

It was clear to the most cursory observer, for example, that the law was not impartial. When Philip Herbert, who held the dual titles of 7th earl of Pembroke and 4th earl of Montgomery, killed Nathaniel Cony in a tavern brawl in 1687, his peers voted in the ensuing trial in Westminster Hall by eighteen to six to convict him of manslaughter rather than murder. This conveniently enabled him to claim 'privilege of peerage', whereby a first conviction for anything other than murder or treason was discounted. The duke of Ormonde warned him that he could only use this provision once, but later that year he was accused of murdering his prosecutor, Sir Edmund Godfrey, and in another drunken brawl in 1680 he killed William Smeeth, an officer of the watch. This time he should have faced execution, but such was the superior solidarity among peers that twenty-four of them petitioned the king for a pardon, which was duly granted. When it came to the trial of William, 5th Baron Byron, in 1765 the numbers were even more overwhelming: 119 peers voted for manslaughter rather than murder and four found him not guilty of any charge, even though it was undeniable that he had run William Chaworth through with his sword in the Star and Garters Tavern, contrary to common law.

Unlike regular courts, where the evidence was weighed in the balance, in a trial by peers it was a man's honour that was in question. Even after his conviction for treason Simon Fraser, 11th Lord Lovat, went to considerable lengths to prove his dignity, rehearsing his forthcoming execution so often that one visitor approvingly commented: 'I could never observe ... the least Shadow of Fear, or indeed any Symptoms of Uneasiness.'[27] A peer's rank was recognized even in his execution. Peers tipped the man who swung the sword (Lovat gave ten guineas) and signalled when they were ready, as if they were still in charge. Executed corpses of commoners were regularly desecrated by the authorities and the crowd, but peers were shown enduring deference. When the earl of Kilmarnock was beheaded as a Jacobite traitor in 1746, his head was 'put in a Piece of scarlet Bays ... and laid with his Body in the Coffin'.[28]

There was only one exception to this rule – 'lunacy', for which several peers were excluded from the Lords. So when Laurence Shirley, the 4th Earl Ferrers, proved as mentally disturbed as his uncle the 3rd earl (who ended his days under lock and key), and was indicted for shooting his steward Mr Johnson in his study at Staunton Harold on 18 January 1760, his peers refused to accept his plea of occasional insanity of the mind and convicted him of murder. He was spared little mercy. He was hanged at Tyburn, not beheaded, and his body was surgically anatomized. Yet even he put on a good show, appearing at the gibbet in his silver-embroidered wedding suit and placing his own head in the specially selected silken noose.

What drove all this preferential treatment was the belief that someone with a title was inherently better than someone without. It was irrelevant that this was often patently untrue. Greed, licentiousness, violence, mendacity or spite never negated the nobility of an entitled man or woman, whose gentility was in the blood. Yes, this was illogical – the equivalent of the Indian rope trick. But so long as others offered deference, the aristocracy stood proud and unchallenged.

That double standards were par for the course is shown by the Lords' treatment of George Sackville, the third son of Lionel, duke of Dorset. Born in 1716, he made his way in life as a soldier, was wounded at the battle of Fontenoy, and saw action alongside the dukes of Cumberland and Marlborough. At the battle of Minden in 1759 he fell out with his commanding officer John Manners, marquess of Granby, the eldest son of the duke of Rutland, and was cashiered out of the army for refusing to obey Granby's order of a cavalry charge against the retreating French. Back in England Sackville demanded a court martial to make his case, but this proved a mistake. He was found guilty and declared unfit to serve in any military capacity whatsoever. At this point Sackville might have considered his public career to be well and truly over – George II even revoked his membership of the Privy Council – but in 1765 George III reinstated him, and in 1769 he inherited a significant fortune from Lady Elizabeth ('Betty') Germain, who had spent much of her fifty years of widowhood at Knole House, the Sevenoaks residence of Sackville's parents. With a seat in the Commons, enough wealth to cut a dash, and a witty, pithy way of speaking (and a new name, having relabelled himself George Germain), in 1775 he was made First Lord of Trade and Colonial Secretary, with responsibility for America, in Lord North's government. Whether the failure of the government's policy on America should be laid at his feet or those of the myopic Prime Minister or the intransigent king is a moot point, but when the government was under threat in 1782 he was the first casualty, asked by North to retire in return for a viscountcy.

Sackville was used to abuse – at one point John Wilkes accused him of being the archbishop of Armagh's catamite – but nothing can have prepared him for the reception he received on his first day in the Lords. Francis Osborne, the marquess of Carmarthen, who had been accelerated into the Lords as son and heir of the 4th duke of Leeds, and who suffered from delusions of grandeur (after nine years as a very ineffectual Foreign Secretary, he presumed to replace Pitt as Prime Minister in 1792), tabled a motion in a heavily attended house on 7 February stating 'that it is highly derogatory to the Honour of this House' that a man who had been censured by a court martial 'should be recommended to the crown to be a fit person to be raised to the dignity of a peerage'.[29] After 'long debate' the House voted to adjourn, but when Viscount Sackville came to take his seat the following Tuesday, Carmarthen tabled an even sharper motion: 'The house of peers being a court of honour, it behoved them to preserve that honour uncontaminated.' Willoughby Bertie, the 'peculiarly eccentric'[30] 4th earl of Abingdon, Charles Lennox, 3rd duke of Richmond, and Charles Fitzroy, Baron Southampton, all agreed and there was a division, which Sackville won by 93 votes to 28. Extraordinarily, nine peers – Carmarthen, Abingdon, the 4th duke of Rutland, the 10th earl of Pembroke, the 12th earl of Derby, the 5th duke of Devonshire, the 6th Baron Craven, the 3rd earl of Egremont and the 2nd earl of Chatham – entered a protest in the *Lords Journal* stating that his elevation was 'fatal to the interests as well as the glory of the crown and to the dignity of the House'.[31] Yet none of them was notably honourable. Chatham was grinding a party political axe on behalf of his younger brother Pitt; Derby was still smarting from his wife's elopement with Germain's nephew, an inveterate rake and 3rd duke of Dorset; Rutland dissipated his life in claret, gambling and womanizing; Pembroke and Devonshire were serially unfaithful to their wives; Egremont kept more than fifteen mistresses by whom he had more than forty children; Richmond was so 'very obstinate, wrong-headed, and tenacious of [his] opinions'[32] that he fell out with all his colleagues and earned universal opprobrium on account of the coal duty monopoly he farmed in Newcastle; and Abingdon was a fanatical self-publicist who considered himself a radical but decried 'that Hellish Doctrine of an Omnipotency of Parliament'.[33]

As for Craven, despite an entirely lack-lustre career, he was famed for his patrician arrogance. Slighted somehow at the county meeting at Abingdon on 7 November 1775, he angrily proclaimed: 'I will have it known there is respect due to a lord,' prompting the satirist William Coombe to write:

> *vulgar brows shall scowl on LORDS no more;*
> *Commons shall shrink at each ennobled nod,*
> *And ev'ry lordling shine a demigod:*
> *By CRAVEN taught, the humbler herd shall know,*
> *How high the Peerage, and themselves how low.*[34]

That was the essence of it. The humbler herd should know that the peerage was entitled to rule.

A

MASTER-KEY

TO THE

RICH LADIES TREASURY.

OR,

The WIDOWER and BATCHELOR's DIRECTORY.

CONTAINING

An exact ALPHABETICAL LIST of the

Duchefs ⎤		Ladies by Curtefie, Daugh-
Marchionefs ⎟		ters of Peers.
Countefs ⎬ Dowagers.		Baronets Widows.
Vifcountefs ⎟		Widows, and
Baronefs ⎦		Spinfters in *Great-Britain*.

WITH

An ACCOUNT of their PLACES of ABODE, Reputed FORTUNES, and FORTUNES they pofsefs in the STOCKS.

By a YOUNGER BROTHER.

—— He took his Stand ——
Upon a Widow's Jointure Land.
HUDIBRAS.

LONDON:
Printed for J. ROBERTS in *Warwick-Lane*,

M DCC XLII.
[Price 1s.]

So keen were noble families to perpetuate and agglomerate their wealth that marriage was seen as a commercial transaction. Noble sons and heirs sought equally noble daughters, and younger brothers trawled the salons and ballrooms in search of rich heiresses. A Master-Key to the Rich Ladies Treasury *was one of several published guides to the respective wealth of available noblewomen.*

Ladies by Curtefie, Daughters of Peers.

Names. Lady	Places of Abode.	Reputed Fortunes	In the Stocks.
Egerton Anne	Cleveland-court	20,000	
Egerton Caroline	Cleveland-court	20,000	
Fitzroy Caroline	Old Bond-ftreet	20,000	
Fielding Eliz.		20,000	
Finch Ifabella	St. James's	20,000	
Finch Martha		20,000	
Finch Efsex		20,000	1000 B
Herbert Marget		20,000	
Herbert Eliz.		20,000	
Hyde Catharine		20,000	
Howard Diana	Soho-fquare	30,000	
Howard Arabella	Soho-fquare	30,000	
Haftings Frances	Leadftow, Yorkfhire	20,000	1000 E. I.
Lenos Georg. Carolina	Privy-garden	30,000	
Lee Charlotte	Hanover-fquare	20,000	
Lee Mary	Hanover-fquare	20,000	
Lee Frances	Hanover-fquare	20,000	
Leflie	New Bond-ftreet	20,000	
Mountague Doddingt.	Conduit-ftreet	20,000	2000 E. I.
Mountague Elizabeth	Conduit-ftreet	20,000	2000 E. I.
Manners Lucy	Grofvenor-fquare	30,000	
Manners Leonora	Albemarle-ftreet	20,000	
Manners Frances	Albemarle-ftreet	20,000	
Mountague Anne	St. James's	20,000	
Shirley Anna	Conduit-ftreet	20,000	1000 S. S.
Sackville Caroline	Whitehall	30,000	
Seymour Frances		30,000	
Seymour Charlotte		30,000	
Shirley Frances	Dover-ftreet	20,000	
Stanhope Lucy		30,000	3000 B.
Stanhope Charlotte		20,000	
Scott Ifabella	Grofvenor-ftreet	30,000	
Scott Charlotte	Grofvenor-ftreet	30,000	
Wentworth Lucy		20,000	
Walpole Maria	Downing-ftreet	80,000	
Yelverton Sufanna		20,000	

CHAPTER 9

WHAT IS A WOMAN WITHOUT GOLD OR FEE SIMPLE?

IN 1700 THE EARLY feminist Mary Astell (who campaigned for women to have more career options than mother or nun) asked what qualifications men looked for in a spouse. 'What will she bring is the first enquiry. How many acres? Or how much ready coin?'[1] Her comments were prompted by the case of Hortense Mancini, the French beauty who had inherited a fortune from her uncle Cardinal Mazarin and married a wealthy, noble general, whereupon the two were made duke and duchess of Mazarin. It was an unhappy marriage and his brutish behaviour led her to flee (without her fortune) to the protection of the duke of Savoy and then into the adulterous arms of Charles II, who gave her a pension of £4,000. Her multiple affairs attracted a fair degree of scandal – she fought a friendly fencing match in her nightgown with her lover Anne, the countess of Sussex, who refused her husband's demands that she repair to the country – but Hortense remained in royal favour up until her death in 1699. Astell took a very clear lesson from the Mazarin marriage and the duke's appropriation of Hortense's fortune.

> To be yoak'd for Life to a disagreeable Person and Temper; to have Folly and Ignorance tyrannize over Wit and Sense; to be contradicted in every thing one does or says, and bore down not by Reason but Authority; to be denied one's most innocent desires for no other cause, but the Will and Pleasure of an absolute Lord and Master . . . is a misery none can have a just Idea of, but those who have felt it.[2]

In an uneven world, that was the danger of an arranged marriage based on financial convenience.

This is not, of course, to say that a noblewoman could not forge a successful and active life for herself. Later in the century the twenty-year-old Elizabeth Robinson refused to believe that 'the wisest and best Men marry for money', declaring: 'I think Sense and Virtue in a Man will induce him to chose prudence & virtue in a woman' and that 'till I meet with a Deserving Man who rightly thinks the price of a virtuous woman above rubies I shall take no other obligation or name upon me.'[3] In another letter, written while staying with the duke and duchess of Portland at Bulstrode, she asked: 'What is a woman without gold or fee simple?' and answered: 'a toy while she is young, and a trifle when she is old'.[4] Two years later she married Edward Montagu, a reclusive bachelor of fifty and wealthy grandson of the earl of Sandwich. Montagu owned an impressive range of properties: Allerthorpe in Yorkshire, Sandleford Priory near Newbury, East Denton Hall near Newcastle (with a string of collieries) and a London house in Dorset Street – and after the death of the couple's only son John aged two in 1744 Elizabeth proved a successful hostess, establishing a famous literary salon, hosting the Blue Stockings Society of England, creating Montagu House in Portman Square, enhancing Sandleford, giving roast beef and Yorkshire pudding to all and sundry at her May Day parties at Montagu House, and handing out parcels to the colliers and pitmen in Denton for twenty-five years after Edward's death (although she complained that their accents were dreadful to the auditors' nerves). Edward's preference for his own company and Elizabeth's intelligence and charm seem to have been well matched as they spent much of their time quite happily apart. Lady Louisa Stuart, a daughter of the 3rd earl of Bute, wrote of her that she had 'quick parts, great vivacity, no small share of wit, a competent portion of learning, considerable fame as a writer, a large fortune, a fine house, and an excellent cook'.[5] Louisa might have added that Elizabeth published two well-regarded books, sponsored several other authors and managed Edward's finances so astutely that his mining operations were bringing in £10,000 a year. It was no small achievement for a woman who had declared: 'I have nothing but myself in the scale, and some few vanities that make me light.'[6]

Although there was no pretence of equality between men and women, many noblewomen of the seventeenth and eighteenth centuries played an active part in political life. Charles II's reign had seen a succession of ennobled royal mistresses wielding extensive power and influence. Barbara Villiers, a not too distant relative of the duke of Buckingham, bore Charles five children while married to Roger Palmer and used her position at court to bring about the downfall of the earl of Clarendon and support the second Dutch war. Her husband was made earl of Castlemaine, and she was made duchess of Cleveland with special remainder to her illegitimate son Charles. In time the baby-faced Frenchwoman Louise de Kérouaille, who was given the title duchess of Portsmouth and the sum of £136,000 in one year alone, replaced her in Charles's affections and in the complex network of court influence. Likewise, the notoriously plain but sharp-tongued Catherine Sedley was made countess of Dorchester by her lover James II. Queen Anne's reign saw a different phenomenon, the rise of the female companion and adviser-in-chief, as her intimate friend, Sarah Churchill, the duchess of Marlborough, virtually dominated the administration, keeping her husband informed of court intrigue while he was on military campaigns, monopolizing ecclesiastical and ministerial appointments, and advising on every aspect of policy – all from the vantage point offered by the posts of Mistress of the Robes, Groom of the Stole,* Keeper of the Privy Purse and Ranger of Windsor Great Park.

In 1784 Lavinia, Countess Spencer, tried to dissuade her daughter Lady Duncannon from entering into disputes on the 'Odious subject' of politics on the grounds that, 'connected as you are, I do not wish you to appear, or to be, uninterested upon it – but in the situation things now are, trust me if you once allow your[self to] argue upon it, you will nine times out of ten say things you will afterwards wish unsaid'.[7] Yet the eighteenth century saw a string of charismatic noblewomen take direct political action – notwithstanding their usual marital obligations. Katherine Murray, for instance, wife of the 1st duke of Atholl and sister

*Formally the Groom of the Queen's Close Stool, the most intimate of offices charged with assisting the monarch with their ablutions.

of the 4th duke of Hamilton, complained in 1702 of complications with breastfeeding which had left her 'fit scarce to do anything' and told Lady Panmure that the birth of 'a huge girl' had 'taken all [my] good blood with her, [which] made me so weak that I was in a few degrees of decay'.[8] Yet she was infuriated by the 'hard treatment we meet from the English' over the failed Darien Scheme,[9] she did not believe 'that any English are serious for an union with Scotland on any honourable terms for us',[10] she actively engineered the election of an opponent of the proposed union with England in the Scottish parliamentary elections for Perth, and she discovered the Queensbury Plot against her husband in 1703. Likewise the duchess of Marlborough reckoned she had a perfect right, as a major local landowner, to try to persuade the voters of St Albans not to elect the Tory John Gape in 1705 by canvassing for Admiral Henry Killigrew instead; and when Gape was returned by the mayor, she had the Committee on Elections and Privileges unseat him in favour of Killigrew and in the teeth of complaints about her electioneering.

Several noblewomen were ardent Jacobites, including Winifred, the countess of Nithsdale, who visited her husband in prison on the eve of his expected execution for his involvement in the rebellion of 1715 and helped him escape, dressed in her maid's clothes; and Lady Anne Farquharson, who was married to the chief of the clan Mackintosh, raised several hundred men for the rising of 1745 and joined them at Bannockburn. Others preferred to take the role of confidante, dispensing political and personal counsel to their husbands and other connections. Lady Charlotte Wentworth was so close to her brother the marquess of Rockingham, Prime Minister in the 1760s, that she advised him on his speeches. Lady Betty Waldegrave was a regular go-between for her lazy brother Lord Gower and her brother-in-law the duke of Bedford. The duke of Portland's love letters to his pregnant duchess in 1766 included a sequence in which he poured out his agonies over whether to resign from government; and by the time Sophia Carteret married William Petty, 2nd earl of Shelburne, she had been well schooled in the intricacies of politics by her father the Earl Granville's confiding letters to her. As for Emily Lennox, who married the 20th earl of Kildare in 1747 and was sister to the 3rd duke of Richmond, it was her ambition that secured her husband the dukedom of Leinster and persuaded him not to resign his £1,500 sinecure, as she cleverly berated him: 'I hear all your enemies . . . are so much delighted at the thoughts of you giving up so good a thing as this in a huff.'[11] In every case, the woman largely derived her position from her marriage; but even arranged marriages could be fruitful and liberating alliances.

✠

It was undeniable that for a man, the best means of staving off the twin perils of poverty and family extinction was a propitious marriage. As the arch-royalist Sir Lionel Tollemache, 3rd baronet of Helmingham Hall, wrote to his son in 1668: 'The action of your life upon which will depend your future happiness is your marriage and choice of a wife. Choose a person of a good family, a comely person rather than a beauty, and of your own religion and a portion proportionate to your present and future estates.'[12] This might have been the family motto. The 2nd baronet had married Elizabeth, who inherited from her brother Charles, 2nd Baron Stanhope, and was known in the family as the 'Stanhope heiress'. The 3rd baronet followed his own advice, marrying the well-educated and comely Elizabeth Murray, the 'Scottish heiress', who inherited Ham House in Richmond and her father's title as 2nd countess of Dysart in 1655. And the young Lionel, who succeeded his father and mother as 4th baronet and 3rd earl, married Grace Wilbraham, the daughter of a wealthy Staffordshire baronet, who inevitably became known as the 'northern heiress'. The 3rd baronet's and his wife's combined fortunes were swallowed up by heavy spending and debt, but thereafter several generations of good marriages – and a few years of frugality – left the Tollemaches in fine financial fettle. When the 4th earl of Dysart succeeded his grandfather in 1727 he came into Ham House, Helmingham Hall, the manors of Harrington and Bentley, and 20,000 acres in Cheshire. Evidently, future happiness depended on marrying well.

With the advent of new means of communication (and, later, new means of travel), exploiting this marriage market became a compulsive obsession. In other European countries laws of derogation banned nobles from marrying outside their class or engaging in commerce or retail on pain of losing their noble status, but in Britain peer pressure and primogeniture were sufficient to ensure that nobles stuck to their own. The statistics are striking.[13] There were 954 English peers born between 1600 and 1800. Their marriage rate was high. Under pressure to provide a successor, 84 per cent of heirs married, as did 63 per cent of younger sons of nobles, leaving 128 peers who never married – whether because they died young, they were Catholic priests (four of them) or they chose otherwise. Of the remaining 826, 224 married twice and 36 three times. Yet only 177 peers married outside their social circle: 244 married the daughters of other English peers, a further 358 married the daughters of knights, baronets, Scottish, Irish or foreign peers, and 47 married the daughters of MPs, clerics and military officers. At no point between 1640 and 1759 did the rate of marriage to social equals slip below 60 per cent; and the figures for the *daughters* of peers between 1700 and 1899 are even starker – 83.7 per cent of Scottish daughters and 87.9 per cent of English married noblemen. Nobody seems to have stopped to ask whether such inbreeding was good for the aristocracy. If anything, it was reckoned that close affinities bred stronger stock and protected the noble bloodline. This led to some extraordinarily close matches between in-laws and cousins. In 1702, for instance, Elizabeth Lyon, daughter of the 3rd earl of Strathmore, married her first cousin Charles, 2nd earl of Aboyne; and in 1777 Anne Duncombe married Jacob Bouverie, 2nd Earl Radnor, who was her mother's stepson (though not her half-brother). As late as 1866 Lucy Lyttelton was quite happy to overlook the fact that her brother-in-law Lord Edward Cavendish, the youngest son of the 7th duke of Devonshire, was about to marry his first cousin Emma Lascelles as it was 'a case of real tried and genuine affection'.[14]

This interweaving of lineages did not happen by accident. The marriage market was a serious business. A single heiress could restock a whole family's aristocratic larder, and every bride was expected to have a substantial portion settled on her, her husband and a prospective son and heir, which would increase the groom's family holdings. Prospecting parents of noble sons had several factors in their favour. What seemed like a constant tragedy afflicting the nobility between 1680 and

1770 – the increased incidence of infant mortality, the lower birth rate and the disproportionate lack of legitimate male heirs – in fact proved a Godsend, as there was a glut of sole and joint heiresses, meaning family fortunes could be consolidated rather than dissipated. In addition, there were new means of finding a rich bride. Starting in 1731, Edward Cave published detailed lists of recent upper-class marriages every month in the *Gentleman's Magazine* and provided a compendious annual index, while *A Master-Key to the Rich Ladies Treasury*, which was published in 1742, laid out the full details of all the 'spinsters' on the market, with their names, their places of abode and their reputed fortunes. Here were enumerated the twelve dowager duchesses, the seventeen dowager countesses, the sixty 'ladies by courtesy' and the many daughters of lesser peers, along with nine pages of other wealthy widows and sixteen of other spinsters – with estimates of their monetary value. Sarah, the elderly dowager duchess of Marlborough, was said to be worth 'millions', and the two sisters Diana and Arabella Howard of Soho Square, the daughters of the 4th earl of Carlisle, were worth £30,000 apiece. Even Maria Walpole, the daughter of the recently retired Prime Minister by his long-term mistress, was included as if she were the legitimate daughter of an earl – and was estimated to be worth £80,000. As the author, an impecunious noble younger brother who had married advantageously, put it: 'Gentlemen . . . in the following Sheets I think [I have] opened a fair Field for Action for you; a fine Choice and a fine Collection of Ladies; – Open the Campaign directly then yourselves.'[15]

There was a great deal of enthusiasm for this market, but plenty of scepticism too. As Henry Fielding put it in 1752, 'in high life, marriage is a mere trade, a bargain and sale, where both parties endeavour to cheat one another'.[16] Tales circulated among the nobility of fortunes made or lost by a good or a bad match – and of matches to rescue fortunes already squandered. Take the case of Frederick St John, who inherited his father's title as 3rd Viscount St John in 1748, when he was just fifteen. Three years later came his uncle's title as 2nd Viscount Bolingbroke, leaving Frederick with large tracts of Battersea that had been in the family for centuries, a handsome house at Lydiard Tregoze in Wiltshire, and a hefty inheritance from his wealthy mother Anne Furnese. He should have been set up for life; but his marriage in 1757 to the popular elder daughter of the duke of Marlborough, Lady Diana Spencer, collapsed under the weight of his heavy drinking, gambling, womanizing and general dissolution. After hypocritically securing a divorce on the grounds of Diana's adultery, he found himself in such debt that he had to sell Battersea. He tried to make £30,000 out of enclosing Sedgemoor; and, when that failed, with a view to meeting his racing costs and gambling losses he resolved 'to marry a rich monster and retrieve his affairs'[17] – a venture in which he laughably failed as a series of heiresses evaded his clutches and he subsided into madness. His son and heir George did no better, marrying his tutor's penniless daughter and having an affair with his half-sister before bigamously marrying his German mistress. The 4th Viscount Bolingbroke led a less complicated life, but his son Henry, who inherited the titles in 1851, continued in the family tradition, living first with the impecunious daughter of a Belgian schoolmaster and then with Mary Howard, the daughter of a blacksmith, whom he installed as housekeeper at Lydiard Park and eventually married. In 1922 their only son Vernon petitioned the Lords to be allowed to take his seat as 6th Viscount Bolingbroke, but by the time of his death Lydiard had been sold to Swindon Borough Council.

By contrast, the Leveson-Gower family started as mere baronets in Staffordshire in the 1680s, but got into the Lords in 1703 and secured an earldom in 1746, a marquessate in 1786 and the duchy of Sutherland in 1833. Theirs was a tale of generation after generation of successful marriages. Sir William Leveson-Gower, Bart*, who held Trentham Hall, married the eldest daughter of the earl of Bath. His son John, the first Baron Gower, married the duke of Rutland's eldest daughter. His son, also John, the first Earl Gower, married Evelyn Pierrepoint, the third daughter of the duke of Kingston-upon-Hull. His son, Granville, the first marquess of Stafford, married Elizabeth Fazakerley, who brought £16,000 with her in 1744 and died two years later; Louisa Egerton, eldest daughter of the 1st duke of Bridgewater, in 1748 (she died in

---

*Baronets added Bt or Bart after their names to distinguish their (hereditary) titles from those of mere knights.

1761); and Susanna Stewart, daughter of the 6th earl of Galloway, in 1768. To top it all, in 1785 Granville's son George, the 2nd marquess, married Elizabeth Gordon, whose parents William and Mary, 18th earl and countess of Sutherland, had died just after her first birthday, leaving her in sole ownership of much of the county of Sutherland; and in 1803 he inherited the estates of his uncle the duke of Bridgewater. It was said of the 1st marquess that 'his vast property, when added to his alliances of consanguinity or marriage with the first ducal families in this country ... rendered him one of the most considerable subjects in the kingdom'.[18] The same was even truer of his son, who was made duke of Sutherland not long before he died in 1833. 'A leviathan of wealth',[19] indeed 'abominably wealthy',[20] he held more than a million acres in Scotland alone (including Dunrobin Castle), along with the family estates at Trentham and Wolverhampton in Staffordshire, Lilleshall in Shropshire and Stittenham in Yorkshire, and Stafford House in London, bringing in an annual income of £200,000.

Several noble families owed their later wealth almost entirely to a single prosperously felicitous match. The earls of Bedford were not poor, but the marriage in 1669 of the 5th earl's son William Russell to Rachel Wriothesley, the co-heiress to the earl of Southampton, added the whole of modern-day Bloomsbury to the Bedford family holdings; and Sir Thomas Grosvenor's marriage in 1677 to Mary Davies, the daughter and heiress of a City scrivener, added the swampy meads of the manor of Ebury (which would later become Mayfair, Park Lane and Belgravia) to the Grosvenor estate of Eaton Hall in Cheshire, a holding that would help raise the family to the dukedom of Westminster in 1831.

One woman was without equal as a matriarchal matchmaker in the eighteenth century: Jane Maxwell. Perhaps her early life conditioned her to marital ambition: when her parents separated, her mother brought her and her sisters up in relative poverty in Edinburgh. As a bubbly and tenacious young woman of eighteen she caught the eye of the handsome 24-year-old Alexander, 4th duke of Gordon, and they married in 1767, producing two sons and five daughters. The couple became mainstays of Tory society, hosting balls and soirées at their homes on Pall Mall and Speyside – Pitt the Younger referred to the duchess as his chief 'whipper-in' – but theirs was a chaotic marriage. The duke had nine other children and eventually took his mistress to live with him at Gordon Castle, and when a prospective match for Jane's daughter Louisa speculated that the girl might suffer from the Gordon family hereditary madness, Jane said she could confidently guarantee that Louisa had not a drop of Gordon blood in her. She was determined that her daughters should marry well. Her contemporary Sir Nathaniel Wraxall said of the duchess that 'no sacrifices appeared to her to be too great, no exertion too laborious, no renunciation too severe'[21] for the elevation of her five daughters. He wasn't exaggerating. Louisa married the son and heir of the conquered but wealthy anti-hero of the American War of Independence, General the Marquess Cornwallis. When Jane secured the heir to the duke of Richmond for her eldest daughter Charlotte, the marriage was hastily performed in her dressing room at Gordon Castle with just two servants as witnesses. She found another ducal coronet for her third daughter Susan, who married William Montagu, 5th duke of Manchester (though he was so incorrigibly unfaithful to her that she left him for a footman after twenty years). As for her youngest, Georgiana, Jane initially had her osprey-like eye on Francis Russell, the widowed 5th duke of Bedford, but when he died in 1802, she cast her net across the Channel at Napoleon's stepson Eugène Beauharnais. Bonaparte would have none of it, but while Jane and Georgiana were in Paris, the previous duke of Bedford's younger brother (now the 6th duke), appeared – and soon the two were married. Plenty of people ridiculed the duchess for her determination, but James Gillray's cartoon of the bold and brassy duchess of Gordon 'hunting the Bedfordshire bull' proved only one duke out – and she beat her arch-rival the duchess of Devonshire to the match. The list of Jane's daughters' marriages to three dukes, a marquess and a baronet was inscribed on her memorial. In her mind at least, it was her greatest achievement.

The biggest fear was a *mésalliance* – a son or daughter legally but irregularly eloping with someone who was financially or socially inappropriate. This was a real possibility, as the Marriage Duty Act of 1695, which attempted to tidy up the law on irregular weddings, prohibited the carrying out of marriages without banns or a licence only for Church of England parish clergy, as opposed to those working in districts such as the area in and around the Fleet Prison, which was considered outside the jurisdiction of the church. In the first half of the eighteenth century dozens of clerics of a variety of persuasions plied their marriage trade here with impunity and the help of the prison warders. It was in the Fleet that the seventeen-year-old Philip Wharton, who had very recently become the 2nd marquess of Wharton, was married in 1716 to Martha Holmes, the daughter of a major-general, without the approval of his mother the dowager marchioness. His father, a leading Whig politician and libertine, would have had few grounds for criticizing him, as he had given his first wife Anne syphilis and seduced Sir Robert Walpole's sister Dorothy, and in 1705 had been accused of drunkenly urinating on the communion table and in the pulpit of the church in Great Barrington in Gloucestershire. To the supercilious classes, though, the subsequent life of the 2nd marquess proved the danger of irregular marriages. Wharton tired of his wife, became a Jacobite, misspent the fortunes that had come to his father from his two wives, invested badly in the South Sea Company and was accused of treason. Although both the Old Pretender and George I gave him dukedoms (respectively of Northumberland and of Wharton), he ended his days in alcoholic poverty in Catalonia in 1731. With tales such as his doing the rounds, these 'Fleet marriages' were a constant concern. As early as 1677 the Lords sent a Bill to the Commons complaining that since fathers had 'no means to avoid such marriages' they often ended up having to be 'reconciled thereto rather than wholly desert their children'. Understandably, the nasty condescension of this argument did not convince the Commons, who rejected seven such Bills over the following decades, so the marriages continued.

In relation to the nobility, the term 'Fleet marriages' was largely a misnomer, as most aristocratic elopers preferred the more refined but equally irregular tiny private chapel in Curzon Street in Mayfair run by the Reverend Dr Alexander Keith. Having been excommunicated and sent to prison in 1743 for running a brisk irregular trade in marriages without the legally necessary banns or licence, thereafter, even though he remained in the Fleet until his death in 1758, he advertised his services at a guinea for a wedding in 'a little new chapel' just ten yards away 'at any hour till four in the afternoon', adding helpfully: 'There is a porch at the door like a country church porch.'[22] This crafty circumvention of the law was not just a scandal to the anxious parents of wild young heirs; it also angered the church, as Keith siphoned off 723 couples from the next-door parish in 1742 and in 1751 his four deputies performed more than 1,300 marriages. But these were not all young rapscallions eloping with chambermaids. When Henry Brydges married Anne Wells at Keith's chapel on Christmas Day in 1744 he was thirty-six, he had a son and a daughter by his first wife – Mary Bruce, the daughter of the 4th earl of Elgin – who had died in 1738, he was an intimate of the Prince of Wales and four months previously he had succeeded to his father's title as duke of Chandos. The circumstances of the couple's first meeting were unusual, though. He had been dining with a friend at the Pelican in Newbury when a fracas arose. An ostler was leading his wife, the innkeeper's daughter, round the yard with a halter round her neck and was trying to sell her to the highest bidder. Out of compassion or, as a contemporary journal had it, 'smitten with her beauty and patient acquiescence in a process which would (as then supposed) free her from a harsh and ill-conditioned husband',[23] Henry offered half a crown and took her as his mistress. It was only when both his first wife and his father died that he dared marry her.

Such was the aristocratic determination to keep nobility in the family that those involved in marriages considered inappropriate were often ostracized. The marriage in 1766 between Henry Somerset, the duke of Beaufort, and Betty Boscawen was considered so unseemly that the dowager duchess was reduced to sitting at home alone unvisited and uninvited, while the young bride's only consolation was that the duke's uncle gave her a pair of diamond earrings, supposedly the only jewels she possessed. This was quite unfair, as Betty was the granddaughter and sister of a viscount, and her father was a much-decorated admiral – but such was the obsession with money and status that the marriage of a poor beauty to a great duke was thought unconscionable. Likewise, when Lord George Bentinck MP, the second son of the duke of Portland, availed himself of Keith's chapel for his marriage to Mary Davies on 29

June 1753, his brother the 2nd duke refused to have anything to do with the couple, as did the first duke's sister, Lady Sophia Egerton, who referred to Mary as Lord George's 'matrimonialised mistress', who had been taken into his keeping after being 'quite common about town'.[24] The most famous 'Fleet marriage' was that of James Hamilton, 6th duke of Hamilton and 3rd duke of Brandon, who met the renowned Irish society beauty Elizabeth Gunning at a party at Bedford House on St Valentine's Day in 1752 and demanded that a clergyman marry them there and then. When he refused, they waltzed off to Keith's chapel, where their marriage was contracted at midnight with nothing but a curtain ring. The groom undoubtedly outranked the bride (whose mother had suggested that she take up acting to stave off poverty), yet when Hamilton died Elizabeth went on to marry another Scottish peer, John Campbell, marquess of Lorne, who succeeded to the title of duke of Argyll in 1770.

With the scandal of the Hamilton marriage ringing in everyone's ears, every duchess and countess fretted about her son or daughter's prospects if these clandestine marriages were allowed to continue. It was not that these *mésalliances* were common. Far from it. But they were common *enough* to disturb the noble equilibrium. John Perceval, for instance, the earl of Egmont, noted that 1745 had seen a string of nobles marrying beneath them, including the dukes of Chandos, Ancaster and Rutland, who had all married their mistresses; the earl of Salisbury, who had married his steward's niece, 'the daughter of a barber and shower of the tombs in Canterbury'; and the earl of Bristol, who had married his late wife's maid.[25]

This affronted sense of noble exclusiveness permeated the government of the day, led by two aristocratic brothers, the Prime Minister Henry Pelham and his older brother Thomas. The two were descended from a string of baronets and the earl of Leicester on their father's side, but, more importantly, their mother Grace was the younger sister of John Holles, 4th earl of Clare and duke of Newcastle. When Thomas and Henry's father died in 1712, Thomas became one of the wealthiest landowners in England, in recognition of which he was made duke of Newcastle-upon-Tyne in 1715. The two boys prospered politically and financially under Walpole, and in 1742 Henry Pelham succeeded the earl of Wilmington as Prime Minister, retaining his brother Thomas as his leading minister in the Lords.

It was only a question of time before a ministerial team with such aristocratic credentials moved to close off the legal loophole that allowed clandestine marriages, and in 1753 the longstanding and uncompromising Lord Chancellor, Philip Yorke, Baron Hardwicke, brought forward a Bill requiring parental consent for marriages by licence for those under twenty-one. It was what the Lords had been calling for since 1677. The Attorney-General, who introduced the Bill in the Commons on 14 May, thought the benefits were obvious. 'What distress', he said, 'some of our best families have been brought into, what ruin some of their sons or daughters have been involved in, every gentleman may from his own knowledge recollect.'[26] But not everyone agreed. Henry Fox was understandably opposed to the measure as he had persuaded Caroline Lennox, the eldest daughter of the 2nd duke of Richmond, to elope with him when she was twenty-one and he was thirty-nine and her mother the duchess had refused even to discuss the matter. Robert Nugent's speech laid bare the whole marriage market; if the Bill were passed, he argued, the Lords

> will thereby gain a very considerable and a very particular advantage; for they will in great measure secure all the rich heiresses in the kingdom to those of their own body . . . I may prophesy that if this Bill passes into a law, no commoner will ever marry a rich heiress, unless his father be a minister of state, nor will a peer's eldest son marry the daughter of a commoner, unless she be a rich heiress.[27]

He was in a good position to know: his father, a commoner, had married the daughter of an Irish baron; his own first wife Emilia was a daughter of the 4th earl of Fingall; and his second, Anne, was the daughter of the wealthy and corrupt financier, politician and South Sea speculator James Craggs. What Nugent did not yet know was that an even greater fortune would come his way when he married his third wife, Elizabeth, the widow of the 4th earl of Berkeley, in 1757. Despite the opposition, the Bill stumbled its way through the Commons and was adopted unanimously in the Lords. Their lordships rejoiced, but the measure remained so unpopular that the Commons twice voted to repeal it, in 1765 and 1781, only to be blocked by the Lords.

✠

The fuss about ensuring that matches were properly arranged and conducted masked a great deal of noble hypocrisy about sex and marriage. Throughout the eighteenth century the courts rigorously enforced the laws forbidding fornication, adultery, buggery, incest, bestiality and bigamy on the common people. Thousands were punished. Countless common adulterers were forced to do penance sitting in the market place wearing a white sheet and carrying a white wand. Women found guilty of bearing an illegitimate child, whose care might fall on the parish, were dealt with even more harshly. Stripped to the waist, they were whipped through the streets tied to the back of a cart. Not content with the rate of prosecution, successive busy-bodying organizations like the Society for the Reformation of Manners, which flourished from 1690 to the 1730s, sought to put a stop to common profanity, debauchery and sexual immorality. On 13 January 1719 the *White-hall Evening Post* reported that during the previous year, thanks to its network of informers, the Society had privately prosecuted 1,253 people for 'lewd and disorderly practices' and 31 for keeping 'bawdy or disorderly houses'. In 1725 it organized raids on molly houses* and, although it lapsed, it was revived in the 1750s with the blessing of the repeat adulterer George II. Bishops were to the fore in the Society. Bishop Richard Smalbroke of St David's, for instance, pontificated in 1727 that

> since that most detestable and unnatural Sin of Sodomy ... has been
> of late transplanted from the hotter Climates to our more temperate
> Country ... it is now become the indispensable Duty of the Magistrate
> to attack this horrible Monster in Morality, by a vigorous Execution
> of those good Laws, that have justly made that vile Sin a Capital
> Crime.[28]

---

*A tavern or coffee house where homosexual men could socialize. One raid on Mother Clap's molly house in Holborn in 1726 led to forty 'notorious Sodimites' being arrested, imprisoned and pilloried and three being hanged at Tyburn.

Twenty-nine temporal lords signed the Society's 1699 manifesto. Most were serious, family-minded types, but several of those signatures might have raised an eyebrow. Fulke Greville, 5th Baron Brooke, was reckoned to be 'always a man of pleasure, with a very good capacity' who 'loved play'.[29] William III had given his fellow Dutchman William de Zuylestein the title earl of Rochford in gratitude for his role in the Glorious Revolution, but there was a seamier past to their friendship. De Zuylestein had seduced Jane Wroth, a maid of honour to Mary, Princess of Orange, in 1681 and had initially refused to marry her, on William's instruction. It was only after Princess Mary pleaded with de Zuylestein that a secret marriage went ahead. And George Booth, 2nd earl of Warrington, who was just twenty-five in 1699 but had inherited his father's titles five years previously, went on to marry Mary Oldbury in 1702. She was the daughter of a City merchant, who brought with her a fortune of £40,000, but the marriage was so unhappy that they lived as absolute strangers to each other and in 1739 he wrote a treatise calling for the legalization of divorce. Neither he nor his wife sounds all that prepossessing. One contemporary reckoned: 'She is a limber dirty fool and he the stiffest of all stiff things.'[30]

The rule for the common people was strict – avoid gambling, sexual incontinence, fornication, extra-marital relations, homosexuality and profanity. Not so for the aristocracy. To the contrary, gambling was a common (not to say endemic) aristocratic pastime, and the nobility were active sexual adventurers who ploughed on with complete impunity, often seeing women (and occasionally men) as little more than sport. On one occasion the 2nd duke of Buckingham invited the husband of a pretty young woman in Newmarket to the local inn so that his friend John Wilmot, 2nd earl of Rochester, could slip past the man's maiden sister dressed as a woman, drug her, rob the house and seduce the wife, before taking her back to the inn, where Buckingham had his way with her as well. The poor cuckolded man took his own life, but the two nobles boasted of the affair for years. Charles Howard, the debauched younger son of the earl of Suffolk, was reckoned to be so 'wrong-headed, ill-tempered, obstinate, drunken, extravagant, brutal'[31] that it was understandable his witty wife Henrietta should maintain an affair with the Prince of Wales, later George II, and eventually leave her husband to set up home in Palladian splendour at Marble Hill. Francis Charteris, who was married to the daughter of the royalist and Presbyterian Scottish judge Alexander Swinton, Lord Mersington, and held large estates in Lancashire and Dumfries, had an extraordinary reputation for usury, cheating at cards, taking bribes, seducing respectable women and blackmailing them, and getting young women pregnant and abandoning them. He was cashiered out of the army several times. Yet his aristocratic credentials afforded him unwarranted protection. When he raped one servant woman at his house in George Street he avoided prison by paying a £600 fine. And when in 1729, aged seventy, he was convicted by an Old Bailey jury of raping another, Anne Bond, he was absurdly excused the death penalty by George II and merely forced to surrender some of his abundant wealth.

Sexual freedom was an accepted part of the (mainly male) noble life. Philip Stanhope, 4th earl of Chesterfield, begged his son to use condoms whatever the 'probability or even attestations of health, nay, of untouched virginity itself',[32] and the duke of Newcastle ensured his son received a lengthy lecture from his doctors on the inconvenience of mercury treatments for syphilis when he ignored the same advice. In 1773 the *Westminster Magazine* complained that William Stanhope, 2nd earl of Harrington, had 'sacrificed all appearance of decency . . . for the lowest amusements at the lowest brothels'.[33] This was before he was caught up in a scandal in 1779 about paying less than the going rate for a woman at the seraglio in King's Place that he frequented four times a week. There were plenty of high-end brothels, deliberately priced so as to exclude anyone but the nobility – and sex clubs, too. In England Sir Francis Dashwood (later Baron le Despenser) and John Montagu, 4th earl of Sandwich, belonged to the Hell-Fire Club, whose motto was *Fais ce que tu voudras* (Do what you will) and whose activities from the 1730s until Dashwood unexpectedly became Chancellor of the Exchequer in 1762 were strictly limited to sexual and gluttonous debauchery. In Scotland Lord Newark, Lord Cardross, the son of the 10th earl of Buchan, and the two Thomas Erskines, 6th and 9th earls of Kellie, were members of the Beggar's Benison, a gentlemen's sex club at which they studied pornography and engaged in collective masturbation between 1739 and 1781.

Even senior figures made light of unmarried and adulterous relationships that would have been frowned on in the lower orders. When Augustus Fitzroy, 3rd duke of Grafton, tired of his second wife Anne he ostentatiously installed Nancy Parsons in her place, despite her reputation as a courtesan, while the slighted duchess chased after the duke of Portland and got herself pregnant by the earl of Upper Ossory. Grafton – at the time Prime Minister, albeit a very ineffectual one – sought a divorce in 1769, and soon afterwards threw Nancy over in favour of the far more respectable Elizabeth Wrottesley, the daughter of the dean of Worcester and niece of the duchess of Bedford – leaving a furious Nancy to pursue the 3rd duke of Dorset before attaching herself to the 2nd Viscount Maynard. Despite being the son of the bishop of Durham, Edward, Baron Thurlow, Lord Chancellor from 1778 to 1793, never married but had a son by Kitty Lynch, the daughter of the dean of Canterbury, and three daughters by Polly Humphries, the daughter of the keeper of Nando's Coffee House, with whom he lived in unmarried domestic bliss in Dulwich. The ebullient and rotund radical politician Charles James Fox, second son of Henry Fox, Lord Holland, who was (briefly) Foreign Secretary three times, had a succession of mistresses before settling on one of the Prince of Wales's former lovers, Elizabeth Armistead, whom he married in secret.

These swing-door aristocratic affairs were far more common than the dreaded *mésalliance*, as the aristocracy allowed themselves considerable leniency in matters of fidelity. In this they took their cue to some extent from the crown. Queen Anne was unusual in refusing to give her secretary of state Henry St John anything more than a viscountcy purely because of his moral dissipation (Oliver Goldsmith said that he was 'noted for keeping Miss Gumley, the most expensive prostitute in the kingdom, and bearing the greatest quantity of alcohol without intoxication').[34] In contrast, George I brought his mistress with him from Hanover, while George II came to an amicable arrangement with his mistress Henrietta Howard's irascible and violent husband the earl of Suffolk – and when he told his wife Caroline of his latest mistress in

1735, she said 'she was sorry for the scandal it gave to others, but for herself she minded it no more than his going to the close stool'.[35] George IV lived for years with one mistress and fathered children by several others, including two marchionesses – and although William IV seems to have been faithful to his wife once he married, he had ten children by the witty Anglo-Irish actress Dorothea Jordan while he was still duke of Clarence.

The relaxed royal sexual ethic filtered down through the aristocracy. The *Westminster Magazine* and *Town and Country Magazine* regularly listed men of note who were engaged in sexual shenanigans, detailing for instance that the earl of Surrey, the duke of Bedford and the Baron Sydney had mistresses who were the daughters of, respectively, a bankrupt attorney, a bankrupt physician and a bankrupt apothecary. When John Sheffield, duke of Buckingham, died in 1721 his will openly referred to several natural children, including a son in Utrecht and two daughters living at home with his duchess. Their illegitimacy did them little harm: the son became a baronet and the elder daughter married a peer. So too the renowned horseman Henry Herbert, 10th earl of Pembroke, had children by two mistresses, one of whom he had seduced in Venice on the night of her marriage to another man. His countess was remarkably relaxed about this, insisting only that the children should not take the name of Herbert – but then the earl was so blasé that he displayed a portrait of another mistress, the Venetian ballerina Giovanna Baccelli, in the marital bedroom at Wilton. None of this stopped him being made a lord of the bedchamber to George III in 1769. He was in good company. John Sackville, the unmarried 3rd duke of Dorset, also had an affair with Baccelli, and commissioned paintings of her by Gainsborough and Reynolds and a nude sculpture, before going on to take Elizabeth, daughter of the duke of Hamilton and Elizabeth Gunning, as his mistress in the late 1770s, despite her being married to the 12th earl of Derby. Her husband refused to divorce her, and such were the unequal and hypocritical rules of the game (wives were still considered their husbands' possessions) that she was shunned by society while the two men were soon reconciled. Dorset then moved on to another mistress, Elizabeth Foster, who also showered her affections on the earl

of Dunraven, the 3rd duke of Richmond and the 5th duke of Devonshire –
with the last of whom she lived for some twenty-five years in a *ménage
à trois* alongside the duchess Georgiana. The Devonshires' household
was in fact one of the more remarkable, as Georgiana bore her husband
a son and two daughters and brought up his natural daughter (Charlotte)
by another lover, but when she became pregnant in 1791 to Charles, the
eldest son of Earl Grey, the child, Eliza, was taken from her and brought
up in the Grey household. Eliza's father Charles calmly went on as 2nd
Earl Grey to be a groundbreaking Prime Minister from 1830 to 1834. As
for another of Elizabeth Foster's lovers, the duke of Richmond, he had
no legitimate children by his duchess, but three natural children by his
housekeeper, each of whom was provided for in his will in 1806.

The point here is not that the aristocracy had scandalous affairs or
engaged in extra-marital sexual relations, but that there was such evident
hypocrisy in action, with the law constantly relaxed for the rich and
titled. Some contemporaries actively promoted and defended this double
standard. The Scottish Enlightenment thinker Adam Smith argued for a
strict moral code for the common people and a looser one for people of
fashion; the new bishop of Chichester in 1731 reckoned that the national
societies devoted to reforming sexual mores should confine themselves
to the lower orders, 'upon whose industry and virtue the strength and
riches of the nation so much depend',[36] and Sir John Fielding said in
1763 that while all sexual indecency was wrong, the worst was 'low, and
common bawdy-houses, where vice is rendered cheap, and consequently
within the reach of the common people, who are the very stamina of the
constitution'.[37]

Nowhere was this hypocrisy clearer than in relation to separation
and divorce. The former had long been accessible through the ecclesiastical
courts, but the latter had not been legally available since the Reformation,
so remarriage was effectively illegal. Until the 1660s, that is, when the
marriage between John Manners, the only surviving son of the 8th earl of
Rutland, who sat in the Commons as Lord Roos, and his wife Anne
Pierrepont, daughter of the marquess of Dorchester, collapsed amid
allegations that someone else had fathered Anne's son, who was baptized
Ignoto ('unknown'). Anne briefly returned to her father's house, but in

1663 Roos was granted 'separation from bed and board' from her in the ecclesiastical courts on the grounds of adultery, and in 1667 he secured a private Act of parliament laying bare what he called her 'foul carriage' and declaring Ignoto and another son bastards. This left Roos without a son and heir; so in 1670 he sought another private Act enabling him to remarry in order that 'his family might be kept up by his posterity, which otherwise would extinguish'.[38] This request was hotly debated, with 'the king as earnest in the setting it on as [his brother] the duke [of York] was in opposing it'.[39] One member of the Commons argued that if such a law could be made for a lord, why not for everyone, as 'a poor man may have a wife as well as a rich man'.[40] The most extraordinarily misogynistic and hypocritical contribution came from Sir Charles Harbord, MP for Launceston, who, in Anchitell Grey's account, stated that 'the worst of whores is a wife-whore'.[41] This was a man of whom Andrew Marvell wrote that he had got £100,000 from the king, having formerly been a solicitor of Staples Inn, 'till his lewdness and poverty brought him to court'.[42] The Bill was eventually carried, leaving Anne destitute and Roos free to marry, which he did twice more, his third wife bearing him the desired son and heir in 1676. The Roos saga opened a way to divorce and remarriage, albeit an expensive and exclusive one. In fact it was so exclusive that nobody else chose to pursue it until 1698, when Charles Gerard, 2nd earl of Macclesfield, was granted a divorce from his countess, Anna, who had given birth to two sons said to have been fathered by Richard Savage, 4th Earl Rivers. In this case the divorce proved a greater release for the countess than the earl, as she remarried and lived until 1753, while he died without legitimate heir in 1701. By then Henry Howard, 7th duke of Norfolk, had used the same process to divorce his wife Mary, the only child and heiress of the earl of Peterborough, again on grounds of adultery. Mary took her father's barony of Mordaunt and his manor of Drayton with her and married her lover, the 'notorious adventurer and gambler'[43] Sir John Germain, in 1701 just after the death of the childless duke.

There was no flood of parliamentary divorces – the next one was not until 1744 – but later in the century the numbers picked up, and in 1779–80 seven volumes of *Trials for Adultery* were published detailing the titillating sexual peccadilloes of the aristocracy. One example speaks for the rest. Francis Osborne, who was known by his courtesy title as marquess of Carmarthen, claimed in January 1779 that his wife Amelia d'Arcy, the only child of the 4th earl of Holderness, whom he had married in 1773, had conducted an affair with a guardsman by the name of Captain Jack Byron with whom she had then run off. Servants were dragged in to testify that they had seen a man in the marchioness's powdering room and stains upon the bed-sheets giving 'every appearance of a man and woman having lain together and been connected with each other that night in the said bed'.[44] As so often, those involved straddled the worlds of high society and high politics. Holderness had been Southern Secretary, a member of the Cabinet for a decade and tutor to the Prince of Wales before his death the year before the divorce; Amelia had inherited the titles of 12th Baroness Darcy de Knayth and 9th Baroness Conyers in her own right on her father's death; and Carmarthen was a privy councillor and Lord Chamberlain of the queen's household – and would go on to be a vain Foreign Secretary, of whom it was said that he was a man of 'higher talents than he was generally supposed to possess'.[45]

Jack and Amelia subsequently married, though he apparently treated her appallingly and she died in 1784, following which Byron married a Scottish heiress, Catherine Gordon, whose £23,500 fortune he managed to squander before dying himself in 1791. In 1798 Catherine and Jack's ten-year-old son George succeeded Jack's uncle, William Byron (known as 'the wicked lord' for having killed a cousin in a duel), as 6th Baron Byron of Rochdale, and inherited the dilapidated Newstead Abbey in Nottinghamshire. He went on to be the notoriously 'mad, bad and dangerous to know' poet, politician and freedom fighter, who, true to his aristocratic pedigree, ran up enormous debts, married an heiress, abused and deserted her, and had a string of affairs with men and women including Lady Caroline Lamb, Jane Harley, the countess of Oxford and his half-sister Augusta before dying at the age of thirty-six fighting in the Greek war of independence. Such was the hypocrisy of the age that when Byron's body was repatriated, huge crowds gathered to honour the author of *Childe Harold's Pilgrimage* and *Don Juan*, but Westminster

Abbey refused to allow him a burial or a memorial on the grounds of his allegedly dubious morality. As in so many other spheres, when it came to sex and marriage, there was one rule for the aristocracy and another for the rest. Anyone who, like Byron, exposed that hypocrisy, was liable to be ostracized. He had, after all, told his mother when he inherited his title at the age of ten that he could not perceive that it had made any difference to him, and he declared in his maiden speech in the Lords: 'You may call the people a mob, but do not forget that a mob too often speaks the sentiments of the people.'[46] Perhaps it is not surprising that he did not gain admittance to the Abbey until 1969.

WANTED

A Hundred

Negro

DRIVERS

To be employed in the

ISLAND OF

BARBADOES

Apply at Har–w——d Houfe.

No Yorkshire Clothier need apply, as they have been found too refractory to be infulted and trampled upon by

The Son of the Proprietor.

☞ *Should the Slave Trade be revived in the next Session of Parliament, with a View to which the Proprietor is labouring to procure for his Son the Representation of the County of York, the Number of Negro Drivers wanted will not be limited, but may extend to Two Thousand at least.*

Printed at the Leeds MERCURY-OFFICE, by Edward Baines.

Many aristocratic fortunes – and palatial mansions – were built on the profits from the slave trade, which the aristocracy fiercely defended through their dominance of both Houses of Parliament. The most notable beneficiaries of the trade were the Lascelles family, whose vast slaving fortune delivered them an earldom and the Harewood estate. When slavery was eventually abolished, the earl of Harewood received £26,309 4s 6d from the state in 'compensation'.

CHAPTER 10

NEGROES, AND GOLD AND SILVER
ON THE SAME FOOTING

O N 18 DECEMBER 1660 Charles II granted the Company of the
Royal Adventurers into Africa a thousand-year monopoly for
'orderly traffic and trade' on the west coast of Africa from Cape Blanco
to the Cape of Good Hope. The charter's list of investors shows the
venture's glittering aristocratic credentials. In addition to the king's
brother and sisters and Prince Rupert, he named the dukes of Buckingham
and Albemarle, the marquess of Ormond, the earls of Bath, Ossory,
Pembroke, St Albans and Sandwich, and four barons; and he put the
company in the hands of the 5th earl of Pembroke, William, Baron
Craven, and four others. Charles called it a 'hopeful' enterprise, not least
because he and his heirs would 'have, take and receive two third parts of
all the gold mines which shall be seized, possessed and wrought'.[1] Yet
initial returns were so poor that in 1663 a new charter was granted to a
similarly aristocratic body of twenty named peers and others, under the
slightly different name of the Company of Royal Adventurers of England
Trading into Africa, extending the territory up to Morocco and adding a
new monopoly on 'the whole, entire and only trade for the buying and
selling bartering and exchanging of for or with any negroes, slaves,
goods, wares and merchandises'.[2]

This was not the first time the crown had sanctioned the slave trade.
Back in 1565 the privateering sea captain Sir John Hawkins and his
cousin Sir Francis Drake sold four hundred illegally captured west
Africans in Borburata on the western coast of modern Venezuela and
took the rewards back to their royally sponsored investors in London.

In 1617 'a good store of neggars'³ was brought to Bermuda to work on the plantations of Robert Rich, the Puritan 2nd earl of Warwick, who was a member of the Virginia Company, one of the original proprietors of the Bahamas and governor of the Bermuda Company. Many other Puritan colonists took the same course, demanding free labour for their plantations so as to assuage domestic demand for sugar, tobacco and cotton. This was a triangle of profit – British goods to west Africa, enslaved Africans to the West Indies and Caribbean crops to Britain – which the British aristocracy raced to exploit. By the time of this second charter the company was advertising 'negroes ... at £17 per head, sound, in lots as customary',⁴ and the British aristocracy was set on its bloodiest course yet.

The original monopoly on African gold and silver* was soon surpassed in value by the trade in slaves. By the 1680s the company (under its new name of the Royal African Company) was exporting five thousand enslaved west Africans a year, and between 1673 and 1711 Barbados, Jamaica, Nevis, Antigua, St Kitts and Montserrat received 90,768 slaves, all of them branded either 'RAC' or 'DY' for the duke of York, their captor and their owner. The RAC lost its monopoly on the African trade in 1697, allowing scores of other British adventurers to join the trade on payment of a 10 per cent levy to the RAC, but in 1713 the *asiento* or agreement entered into as part of the Treaty of Utrecht guaranteed the newly created South Sea Company (SSC) thirty years as sole provider of 4,800 slaves a year to the Spanish colonies. The fatal flaw in the agreement was its assumption of a lasting peace with Spain. In 1714 the SSC carried 2,680 slaves provided by the RAC, and in 1716–17 it transported another 13,000 to Spanish plantations. Then, in 1718, war with Spain recommenced and two years later the SSC collapsed under its own oversold stock in the South Sea Bubble; but the demand for slaves increased exponentially. In ending the RAC monopoly, parliament had expressly intended to boost mainland American plantations and expand the slave trade. It succeeded. English slave

---

*Hence the 'guineas' that started to be coined in 1663 and the Royal African Company logo of an elephant with a castle on its back.

traders made thirty-nine passages in 1686, but in 1729 they made eighty-one.

Although many slave traders were merchants and financiers, aristocrats were nearly always lurking in the background. Even those who espoused progressive views on an Englishman's rights actively engaged in the trade. Philip Herbert, 5th earl of Pembroke, sat as a member of the Commons when the Lords was abolished in 1649 and acted as an assessment commissioner during the protectorate, yet in search of funds to replenish his father's depleted estates and refurbish Wilton after the Restoration, he was a prime mover in the establishment of the Company. The 2nd duke of Buckingham invested heavily in each of the monopoly companies. Anthony Ashley Cooper, the self-confident leader of the Country Party who as the earl of Shaftesbury opposed arbitrary rule in England, part-owned a 205-acre plantation in Barbados with nine slaves from 1646 to 1655, held a fourth share in 1646 in the *Rose*, which was almost certainly engaged in the Guinea trade, and invested £2,000 in the RAC. The aristocratic involvement in slavery continued in the eighteenth century. The SSC was the invention of Queen Anne's favourite minister, Robert Harley, who was rewarded by being made its first governor and earl of Oxford. John Campbell, 2nd duke of Argyll, was a director of the SSC and Charles Montagu, Baron (and later earl of) Halifax, was an early investor who intervened directly to ensure that a legislative attempt to end the *asiento* monopoly in 1713 was derailed. So overwhelming was the RAC's support in the House of Lords that the company's directors told one of their agents: 'You may rest assured no act of Parliament will ever pass in favour of interlopers for an open trade.'[5] And when the RAC required a massive recapitalization in 1720 James Brydges, duke of Chandos, successfully reached out to his aristocratic friends. His plan was to refocus the company on mineral and botanical research in Africa – but scores of aristocrats invested without questioning that the RAC would continue in the slave trade.

Profiteering peers were to be found at both ends of the trade. Many were proprietors, investors and royal governors in the American colonies who expressly promoted colonization on the back of slavery. In 1663, for instance, the king awarded the as yet un-settled Carolina to a group of lords proprietors including Shaftesbury, the supercilious Lord Berkeley of Stratton, the earls of Craven and Clarendon, and Sir George Carteret. All of them had City money to invest and ideas to impose. When Shaftesbury had his friend John Locke draft the *Fundamental Constitutions of Carolina* they included a highly contradictory set of principles. On the one hand the colony would tolerate religious and political dissent, and the rights of native Americans would be respected because their 'idolatry, ignorance, or mistake gives us no right to expel or use them ill'. Yet the lords proprietors insisted on creating a clearly defined hereditary landowning nobility in Carolina with the titles of landgrave and cazique, and stated unambiguously that 'every freeman of Carolina shall have absolute power and authority over his negro slave of whatever opinion or religion whatsoever'.[6] The fact that Shaftesbury spent much of the 1670s campaigning against absolute power and authority in England seems not to have troubled him as he also enabled the sale of native American slaves in 1677.

It was the same in Maryland, which was a proprietary colony belonging to Cecil Calvert, 2nd Baron Baltimore, thanks to a charter from Charles I allowing him to create a safe haven for English Catholics. Cecil himself preferred to remain in his stately home at Kiplin Hall in Yorkshire, while his younger brother Leonard and his son Charles, later the 3rd baron, exercised his father's full palatinate powers in Maryland; and, for all their commitment to religious tolerance, as soon as the tobacco trade ran out of settlers the Calverts legislated to allow Maryland to become a slave colony. The first enslaved Africans arrived in 1642, miscegenation was made illegal in 1661 and in 1664 it was decreed 'that all negroes or other slaves already within the Province, and all negroes and other slaves to be hereafter imported into the Province shall serve *durante vita*. And all children born of any Negro or other slave shall be slaves as their fathers were for the term of their lives.' They went further. 'Forasmuch as divers freeborn English women, forgetful of their free condition and to the disgrace of our nation, marry Negro slaves ... whatsoever freeborn woman shall marry any slave ... shall serve the master of such slave during the life of her husband ... and all the issue of such freeborn women so married shall be slaves.'[7] The effect of the measure was that although the Irishwoman Eleanor Butler originally arrived in Maryland in 1681 as one of Lord Baltimore's indentured servants, when she married a slave on her master's estate she and their offspring became slaves for several generations. In other words, slavery was as hereditary as a noble title, and just in case there should be any doubt, it was added in 1692 that the children of female slaves, whatever their parentage, would also be slaves. Thus, for the first time in English common law, your social status could be determined by your mother, not your father – which was convenient, as many white English planters had raped, seduced or otherwise sired children by black slaves and the Calverts did not want such children to be free, not least because in 1679 a single male slave would sell for 8,000lb of tobacco, or £33.

Several other slave colonies were established and run by peers. Francis, 5th Baron Willoughby of Parham, was twice governor of Barbados when it was under constant assault by the French (1650–1, 1663–6) and from there colonized Willoughbyland (later Suriname) as lord proprietor with the earl of Clarendon's second son Laurence Hyde (later earl of Rochester) and three thousand slaves. When Willoughby died in a hurricane aboard his flagship *Hope* his title and post as governor went to his younger brother William, and he left estates in Barbados, Antigua and Suriname to his three daughters, who were married to peers, and to his nephew Henry, who was governor of Antigua. The province of Virginia, which was largely dependent on slaves, also had a string of noble governors in the eighteenth century, each of whom (even those who never crossed the Atlantic) made a profit out of his tenure. They included Sir William Berkeley, younger brother of Lord Berkeley of Stratton; Thomas, 2nd Baron Colepeper, who owned much of the northern neck of Virginia and was dismissed when he illegally appropriated £9,500 from the Virginia treasury; William Keppel, 2nd earl of Albemarle, who never visited despite being governor for seventeen years; John Campbell, the unmarried and largely ineffectual 4th earl of Loudon, who did at least reside in Virginia between 1756 and 1758; Jeffery, Baron Amherst, the glamorous captor of Fort Ticonderoga and Montreal who, at a key point in the American War of Independence, considered sending smallpox-infected blankets to the native Americans;

and John Murray, 4th earl of Dunmore, a Scot who at the height of the colonists' rebellion offered freedom to any Virginian slave who fought for the crown, shortly before fleeing for safety in New York and England, whence he returned in 1787 to be governor of the Bahamas. For each of them slavery was the currency that kept his colony in business. Their argument was simple. As Nicholas Spencer, who owned a plantation at Nomini Creek, put it: 'The low price of Tobacco requires it should be made as cheap as possible, and that Blacks can make it cheaper than Whites.'[8] All that was lacking was the milk of humankind-ness, which was a point the political philosopher Montesquieu (full name Charles-Louis de Secondat, Baron de la Brède et de Montesquieu) made with his characteristic sarcasm in 1748. 'It is impossible for us to suppose these creatures to be men,' he said, 'because allowing them to be men, a suspicion would follow that we ourselves are not Christians.'[9] Few eighteenth-century peers quailed at this trade in humanity. Pitt the Elder thought of the slave colony estates as part of the landed wealth of England, Admiral Nelson claimed that the trade was necessary to supply the Royal Navy with seamen, and in the upper echelons of British society enslaved Africans were considered property, just like a farm, a herd of cattle or a wife.

Many noble households in England acquired black servants and showed them off as a quaint sign of their supposed magnanimity. Louise de Kérouaille had herself painted in 1682 with a black child playing at her lap. Charles Howard, 7th earl of Suffolk, owned a slave he named Scipio Africanus, after the Roman general, who died in 1720. Catherine Hyde, the eccentric and beautiful duchess of Queensberry, renamed a ten-year-old boy from St Kitts whom she was given in 1764 Julius Soubise and trained him to ride, fence, sing, act, play the violin and strut his stuff about town (until he fled to India, where he founded a riding school in 1777). Ignatius Sancho, who had been born on a slave ship bound for New Grenada in 1729 and had been brought to England by his owner at the age of two when his parents died, was first put to work as a servant for three maiden sisters in Greenwich but, having been encouraged to learn to read and write by a near neighbour – John Montagu, 2nd duke of Montagu, who had been a very unsuccessful governor of Saint Lucia and Saint Vincent in the 1720s – he became butler to the duchess. He later went on to be valet for Montagu's heir, his son-in-law George Brudenell, and ended up as a grocer, prolific letter-writer and abolitionist. So too in 1766 Sir John Lindsay, grandson of the 5th Viscount of Stormont, brought his natural daughter Dido Belle, whose mother Maria was an enslaved African woman in the West Indies, to England, where she was raised at Kenwood House by Lindsay's maternal uncle William Murray, earl of Mansfield, and his countess, who had no children of their own. Dido's arrival at Kenwood may have helped usher in the end of slavery, as in 1772 Mansfield, who was Lord Chief Justice of the King's Bench, had to adjudicate in the case of a slave called James Somersett, who had escaped his American 'owner' Charles Stewart on English soil. The American had recaptured him and wanted to ship him out for sale in Jamaica, but abolitionists argued that since neither common law nor statute law allowed for slavery in England, Stewart could not force Somersett to set sail. Mansfield (reluctantly) ruled that since slavery could not be justified on any moral or political basis and there was no 'positive law' allowing it, 'whatever inconveniences, therefore, may follow from a decision, I cannot say this case is allowed or approved by the law of England; and therefore the black [sic] must be discharged'.[10] Nearly fifteen thousand Africans living in Britain earned their freedom by this judgement.

One aristocratic family exemplifies the outstanding wealth that could be made directly or indirectly from slavery. The Lascelles family had been prominent in Northallerton in Yorkshire since the thirteenth century and included several MPs in their lineage, but at the start of the eighteenth century George Lascelles and his brothers Henry, Daniel and Edward made their way to Barbados, where they engaged in the triangular trade. What with their own plantations and the valuable post of collector of customs for the port of Bridgetown, which one or other of them held for three decades from 1714, the brothers made a fortune, all of which would have been impossible without their first cargo of one hundred enslaved Africans aboard the *Carracoe Merchant* in 1713. When Henry returned to England he further enhanced the Lascelles fortune by lending £226,772 to plantation owners between 1723 and

1753 and reaping the benefits of mortgage defaults and foreclosures, which brought him yet more property (including slaves). As befitted his new wealth, he bought a large house in Richmond upon Thames and the Harewood estate near Leeds; but, fearing blindness, he took his own life in 1753 aged sixty-three. His son Edwin initially sold the Caribbean plantations, remodelled his houses at Darrington, Goldsborough and Plompton, and built a magnificently respectable palace at Harewood with a thousand-acre garden landscaped by Capability Brown. Then, from 1773 onwards, with a credit crisis hitting the West Indies, he started accumulating estates again. By 1787 he had 27,000 acres in twenty-two plantations in Barbados, Jamaica, Grenada and Tobago – all worked by 2,947 slaves. The seal was set on Edwin's social respectability when he was made Baron Harewood in 1790, but despite two marriages he died childless in 1795, whereupon Harewood House, the slaves and the plantations passed to his cousin Edward, an equally respectable Whig MP for the pocket seat of Northallerton. This Edward stoutly defended the planter interest and voted against abolition in 1796 just before being made Baron Harewood in his turn, to which title was added an earldom in 1812. Edward's second son Henry was returned for one of the county seats in Yorkshire in 1796 and 1801 (ironically enough, alongside William Wilberforce), but in 1807 the election was contested for the first time for half a century, thanks to local opposition to his father's slave interests – and this time even the £100,000 he spent on the campaign could not save him from defeat by the out-and-out abolitionist Viscount Milton, the 21-year-old son of the immensely wealthy 4th Earl Fitzwilliam. But the Lascelles were not to be thwarted. The earl bought Henry the seat of Westbury and kept slaves well into the new century, as one document from 1825 proves: 'Henry, Earl of Harewood . . . by these presents doth give grant and confirm unto the said Richard Harding, and his heirs, all those three Mulatto slaves whose names and sexes are as follows, that is to say Polly-Kitty (a Woman) John Thomas (a Boy) and Betsey Ann (a Girl) with the issue and increase of the said several slaves hereafter to be born.'[11]

As the Lascelles eminently demonstrated, the aristocracy spent the profits of the slave trade with abandon. Alan, earl of Bathurst, built

Cirencester Park between 1714 and 1718 out of the money his father Benjamin had made as deputy governor of the Leeward Islands and a major shareholder in the RAC. Henry Howard, 6th earl of Suffolk, oversaw the transportation of 54,000 enslaved Africans during his spell as President of the Board of Trade and Plantations between 1715 and 1718; the profits passed through his son, the 7th earl, and ended up with his brother Charles, the 9th earl, who proved a drunken and abusive husband to Henrietta Hobart. She consoled herself by lavishing profits from the additional £8,000 of SSC shares awarded to her by her lover George II and her own investments in its French equivalent, the Compagnie des Indes, on the elegant Palladian mansion Marble Hill House on the Thames – and fitting it out at great expense with slave-harvested mahogany. Dodington Park in Gloucestershire, Greys Court in Oxfordshire, Brentry House in Gloucestershire, Stocks in Hertfordshire and Farley Hall in Berkshire – among many other grand houses across the country – all benefited from the profits of slavery.

✠

Even as the national clamour against slavery grew, the aristocracy clung tenaciously to their human property and set their faces against abolition of either the trade in slaves or slavery itself. When Sir William Dolben, the MP for Oxford University, introduced a Bill in 1788 to prevent overcrowding on slave ships, he was immediately opposed by one of the Liverpool MPs, Richard Pennant, who held an Irish title as Baron Penrhyn and owned six sugar plantations in Jamaica (as well as large tracts of Caernarvonshire). The Commons approved this very minor temporary measure, but a string of Lords lined up to attack it. The naval hero Lord Rodney reckoned it would be better to reward traders for delivering their catch in mint condition rather than penalizing them for overcrowding. The military hero of the siege of Gibraltar, George Eliott, Baron Heathfield, suggested that Africans got just as much fresh air on the passage across the Atlantic as soldiers did in their tents. The Home Secretary Thomas Townshend, Baron Sydney, whose plan to settle convicts at Botany Bay was rewarded with the naming of Sydney Town in his honour, argued that the trade was salutary 'because it brought the negroes from a barbarous native tyranny to the decidedly improved conditions in the islands'.[12] And Edward, Baron Thurlow, the arrogant and sarcastic Lord Chancellor, pronounced that he disliked the Bill because it was merely the product of a 'five days fit of philanthropy'.[13] When the Lords tried to insist on a wrecking clause compensating traders for their losses the Commons effectively over-ruled them, but subsequent Commons measures received short shrift from the Lords, who endlessly demanded more time to gather evidence. When a slightly more comprehensive Bill for Limiting the Slave Trade was debated in the Lords in 1799, the Lord Privy Seal, John Fane, 10th earl of Westmorland, whose grandfather and aunt had both married into planter families, argued that he had a superior duty to any consideration of 'animated descriptions of the miseries of the slave trade', namely 'to protect the rights, the property, the interests of the subjects of England, the commerce of the merchants, the property of the planters of the West-Indies'.[14] It was self-serving nonsense, but since just 25 peers voted for the Bill and 32 against, with 36 proxies on either side, 'the bill was consequently thrown out'.[15] When after many attempts William Wilberforce managed to secure the third reading of an abolition Bill in the Commons in June 1804, the Lords failed even to consider it before the end of the session.

Opposition in the Lords was eventually overturned thanks to two astute tactical decisions. First, the precarious new government led by the abolitionist William, Baron Grenville, capitalized on the victory at Trafalgar by bringing forward a crafty Foreign Slave Trade Bill, which purported to lay siege to British subjects aiding and abetting French colonial interests but actually limited all British slave traders. This was carried without undue fuss in the Lords (by 43 to 18). And then on 2 January 1807 Grenville introduced the Abolition Bill in person in the Lords, thereby tickling the aristocratic sense of superiority. Prince William, the duke of Gloucester, backed Grenville, expressing his 'abhorrence and detestation of this abominable traffic in human blood',[16] but the duke of Clarence (later William IV), George Douglas, 16th earl of Morton, and the Lords Eldon, Sidmouth and Hawkesbury (the last of whom would become Prime Minister as the 2nd earl of Liverpool) all spoke against. John Jervis, Britain's imaginative naval commander in successive wars, who had been made earl of St Vincent after his victory there in 1797, claimed that 'the West-India islands formed Paradise itself, to the negroes, in comparison with their native country'.[17] At least he had direct experience of the trade, though possibly not with great success, as his nephew and heir Edward Ricketts told the Commons in 1804 that when he took over the management of his uncle's Jamaican plantations at Canaan he had found them in a very reduced situation and he had set about recruiting ninety 'new Negroes to the estate'.[18] Westmorland returned to the crease, too. 'If such a system were acted upon,' he ranted, 'no property could be reckoned safe which could fall within the power of the legislature ... the very freehold estates of the landholders might be sacrificed to field-preaching and popular declamation ... and though he should see the presbyterian and the prelate, the methodist and field-preacher, the jacobin and the murderer unite in support of it, in that house he would raise his voice against it.'[19] This time, though, the government had rallied its troops in support of the Bill, which was carried thanks to a much larger attendance with 72 in favour (plus 28 proxies) and 28 against (plus 8 proxies) – a majority of 64.

This did not deliver emancipation, though, and over two decades passed before that campaign was given a jolt in the arm by an eleven-day slave strike in Jamaica at Christmas 1831 and the bloodshed that followed. Sixty thousand downed tools before being savagely attacked by the plantations' militia, and in the ensuing crackdown 207 rebels were killed and over three hundred were executed, leading to two parliamentary inquiries back in London and a final if reluctant decision by the Prime Minister, Earl Grey, to push for full emancipation in stages between 1838 and 1840. As in 1807, the government launched its Bill in the Lords, where the debates were cantankerous. There were tasteless rows about the relative values of slaves in Demerara and in Jamaica. Peers demanded massive sums in compensation. Yet more evidence was sought as yet another means of delay. The otherwise successful lawyer William Best, Baron Wynford, maintained that he had formerly voted for the abolition of the trade, but opposed this measure because he doubted that 'slaves could be induced to work upon sugar estates for any wages except such as would be too high'.[20] His memory clearly failed him, as he had not been a member of either house back in 1807, but his views became more extreme as the debates went on. From the armchair in which he was confined by his gout, he railed that 'the formal consent of the slave ought not to be required as an essential condition in his being removed from one estate to another',[21] and called the Bill 'an act of tyranny as regards the West India proprietors, which is not to be paralleled'.[22] Edward Ricketts, now the 2nd Viscount St Vincent, presented a long petition against emancipation 'from proprietors, merchants, ship-owners, manufacturers, traders, mortgagees, annuitants and others interested in the preservation of the British West Indies colonies',[23] and demanded that 'negroes, and gold and silver [be] put on the same footing'.[24] One of the Irish representative peers, Somerset Lowry-Corry, 2nd Earl Belmore, who had just returned from a spell as governor of Jamaica during which he had violently put down an even fiercer slave rebellion than that of 1831, claimed he was all in favour of ending slavery but that, 'in deprecating a state of slavery, I must, at the same time, distinctly disclaim any concurrence in the exaggerated statements of cruelty described as habitually practised towards the slaves, tending, in my opinion most unjustly, to calumniate a large proportion of our countrymen, whose labour and enterprise have so greatly contributed in advancing the power and wealth of this nation'.[25] Since the Privy Council trade committee had produced evidence as early as 1789 that 4.5 per cent of those captured died before they left Africa, 12.5 per cent died on the passage and 33 per cent died in their early months on the plantations – a shocking mortality rate of 50 per cent – it is difficult to credit Belmore with any of the common attributes of humanity.

One debate showed the peers in a particularly poor light. Edward Harbord, 3rd Baron Suffield, whose argument was that 'slavery is essentially iniquitous',[26] tabled an amendment to outlaw corporal punishment of females and recounted an instance in 1830 from Exuma in the Bahamas, when forty-four slaves belonging to John, Baron Rolle, had tried to escape in a boat and had been chased down and captured. Rolle's agent John Lees had had five of the men sentenced to fifty lashes each, and a boy and eight women sentenced to thirty-eight lashes each.

One of the women was pregnant; two others had babies. Astoundingly, some argued that women had to be subject to such corporal punishment. The Bahamian House of Assembly argued that 'until negro women have acquired more of the sense of shame that distinguishes European females, it will be impossible, in respect of them, to lay aside altogether punishment by flogging'.[27] Belmore agreed, arguing that without corporal punishment there would be no means of punishing women other than imprisonment and 'to imprison the slave is to punish the master'.[28]

The duke of Wellington was flatly opposed to emancipation, as was his former Lord Privy Seal, Edward Law, 2nd Baron Ellenborough. So angry were they when the measure was carried that they entered a protest against it, along with other peers. Wellington had also made the point that, unable to stop the measure, 'our object . . . is to render [it] as palatable as possible to the West India proprietors'.[29] Key to this was the compensation that slave-owners now demanded and peers were eager to approve. The list of shameful demands for and awards of compensation to the aristocracy is lengthy. Richard Plantagenet Temple-Nugent-Brydges-Chandos-Grenville, the already phenomenally wealthy 2nd duke of Buckingham and Chandos, asked for £20,000 in 1819 and was granted £6,630 5s 6d for the 114 slaves on his Hope Estate in Jamaica. William Vane, duke of Cleveland, and his son Lord William Poulett were awarded £4,854, 16s 9d for the 233 slaves on the Lowther estates they had inherited in Barbados. Baron Rolle received £4,333 6s 9d. The 8th earl of Northesk received £3,529 8s 10d for 200 slaves at Canaan estate in Jamaica. Charles, 2nd Earl Talbot, was given two awards for estates in Jamaica, totalling £4,660 18s 6d. General Sir Edward Cust walked off with £5,029 7s 8d thanks to his mother-in-law's planter holdings in British Guiana – and his brother John, Earl Brownlow, shared the same figure with Wilbraham Egerton MP of Tatton Park in Cheshire. James Grimston, 2nd earl of Verulam, had two estates in Jamaica, for which he received £7,359 18s 4d. Lawrence Dundas, whose father was the first Baron Dundas and whose grandfather had made so much money as a wine merchant and army contractor that he was able to buy extensive British estates and two West Indies slave estates in Dominica and

Grenada, was granted £8,135 4s 6d. And, to cap it all, Henry Lascelles, 2nd earl of Harewood, whose six estates held 2,554 slaves, received £26,309 4s 6d. All in all £20 million was paid in 'damages', and £10 million of it stayed with absentee British landlords. Like Nye Bevan's reluctant doctors at the creation of the National Health Service in 1948, the landed British slave-owners had their mouths stuffed with gold and the ordinary British taxpayer footed the bill.

There was another pernicious aspect of the slave trade, as successive governments allowed it to skew foreign policy towards war and regularly deployed troops, munitions and ships to further or to protect it. William Beckford – plantation owner, City alderman, MP and campaigner for liberty (for Englishmen) – openly advocated a 'blue water' strategy of total domination of the Atlantic in 1748, on the grounds that thereby 'we may conquer from our enemies, they can conquer nothing from us and our trade will improve by a total extinction of theirs';[30] his argument became a central rationale for the Atlantic segment of the Seven Years War, which began in 1756. Pitt the Elder expressly referred to his desire to attend to 'the complaints of your despairing merchants, the voice of England'[31] (i.e. the plantation owners and the traders whose wealth depended on slavery), and wrote to Thomas Cumming, who had been trading in ivory, gold dust and slaves along the coast of Senegal, promising his 'best assistance in obtaining an exclusive charter in your favour';[32] and in 1758 a hare-brained expedition was mounted under Captain (later Viscount) Augustus Keppel to seize the island of Gorée and Fort Louis on the Senegal river from the French, in large part because it was thought this would consolidate British control of the slave trade. This obsession with the slave-enabled sugar trade also infected policy on the American colonies and perpetuated the War of Independence long after the British should have abandoned it and sued for peace. As late as 1779 George III wrote to his incompetent and corrupt First Lord of the Admiralty, John Montagu, 4th earl of Sandwich, that 'if we lose our sugar islands it will be impossible to raise money to continue the war'.[33] It is true that the West Indies interests were substantial. By one reckoning, they represented 15 per cent of the country's overseas trade in 1780. But major deployments of forces to defend Caribbean interests from the

French in the 1790s led to sixty thousand British casualties – and still the British aristocrats, absentee landlords that they were, could not see that the trade was immoral and the policy unsustainable. Blind to the moral imperative behind reform, they saw their own wealth and right to property as the sole determinants of British public policy.

The twin revolutions in America and France caused consternation among the British aristocracy, who feared democracy as much as the guillotine. They waged unnecessary wars abroad and introduced harsh laws at home solely to defend their wealth, power and prestige.

CHAPTER 11

THE INFLUENCE OF PROPERTY
FAIRLY EXERCISED

O N SATURDAY, 4 JULY 1789 Gouverneur Morris chatted after dinner
in Paris with Gilbert du Motier. They were an intriguing pair.
Gouverneur had been brought up in a wealthy family in New York and
was now thirty-seven. He was a close friend of George Washington, and
although he did not fight in the War of Independence, thanks to a coaching
accident which left him with a wooden leg, he was a loquacious delegate
to the Constitutional Convention in 1787 and was one of five members
appointed to draft the new American Constitution. He was in Paris
doing business, womanizing and watching events unfold. As for the 31-
year-old Gilbert, few Frenchmen had such a noble pedigree. His maternal
great-grandfather was the comte de la Rivière and had apartments in the
Palais de Luxembourg, his father held one of France's oldest titles as
marquis de Lafayette, and his wife Marie was the daughter of the duc
d'Ayen. By the age of thirteen he had inherited his father's title and lands
which brought in 150,000 livres a year. Inspired by talk of liberty – or
by hatred of the British, who had killed his father in battle at Minden –
he sailed for America in 1777 in search of military glory and fought at
Brandywine, Albany, Rhode Island and Yorktown. Back in France, he
was appointed to the Assembly of Notables by Louis XVI in 1786 and
elected to the Estates General as a noble in 1789.

Recent events were on both men's minds. Lafayette had supported
the transformation of the Estates General into the National Assembly on
17 May and was drafting a new constitution with the long-distance
advice of Thomas Jefferson. Morris urged Lafayette to 'preserve if

possible some constitutional Authority to the Body of Nobles as the only means of preserving any Liberty for the People. The current is setting so strong against the Noblesse that I apprehend their Destruction, in which will I fear be invoked consequences most pernicious, tho' little attended to in the present Moment.'[1] A week later Lafayette published his declaration of rights. It was an unmistakably egalitarian tract; but, as Morris had urged, there was no mention of the evils of hereditary power and offices, of primogeniture and entails, which had so infuriated the elected deputies earlier in the year. This was merely a stay of execution, though. When the National Assembly debated on 19 June 1790 how to commemorate the fall of the Bastille, Joseph-Marie Lambel demanded that 'today [should be] the graveyard of vanity' and that 'it should be forbidden for any person to assume the qualities of Count, Baron, Marquis etc.'.[2] Even those with aristocratic connections condemned the nobility. Charles de Lameth, a former retainer of the comte d'Artois, thought titles were 'puerile distinctions', and the comte de Montmorency considered liveries and coats of arms 'vain ostentations'. As the Assembly abolished the French nobility, a sole voice, that of the Comte Landenberg-Wagenbourg from Alsace, argued that no noble could ever subscribe to this, because 'they will know they live with the blood with which they were born, and that nothing can prevent them from living and dying as gentlemen'.[3]

And die they did. Thomas de Mathy, marquis de Favras, was arrested on Christmas Eve 1790, condemned on 18 February 1791 and, since egalitarianism had been extended to capital punishment, hanged the following day in front of a crowd of fifty thousand. When the Great Terror came in June 1794 the Committee of Public Safety sent thirteen hundred souls to Madame Guillotine in six weeks, at least 473 of whom were nobles, including 51 women. By then, Morris was America's minister plenipotentiary to the revolutionary government, and he kept his views on aristocracy to himself. Although he resolutely continued to use a carriage when such vestiges of aristocratic privilege were banned, he is said to have responded to the angry cries of 'An aristocrat!' that followed him down the street by opening the carriage door, thrusting out his wooden leg and shouting: 'An aristocrat! Yes, truly, who lost his leg in the cause of American liberty' – at which the mob apparently applauded wildly.[4] As for Lafayette, he was in a Prussian prison when his wife's sister, mother and grandmother were guillotined in 1794. Adrienne narrowly escaped execution thanks to Gouverneur's assistance, and in later years she helped turn the convent garden at Picpus in Paris, where the aristocratic bodies had been dumped, into a shrine to France's lost nobility. She was laid to rest there in 1807 and in 1834 Lafayette joined her. An American flag has flown over his tomb since the Americans pledged to liberate France on 4 July 1917.

✠

The twin revolutions in America and France were a shock to the British aristocracy. The former directly threatened their dominions and the latter menaced their status. Both questioned the old Whig doctrine that the aristocracy was the best guarantor of liberty. True, they could claim that the British monarch was bound by the constitution. But the new republican and egalitarian principles flowing out of America and France threatened to shake the foundation stones of the landed hereditary nobility.

The aristocracy's response was twofold: unremitting warfare abroad and repression at home. Both were utterly hypocritical. The central tenet of the Glorious Revolution had been government by consent and they had long criticized the arbitrary Catholic monarchism of the French, but the aristocracy responded to the American colonists' call for 'no taxation without representation' with gunfire, and although some brave souls such as Charles James Fox, Thomas Paine and Mary Wollstonecraft hoped that the revolution across the channel would generate a British-style constitutional monarchy, they started a very expensive war with revolutionary France in 1793. The British government was notably more successful in the latter case than the former, of course, but it was clear in both cases that the aristocracy was fighting to defend its interests.

That was not the end of the hypocrisy. Time and again British governments dominated by aristocrats resorted to severe repression across the country, silencing anything that hinted of democracy or mob rule. When groups of poachers with blackened faces had targeted the estates of the bishop of Winchester and the earl of Cadogan (and wine bound for the Prince of Wales) in the 1720s, the peerage had demanded and secured draconian measures in the form of the sanguinary Black Act, which introduced the death penalty for over fifty property-related offences, including being caught in a forest in disguise. When John Wilkes tried to open up parliamentary debates to public scrutiny in the 1768 he was imprisoned and his supporters were fired on by troops in St George's Fields in Southwark; and when George Gordon, the eccentric youngest son of the 3rd duke of Gordon, led the Protestant Association in protest against the Papist Act in 1780, 285 rioters were shot dead and two dozen or so more were executed. Pitt the Younger's government was equally draconian. When revolutionary France executed Louis XVI, Pitt banned all meetings of more than fifty people as 'seditious' and condemned Thomas Paine, the author of *Rights of Man*, for advocating principles that 'struck at hereditary nobility, and which went to the destruction of monarchy and religion and the total subversion of the established form of government'.[5] Hot on the heels of the Seditious Meetings Act came another imposing deportation for up to seven years for anyone found to have expressed, published, uttered or declared 'any Words or Sentences to excite or stir up the People to hatred or Contempt of the Person of his Majesty, his Heirs or Successors, or the Government and Constitution of this Realm'.[6]

Pitt's clampdown at home and his war overseas were not surprising. He was the son of an earl and he believed in the aristocracy. Between 1784 and 1801 he appointed as his ministers four dukes, three marquesses, nine earls, one viscount, four barons and just one commoner, William Windham, and he created or promoted 130 English peers, taking the peerage from 195 to 273. In earlier generations such inflation had been criticized, but now the complaints were decidedly muted as the new peers gave him a strong bulwark in the Lords against his more radical opponents and helped perpetuate the aristocratic dominance of the nation. That was not all. The forty-five Scottish seats in the Commons gave Pitt an additional buffer, as the total electorate for these amounted to little over four thousand, which left them open to aristocratic influence. By 1796 Pitt's Secretary for War and corrupt Scottish parliamentary fixer Sir Henry Dundas (later Viscount Melville) had persuaded the duke of Buccleuch, the earl of Fife and the earl of Eglinton to put their Commons seats at his disposal, giving him control of all bar four Scottish MPs. As if that were not enough, many a British and Irish peer had his hand greased to secure the passage of the controversial union of the two kingdoms in 1801. So even though Arthur Hill, the 2nd marquess of Downshire (who also had a British title as earl of Hillsborough), opposed the Union and took his own life when he was consequently sacked as privy councillor and governor of Down, he still received £52,000 'compensation' for the seven Irish seats he owned. George Forbes, 6th earl of Granard, was granted £30,000 for his four seats, plus a seat in Westminster as Baron Granard and the very lucrative post of clerk of the crown and hanaper in Ireland (an officer in the Irish chancery), all in the hope of overturning his vehement opposition to the Union. Charles Loftus was bumped up from earl of Ely to marquess (in the Irish peerage) and received £45,000 for his six seats, plus a British title as Baron Loftus. Richard Boyle, 2nd earl of Shannon, pocketed £37,000, Henry Ellis, 2nd Viscount Clifden, £30,000 plus a special remainder for a British peerage; the slave-trading Earl Belmore and the philandering 5th duke of Devonshire netted £30,000 each; and John Bingham, one of the MPs for Tuam, swapped the two seats in his control for £8,000 plus a now largely redundant Irish peerage as Baron Clanmorris. In all, Pitt's Chief Secretary for Ireland, Robert Stewart, Viscount Castlereagh, budgeted on spending £1.5 million of Irish Treasury funds in this way. These *douceurs* were not even a very reliable form of inducement: John Browne, 3rd earl of Altamont, complained to Richard Bingham, 2nd earl of Lucan, that although George Rochfort, 2nd earl of Belvedere, 'has touched Government cash' to the tune of £15,000 he 'possibly may not exert all his influence to give value in return for it'.[7] Altamont and Lucan knew the rules of the game, though. Altamont's vote was worth a promotion to marquess of Sligo and knight of the Order of St Patrick, and Lucan's got him a seat as an Irish representative peer from 1802 until his death in 1839.

This substantially enlarged House of Lords, with twenty-eight Irish representative peers elected for life and four Irish bishops, totalled 347, and substantially strengthened the aristocratic grip on power. This could now be readily deployed to enforce further draconian measures, such as another Seditious Meetings Act (which made such meetings a capital offence), a Treason Act and the suspension of habeas corpus, all of which were introduced by Lord Liverpool's government in 1817 on the pretext that, as Lord Sidmouth put it: 'Clubs had also been established in every quarter under the ostensible object of parliamentary reform ... [and] a very large proportion of them indeed had parliamentary reform in their mouths, but rebellion and revolution in their hearts.'[8]

The extraordinary degree to which the nobility still held sway in the land was laid bare in 1820 by the former wool-sorter turned journalist and polemicist John Wade in his work *The Black Book, or Corruption Unmasked!*, which sold fifty thousand copies. Inspired by the ideas of Tom Paine and Joseph Priestley, and funded by the radical philosopher Jeremy Bentham (who argued for the abolition of the monarchy and the aristocracy), Wade relentlessly pursued instances of inequality and corruption. 'At no former period of history', he complained, 'was the power of the Aristocracy so absolute, nor did they enjoy a tithe of their present advantages.'[9] He railed against primogeniture and entails, asking: 'What right had an assembly of half-civilised men, some five hundred years ago, to tie up the great estates of the country in perpetuity; to enact that, whatever changes of society might intervene, they should never be subdivided nor severed from their lineal heirs as long as they endured?'[10] This was a system that enriched one person and left the rest of the family destitute. 'Hence they are thrown, like mendicants, on the public for support; but they are unlike mendicants in this – that the public has no option whether they will support them or not.'[11]

Wade had other complaints. The aristocracy enjoyed preposterous privileges – free postage, freedom from arrest for debt and from bankruptcy, freedom from enforced sequestration of assets for in-solvency, the right to swear on their honour rather than their oath, the right to sue for the slightest aspersion cast on their dignity and the right to trial by other peers. They had secured heavy import duties on foreign agricultural goods that might compete with their own produce, but low tariffs on luxury imports that they wanted to buy and did not produce.

Most importantly, they had rigged taxation to their own advantage. The rules on inheritance meant that if a lord succeeded to an entailed estate of £100,000, he would not pay a single shilling in tax, but the son or daughter of a rich merchant who inherited £100,000 would have to pay £1,500, or £2,250 if there were no will. Likewise, a man who bought a cottage for £10 had to pay 10s or 5 per cent of the cost in stamp duty, but a lord who bought an estate for £50,000 would pay only £450, just 0.9 per cent of the purchase price. Even the window tax was unfair. A house was charged 4s 6d for every window above eight, while a mansion paid just 1s 6d for each window over and above 180.

How could such unfairness be sustained? The answer lay in the vicious circle of aristocratic supremacy. As John Cartwright, one of the earliest campaigners for constitutional reform, put it, thanks to the aristocracy's continuing grip on both the Lords and the Commons, there were 'two hereditary houses instead of one'.[12] John Wilson Croker admitted as much when he reminded the Prime Minister George Canning in 1827 'how powerful the aristocracy is . . . and how necessary it is to have a fair proportion on the side of a Government'.[13] Wade's conclusion was equally clear. The nobility wrote the rules to benefit themselves; and, 'instead of bearing the burthen of taxation, which, in fact, is the original tenure on which they acquired their territorial possessions, have laid it on the people'.[14]

✠

Ironically, it was an aristocrat who precipitated the first limited reform of the system. Born at Fallodon Hall in 1764, Charles Grey spent much of his youth when his father was away on military campaigns in the dour but impressive nearby medieval surroundings of Howick Hall with his bachelor uncle Sir Henry. The Greys were an old and long-established Northumbrian family, but it was Charles's father's military success that brought them their first title as Baron Grey of Howick in 1794, upgraded to Earl Grey and Viscount Howick in 1806. The following year the 78-year-old earl died and Charles, who had sat in the Commons from the age of twenty-two, joined the Lords as the 2nd Earl Grey. His personal and political inclinations were on the conservative end of Whiggery; yet he supported Catholic emancipation and parliamentary reform. Having served briefly as Foreign Secretary, he endured twenty-three tedious and depressing years in opposition. But in 1830 George IV, who always vetoed any thought of Grey becoming a minister, died and in the subsequent session of the new parliament Grey goaded the Tory Prime Minister, the duke of Wellington, into asserting that he could never support *any* measure of parliamentary reform whatsoever. Within weeks the duke's government was defeated and Grey replaced him.

Grey's administration was every bit as aristocratic as Wellington's. He admitted his preference for aristocrats to Princess Lieven, 'for that class is a guarantee for the safety of the state and of the throne'.[15] Sitting around his Cabinet table were the 6th earl of Carlisle, the 3rd marquess of Lansdowne, the future 3rd Earl Spencer, the 3rd Baron Holland, the 3rd Viscount Palmerston, Viscount Goderich and Baron Melbourne. His Postmaster-General was the virulent Tory opponent of Catholic emancipation and stout defender of the corn laws, Charles Gordon-Lennox, 5th duke of Richmond. The Lord Chancellor, Henry, Baron Brougham, was a recent ennoblement, but his family had long been well ensconced at Brougham Hall in Westmorland and had owned estates in Cumberland for centuries. The Lord Privy Seal was Grey's son-in-law John Lambton, whose recently minted title as earl of Durham doffed the cap to his vast inheritance of the 17,000-acre colliery lands around Lambton Castle in County Durham, and who was reported to have said that 'he considered £40,000 a year a moderate income – such a one as a man might jog on with'.[16]

Clearly this was no band of revolutionary sans-culottes, yet it tackled the problem of corrupt and rotten parliamentary seats and the under-representation of growing cities such as Birmingham, Manchester, Leeds and Liverpool. Previous attempts at reform had failed, but public pressure had grown and now, ever the cautious aristocrat, Grey wanted a Bill that would do 'as much as is necessary to secure to the people a due influence in that great council in which they are more particularly represented . . . guarding and limiting it, at the same time, by a prudent care not to disturb too violently, by any extensive changes, the established principles and practice of the constitution'.[17] Grey knew that it would not be plain sailing. After all, Wellington's government had only just fallen on this very subject, and the duke was likely to be a hardy opponent in the Lords. Little can have prepared Grey for the battle that ensued, though. Up against the vested interests of the aristocracy, whose families held dozens of Commons seats, the government's leader in the Commons, Lord John Russell, a younger son of the 6th earl of Bedford, secured a single-vote majority for the second reading of the Bill; but when he began to lose amendments and procedural motions, Grey pulled the Bill and demanded a new election. The tactic worked. When the Commons returned in September 1831 the reformist Whigs had won virtually every seat that had a proper electorate and the Tories were reduced to their rotten core; so a second attempt at reform went far more smoothly and the Bill enjoyed Commons majorities of more than a hundred.

When Grey opened the debate in the Lords on 3 October, though, Hansard recorded that 'the utmost stillness pervaded the air', partly because everyone knew that his favourite grandson's funeral cortège was under way as he spoke. His long, uncomfortable speech dealt directly with the peers' vested interests. 'I deny', he said, 'that the power of returning Members to Parliament is to be considered in the nature of property. It is not property, but a trust; and there can be no greater mistake than to confound the obligation of a trust with the rights of property.'[18] This stuck in the noble craw. The only moment during Grey's speech that elicited a hearty cheer was when he asked: 'Had it not been said that the measure now before your Lordships ought, in consequence of the disfranchising part of it, to be denominated a measure of spoliation and robbery?' It was a rhetorical question, but the peers sarcastically cried 'Hear, hear!'[19] The debate went on for five days, and every day lords presented petitions from their area of influence. Sometimes they clashed. The duke of Devonshire and the marquess of Londonderry disagreed about the views of the people of Derby. The duke of Newcastle and Lord Holland had counter-petitions from Nottingham. The marquess of Salisbury questioned the validity of the earl of Sefton's 17,600 Liverpudlian signatures in support of the measure. The earl of Eldon had a petition from Norwich with 3,500 signatures against; the earl of Albemarle had 11,750 signatures from Norwich in favour. The debates were testy. The marquess of Bute argued against Grey that although peers did exercise an influence, 'it was nothing but the influence of property fairly exercised'.[20] The earl of Harrowby claimed that peers' nomination rights must stem from their property, not from their rank. Wellington stated that he wanted a parliamentary system 'in which property, and particularly property in land, should be preponderant', because it was only by the influence of property over the elections of MPs and the proceedings of the Commons 'that the great powers of such a body as the House of Commons can be exercised with discretion and safety'. Otherwise, he feared that 'property, and its possessors, will become the common enemy'.[21] One relative newcomer to the Lords, James Stuart-Wortley, who was reckoned to be the epitome of the 'spirited, sensible, zealous, honourable, consistent country gentleman',[22] went further. A grandson of a former Prime Minister, the 3rd earl of Bute, he had been colonel of the 12th Foot before sitting as MP for the corrupt borough of Bossiney from 1797 and becoming Baron Wharncliffe in 1826. His argument reeked of privilege. If there were to be no possibility for any man to arrive at a seat in the Commons except by the favour of the people, it 'would become too much the image of the people; and, being so, it would be impossible that 300 or 400 titled persons should have the power of arresting its movements'.[23] In short, the Bill represented 'the subversion of the monarchy and . . . the destruction of the House of Lords'.[24]

Crowds gathered early outside parliament to hear what the Lords had decided on the fifth evening of debate, Friday 7 October, but it was not until five o'clock on the Saturday morning that Grey rose to have the final say – and the vote came at 6.30 a.m. It was a high turnout. When the numbers were counted, 158 were 'content' – but 199 were 'not content', so the second reading was lost. The mood among the more newly entitled was against reform: peers whose titles had been created before George III voted 60 to 51 in favour of the Bill, but Pitt's creations, the representative peers and the crown-appointed bishops voted 74 to 32 against. There was danger in the air. The duke of Newcastle's home at Nottingham Castle was burned to the ground (for which he later demanded and received £21,000 in damages, despite never rebuilding it). Rioters attempted to do the same to the magnificent nearby Wollaton Hall, where Henry Willoughby, 6th Baron Middleton, had recently enclosed additional acres in his deer park and spent thousands of pounds on refurbishments. And at Colwick Hall, the home of the Musters family, enraged commoners smashed every window in the entrance hall, tore a portrait by Romney to atoms, attempted to set off a canister of gunpowder and forced the lady of the house to hide in the shrubbery in the rain – from which affront she was said to have died four months later. In Paris, Harriet, Viscountess Granville, the daughter of the 5th duke of Devonshire and wife of the stuffy British ambassador, shuddered when she read in *Le Temps* that the Lords, like the old French nobility in 1789, 'have made their own 25 July'.[25]

Grey's response was to prorogue parliament and try again with a third Bill. This one positively billowed through the Commons, but when the king declared himself reluctant to create sympathetic peers to carry it through the Lords, Grey resigned and Wellington was left floundering as the country began to demand the complete abolition of the nobility. Fearing anarchy, Wellington capitulated, Grey was reappointed, and when the Bill reappeared in the Lords enough opponents absented themselves for the measure to be carried. This was hardly republicanism. The Bill made no provision for a secret ballot. Many borough seats remained in the pocket of the local lord. Voters had to own property worth £10, county MPs £600. And it soon became apparent that if there were more voters, there were more votes to buy and sell. The influence of the Lords had been touched but not destroyed, and Grey's innate conservatism had ensured that a minor, evolutionary measure staved off clamour for more substantial reform.

✠

One man's history best exemplifies the corruption of borough-mongering. James Lowther was just nine when his father died, leaving him his baronetcy, valuable plantations in Barbados, and the extensive estates in Westmorland that he had bought for £30,000 from the duke of Wharton. James received another windfall when he was fifteen, as his cousin Henry

Lowther, 3rd Viscount Lonsdale, died childless, leaving him Lowther Hall, Appleby Castle and a further slice of Westmorland. A third bounty came before his twenty-first birthday in the shape of the Cumberland lands of the Lowther family of Whitehaven – making him one of the wealthiest commoners in the land. James sat as an MP for twenty-three years and was constantly engaged in purchasing and manipulating seats. In the Appleby constituency the vote lay with a hundred or so burgage tenements, the majority of which belonged to the Lowther and Tufton families. At first this meant a battle with the earl of Thanet, but soon Lowther's financial clout secured him the seat. Then he bought Cockermouth for £50,000. In 1761 he returned eight MPs, two each for Cumberland, Westmorland and Cockermouth, and one each for Carlisle and Appleby. In 1784 he managed nine, including two for Haslemere, a seat he had bought in 1780, and in 1784 he had twelve. He splashed money on elections – £15,000 at Appleby in 1754, £25,000 in Cumberland and Carlisle in 1768 and £25,000 in Lancaster alone in 1786 – and tried to rig the poll by threatening to transplant 600 Irishmen to Westmorland in 1773 and getting the corporation of Carlisle to appoint 1,400 additional freemen to swing the vote in 1784.

What was the point of all this political engineering? In part he simply enjoyed exercising dominion over others. But there was something else. Early wealth rendered him arrogant and seems to have deprived him of a moral sense in virtually any aspect of his life. He married the daughter of the earl of Bute, but was serially unfaithful to her; he kept his mistress's body putrefying on her bed when she died, and was only reluctantly persuaded to allow her to be buried. He was renowned as a harsh and avaricious landlord, and he used parliament to protect his and his family's interests. He was made earl of Lonsdale in 1784 and in 1797, in an attempt to prevent the extinction of his family line, he insisted on additionally being made Viscount Lowther with a special remainder to the heirs male of his deceased third cousin. It was said that he was one of the most worthless men in the kingdom, yet he prospered thanks to his extremely jealous guarding of his own interests.

The charge sheet against this self-perpetuating ascendancy was best laid out, inadvertently, by David Murray, 3rd earl of Mansfield:

It is said, the House of Commons, of whose Members a great proportion are the nominees of Peers, or great landed proprietors . . . for their own advantage, supported the Ministers who plunged the country into an unjust and unnecessary war. British blood was shed, treasure lavished with profusion in ill-concerted expeditions, heavy taxes were imposed, and our Debt considerably increased. At last the war of long continuance was brought to a close, a peace was signed which gave to Britain no useful addition to her territorial possessions – merely the solitary advantage of having imposed upon France a ruler whom she detested, and having become the ally of all the despots in Europe, leagued together for the oppression of their subjects, and the destruction of civil liberty, while her own subjects were oppressed with a debt so onerous, that our commerce, our agriculture, and all our resources were crippled for ever – this could not have taken place with a reformed Parliament.[26]

Mansfield was speaking against the second Reform Bill in 1831, but the point could hardly have been made better.

La galerie

Croupades sur les Voltes a mán. gauche

One of the defining features of the aristocracy was that their wealth and status meant they could afford to eschew work. The members of this leisured class found expensive ways to disport themselves in riding, hunting, shooting and gambling – entertainments that they jealously guarded. Many of the complex equestrian manoeuvres laid out in the duke of Newcastle's book from 1658 are still part of modern dressage. Here he is seen in front of his castle at Bolsover.

CHAPTER 12

THIS LORD LOVES NOTHING BUT HORSES

IN 1772 THE ALREADY well-established painter George Stubbs made his way back to Yorkshire to spend several months as a guest of Charles Watson-Wentworth, 2nd marquess of Rockingham, at his country home, Wentworth House, near Rotherham. Wentworth was very grand. The original Jacobean manor house had been transformed beyond recognition by Rockingham and his father, the first marquess, who had given it the most finely proportioned rooms in England and the longest façade in Europe, largely out of a competitive desire to eclipse their relatives, the earls of Strafford, who occupied another nearby country home, Wentworth Castle. The new walls needed decorating, so Rockingham commissioned Stubbs to paint portraits – not of himself or his family, but of his horses. One painting, now in the National Gallery in London, is particularly striking: it shows a solitary chestnut stallion, the thoroughbred Whistlejacket, rising impressively on its hindquarters to a levade while looking straight out at the viewer. Whistlejacket was famous for having won several races for Rockingham, including the King's Plate at Newmarket in 1755 and a four-mile race at York in 1759, but what is especially striking is that the portrait has neither Rockingham nor his ancestral home in the background. Rockingham had a lengthy career in politics and was twice Prime Minister, but it seems Horace Walpole was right when he said that 'this Lord loves nothing but horses'.[1]

Rockingham was not alone. Horses have always been an aristocratic obsession. Anglo-Saxon eorls measured their wealth and status in terms of their horse gear. Norman barons arrived on horseback as *chevaliers*.

The Master of the Horse was always one of the king's closest confidants, ranking third in the royal household and running the royal stables, coach-houses, stud, mews and kennels. In part this was just military necessity. A horse gave a noble a clear advantage in battle, allowing him to charge down the enemy and move freely around the battlefield. Five feet above the common foot-sloggers, he could oversee them, lead them, signal to them and if necessary flee the field. Well into the twentieth century the cavalry was thought to outrank the infantry in terms of military acumen, strategic significance and social standing. In peacetime, too, horses were an aristocratic prerequisite. From the vantage point of a well-made and elaborately decorated saddle a lord could survey his estates, visit his neighbours, and address his tenants without fear of contradiction. A horse was not just a means of transport; it was a symbol of wealth and authority.

More than that, though, horsemanship became an emblematic aristocratic pastime and as vital a social skill for a Stuart courtier as fencing and dancing. All the best young nobles went to Paris or Naples to master the precision horsemanship known as *manège*, and successful favourites like the duke of Buckingham not only hunted regularly with the king but also invested heavily in stud farms such as Helmsley (which had been in Buckingham's wife's family for centuries). The most notable example is William Cavendish, successively the earl, marquess and duke of Newcastle, who was taught *manège* by the French master St Antoine and devoted himself to horses. He built magnificent riding stables at Welbeck Abbey in 1623–4 and hung them with twelve exceptional portraits of horses, each measuring five feet by six feet; he built a riding school at Bolsover Castle in 1630–4 and drew up plans for another in London which never came to fruition; and he spent his exile during the Commonwealth turning the artist Rubens' former home in Antwerp into a riding academy and publishing a beautifully illustrated book on *manège* entitled *Méthode et Invention Nouvelle de Dresser les Chevaux*. The corvets, voltoes and terra terra movements that he described in his book and performed on his favourite Spanish horse, Le Superbe, became staple elements of modern dressage. Cavendish commissioned a commanding mounted portrait of himself performing a leaping capriole with Bolsover Castle in the background; and when his descendant William Cavendish Bentinck became 3rd duke of Portland and inherited Welbeck in 1767, he, like Rockingham, commissioned Stubbs, in this case to provide two equestrian paintings. In one Portland is seated on a fine grey horse outside the stables, and in the other he and his wayward younger brother are watching a groom training a young horse at a jumping bar. The message of calm aristocratic authority achieved through fine breeding was deliberate.

✠

Horses brought another aristocratic thrill – racing. Originally this had been a purely local sport as neighbouring peers challenged one another, but when Charles II instigated the King's Plate at Newmarket in 1666 and Anne launched the racecourse at Ascot with a race entitled Her Majesty's Plate in 1711, racing acquired an added lustre. Peers became so addicted to the thrill of the turf (and to the gambling that went with it) that they sponsored much larger races with more contestants on their own estates, shortened the courses and raced younger horses – all adding to the excitement. By 1753 there were three grand race meetings a year at Newmarket. In 1776 Rockingham declined a proposal made at dinner at the Red Lion in Doncaster that an annual sweepstake race be inaugurated in his name and insisted it be named instead after the event's proposer, Anthony St Leger: later that year Rockingham's own filly, Allabaculia, won the first St Leger Stakes. Two years later Edward Smith-Stanley, 12th earl of Derby, came up with the idea of an annual race to be held on one of his several estates, The Oaks in Carshalton near Epsom. Derby's sporting interests were notorious and all-embracing, as he was equally devoted to the turf, the crease, the chase and the cockpit – and their attendant bookmakers. Derby's horse Bridget won the first Oaks Stakes in 1779, and in 1780 he founded another race for colts, unsurprisingly thereafter known as the Derby Stakes. The predominance of the peerage is evident in the list of early winners of these classic races. In its first thirty years the Oaks was won five times by horses belonging to dukes, fourteen times by earls, four times by baronets and just seven times by wealthy commoners; and the Derby was won twenty-six times by peers or baronets in the thirty years between 1780 and 1810.

The aristocratic enthusiasm for horse-racing continued unabated in the nineteenth century. In 1802 Charles Lennox, the reformist 3rd duke of Richmond, started races at Goodwood to entertain himself in his old age; in 1821 'Radical Jack' Lambton, later the earl of Durham, built Lambton Park for the Lambton Racing Club; in 1829 William Molyneux, 2nd earl of Sefton, known as 'Lord Dashalong', leased land at Aintree to a Liverpool hotelier for a series of flat races; in 1830 Wrest Park, the home of the countess de Grey and her heir Thomas Robinson, 3rd Baron Grantham, hosted the first St Albans Grand Steeplechase; in the 1830s and 1840s the successful racehorse owner and staunch Conservative politician Archibald Montgomerie, 13th earl of Eglinton, held private races on his estates in Ayrshire; and in 1836 the races at Aintree included a Liverpool Grand Steeplechase, which in time became the Grand National.

A race meeting became a grand occasion – a fixed point in the social calendar at which the great and the would-be great could see and be seen. Upper-class families traipsed out of London for the races at Epsom and Ascot, and lined up for a sight of the monarch or a noble like Hugh Lowther, 5th earl of Lonsdale, who would appear in an unmistakable canary-yellow carriage at Ascot and splash out on lavish entertainment at Epsom. Peers added to the sense of occasion by holding social events around the races. Successive dukes of Richmond held a ball at the end of the race week at Goodwood, the earls of Sefton and of Derby held competing house parties at Croxteth Hall and Knowsley for the races at Aintree, and during the meetings at Redcar the Lowther family would host friends at Wilton Castle. New facilities were added to racecourses, often by aristocratic subscription. Doncaster gained betting rooms, which in 1827 were so crowded that 'noble lords were constrained to stand on tables and chairs',[2] and assembly rooms, where 'nearly all the nobility [attended] the ball on race week Monday' in 1829. By the middle of the century it was common for newspapers to publish lists of 'the company' in attendance and comment that peers had been seen mixing with the crowd. The 14th earl of Derby, for instance, who was Conservative Prime Minister three times in the 1850s and 1860s, was seen at Newmarket 'in the midst of a crowd of blacklegs, betting men, and low characters of every description, in uproarious spirits, chaffing, roaring and shouting with laughter'.[3] Quite how genuinely comfortable the earl was in these circumstances is difficult to gauge, although a comment on his relationship with his talented trainer John Scott is suggestive: *Baily's Magazine* remarked on 'the most perfect understanding and respect which the one felt for the other', but added that 'there was none of that *undue familiarity* which too frequently exists between an owner and his trainer'.[4] Sometimes the pressure to attend became an irritant. When John Manners, 5th duke of Rutland, failed to attend the Leicester races in 1850, people complained that 'the country gentlemen and ladies seem entirely to have forsaken our racecourse'.[5] Charles, Viscount Milton, wrote to his father, the Whig leader William, 4th Earl Fitzwilliam, that he hoped not to receive any recommendation to go to York races as he had no intention of stirring unless he was very much pressed. His father cannot have been very impressed. He had inherited Rockingham's estates, stables and stud, he was a successful racehorse breeder in his own right, and when William Cavendish, the bachelor 6th duke of Devonshire, turned up at Doncaster races in 1827 with the same equipage as himself, namely a coach and six with twelve outriders, he deliberately eclipsed the duke by appearing the next day with two coaches and six attended by sixteen outriders.

Part of the appeal of the turf was the relief of the boredom that afflicted the under-occupied, with betting lending a frisson to an otherwise dull life. But peers found other exclusive equestrian ways of entertaining themselves, too. The early nineteenth century saw an expensive new craze: carriage-driving clubs. The first of these, the Bensington Driving Club, was founded in 1807 and presided over by Thomas, Viscount Cranley, before he became the 2nd earl of Onslow. In addition to his efforts as an amateur cricketer (and some very occasional appearances in the Commons during his thirty-one years as an MP), 'Tommy' drove at speed a funereally black phaeton drawn by four black horses, prompting a satirical poem on his general uselessness:

> *What can Tommy Onslow do?*
> *He can drive a coach and two.*
> *Can Tommy Onslow do no more?*
> *He can drive a coach and four.*

Like the Bensington, the Four-in-Hand Club, founded in 1808, was little more than a riotous aristocratic drinking club. It had ludicrously pedantic rules. Gentlemen drivers had to wear an ankle-length drab coat with three pockets and mother-of-pearl buttons, a blue waistcoat with yellow stripes, and plush knee-length breeches. They would gather in George Street, Hanover Square, and drive the twenty-five miles to the Windmill in Slough, 'where a sumptuous dinner awaited them; after which they returned to London, in high spirits, and not unfrequently somewhat overcome by the quantity of sound port wine'.[6] The whole point of the club was the ostentatious display of the noble carriages, horses and livery. Its members were among the most dissolute young nobles in town: Henry Somerset, later the 7th duke of Beaufort, whose younger brother the Tory politician Granville Somerset was an equally devoted sportsman and rider after hounds, despite a disfiguring riding accident in his youth; the earl of Sefton, who was described as 'a man of considerable taste' and 'a capital horseman';[7] and Henry Barry, unkindly nicknamed 'Cripplegate' because of his club foot, who had inherited his brother Richard's title as 8th earl of Barrymore along with some of his rakish ways, Richard having been known as 'Hellgate' for his habit of driving teams of horses at speed through London's streets and spending his fortune on betting and prostitutes. Bringing up the rear was the hard-drinking Colonel William Berkeley, who had almost certainly been born out of wedlock but still claimed his father the libidinous 5th earl of Berkeley's several titles – to no avail. The colonel, who was eventually granted a newly fabricated title as Earl Fitzhardinge in 1841, was reckoned to be 'a very dissipated young man',[8] 'a vulgar, narrow-minded man [whose] great pleasure seems to be to act the sort of King of Cheltenham, where all the vulgar misses make a great piece of work with him,'[9] and 'an arrant blackguard' who was 'notorious for general worthlessness'. The club barely lasted twenty years, but such was the demand for noble roistering that another extravagant horseman, George Stanhope, 6th earl of Chesterfield, whose political career consisted of a five-month spell as Master of the Buckhounds under Sir Robert Peel and who won the Oaks in 1838 and 1849 and the Grand National in 1843, founded the Richmond Driving Club in 1838 with the sole purpose of driving carriages in an ostentatious procession from Chesterfield House in Mayfair to the Castle Hotel in Richmond. Showing off was always fun, but showing off with horses was even better.

There was another aspect of keeping horses that appealed to the hereditary nobility, as breeding thoroughbreds for their refinement and their speed on the racecourse was akin to the age-old preoccupation with human pedigrees. The stud farm and the debutantes' ball were close cousins, as peers obsessed about their horses' ancestry and bloodlines. The dukes of Newcastle, Grafton, Cumberland, Bedford and Rutland and the earls of Egremont, Abingdon and Grosvenor ran successful studs at Welbeck, Euston Hall, Windsor, Cranbourne, Woburn, Cheveley, Petworth and Eaton Hall. The most successful of the noble breeders was Archibald Primrose, who became the 5th earl of Rosebery in 1868 and flamboyantly boasted in his youth that he had three ambitions: to marry the richest woman in England, to become Prime Minister and to win the Derby. He achieved all three; and the first, his marriage to Hannah, the daughter of Baron Meyer de Rothschild, undoubtedly helped him succeed in the other two, especially as she brought with her the successful Rothschild stud at Mentmore near Leighton Buzzard, which complemented his own stud at Durdans near Epsom. The result was that in 1894, when he briefly held the premiership, his colt Ladas won the Two Thousand Guineas and the Derby; the following year he won the Derby and the St Leger with Sir Visto; and in 1905 he had his third Derby win with Cicero. When his Mauchline won the 1897 Gimcrack Stakes at York, he advised those assembled for the anniversary dinner at the Station Hotel against spending their time and money on the turf, on the grounds that 'the apprenticeship is exceedingly expensive ... the pursuit is too engrossing for any one who has anything else to do in this life ... and ... the rewards, as compared with the disappointments, stand in the relation of, at the most, one per cent'.[10] He was being unnecessarily arch, still smarting from the drubbing he and the Liberals had received in the general election of 1895. Even so, several peers admitted that, like him, they were far more interested in the hereditary process of improving the breed, which they thought of as a form of national service, than in attending or winning races. In the case of James

Carr-Boyle, 5th earl of Glasgow, it was just as well that he did not care too much about winning. His stubborn insistence on particular bloodlines proved misguided, as he never won a major race – and his foul temper led to his unnecessarily shooting unsuccessful horses on the spot (and throwing a waiter out of the window at the Black Swan in York, for which he had £5 added to his bill). As for Rosebery, he made clear at York that his ambition was to breed 'the horse of the century', because so far as he was concerned, 'the amusements of the turf do not lie on the racecourse – they lie in the breeding of a horse; in that most delightful furniture of any park or enclosure, the brood mare and the foal; in watching the development of the foal, the growth of the horse, and the exercise of the horse at home'.[11]

✠

Horse-racing was an expensive aristocratic pastime, but its close cousin hunting could become even more of an obsession. For many, indeed, it became their raison d'être. Take the Cravens. When William, Earl Craven, started building a mansion at Hamstead Marshall on the Berkshire Downs as a palace for his heart's love, Elizabeth Stuart, the 'Winter Queen' of Bohemia, he added a Dutch-looking hunting lodge in the middle of the extensive woodlands, which became known as Ashdown House. Elizabeth died before either mansion or lodge was completed, Craven died unmarried at the age of eighty-nine in 1697, and Hamstead Marshall was burnt down in 1718, but for centuries Ashdown remained a huntsman's idyll, from which successive Cravens went out riding and hunting. When *Baily's Magazine* published a character sketch of William's descendant, the 31-year-old George, 3rd Earl Craven, in 1872, it made clear quite how central these country sports were to the Victorian nobility. Although, like every self-respecting member of the nobility, he attended the London season with his countess Evelyn, George much preferred to go hunting at Ashdown, where he was joint master of the Old Berkshire hounds, or riding at Weathercock Hill (where his father had re-inaugurated the Lambourn Racehorse Meeting) or at his other home, Coombe Abbey in Warwickshire. He was, in the eyes of *Baily's*, the epitome of the noble English gentleman. 'Warmly attached to all field sports, but pre-eminently to hunting . . . he is a good shot, a keen angler, popular with all classes . . . and whether by the covert side on Kingston Warrens, with the greyhounds on the slips, or over a Lancashire moor, Lord Craven holds his own in those sports which are in some way the heritage of an English gentleman.'[12] His father had been a keen sportsman too, having started the Craven Cricket Club, served as president of the Marylebone Cricket Club and won the Grand National with his own horse Charity (ridden by Horatio Powell) in 1841, but the 3rd earl was an even braver horseman. As *Baily's* put it: 'In the field Lord Craven is a very determined rider, crashing through strong places which would infallibly turn over a lighter or less powerful horseman.'[13] Craven did have one other achievement – the Craven A brand of cigarettes was named after him – but hunting was his life: although he was a member of the House of Lords for nearly seventeen years, it took him two years to take his seat and there is no record of his ever appearing there again, let alone speaking.

Craven was far from exceptional in his devotion to hunting. From time immemorial monarchs had revelled in the pursuit and slaughter of wild animals, and it had been a special honour to accompany the king out hunting. Their poets regularly eulogized hunting as an aspect of chivalry. Chasing a wild stag with hounds and felling it with an arrow required courage, talent, stamina and prowess, the nobility argued, and the crown claimed for itself exclusive hunting rights through strict forest laws. Only the king or queen could hunt wherever they chose – including on land sub-tenanted by others – and only they could take rabbits, deer, hares, pheasants and partridges. In the seventeenth century the Winter Queen's father, James I, devoted so much of his time to hunting that his nobles complained at his absence from the Council table; he died at his favourite hunting lodge, Theobalds. Right up until the outbreak of civil war, Charles I wandered from one lodge to another, devoting whole weeks to hunting at Theobalds, Royston, Newmarket and Oatlands, or on his nobles' estates up and down the country. The nobility followed suit. Landed families enclosed common fields in large private parks and stocked them with tame deer, seen no longer as wild game but now as private property. When civil war came, ordinary people took their chance to trap and kill game for their own consumption, including many of the royalist nobility's bucks and roes.

The aristocracy's response after the Restoration was vicious. In 1671 it forced through a new Game Act, which forbade anyone other than a 'qualified person' from killing 'game'. Since the Act limited the former to those who owned land worth more than £100 a year, plus the eldest sons of esquires, knights and nobles, and extended the latter to include all partridges, pheasants, hares and moor fowl, this was a very exclusive Act. As deer were now formally classed as property, their illegal capture was not merely poaching but theft, and therefore attracted even harsher punishment. Another clause was particularly pernicious, as it extended the right to roam and hunt wherever one chose to all 'qualified persons'. That meant every noble in the land could trample over his neighbours' and tenants' land and seize whatever game he fancied with complete impunity. Over the next fifty years the aristocratically dominated parliament added to the statute book another twenty-four laws restricting hunting to themselves. In 1671 they determined that only they could own 'snares, nets, or hare-pipes, or keep greyhounds, ferrets, coney-dogs and lurchers';[14] in 1691 they gave themselves new powers to fine, imprison or pillory poachers; in 1707 they banned anyone other than themselves from possessing hares, partridges and pheasants; in 1711 they introduced new penalties for hunting at night; and in 1723 they restored the death penalty for stealing deer.

There were objections. The eighteenth-century Tory jurist Sir William Blackstone despaired that although 'the forest laws established only one mighty hunter throughout the land, the game laws have elevated a Nimrod in every manor'.[15] The Victorian Anglican priest and essayist Vicesimus Knox condemned the 1671 Act for having created a breed of 'petty princes', who 'claim the privilege of prowling for prey, without control, on their neighbour's land'.[16] And those who believed the laws illogical simply ignored them, not least because the aristocracy could not possibly hunt down enough hares to prevent their being a major nuisance to farmers and because many rural commoners understandably believed that hunger trumped property rights. As the founder of the National Agricultural Labourers Union, Joseph Arch, put it in his autobiography in 1898, 'we labourers did not believe hares and rabbits belong to any individual, nor any more than thrushes and blackbirds do'. Nor had hares been created 'exclusively for one class of the community'.[17]

Landlords' response to the flouting of the law was brutal: they installed vicious man-traps like the 'Body-Squeezer' and the 'Thigh-Cracker' and spring-guns that fired indiscriminately when a tripwire was triggered. The morality of this was, to many aristocrats' minds, beside the point. As the philanthropist, abolitionist and all-round radical Edward Harbord, 3rd Baron Suffield, who loved field sports but successfully campaigned to make spring-guns illegal, explained to a friend in 1823: 'The whole system ... is one of *exclusion*, it is founded upon exclusive rights, it is supported upon selfish principles, and its chief enjoyment consists in the possession of that which your neighbour has *not* and perhaps *can not* have.'[18] Suffield died in 1835 when his horse stumbled, threw him and rolled on top of him on Constitution Hill – thus suffering the same fate, so his family recalled, as an eighty-year-old ancestor, John Harbord, whose pony had stepped into a rabbit-burrow when returning from a shoot and had killed him 'on the spot'.[19]

Practical changes to hunting altered its social dynamic and purpose. Coursing, the practice of chasing deer, hares or rabbits with sight-hounds, had been an aristocratic pastime for centuries; King Cnut had ruled that only gentlemen should be allowed to keep a greyhound and Thomas Howard, 4th duke of Norfolk, had drawn up a set of coursing rules, *The Laws of the Leash*, in the reign of Elizabeth I. By the time of George III, though, coursing was largely restricted to hares, with two greyhounds set on to chase a single hare and the killer hound being declared the winner – yet another opportunity for betting. In 1776 the notoriously eccentric and ultimately insane George Walpole, 3rd earl of Orford, established the first modern coursing club at Swaffham in Norfolk along with twenty-five colleagues, each of whom named a hound with a different letter of the alphabet. Others followed.

A similar process happened with the hunting of game birds. In older times pheasants and partridges had been snared with nets at ground level, but in 1735 the *Sportsman's Dictionary* started to refer to the new practice of 'shooting flying'. By the end of the century more accurate, faster-loading guns made it easier to bag large numbers of birds by adopting the French practice of a 'battue' shoot, in which beaters and shooters all marched towards the coverts where the birds were hidden and the shooters took aim at the birds as they flew away. Some, like one commentator of 1792, thought that 'the rage for shooting was never at a higher pitch than at present and the art of shooting flying is arrived at tolerable perfection',[20] but others considered such an unfair practice 'unworthy of any gentleman aspiring to the title of an English sportsman'.[21] Such considerations barely made the nobility pause before reloading as they adopted another innovation – the drive hunt, in which the beaters drove the birds towards the shooters, thereby making them fly higher and faster. These changes made a dramatic difference. *The Times* reported in 1836 that a single battue shoot at Lord Mostyn's estate at Pengwern in Flintshire had taken five hundred head of game. In 1840 James Harris, 2nd earl of Malmesbury, reckoned the total number of animals he had killed across thirty-nine years of shooting was 54,082. There was even a frisson of shame about these numbers. In his later years George Thomas, 6th earl of Albemarle, a Liberal politician who had served as an equerry to Prince Augustus, duke of Sussex, and private secretary to Lord John Russell as Prime Minister, recollected shooting at Holkham in Norfolk in the 1820s when 'the quantity of game killed in three months was probably not much more than it is now the fashion to slaughter in as many days'.[22] He knew what he was talking about. He had been brought up at his father the 4th earl's residence Elvedon Hall, where five thousand birds were bagged every year.

This mass slaughter meant that estates had to adopt careful strategies for preserving their stock of birds, solely so as to kill them. Thus, towards the end of the eighteenth century, the earl of Pembroke paid a shilling for every wild pheasant egg brought in to be hatched at Wilton; the duke of Richmond spent £385 a year on stock preservation at Goodwood, importing more than a thousand eggs from France and eradicating three hundred rats, hawks, owls, pole-cats and other predators; and similar figures were spent at Audley End and Longleat. Yet again the exclusive rights of the landowning class were jealously guarded. In case a tenant might get some idea into his head that he had a right to some of the game on the land he rented, leases were drawn up that stipulated that all game was the preserve of the landlord and that tenants should not allow anyone on to their land except those of some consequence. So, in 1770, Thomas Bruce, the young 7th earl of Elgin, was advised that since there was a shortage of game on his estates, it would be perfectly legitimate to forbid access to anyone other than 'persons of some consequence'.[23] James Grimston, earl of Verulam, was so jealous of his game at Gorhambury near St Albans that he angrily pronounced in the 1820s that all the game birds on the estates were his – and that if necessary he had plenty of gamekeepers to enforce his rights. This protectiveness could be something of a double-edged sword. In 1787 the young earl of Darnley was advised 'not so closely [to] imitate his Father's example in the preservation of game, as to deprive himself of that influence in the country to which he was justly entitled by his rank and fortune'.[24]

By the nineteenth century shooting was a form of country entertainment, and shooting parties became a fixed part of the noble calendar. A couple of instances a hundred years apart give the general impression of its enthusiastic embrace. In January 1822 Granville Leveson-Gower, a former ambassador to Russia and France, and a man described as 'the original stuffed-shirt – starch outside, sawdust within',[25] hosted a shooting party at Wherstead in Suffolk. He was not as grand as his elder half-brother, the exorbitantly wealthy duke of Sutherland, but he had been made a viscount in 1815 and Wherstead had better hunting than his main home Stone Park in Staffordshire. His guests included the Master-General of the Ordnance – and notoriously bad shot – the duke of Wellington (who held shooting parties of his own at Stratfield Saye); the recently appointed under-secretary for Foreign Affairs, Richard Meade, 3rd earl of Clanwilliam; the writer and politician George Lamb, who was the younger brother of the second Viscount Melbourne; and Gower's young son Frederick. The *Sporting Magazine* rejoiced that 'His Lordship's very extensive preserves afforded abundant sport; and we understand upwards of two hundred head of game, comprising pheasants and hares, were bagged each day. The pheasants killed were almost all cock birds, and being disposed in regular order presented to the eye of the sportsman a most gratifying spectacle.'[26] To be precise, on the first day the group bagged 2 partridges, 151 pheasants, 6 woodcocks, 70 hares and 36 rabbits. The event was such a success that Wellington returned the following year, when he accidentally shot his host in the face and a doctor had to be called from Ipswich to remove as many of the pellets as possible. Nearly a century later Francis, 7th Earl Cowper, died as one of the wealthiest men in the land, with 37,869 acres to his name and homes at Brocket Hall, Wrest Park and Panshanger. Having no children, and having lost his brother, two sisters and two brothers-in-law, he left Panshanger to his niece Ettie (Ethel) Fane. She and her husband, the politician and sportsman William Grenfell, Baron Desborough (he swam Niagara Falls, fenced, rowed, punted, played cricket and tennis, climbed the Matterhorn and shot big game in Africa), already had another grand home at Taplow Court in Buckinghamshire, so Panshanger was little more than a holiday home, but in 1914 their shooting parties there despatched more than 7,000 pheasants, 1,000 partridges and 250 hares.

Foxes had long been killed out of necessity as inedible pests by farmers and estate managers, but when the hunting of wild deer declined thanks to the enclosure of fields and forests, the landed class began to look to foxes to replace their lost thrills. This brought a different logic to the business of breeding horses and hounds, as, unlike hares, which run straight and lay little scent, foxes seek cover but lay a discernible trail, which scent-hounds can follow. Hounds would now be bred for their speed, stamina and nose. Thomas Boothby of Tooley Park in Leicestershire was probably the first to take hunting down this avenue, but when his son-in-law Hugo Meynell bought Nether Hall while still a minor in 1753, near the open-wooded Charnwood Forest in Leicestershire, and renamed it Quorn Hall, he amalgamated Boothby's pack with another he bought from Henry, 7th Baron Arundell of Wardour, thereby creating the Quorn Hunt. Meynell transformed the hunt. Instead of hunting when the fox was tired and sluggish after its early morning meal, he initiated meetings in the mid-morning, when it would run further and faster. He introduced rituals – the blooding of initiates, the award of the brush to the first huntsman on the scene of the kill and the presentation of the carcass to the hounds – and his form of hunting rapidly caught the imagination of the aristocracy, for whom it became more a passion than a pastime. Several peers and members of the hereditary gentry started or led fox hunts. Charles Fitzroy, 2nd duke of Grafton, set up a pack in the early part of the eighteenth century and his son was such an ardent lover of the chase and the turf (and his mistress) that his political career suffered. The Tarporley Club founded in Cheshire in 1762 included among its members the Earl Grosvenor, Viscount Combermere, Lord Delamere and sons of the earls of Stamford and Barrymore. In 1765 John, Earl Spencer, bought new hounds for the existing pack at Pytchley, of which he was master, and started a regular pattern of alternating the hunting between Pytchley and his house at Althorp. He hunted almost up until his death and was succeeded as master by his son the more cerebral 2nd earl. So too the 4th Earl Fitzwilliam started a pack at Milton in 1769 and was followed as master by his son the 5th earl in 1833. By 1781 the noted huntsman Peter Beckford could state without fear of contradiction in his popular book *Thoughts on Hunting* that 'foxhunting is now become the amusement of gentlemen: nor need any gentleman be ashamed of it'.[27] In 1787 William Vane, 3rd earl of Darlington (later duke of Cleveland), founded the Raby pack with which he hunted across Yorkshire and County Durham, managing to clock up ninety-one days hunting to hounds and forty-nine kills in the 1804–5 season alone. To cap it all, the Prince of Wales took to fox-hunting in 1793. By 1850 there were well over a hundred packs, fourteen of which were each directly and solely funded by the local lord.

The popularity of the new sport produced a sharp irony. Far from eradicating foxes as predatory vermin, hunts went to considerable lengths to make sure there were enough foxes to hunt. Fitzwilliam paid between three and four guineas for a bred fox; foxes were imported and sold at Leadenhall Market; hunts protected foxes from being stolen and attacked farmers who killed them without a hunt as 'vulpicides'. The social nature of the hunt was enhanced, too. In 1769 the Tarporley Club in Cheshire swapped their blue coats for red, and soon tight scarlet coats with five brass buttons became standard. The number of riders in 'the field' rose, often reaching several hundred once horseboxes were installed on trains. With so many horses galloping and leaping in close proximity, there was a real sense of danger, which thrilled the fast set of young nobles, who paid little consideration to the crops, walls, fences and gates that were damaged or trampled underfoot. A court ruling of 1788 gave them freedom to ride over any man's enclosure with impunity, but when George Capel, 5th earl of Essex, barred the gate on his estates at Cassiobury to his half-brother the Revd William Capel at the head of the Old Berkeley pack and the hunt ran riot, the earl sued his brother for trespass and won when the judge, Lord Ellenborough, decided that the issue at hand was whether the defendants were truly intent on killing vermin or were merely disporting themselves.

Some have argued that fox-hunting was the most inclusive of blood sports as no noble qualification was required to participate. Yet hunting attire, hunt horses and packs of hounds were prohibitively expensive for anyone other than the wealthy. Nor, in theory, were women excluded from fox-hunting, although the hard riding demands of leaping ditches and fences made it difficult for women to participate while dressed in long riding habits and seated to one side, and plenty of huntsmen looked down their noses on women who hunted. Nevertheless, Emily, the dowager marchioness of Salisbury, was such a regular participant that she succeeded her husband as master of the Hatfield Hunt after his death in 1823 despite being seventy-two, and was painted by James Pollard taking the field at Hatfield the following year dressed in a sky-blue riding habit and surveying the scene from an eyeglass on the top of her whip. Charles Brindley, writing under his pseudonym of Harry Hieover, reckoned that she 'rode as straight as I have held any gentlewomen should ride ... and nothing was done that could for a moment compromise the marchioness, the wife of the noble owner of the pack'.[28] In 1836 *The Times* commented that it was not aware 'of any picture more beautiful than an elegant female on horseback',[29] and according to the *Sportsman* in 1838, Lady Elizabeth Belgrave (later Countess Grosvenor and marchioness of Westminster) often joined the Cheshire hounds at Eaton Hall and 'witnessed the find, and if it so happened that lanes or other means of keeping near the hounds without the necessity of jumping, happened to occur, she continued to follow, and under such circumstances we once observed her up at the death'.[30] Likewise Lady

Helen Lowther, the daughter-in-law of the 2nd earl of Lonsdale, rode to hounds with the Melton Hunt in Leicestershire, and Kate Stanley, later Viscountess Amberley, wrote home after her first hunt that she much preferred fox-hunting to parties.

This criticism may seem unfair. After all, many thousands of ordinary members of the public enjoyed attending the race meetings that the aristocracy initiated and, certainly in the early days, people hunted out of necessity. But the illogicality of how hunting developed cannot be avoided. Noble deer parks entailed fences, and when deer could no longer roam from forest to forest and were penned in, it was difficult to argue that chasing them was a noble pursuit. Often a tame deer would be released and recaptured once the pretence of stalking it was done. Likewise foxes would be bagged and released for a hunt when they were tired and pungent. Changes in gun manufacture made possible the mass slaughter of game birds, so their eggs had to be imported and hatched artificially under pullets. The hunting of foxes was never a utilitarian business, and its impetus lay entirely in the thrill of the chase rather than the eradication of vermin. In effect, hunting had become less the honourable pursuit of wild game and more a wild game to entertain the well-heeled. As one gentleman argued in 1817, hunting had a logic to it when 'wild animals were chased over wild country by wilder men', but when the object was 'a valuable, half-tame, and exotic bird . . . guarded in its coverts by legions of gamekeepers' it made little sense to keep the game laws.[31] Moreover, it was not that the aristocracy did not have moral qualms about killing sentient creatures. They did. Parliament banned cock- and dog-fighting and the baiting of bulls, bears and badgers in the Cruelty to Animals Act of 1835 – but these were working-class pastimes; the chasing, hounding and killing of wild animals, whether edible or not, was left untouched by legislation for the simple reason that those who drafted the legislation liked to stalk, shoot and ride to hounds. It is difficult not to spy hypocrisy. When it was mooted in 1796 that the property qualification for hunting should be removed, Sir Richard Sutton, Bart, a client of the 2nd duke of Newcastle and a man described as 'a man of coarse and almost rugged exterior',[32] said that he was opposed to the measure because it would favour poachers who were 'a class of person much too insolent already'.[33]

The aristocracy has always been in thrall to its own antiquity and enjoyed displaying its opulence to the common herd. One particular brand of aristocratic condescension embraced by a set of Victorian nobles known as 'Young England' tried to revive the 'olden times' and live by a code of noblesse oblige. Dilapidated ancestral mansions like Haddon Hall (one of the duke of Rutland's several properties) were romanticized – along with the medieval era and its old nobility.

CHAPTER 13

LEAVE US STILL OUR OLD NOBILITY

WHEN ELIZABETH HOWARD MARRIED John Manners, the 5th duke of Rutland, in 1799 she was already well accustomed to the luxurious, wealthy and peripatetic life of the English nobility. Her father, the 5th earl of Carlisle, had spent much of his youth carousing round Europe and much of his early married life at the card tables and louche salons of London, retiring to his mansion at Castle Howard only to let his agricultural rental income catch up with his debts. But having taken his seat in the Lords in January 1770, and having largely reined in his financial exuberance, he discovered a political ambition that led to six years as a minister, including two successful years in Dublin as a grandiose Lord Lieutenant, the king's chief governor and viceroy in Ireland. What with the obligatory annual spell at his London home, 12 Grosvenor Place, for the parliamentary season, and regular visits to his other properties, most notably the dilapidated priory at Lanercost and the equally tired Naworth Castle in Cumbria, which was described in 1801 as 'a true specimen of ancient inconvenience, of magnificence and littleness',[1] he was, like most of his peers, constantly on tour.

Elizabeth's young husband was just as grand as her father. The celebrations for his coming of age at Belvoir Castle on 4 January 1799 had been the talk of the nation. The Prince of Wales had attended, as had the 5th duke and duchess of Beaufort and their son the marquess of Worcester, the 5th duke of Argyll and his son, the marquess of Lorne, the earls of Westmorland, Winchelsea and Exeter, and a caravanserai of seventy coaches full of other gentlefolk. Even the regency rake Beau

269

Brummell made an appearance (only to be described as 'not altogether effeminate [as] he could both shoot and ride').[2] No expense was spared. The house was decorated with artificial flowers, variegated lights and transparencies with allegorical motifs. Six bullocks and sixteen sheep were roasted for all the servants who had ever worked on the estate, and saddles of mutton and hot plum-puddings were served up for Rutland's tenants. After dinner at six, the duke and his mother, who was 'dressed in a profusion of diamonds', presided over a firework display with rockets, 'brilliant suns and stars', vertical wheels and the Rutland coat of arms displayed 'in rayonant fire'. The dancing carried on until daylight, when it was found that several guests had got so drunk that they had lost their footing on the steep hill up to the castle and had 'slept in the fields till morning and suffered severely for their folly by the frost'.[3]

Just under four months later, on 22 April, Elizabeth and John were married, and when within a few weeks he departed to join his regiment in Ireland, she wrote to her 'dearest my beloved Duke' that she hoped 'that when we meet, it will be to never, never part'.[4] The duke protested similar affections, but in fact the two were regularly apart. Often he was in London, 'on business', or with his regiment in Ireland, or hunting for weeks on end with the Belvoir or at the largely dilapidated Haddon Hall, or studying his thoroughbreds' form at Cheveley Park. On other occasions, when she was not pregnant with one of their ten children, the duchess was taking the sea air at Yarmouth or Ramsgate or entertaining at their sumptuous London home, 16 Arlington Street, where her neighbours included the earl and countess of Yarborough (at no. 17), the marquess and marchioness of Salisbury (at no. 20), the duke and duchess of Beaufort (at no. 22), the earl and countess of Bath (at 80 Piccadilly) and the marquess of Lansdowne nearby in Berkeley Square.

Although Elizabeth was thoroughly aware of the need to produce a healthy son and heir – a feat that proved elusive until the birth of their eighth child, Charles, in 1815 – that was not her only role. The Rutlands' several homes provided a full-time occupation for a wife with as keen an artistic flair as Elizabeth. The hiring and firing of staff lay largely in her hands, as did the day-to-day management of budgets, provisions, repairs and entertainment. In addition, Elizabeth took a particular interest in the major refurbishments of the ducal properties. She set about refashioning Belvoir and its gardens with the assistance of the fashionable architect James Wyatt, who had already built or rebuilt noble houses in the neo-gothic ecclesiastical style at Wycombe Abbey, Fonthill Abbey and Trentham Hall. Wyatt died in 1813 and in 1816 a fire tore through much of Belvoir, doing at least £120,000 worth of damage and destroying several of the Rutlands' Old Masters; but little daunted, Elizabeth started afresh with a new architect, Sir James Thornton. This became her passion. She energetically supported a string of other building projects. She was 'enchanted' at the idea of 'a National Gallery, for Pictures and Statues',[5] she campaigned for the building of a new embankment quay on the north of the Thames (though she came to abhor gothic, which she thought 'very beautiful in its way for Churches and Cathedrals, but not in the least appropriate for Quays'),[6] and she tutored her intimate friend the young duke of York into rebuilding Godolphin House on the Mall as York (later Lancaster) House according to her preferences. The sums spent at Belvoir were significant – another £82,000 (£7.3 million in 2017) on top of the restorations after the fire – but the work was so slow that when the duchess died of a burst appendix in 1825 it was left to her grieving widower to complete her designs. Not until 1829 was he able to invite friends for his birthday celebrations and the opening of the completed works. Wellington's friend Mrs Arbuthnot was full of admiration for the newly named Elizabeth Saloon: 'It is the most magnificent room I ever saw ... At the end of the room, in front of an immense looking glass, is a marble statue of the late Duchess, exceedingly like her. It is very proper to have her there for she was the builder of the castle, & Belvoir is indebted to her for all its beauty & decorations.'[7]

The proliferation of grand country houses and the parliamentary and social requirements of 'the Season', which ran from April to August, meant that this pattern of perpetual peregrination was the aristocratic norm. It was certainly the case with the dukes and duchesses of Devonshire well into the twentieth century. Their two main homes were Chatsworth in Derbyshire and Devonshire House on Piccadilly in London, and each was as grand as the other. Chatsworth, the creation of Bess of Hardwick, had come to William Cavendish, the first earl of

Devonshire, when he bought it from his elder brother for £10,000 after their mother's death in 1608, since when it had grown out of all proportion, especially under the profligate eye of the unmarried and unassuming 6th duke, who added a wing, created an enormous conservatory and increased the family collection of books and sculptures. By the time the Liberal Unionist politician Spencer Cavendish – known as 'Harty-Tarty' after his courtesy title as marquess of Hartington – became the 8th duke in 1891 and married his long-time mistress, Louise, the widow of the duke of Manchester, the following year, Chatsworth was probably the greatest country house in England. Devonshire House was in the same league. The original building on the site between Stratton and Berkeley Streets had been built by Baron Berkeley of Stratton and had been the home of one of Charles II's mistresses, the duchess of Cleveland, before the duke of Devonshire purchased it in 1696. A fire in 1733 had enabled the duke to rebuild it in the austere Palladian fashion, and his successors had poured money into modish upgrades. In addition to a library worthy of Alexandria and eleven gilded state rooms, it gained porticoes, an external double staircase, a matching internal 'crystal' staircase with a glass handrail and newel posts (thanks to the ubiquitous James Wyatt), a saloon with a domed ceiling, and a double-height ballroom lined in gold brocade. It was here that the Devonshires spent the London Season, attending parliament and flitting from one ball to another. Within three decades of the 8th duke's succession it was gone, demolished in 1924.

The whole point of these houses was ostentatiously impressive (and impressively ostentatious) entertainment, and the Devonshires took their role seriously. On 2 July 1897, keen to promote her husband the Lord President of the Council as a possible successor to the marquess of Salisbury as prime minister, the duchess held a ball at Devonshire House to commemorate Queen Victoria's diamond jubilee, and instructed the seven hundred guests to appear in 'allegorical or historical costume dated earlier than 1820'. Fancy-dress parties were becoming popular – the countess of Warwick had held one at her castle in 1895 – but Louise's cast list was particularly impressive, including members of several royal families. Two hundred guests were photographed in their costumes, including the duchess of Newcastle as Princess Dashkova; the marchioness of

Londonderry as the Empress Maria Theresa; and Winston Churchill's American mother Jennie, who appeared as the Empress Theodora, wearing a gown by the haute couture designer Charles Worth and a crown with diamond and emerald pendants. Some of the guests had difficulty with their costumes. Lady Helena Gleichen, the artistic daughter of a German count, ditched the idea of coming as St Elisabeth of Hungary on the grounds that the headdress made her look disreputable, and appeared as Joan of Arc instead (with Sir Arthur Sullivan carrying her helmet before her) – and her mother was disconcerted to hear that her own character, the Margravine of Anspach, although an ancestor, 'was not at all respectable'.[8] As for the duke of Devonshire, he greeted guests as the Emperor Charles V, while Louise was borne aloft on a precarious palanquin, dripping in pearls as Zenobia, queen of Palmyra. *The Times* thought 'nothing more harmonious could well be imagined',[9] but not everyone enjoyed the event. It was so hot and congested that many wearied of the charade, and Princess Alexandra (dressed as Marguerite de Valois) declared herself horribly bored. Consuelo Vanderbilt, the American heiress who had very reluctantly married the 9th duke of Marlborough two years earlier (and came dressed as the wife of the French ambassador at the court of Catherine of Russia), recounted her walk home to Spencer House across Green Park: 'On the grass, lay the dregs of humanity. Human beings too dispirited or sunk to find work or favour, they sprawled in sodden stupor, pitiful representatives of the submerged tenth. In my billowing period dress, I must have seemed to them a vision of wealth and youth, and I thought soberly that they must hate me. But they only looked, and some even had a compliment to enliven my progress.'[10] Consuelo and Louise, incidentally, were never great friends. The American, whose marriage was annulled in 1926, described the 'double duchess' as 'a raddled old woman, covering her wrinkles with paint, and her pate with a brown wig. Her mouth was a red gash, and from it, when she saw me, issued a stream of abuse.'[11]

Devonshire House was an impressive home for the height of the season, but almost as soon as parliament rose in July the Devonshires decamped to Eastbourne, where they spent a month at Compton Place, a well-appointed house that had come to the 7th duke in 1858 and was said to have one of the most opulent bedrooms in England. Then, for the start of the grouse shooting on the 'glorious twelfth' of August, they moved on to Bolton Abbey in Yorkshire; and from September to early spring they were at Chatsworth. To complete the year's tour the duke and duchess would spend the later part of the spring at the 700-year-old Lismore Castle in County Waterford, which had been in the family since 1758 and had been transformed by the 6th duke into a commodious and romantic gothic revival fortress; and after a few weeks here fishing for salmon in the Blackwater river, they would return to London in April for another season.

Few members of the nobility had quite so many properties as the Devonshires, but the annual progress from London to the country and back again, with a visit to another noble house for good measure, was a settled aspect of Victorian aristocratic life. Just as the Rutlands had Belvoir, Cheveley and Haddon, the Norfolks had Arundel Castle and Worksop Manor, the Portlands had Bolsover Castle and Welbeck Abbey, the earls of Portsmouth owned Hurstbourne Park in Hampshire and Eggesford in Devon, and the Talbot earls of Shrewsbury had the baroque masterpiece Heythrop Park in Oxfordshire (until it burnt down in 1831), plus Grafton Manor near Bromsgrove and two properties in Staffordshire: Augustus Pugin's gothic creation Alton Towers, and the Jacobean mansion Ingestre Hall. At the very top of the scale were the dukes of Sutherland. The 1st duke rebuilt Lilleshall Hall in Shropshire and purchased the newly completed York House in the 1820s; the 2nd commissioned Sir Charles Barry to transform Trentham Park near Stoke-on-Trent, Dunrobin Castle near Golspie and Cliveden in the Chilterns, leaving them with five palatial properties dotted across the kingdom.

It was not just the wealthy aristocrats who toured these properties. Even before the railways, it became fashionable for the shopkeeping and middle classes to visit the homes of the aristocracy, a pastime made all the easier by the fact that the owners were rarely in residence. Some aristocrats liked showing off their collections of international booty to their peers and the general public. Thomas Howard, 21st earl of Arundel, created a gallery at Arundel House on the Strand in the early seventeenth century so as to exhibit his collection of ancient marbles; in the 1730s and 1740s James Brydges, duke of Chandos, whose period as Paymaster-General of the Forces abroad during the War of the Spanish Succession netted him a dodgy fortune, actively encouraged visitors to the vast edifice he constructed at Cannons, and charged them to see his marble bathrooms and his collection of Caravaggio, Raphael, Poussin and Michelangelo; and when George Herbert, 11th earl of Pembroke, commissioned Wyatt to modernize Wilton House in 1801 he expressly asked for more space to exhibit his paintings and sculptures. But the advent of the steam engine in the mid-nineteenth century provided the aristocracy with a huge new opportunity to show their wares. The growth in this stately home industry was exponential. Horace Walpole reckoned that fewer than three hundred visitors came to his cornucopic Strawberry Hill in the 1780s and 1790s; by the 1820s at least six thousand visitors to Leamington were making a detour to Warwick Castle every year, in the 1840s Chatsworth regularly coped with eight hundred visitors every Sunday in the summer months, and Knole House saw its admissions rise from five hundred a year at the start of the century to five thousand by the 1860s. The paraphernalia of modern tourism became ubiquitous. Guide-books recounted the aristocratic history of each property and detailed the fine furnishings and artworks. County guides like the *Murray's Handbooks* and Methuen *Little Guides* suggested where, when and how to visit and established a well-trodden circuit. This day-trip business was lucrative. Railway companies advertised cheap excursion trains to Chatsworth to see the great conservatory, or to Alton Towers to see the display of rhododendrons and listen to the earl of Shrewsbury's band, and when at the turn of the century Henry James visited Kenilworth, he found 'a row of ancient pedlars outside the castle-wall, hawking twopenny pamphlets and photographs . . . and the usual respectable young woman to open the castle-gate and to receive the usual sixpenny fee'.[12]

So, in the 1830s you could see Cobham Hall, the home of Emma, the dowager countess of Darnley, with its picture gallery and dining room by James Wyatt, its mock-Jacobean library and its Elizabethan façade, any Friday between the hours of eleven and four, all for a shilling ticket purchased at a nearby Gravesend bookseller. Likewise, in the 1850s the regulations for viewing Woburn Abbey, the country seat of the duke of Bedford, stipulated that on application to a Mr Bennett at the park farm office between ten and three in summer and ten and two in winter, visitors could obtain up to two tickets admitting six persons each so long as they left their 'sticks, whips, parasols or umbrellas' in the waiting-room.[13] As for Eaton Hall in Cheshire, Robert Grosvenor, the 1st marquess of Westminster, spent two decades transforming it at great expense into a spectacular gothic mansion and was rewarded with three or four thousand visitors a year in the 1840s. His son Richard, the 2nd marquess, had another set of alterations done, which left *Murray's* unimpressed: 'the style, Florid Ecclesiastical Gothic, was a mistake ... and although nearly a million has been expended on it, the result is not satisfactory'.[14] Visitor numbers duly declined until the 3rd marquess, Hugh (duke from 1874), spent another £800,000 on a third major rebuilding by Alfred Waterhouse. Nikolaus Pevsner pronounced 'this Wagnerian palace the most ambitious instance of Gothic Revival domestic architecture anywhere in the country';[15] and the tourists agreed, seventeen thousand of them turning up every year by 1891. The profits supposedly went to local institutions, but the impetus for the revamp of Eaton Hall was not charity. The Grosvenors were as likely to be at Grosvenor House in London or Motcombe House in Dorset or touring on the continent as in residence at Eaton, so it is difficult not to come to the conclusion that this extravagance was another bid for attention in another phase in the aristocratic passion for displaying their status and opulence.

Open access did occasion some inconvenience for their lordships. Such was the racket when staff laid protective druggets over the carpets three days a week for tours of the state rooms at Blenheim that Alfred Spencer-Churchill, the son of the 6th duke of Marlborough, fled to his room. At Ashburnham Place in Sussex the lady of the house was nearly knocked down a flight of stairs by sightseers and consequently decided to close it to the public; and in 1843 a visitor stole a small but valuable brown crystal from the conservatory at Chatsworth. When Harriet, the widowed countess Granville, visited her sister Georgiana, the countess of Carlisle, at Castle Howard in 1853 she wrote to her nephew George of her experience of meeting the tourists. 'The cheap excursion trains

N?.3. *Elevation of the South Front of Wentworth Castle, in Yorkshire, The Seat of The R.t Hon.ble the Earl of Strafford.*

Horses – and hunting – have been a perennial passion for the aristocracy. Emily, the dowager marchioness of Salisbury, took to the field at the head of the Hatfield Hunt (**top**) in her seventies in 1824. A few years earlier, when the 2nd marquess of Rockingham rebuilt Wentworth-Woodhouse (**above**) with the longest façade in Europe, he commissioned portraits of his favourite horses for the empty walls, including Whistlejacket (**left**) by George Stubbs.

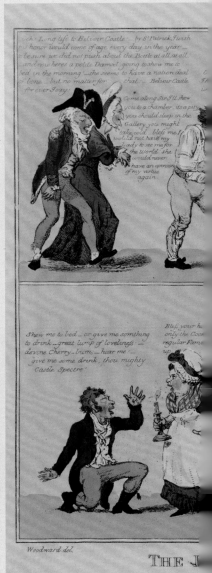

Many noblewomen ran several households
simultaneously and were skilled designers.
Elizabeth, the duchess of Rutland (**above**),
died before the works on Belvoir Castle
and the drawing room she now graces were
completed. There was considerable hypocrisy
about sex: while the laws against adultery
were vigorously enforced against the lower
orders, many peers openly kept mistresses –
and the 10th earl of Pembroke displayed a
naked statue of his lover Giovanna Baccelli
(**top**) in his marital bedroom at Wilton Park.

Almost invariably in Britain the whole aristocratic inheritance went to the eldest son. This placed a heavy onus on noble wives to produce a male heir, whose coming of age was extravagantly celebrated. At the 5th duke of Rutland's party at Belvoir Castle in 1799, the riotous drinking went on till the morning.

The parliamentary season required that the nobility keep palaces in the capital, but like many others the duke and duchess of Devonshire lived a peripatetic life travelling between their several country properties, including Chatsworth House (**left**) and Lismore Castle in County Waterford (**below**), . . .

. . . and every year marking the start of the grouse shooting on the 'glorious twelfth' of August with a visit to their 30,000-acre moorland estate at Bolton Abbey (**below**).

Aristocrats gave full rein to their narcissism and extravagance, spending lavishly on costumes, jewellery and portraits. For her 700-guest fancy dress ball in 1897 the duchess of Devonshire dressed as Zenobia, queen of Palmyra (**left**), while Daisy Brooke, the countess of Warwick (**below**) scandalized Society by appearing at the 1902 coronation without any diamonds.

SAVE

MENTMORE FOR THE NATION

The twentieth century saw peers pleading poverty and seeking public subsidies for their redundant palaces. When the government refused to buy Mentmore Towers from the earl of Rosebery in 1977 (**left**) he sold the contents for £6.5 million. Devonshire House on Piccadilly (**below**) was dismantled in 1924. The marquess of Shelburne sold Lansdowne House on Berkeley Square in 1929 and its neoclassical dining room (**bottom**) was purchased by the Metropolitan Museum of Art in 1954.

A string of cack-handed political interventions contributed to the aristocracy's fall from grace. Several British peers flirted with Italian fascism, the 7th marquess of Londonderry (**above, left**) repeatedly visited Hitler, whom his marchioness described as 'simple, dignified, humble', and the 11th marquess of Lothian (**left**) praised Neville Chamberlain for refusing to believe that 'the Nazis were incorrigible'.

Today the marquess of Cholmondeley (**top left**) is still guaranteed a seat in the House of Lords, the duke of Westminster (**left**) remains the world's richest man under 30, the duke of Marlborough's funeral at Blenheim (**above**) was conducted with customary pomp, and the racist Viscount St Davids (**below**) was imprisoned in 2017 for offering £5,000 to anyone who would 'accidentally' run over Gina Miller.

enchant me,' she wrote. 'They sit about with their baskets of provisions as if it were the Bois de Boulogne ... One lady from Wakefield told me it was all very fine, but that she looked in vain for Lord Carlisle's picture.'[16] And when Harry Vane, 2nd duke of Cleveland, bought Battle Abbey in 1857 he was considerably put out that eight hundred visitors a day came to the house 'and peered through the window of the study ... till they fairly stared him out of countenance'.[17]

Yet there was a growing feeling that the aristocracy had a duty to the nation to open their doors. When a fire ripped through Warwick Castle on Sunday, 3 December 1871, a restoration fund was established to help out the straitened earl of Warwick. John Ruskin was scandalized and wrote to the *Daily Telegraph*: 'If a noble family cannot rebuild their own castle, in God's name let them live in the nearest ditch till they can.'[18] But the newspaper responded that the public should contribute on the grounds that 'an earl of Warwick who would make his whole castle his own in the spirit of an inhospitable curmudgeon, who would shut out all eyes but his own from the feast within his walls, is a being so opposed to every English tradition that it is difficult to realise him'.[19] *The Times* was even more forthright in defence of the embarrassed earl, declaring that the great unwashed should be grateful. 'The public,' it thundered,

> a chartered libertine, steps in and enjoys a glimpse of Paradise – as much as is good for any of us – at the moderate cost of a shilling a head for a party of five ... If there should happen to be among us any survivors of the good old stock exhausting themselves to keep up a monument of England as it used to be, some of us may be thankful for the opportunity to allow ourselves not unworthy of the country we have the good fortune to live in.[20]

In the end the earl got £9,000, the hall was restored and the tours started up again, with the added attraction of the tale of how the earl's younger children and their governess had fled the fire over a rooftop.

The tone of the guide-books was intensely sentimental. William Howitt's *Visits to Remarkable Places*, for instance, claimed in 1840 that visitors to Penshurst Place, the home of the Sidneys, 'know they will not only tread the same ground, and gaze on the same scenes as these patriots and heroes, but that these noble spirits have themselves collected for their recreation, works of art which would make the spot one of the strongest attraction, even if it were not hallowed by their memories.'[21] Howitt went on to promise: 'Here you will see Sir Philip Sidney, as the boy and the man; you walk under his oak ... you see Algernon Sidney, not merely as the stern patriot, planning the overthrow of monarchy, but as the delicate child of a stately line, daintily fed in his separate chamber.'[22] Likewise, the *Penny Magazine* commented that standing in the great hall at Knole 'at once makes us centuries older; we not only think of, but feel with, the past. The loneliness seems suddenly to be broken, the bustle of countless attendants going in and out begins, the tables groan with the profusion of the feast, bright jewels and still brighter eyes begin to sparkle.'[23]

Some sought to capitalize on this romantic attitude towards the past, most notably the second surviving son of the 5th duke of Rutland and his duchess, Lord John Manners, who in the early years of Victoria's reign formed a loose grouping of Tory MPs, including Disraeli and George Smythe, the son of the diplomat 6th Viscount Strangford, that was known as 'Young England'. Manners loved to hark back to the times of yore. He liked Gilbert Scott for his gothic architecture and Sir Walter Scott for his Tory romanticism. He published poetry, in which he detected portents 'in these our days of restlessness and strife', and warned

> that England once again may hear,
> The shouts of Roundhead and of Cavalier.[24]

An unambiguous royalist, who cited Strafford, Laud and the Stuart kings as his heroes, he declared in another poem:

> Let wealth and commerce, laws and learning die,
> But leave us still our old Nobility![25]

In addition to his support for a nostalgic re-creation of the Olympic Games sponsored by his second cousin John Weld, 2nd Baron Forester, at Much Wenlock, Manners made much of the historical connections of Haddon Hall, his family's ancestral seat, which had remained largely uninhabited and untouched – and was consequently a particular favourite on Thomas Cook's tours. The *Derbyshire Courier* recounted one event he held at the Hall on 26 August 1848, when he indulged in a bout of intense nostalgia. Haddon had not been lived in for more than a century, he said, yet it 'laughed at Time's decay'. Warming to his theme, he enjoined his audience to 'cultivate every opportunity that may be offered you to reunite the old ties of loyalty, and affection, and good fellowship; let the rural fete and the cricket match, the merry-making and the dance, be celebrated on your lawns and in your parks.' There were cheers at this point, so he carried on: 'While other less-favoured nations are tossed on the stormy billows of revolution and civil war, England shall sit secure on her island throne.'[26]

This *noblesse oblige* was Manners' driving political instinct. He sat as an MP off and on from 1841 until 1888, when his elder brother died unmarried, leaving him as the 7th duke. He was a minister throughout the Derby and Disraeli administrations and Chancellor of the Duchy of Lancaster from 1886 to 1892 under Salisbury. His viewpoint was unremittingly patrician – he believed in a strong monarchy bound to an established church – yet many of his instincts had an egalitarian hue. He argued in favour of holidays for workers, he toured the industrial areas of Lancashire and he supported reform of factory conditions. When Anthony Ashley-Cooper, Lord Ashley, brought forward his Factories Bill in the Commons in 1847 with its maximum ten-hour day, Manners supported him, pronouncing in a very long speech that 'the Tory Gentlemen of England ... had fought the fight of the poor against the rich, and had been fellow-soldiers with the weak and defenceless against the mighty and the strong, and to the best of their ability, had wielded the power which the Constitution reposed in them, to protect and defend the working-people of this country'.[27] None of this made him a radical. He expressly stated that 'he conscientiously believed all revolutions to be wrong'.[28] If anything, his was a wistful hope of a return to a time when landlord and peasant united in common pursuits like archery and dancing. Moreover, the *noblesse oblige* of these Tory Gentlemen of England had its limitations. It could not countenance social action, for instance; so when the black workforce erupted in Jamaica in

1865 Manners was in favour of harsh recriminations, and when the Reform League clamoured for more parliamentary reform in England the following year he strengthened the Home Secretary's resolve to retaliate with force. His belief in the inherent rights of the landed nobility made him a stout defender of the corn laws, and an early advocate of tariff reform and protectionist imperial preference as opposed to free trade. When a title finally came his way on the death of his brother, he sold Cheveley in 1893 claiming poverty, even though he was granted a pension of £1,200 a year from the government on retiring from public office.

Manners was not alone in this elevation of *noblesse oblige* as a national virtue. Disraeli exalted it in his novel *Coningsby* and in his assault on Peel's repeal of the corn laws in the 1840s. George Smythe, who was first elected to parliament in 1841 and broke with Disraeli and Manners by taking a post as under-secretary for foreign affairs in Peel's government in January 1846, was a similarly romantic Tory who believed in a regenerated aristocracy as the best bulwark against the rising tide of democracy. Smythe did not exactly live up to these high ideals, though. Within weeks of becoming a minister he was mired in scandal as it was rumoured that he had got the 3rd earl of Orford's daughter Dorothy Walpole pregnant and was ignominiously refusing to marry her; so after Peel's government fell in June he left for the continent. This was not Smythe's only liaison. He had affairs, among others, with the countess of Tankerville when he was twenty-two and she was fifty-seven, with the future countess of Stamford and Warrington, with the seventeen-year-old daughter of the Russian Count Stackleberg and with a couple of City heiresses. He provided Disraeli with a draft eulogy on Wellington, which was almost entirely plagiarized, and in 1853 he was found guilty of serial electoral corruption. His father had been little better, having sired several natural children and squirrelled away all his property to them by the time he died in 1855, leaving his formal heir with little more than his titles. Lord Lyttelton described George as a 'splendid failure', and even his mother lamented that 'when a man's ambition is dead, he has ceased to believe in himself'.[29]

✠

The Victorian aristocracy loved mythologizing a glorious past when lord and tenant had merrily wassailed together. For the hymn-writer John Mason Neale in 1853 this was the central story of Good King Wenceslas, who brought food and wine for the poor peasant gathering winter fuel:

> *Therefore, Christian men, be sure, wealth or rank possessing,*
> *Ye who now will bless the poor, shall yourselves find blessing.*

For another hymn-writer, Mrs Cecil Alexander, the message was even clearer:

> *The rich man in his castle,*
> *The poor man at his gate,*
> *God made them high and lowly,*
> *And ordered their estate.*

But you didn't have to go to church to get the *noblesse oblige* message. You could pick up Joseph Nash's *Mansions of England in the Olden Time* and see romanticized illustrations of Roundheads and Cavaliers happily sword-fighting on the grand staircase at Aston Hall, or ladies blissfully chatting in the cartoon gallery at Knole, or peasants, knights and lords revelling together in the banqueting hall at Haddon. This last image was the source of endless aristocratic romance. By the middle of the century an elaborate myth had taken hold, according to which the young Elizabethan heiress of Haddon, Dorothy Vernon, fell in love with John Manners, the second son of the earl of Rutland, defied her father, and eloped with her lover during a crowded ball in 1563. Guide-books pointed to the route the suitors had supposedly taken, a short story was published in 1849, and in 1892 Sir Arthur Sullivan produced a light opera *Haddon Hall* and moved the drama to the civil war for added effect. Next came a novel, *Dorothy Vernon of Haddon Hall*, then a play, and in 1924 a film starring Mary Pickford and Douglas Fairbanks. Manners' paeans of praise to the Olden Times had borne fruit to such an extent that, writing in the late twentieth century, Sir Nikolaus Pevsner said that 'he would indeed be hard put to it if he were asked to define what in the sensations of a first visit to Haddon Hall is due to the aesthetic and what to extraneous values'.[30]

Noblesse oblige was itself a convenient myth in a time of growing discontent about the inequities of society, when the aristocracy still wielded unfettered power, both as members of the House of Lords and in ministerial office. Although the number of government posts was far exceeded by the number of peers (by 1880 there were 431 members of the Lords, plus seven peeresses, 41 Scottish peers and 101 Irish), the landed aristocracy still held the majority of them. The premiership was almost constantly in aristocratic hands. Between 1852 and 1902 the Prime Minister was a member of the Lords for twenty-eight years out of fifty – and that is excluding nine years under Palmerston, who was an Irish viscount, and thirteen under Gladstone, whose merchant father received £106,769 in compensation for his 2,508 slaves in 1834 and owned Fasque estate in Scotland. Gladstone gave aristocrats eight out of fourteen seats in the Cabinet in 1880 and Salisbury eleven out of sixteen in 1885; in 1902 Salisbury's nephew Arthur Balfour appointed nine peers to his team in addition to six other members of the landed elite. Every single Foreign Secretary from 1809 until the appointment of Ramsay MacDonald in 1924 was a member of this titled landowning elite.

As for the House of Commons, it remained firmly in the aristocratic grip even after the parliamentary Reform Acts of 1832, 1867, 1884 and 1885. The 1892 parliament, for instance, included sons of the dukes of Richmond, Marlborough, Abercorn and Rutland, the marquesses of Bristol, Exeter, Waterford and Downshire, the earls of Derby and Wemyss, the Earls Manvers, Howe and Spencer, Viscount Hambledon, and the Barons Newton, Ashcombe, Coleridge, Scarsdale and Montagu of Beaulieu. With other aristocratic relatives aplenty – one estimate reckoned that sixty families supplied a third of the house – the Commons still felt like the embodiment of the landed interest.

A century after the French Revolution, the United Kingdom was unique in the world in preserving this aristocratic political predominance. France, where titles had been abolished, had fewer than a thousand estates of more than 1,000 acres and barely any of more than 10,000. The fact that ennoblement in the UK brought a seat in the Lords meant there was a theoretical if unstated limit on the number of peers, which gave a noble title the added lustre of exclusivity. The same was not true elsewhere. Italy had twelve thousand hereditary nobles by 1906, Prussia had well over twenty thousand, the Austro-Hungarian Empire a quarter of a million and Russia six hundred thousand. There was a reason for this. While the UK had retained the system of entails and primogeniture, so that title and estates remained together, Spain had outlawed entails and primogeniture in 1834, Russia and Prussia had virtually ceased to use them, and in most countries both patrimony and title were constantly being divided.

The British aristocracy, then, was uniquely powerful and prestigious. Its members went to the same schools and colleges, they joined the same clubs, they enjoyed the same pastimes. They retained substantial privileges, most notably the right to be tried by their peers rather than in a common court of law. This was not invoked very often – there were only six such trials after 1750 – but a particularly egregious example of its abuse occurred in 1841. James Brudenell, 7th earl of Cardigan, exhibited all the worst traits of a Victorian peer. He gambled excessively at his London clubs, he engaged in endless affairs with other men's wives, he resorted to violent punishments to instil discipline in the 11th Hussars, whose command he bought for £40,000, and he spent wildly on lavish entertainment at his country seat of Deene Park and on his steam yacht *Dryad*. At his death he left debts of more than £365,000. Most famously, in the Crimean War he acrimoniously fell out with his brother-in-law and superior, the earl of Lucan, and led the notorious cavalry charge straight into Russian cannon fire at Balaclava in 1854 that saw 113 out of 673 men killed and another 247 seriously injured. His bravery – or bravado – was rewarded with banquets and toasts and the sash of a Knight Commander of the Bath, all of which ignored the fact that in his patrician arrogance Cardigan had deemed the lives of lesser mortals dispensable. The hypocrisy at the heart of the British system was nowhere more evident than when Cardigan fought a duel in 1840, wounded his opponent and was tried 'before the right honourable the House of Peers in full Parliament, for felony on Tuesday the 16th day of February 1841'.[31]

The trial was laden with ceremonial: the Serjeant entered the

Chamber with the mace, followed by Black Rod with the Lord Steward's white staff of office, Garter King of Arms with his sceptre and the Lord Chief Justice, Thomas, Baron Denman, playing the role of Lord High Steward for the day in the absence of the Lord Chancellor. There was a roll call, beginning with the youngest baron, before Denman took his place in a chair of state placed on the second step of the throne. The curiously worded charge was read out, namely that Cardigan had 'with a certain pistol, then and there loaded with gunpowder and a leaden bullet, at and against one Harvey Garnett Phipps Tuckett ... then and there feloniously and unlawfully did shoot, with intent thereby, then and there feloniously, wilfully and of his malice aforethought, the said Harvey Garnett Phipps Tuckett to kill and murder'.[32] The proceedings, which lasted a single day, were a charade. At the outset the prosecuting Attorney-General, Sir John Campbell, made an extraordinary admission. 'I am rejoiced to think', he said, 'that the charge against the noble prisoner at the bar does not imply any degree of moral turpitude, and that if he should be found guilty the conviction will reflect no discredit upon the illustrious order to which he belongs.'[33] Quite why attempted murder should not incur the charge of moral turpitude in Campbell's eyes one cannot imagine (especially given that, as a censorious Lord Chief Justice, he was later the chief author of the Obscene Publications Act). Cardigan's defence was equally ludicrous: 'No proof has been adduced that the party at whom the loaded pistol was directed bore that name.' In other words, Cardigan had shot someone, possibly even a man called Captain Tuckett, but possibly not the person named on the indictment, Harvey Garnett Phipps Tuckett. This was clearly preposterous, but in his long summation speech Denman effectively told the peers to acquit Cardigan, and cannot have been surprised when, one by one, starting with John, Baron Keane, all 120 of them, including five dukes, one royal duke, the Lord Privy Seal and the Lord President of the Council, pronounced Cardigan 'not guilty, upon my honour'. Once a delighted Cardigan had been released, the white staff was returned to Denman, who, 'holding [it] in both his hands, broke it in two, and declared the commission to be dissolved'.[34] So pleased with the proceedings were those involved that the Lords ordered that a verbatim account be published; but many others thought the whole business stank of aristocratic complicity. Some suggested the Attorney-General had deliberately included the full name on the indictment so that the earl could get off on a technicality; others contrasted the outcome with Campbell's merciless prosecution of the Newport Chartist John Frost for high treason the previous year. Clearly there was one law for the rich and another for the rest.

Quite how deluded was the concept of the benevolent aristocracy is best exemplified by the largest landowners of them all, the duke and duchess of Sutherland. Their marriage in 1785 had stitched together a phenomenal family fortune, as George Leveson-Gower, 2nd marquess of Stafford, was heir to both the Leveson-Gower estates in Staffordshire, Shropshire and Yorkshire and to those of his childless maternal uncle the 3rd duke of Bridgewater; and his bride, Elizabeth Gordon, was sole heiress at the age of one to the 18th earl of Sutherland. When the marquess came into his double inheritances in 1803 he was reckoned to be the richest man in the realm. Yet that, it seemed, was not enough. Over the next few years he and his wife embarked on a remarkable phase of 'improvements' to their very extensive Scottish estates. Hoping to turn their lands to more efficient forms of agriculture and substantially increase their rental income, they spent two decades enclosing lands, ousting crofters and tenants from their highland smallholdings and forming larger sheep farms which they let to the highest bidders. In the first phase they offered ninety families who were evicted from the parishes of Farr and Larg smaller plots fifteen miles away on the coast, but when they appointed Patrick Spellar as their factor in 1809, thousands more were removed from Dornoch, Rogart, Loth, Clyne, Kildonan, Strathnaver and Golspie. Again, there were offers of scraps of moor and bog land, but when persuasion failed, harsher measures were introduced. Summonses were served, the army was called in and homes were burnt to the ground lest any of those ejected should think of returning. The poor tenants were not even allowed to take the timbers from their crofts. When one evicted couple died, Spellar was acquitted of manslaughter.

The accounts of witnesses were harrowing. As one Sutherland stonemason recounted:

> A dense cloud of smoke enveloped the whole country by day, and even extended far out to sea. At night an awfully grand but terrific scene presented itself – all the houses in an extensive district in flames at once. I myself ascended a height about eleven o'clock in the evening, and counted two hundred and fifty blazing houses, many of the owners of which I personally knew, but whose present condition – whether in or out of the flames – I could not tell.[35]

The duchess was no more moved than Marie Antoinette had been at the lack of bread in Paris. 'Scotch people', she wrote to friends in England around this time, 'are of happier constitution and do not fatten like the larger breed of animals.'[36] The clearances went on for years, forcing thousands to scratch for a living on worthless land or emigrate. The declared aim had been to put the local economy on a stable and profitable footing – and thereby further to enrich the Sutherlands. It failed miserably on both counts. Between 1811 and 1833 the couple spent £60,000 on the project, with virtually no return at all. Yet the damage done to the lives of the poorest tenants was incalculable. Such was the pall of fear that the duke and duchess cast over the poor tenantry that when the duke died at Dunrobin Castle in 1833 the day of his funeral was ordered to be kept as a fast-day even though it was the height of the important herring-fishing season, and a year later every tenant was required to pay a shilling for a monument to the late duke.

Donald McLeod was doubtless speaking for many others when he condemned the Sutherlands: 'I agree . . . that the Duchess of Sutherland is a beautiful accomplished lady, who would shudder at the idea of taking a faggot or a burning torch in her hand, to set fire to the cottages of her tenants, and so would her predecessor, the first duchess of Sutherland . . . Yet it was done in their name, under their authority, to their knowledge, and with their sanction.'[37] The duchess to whom he was then referring was Harriet Howard, daughter of the 6th earl of Carlisle, who had married her cousin George in 1823. The 1841 census recorded that Harriet and George employed forty-one servants at

Stafford House, where the complement of thirty-six in 1851 included a tutor, a governess, a secretary for the duke, a confectioner, a cook, eight housemaids and three kitchen-maids; and in 1861, with the duke dead and the dowager duchess at Cliveden attended by thirty-one servants, the family had ten servants at Trentham and eighteen at Stafford. Harriet was a noted campaigner against slavery in America. She regularly hosted meetings at Stafford House and Dunrobin with the likes of Harriet Beecher Stowe, the author of *Uncle Tom's Cabin*. At one meeting at Stafford House on 26 November 1852 Harriet read out an uncompromising address, which was later signed by half a million British women (including the duchesses of Bedford and Argyll, the dowager duchess of Beaufort, and Ladies Palmerston, Shaftesbury, Dover, Cowley, Ruthven and Belhaven), in which she claimed that 'all will readily admit that the state of things to which we allude is one peculiarly distressing to our sex'.[38] Plenty took issue with the duchess. Thomas Carlyle, a supporter of slavery, snootily referred to 'Aunt Harriet's Cabin, so they now call the Duchess's grand palace'.[39] Lady Janet Kay-Shuttleworth, who had inherited the beautiful Elizabethan Gawthorpe Hall near Burnley at the age of four months and whose husband, Sir James, was the author of *The Moral and Physical Condition of the Working Class Employed in the Cotton Manufacture in Manchester*, railed at Harriet, suggesting that the American people should ignore the duchess and her friends unless and until the British upper classes ended 'the neglect, ill-usage and starvation payment' of governesses. 'Let us reform our schoolrooms, and we may expect them to reform the cabins of their slaves,' she ended.[40] Even Karl Marx waded in: 'The enemy of British Wages Slavery has a right to condemn Negro-Slavery; a Duchess of Sutherland, a Duke of Athol [*sic*], a Manchester Cotton-lord – never!'[41] Marx was grinding his axe with characteristic ideological venom, and the duchess was genuine in attacking the evils of slavery; but after the Highland clearances it is difficult not to sympathize with the anonymous writer to *The Times* who pointed out that, since the British aristocracy lived in glass houses, perhaps 'they should not throw stones at Americans'.[42]

In the twentieth century many peers found their ancestors' ostentatious palaces surplus to requirements. When the duke of Sutherland failed to offload Trentham Hall, with its grand semicircular, arcaded entrance and two carriage porches, to the local council in 1907 he plundered it for salvage and abandoned its slowly decaying carcass.

CHAPTER 14

TATTERED REMAINS OF OLD GLORY

A T NOON ON 15 August 1848 the auctioneers opened the bidding on 7,122 lots at Stowe House in Buckinghamshire. They were acting on behalf of the bailiffs, as Richard Temple-Nugent-Brydges-Chandos-Grenville, 2nd duke of Buckingham and Chandos, had collapsed under the weight of his debts. His rotund father had inherited broad acres and a healthy bank balance, but he had bought more land so as to enhance his chance of a dukedom and spent liberally on purchasing Old Masters and entertaining young mistresses. When he died in 1839 he had a ducal coronet on his coffin, but his estates were heavily encumbered by debt. The 2nd duke was just as profligate. He borrowed against his expected inheritance and spent thousands of pounds on bribing the electorate, even when his parliamentary seat was uncontested. Like his father, he loosened his purse-strings for several lovers, including one woman who had to be bought off and was committed to Bedlam, another who bore him a child in Paris, and Mrs Henrietta Parratt, the wife of the clerk of the journals of the House of Lords. As duke, he spent so extravagantly at Stowe that Queen Victoria was scandalized when she visited in 1845, complaining to Albert that she had no such splendid apartments in either of her palaces and commenting on the bedroom carpet: 'I know this carpet. I have seen it before – it was offered to me, but I did not like to spend so much money on one carpet.' [1] The duke enjoyed a brief political career as Lord Privy Seal for five months until resigning in February 1841 over reform of the corn laws to cast himself as the stout defender of the country interest. As the hungry 1840s progressed, his finances teetered on the brink of collapse. Since most of the family estates were bound up in strict settlements, he tricked his son and heir, the marquess of Chandos, into un-entailing them – thereby allowing him to raise vast additional sums. He even borrowed to pay interest on old debts, so that in the nine years after his father's death he racked up an extra £950,000 of debt. On 17 May 1847 the truth was laid out for the young marquess: the total debt of £1,464,959 11s 11d (equivalent to £139.5 million in 2017) was unserviceable. Chandos now took control. Buckingham House, Avington, Aylesbury, Lillingston and lands in Hampshire were sold. It was not enough. The creditors demanded that Stowe be sold, and on 22 July the notice of sale was advertised. Every movable item was to go. Furniture, carpets, statuary, artworks, bed-linen, chamber-pots, kitchen utensils, a black and gold marble bath, eight tiger skins from the saloon, and even the mattresses, bolsters, pillows and blankets from the maids' bedrooms.

The forty-day sale was an event in itself, as the public came in their thousands to gawp or pick up a bargain. For fifteen shillings they got a catalogue and admission for four. Disraeli speculated that Stowe was too out of the way for a successful sale, but thirteen peers attended including the Prime Minister's elder brother, the 7th duke of Bedford, who ate his sandwiches sitting on the steps. Some days were especially well attended by noble collectors, who had an eye on specific pieces. The duke of Hamilton bought the *Laocoon* by Carbonneau, the earl of Tyrconnel picked up a Zoffany portrait of his great-aunt Alicia, countess of Egremont (now at Petworth House), Buckingham's brother-in-law Lord Breadalbane bought Van Dyck's *Le Marquis de Vieuville* for 210 guineas (sold in New York in 2000 for $772,500), and the duke of Sutherland acquired a Holbein and a Van Dyck. Even Queen Victoria took an interest. When a statue of Venus arranging her hair as she steps out of the sea, which the first duke had brought back from the Caracalla baths in Rome, came up on the sixth day of the sale, Victoria's agent bought it and had it shipped to Osborne House as a birthday present for Albert. It is still there.

Many indulged their *Schadenfreude*. Charles Greville, the aristocratic Clerk to the Privy Council, struck an acerbic tone, declaring that it was 'altogether a painful monument of human vanity, folly, and, it must be said, wickedness, for wickedness it is thus recklessly to ruin a great house and wife and children'.[2] *The Times* attacked 'the destroyer of his house' for having 'struck a heavy blow at the whole order to which he unfortunately belongs . . . a man of the highest rank . . . has flung away all by extravagance and folly, and reduced his honour to the tinsel of a pauper and the baubles of a fool'.[3] One MP, John Evelyn Denison, snootily commented: 'Bad Taste reigns triumphant and lords it in every department . . . For a Man to have ruined himself for such things is a great aggravation of the offence.'[4] As for the duke himself, he showed little remorse and constantly badgered his son for a greater monthly allowance. When he died on 29 July 1861, he was his son's guest at the railway hotel at Paddington, as Chandos had been making a living as chairman of the Great Western Railway.

The Stowe sale exposed the frailty of a great house. It was all the more shocking because broad acres still meant deep pockets well into the second half of the nineteenth century and the landed aristocracy remained in a remarkably secure position. True, many radicals and liberals complained at the injustice of so much wealth being in the hands of so few individuals, but when the Liberal MP John Bright claimed in the 1860s that more than half of Britain was owned by 150 men, the response of the government, prompted by the patrician 15th earl of Derby, was to commission an independent assessment of land ownership in Britain and Ireland in 1871. Derby expected his 'new domesday book' would prove Bright and the critics of the aristocracy wrong; but, in a delightful irony, when the figures were published it was clear that Bright's only error lay in understating the case. In fact, five thousand people owned three-quarters of the land, a quarter was in the hands of 710 individuals, and twelve peers owned more than four million acres. In Buckinghamshire, seven peers owned one-seventh of the land. In Scotland, all bar 5,295 of the 1,299,253 acres in the county of Sutherland belonged to seven peers, and 90 per cent of the county belonged to the duke. It was a phenomenal accumulation of wealth, especially considering that the assessment did not include other forms of wealth, such as liquid holdings or the urban estates of the dukes of Bedford and Westminster in London and the earls of Sefton and Derby in Liverpool. Twenty-nine peers (twelve dukes, five marquesses, eight earls, two viscounts and two barons) luxuriated in an annual income from land of more than £75,000 each, and the dukes of Westminster, Buccleuch, Bedford, Devonshire and Northumberland all had incomes of more than £175,000 each (equivalent to £18.2 million in 2017).[5]

Some thought this precisely as things should be. As Thomas Carlyle put it in 1843: 'It is well said, "Land is the right basis of an Aristocracy", whoever possesses the Land, he, more emphatically than any other, is the Governor, Viceking of the people on the Land. It is in these days as . . . it will in all days be.'[6] He was right in one sense. Land had been a reliable investment for the aristocracy. It granted social status, it provided secure rental income from tenant farmers, and it afforded new revenues through mineral extraction and game. Well husbanded, it paid for every luxury one could want. With advances in agricultural methods bringing ever higher returns and rents running at an all-time high in the early 1870s, this landowning aristocracy – unlike that of many other European countries – was sitting pretty.

But then came a devastating agricultural depression, starting with a poor harvest in 1875 that left countless tenant farmers unable to meet labourers' wages or landlords' rents. One bad harvest could have been weathered; but the harvests of 1877 and 1878 were just as poor, and 1879 was so wet that crops festered in the field. Farmers begged landlords for a reduction in their rents, and when that failed, they defaulted and went bankrupt. The experience in Essex was typical. The *Chelmsford Chronicle* recorded that the harvest festival in 1879 was conducted with 'no attempt having been made at decorating the edifice and none of the more joyous harvest songs having been sung'. As the preacher, the Revd Sir J. C. Hawkins, Bart, pointed out: 'The series of bad harvests which had culminated in the unparalleled poor harvest of this year had brought great distress upon farmers and all connected with agriculture.'[7]

This disaster fostered a new militancy, setting tenant farmers against their landlords at the same time as British agriculture faced a sustained new challenge from overseas. The railways had opened up the prairies of America, Canada, Argentina, Australia and New Zealand, where enormous farmsteads now found it easier to transport goods to port and then to Britain at much lower prices on new steamships equipped with refrigeration. The change was rapid. In 1873 it cost £3 7s to transport one ton of grain from Chicago to Liverpool; in 1884 it cost just £1 4s. Wheat and flour imports rose by 90 per cent between 1871 and 1900, butter and cheese imports by 110 per cent and meat imports by 300 per cent. The effect on prices was equally spectacular. British farmers had been selling wheat at between 50 and 55 shillings a quarter, but in the 1880s they were lucky to get 27 shillings and in 1894 they were selling at 22s 10d. As the 11th duke of Bedford put it in 1897: 'Cheap marine transport ha[s] ... thrown open the English market to the cereals of four continents.'[8] The Liberal Unionist MP Joseph Chamberlain made the point in a campaign speech in January 1885: 'I suppose that almost universally throughout England and Scotland farming has become a ruinous occupation.'[9]

The trouble for the aristocracy was that they were heavily invested in land. As Charles Milne Gaskell, a wealthy Liberal MP who lived at Thornes House in Wakefield and Wenlock Abbey with his wife Catherine, the daughter of the 5th earl of Portsmouth, wrote in 1882: 'For many years the landowner has been credited with the possession of the most valuable form of security; no other class of property has been supposed to vie with his, and among its chief recommendations has been the fact that it could not "run away", and the supposition that it was always increasing in value.'[10] None of this was now true, though. Gaskell reckoned that the only answer was 'to lead a simpler life, to restrict ... expenditure'; but, as history had regularly proved, this was a practice for which the aristocracy had little appetite and no aptitude.

✠

The hegemony of the landed aristocracy did not just die of natural causes, though. Successive governments laid siege to the landed interest, and the aristocracy responded by hiding in the bosom of the Conservative party in an ill-conceived attempt at self-preservation. The battle in the 1840s over repeal of the corn laws, which protected the landed agricultural interest by imposing tariffs on imported corn, had pitted the pro-reform Conservative Prime Minister Sir Robert Peel against many in his own party, including Benjamin Disraeli. But the real battle started under the Liberal leadership of William Ewart Gladstone, although he was hardly a natural revolutionary. His father owned an estate in Scotland and sent him to Eton; and, having unsuccessfully courted a couple of aristocratic daughters, he married the daughter of a baronet, Sir Stephen Glynne of Hawarden Castle in north Wales. Having started his political life as the glowing hope of the young Tories, he campaigned against the abolition of slavery, opposed factory reform, defended the interests of the Church and served as a minister under Peel, Aberdeen and Palmerston.

Yet later, with the High Anglican zeal of a convert, he became an ardent advocate of free trade, an opponent of protectionism and all the aristocratic landowning baggage that went with it. His Conservative adversary Robert Gascoyne-Cecil, 3rd marquess of Salisbury, claimed that for the Lords to be 'a mere echo and tool of the House of Commons, was slavery',[11] and used the Conservatives' majority in the upper house to block the Commons; but when Gladstone won the general election of 1880 with a large majority, he was determined to dismantle the landowners' hold on the political system. First came the Ground Game Act, which repealed the last vestiges of the unjust hunting laws of 1671. That was followed by an Irish Land Bill, which gave Irish tenants unprecedented rights to fair rents, fixity of tenure and free sale (the three Fs for which the Irish Parliamentary Party had been campaigning) and led to the apoplectic resignation of the Lord Privy Seal, George Campbell, the 8th duke of Argyll, who complained that it meant 'death to ownership of land in Ireland'.[12] In 1883 came the Agricultural Holdings Act, which compensated tenants for improvements they made to their lands during their tenancy, followed by four additional, highly controversial measures: the Corrupt and Illegal Practices Prevention Acts of 1883 and 1885, which prevented local magnates from bribing and treating the local population or preventing their employees from voting, and the two electoral reform Acts of 1884 and 1885, which doubled the franchise from three million to six million by setting a universal £10 threshold for voting and redistributed seats from the over-represented countryside to the new urban areas. This was a major incursion into the political power-base of the aristocracy, who thereby lost control of a large number of seats in the Commons. The Liberal President of the Board of Trade and mayor of Birmingham, Joseph Chamberlain, praised it as 'a revolution which ha[d] been silently and peacefully accomplished', and celebrated the outcome: 'the centre of power has been shifted and the old order is giving place to the new'.[13] But not everyone agreed. Lord Randolph Churchill, the third son of the 7th duke of Marlborough, questioned: 'Are we being swept along a turbulent and irresistible torrent which is bearing us towards some political Niagara, in which every mortal thing we know will be twisted and smashed beyond all recognition?'[14] Yet again the Lords tried to delay reform; but when a national outcry ensued, a People's League for the Abolition of the Hereditary Legislature was formed, and their lordships were likened in the Commons to 'Sodom and Gomorrah, and to the collective abominations of an Egyptian temple',[15] they capitulated.

When Salisbury won most seats but not a majority in the Commons in the election of 1886, the Liberal Unionists insisted on another reform that posed a direct threat to the status of the aristocracy as a precondition of supporting the government. Thus far landlords had enjoyed almost exclusive control of local matters through the lords lieutenant and magistrates who formed the county courts of quarter sessions. There had been limited changes with the introduction of poor law guardians and incorporated boroughs such as Birmingham; but now the Liberal Unionists demanded that all these powers be handed to elected councils. The resulting Act of 1888 created forty-seven administrative counties, fifty-nine county boroughs and a new London County Council, all run by councillors elected every three years and the aldermen they nominated, who were vested with the power to levy rates, license theatres, run reform schools and asylums, ensure sanitation, repair roads and bridges, and regulate weights and measures.

Salisbury nostalgically ruminated that because 'the incomes of country gentlemen are not now obtained without difficulty', they would probably be 'less prominent themselves in attending to public affairs'.[16] He was only partly right. Yes, the lords lieutenant became largely ceremonial figures, and the 1894 Local Government Act went even further, setting up nearly seven thousand elected urban and rural district councils. Yet plenty of aristocrats resumed their old roles in the new structure. When the new Hampshire County Council met for the first time in 1889, everyone expected the Lord Lieutenant of the county, Henry Herbert, the 4th earl of Carnarvon, proprietor of nearby Highclere Castle and 36,000 acres in six counties, to take the chair – not least because, as he pointed out in a letter that was read out to the assembled councillors, he had travelled back home from Italy expressly to do so. His doctor's instructions, however, prevented 'Twitters' (he suffered from severe nervous tics) from attending, and the Lord Sheriff took his place while the councillors elected twenty-five aldermen.[17] The list of the new aldermen proves how tight the grip of the local landowners remained: they included two barons plus the sons and heirs of the earls of Selborne and of Portsmouth, a descendant of the dukes of Beaufort, two admirals, a colonel, five MPs and David Carnegie, who despite being a Scottish representative peer, as the 10th earl of Northesk, lived in his much renovated Hampshire home, Longwood House. The council was subsequently chaired from 1904 to 1909 by Henry Paulet, 16th marquess of Winchester, from 1927 to 1937 by James Harris, 5th earl of Malmesbury, and from 1973 to 1977 by Queen Elizabeth II's friend and horse-racing manager, another Henry Herbert, Lord Porchester, later the 7th earl of Carnarvon. Other counties followed very similar patterns. The 11th duke of Bedford was chairman of his county's council from 1895 to 1928. In Kent the *Maidstone and Kentish Journal* claimed that 'the Council Chamber presented a novel and striking appearance' thanks to the 'noticeable absence of some of the leading magistrates',[18] but in truth little had changed other than the seating plan, as the first chairman was the sitting chairman of the East Kent quarter sessions, Edward Knatchbull, Baron Brabourne. In similar fashion the dukes of Bedford, Sutherland and Marlborough had themselves elected mayors of, respectively, Holborn, Longton and Woodstock, and the earls of Pembroke, Derby and Lonsdale and the Earl Cadogan were mayors of Wilton, Liverpool, Whitehaven and Chelsea. Some took several mayoralties: the duke of Devonshire was mayor of Eastbourne, Chesterfield and Buxton, the duke of Norfolk was mayor of Westminster, Sheffield, Llanelli and Arundel, the earl of Derby was mayor of Liverpool and

Preston, and the marquess of Bute was mayor of Cardiff and Rothesay. Peers took a particular interest in the London County Council, whose first chairman was the 5th earl of Rosebery, and whose early aldermen and councillors included a duke, three other earls and six barons.

The aristocracy was not, then, immediately elbowed out of its role in local government; but the battle over the budget presented by David Lloyd George in 1909 gave them a very sharp blow to the collective solar plexus. The row had been brewing for some time. When the Conservative peers threw out Gladstone's Irish Home Rule Bill in 1893 by 419 to 41 and then performed radical surgery on two other Bills, Gladstone told the Commons in his final speech that 'a solution will have to be found for this tremendous contrariety ... between the representatives of the people and those who fill a nominated or non-elected Chamber'.[19] His immediate successor, Rosebery, agreed. He was convinced, he told his Liberal colleagues on becoming Prime Minister in 1894, that 'a chamber so constituted is an anomaly and a danger; and the conviction of that fact ... has been deepened and strengthened by the unhappy chapter of accidents which has turned the House of Lords from a body of hereditary legislators more or less equally divided in party, into one great Tory organisation.'[20] This was the heart of the matter. The peerage, which had once been so strongly dominated by Whigs, had swung almost to a man behind the Conservative party and was now 'at the beck and call of a single individual'.[21] So when that individual, Salisbury, returned to power the following year and won another election in 1900, he and his nephew and successor Arthur Balfour enjoyed a ready-made majority in the Lords; but when the Liberals won a landslide under Henry Campbell-Bannerman in January 1906, the stage was set for a confrontation.

The early legislation set the tone. In the dying moments of the last Liberal government, the Chancellor of the Exchequer, Sir William Harcourt, had introduced a comprehensive 'estate duty' on all inheritances. Rosebery had initially accused Harcourt of attempting to woo the masses and only reluctantly agreed to the measure, and Queen Victoria thought that her Chancellor was 'actuated by spite to, and a wish to injure, the landed proprietors'.[22] But such exaggerated reactions mask the fact that some form of inheritance duty had been in place for centuries. From 1694 a fixed stamp duty was levied on all wills entered in probate, from 1780 beneficiaries paid a graduated legacy duty on any personalty (personal property other than land) they inherited, from 1853 a succession duty had also applied to inherited realty (personally owned land), and in 1889 an estate duty was introduced at 1 per cent on estates (rather than individual legacies) worth more than £10,000 – though this last measure was intended to last only seven years to pay for the growing needs of the navy. When Harcourt introduced his new estate duty on a sliding scale up to 8 per cent for estates worth more than £1,000,000, the wealthy complained, but the Lords let it pass as it did not apply to settled or entailed (i.e. their) estates. Victoria's attack on Harcourt's motives was particularly unfair, as he and his son Lewis had to pay substantial death duties. The Queen may not have liked it, but even people who benefited from the old regime were now questioning hereditary wealth – as became abundantly clear when H. H. Asquith presented his budget in 1907, for the first time setting a higher rate of taxation on unearned income. Conservative peers like Malmesbury denounced such 'attacks upon landlords [as] violent, uncalled for and unjust',[23] but the Liberals were determined.

As if that were not enough, on 3 April 1908 the terminally ill Campbell-Bannerman resigned as Prime Minister, and four days later Asquith, as his successor, appointed David Lloyd George to the Treasury. A man of strong passions and romantic political cadences, Lloyd George was unambiguous about his desire to tackle 'the antiquated, sterilising and humiliating system of land tenure' so as to secure 'the emancipation of the Welsh peasant, the Welsh labourer, and the Welsh miner'. In a speech in Cardiff in October 1906 he had claimed that

> the present state of things on the land means that the sustenance of the labouring man is often sacrificed to the sport of the idle few ... This vicious system of land ownership accounts for the exodus from the country ... for the unemployment which comes from the sturdy countryman earning the bread that is meant for the townsman; for overcrowding ... which makes our towns and industrial villages hideous to look at and unhealthy to dwell in.[24]

It was only a matter of time before the new Chancellor set himself against the serried ranks of the aristocracy. When he introduced his 1909 budget on 29 April he called it a 'war budget' as it sought to 'raise money to wage implacable warfare against poverty and squalidness',[25] but it also represented a direct assault on the finances of the nobility. He increased the top rate of estate duty to 15 per cent, he introduced a higher rate of income tax for incomes above £2,000 and a super-tax for those over £3,000 (equivalent to around £330,000 per annum in 2017); he levied a tax on undeveloped land and minerals, and a 20 per cent appreciation tax on the value of land (backed up by a new national system of land valuation). As he put it: 'Is it too much, is it unfair, is it inequitable, that Parliament should demand a special contribution from these fortunate owners towards the defence of the country and the social needs of the unfortunate in the community, whose efforts have so materially contributed to the opulence which they are enjoying?'[26] Nobody could be in any doubt that he was taking a very direct aim at the hereditary aristocracy, but few expected the Lords to play into the government's hands with quite such spectacular ineptitude as they then showed.

The sequence of events is briefly told. The Conservative and Unionist peers were so incensed that they voted down the Finance Bill by 350 votes to 75 on 30 November. Asquith went to the country in January 1910 demanding a mandate under the banner 'people versus peers'. He did not win another landslide, but he came back into power with two more seats than the Conservatives, and with active Irish and Labour Party support he effectively still had a Commons majority; so Lloyd George re-presented his budget, and, since the peers had vowed to let it pass if and when the matter had been put to the constituencies, the Lords agreed it on 28 April 1910. This resolved the budget question; but there remained the bigger constitutional matter of the respective powers of the two houses. The Irish feared the Lords might veto home rule, Labour was committed to abolition of the upper house, the majority of the Liberals were affronted that a hereditary house could block the democratic will of the people – and the Conservatives under Balfour opposed any diminution in the powers of the Lords. Twenty-one meetings were held during the summer of 1910 in an attempt to find a compromise, but when it became clear that a Parliament Bill would be blocked in the Lords, Asquith demanded another election in December. This too produced a hung parliament with the Liberals as the largest party, so the Parliament Bill was reintroduced. It stipulated that the Lords would no longer have the right to delay a money Bill for more than a month, and that they could reject any other public Bill that had been carried by the Commons only twice over two years before it became law without their consent. When peers and their friends and relations in the Commons objected to the Bill, Asquith threatened the creation of four hundred peers to carry it; but when it came to the crunch the Conservative leadership abstained, and the 'diehards' and 'ditchers' were outnumbered in the Lords by 131 to 114.

Some of the howls of protest were spectacularly ill judged. One peer complained about Lloyd George's 'vulgarity', another accused Churchill of 'cant'.[27] The 8th duke of Rutland called the whole Cabinet 'a pirate crew of tatterdemalions' who were attempting 'but vainly, to hide the red flag of Socialism, beneath which they actually sailed, under the ensign of that older and nobler Liberalism which they had so befooled and defaced. (Cheers).'[28] The 9th duke of Beaufort announced in Cirencester that he wanted to set a pack of twenty hounds on them. The 6th earl of Portsmouth, who had been the Liberal under-secretary for war, told a gathering in Devon that the policy of the government of which he had been a part was 'an unscrupulous appeal to ignorance and class hatred to destroy the social fabric and the Constitution which had made this country great, prosperous and free'.[29] Leaving one heated discussion, the diminutive octogenarian Hardinge Giffard, earl of Halsbury, a Conservative former Lord Chancellor, proclaimed that if the Parliament Bill proceeded the result would be 'Government by a Cabinet controlled by rank Socialists'.[30] In the Commons, Asquith was boisterously and endlessly accused of being a fraud and a traitor, and the marquess of Londonderry's son Viscount Castlereagh called the budget 'as tyrannical and inquisitorial a method as it is possible for the brain of man to devise'.[31]

The peers might have been impressed by their own arguments, but others saw all this outrage as merely offensively selfish special pleading. John Buchan excused them on the grounds that 'looked at from a narrow and selfish standpoint the attitude of the House of Lords is quite understandable. It is a house of landlords fighting for what it regards as its own.'[32] But many thought that was precisely the – very obnoxious – point. As the *Standard* pointed out, the Lords included 147 major landowners, 39 captains of industry, 35 bankers and 35 railway directors. They were acting solely in their own interests and without regard to the wider needs of the nation. There was also something rather undignified about dukes and earls scurrying around London from a caucus meeting in one aristocratic palace to a campaign dinner in another. They boasted of the turnout at these events, but to the public it felt as if the peerage had lost sight of the common cause and were behaving like a grubby but exclusive trade union intent on self-preservation.

✠

On the eve of the First World War, a battered but defiant aristocracy found itself running out of money and power, with its stock of deference running dry. Footage of the 1896 Derby, of Victoria's diamond jubilee celebrations and Edward VII's coronation had shown them in all their finery; and newspapers had begun to run regular stories detailing not just their births, deaths and marriages, but their every move. The illustrated weekly journal the *Sketch*, for instance, first appeared in 1893. Entirely and slavishly devoted to the activities of 'Society', it featured photographs of the aristocracy and other celebrities along with titbits of gossip. One regular piece entitled 'still unmarried – some bachelor peers' in 1905 included photographs of the 2nd Baron Loch (born 1873), the 6th Viscount Doneraile (born 1866), the 4th Baron Tenterden (born 1865) and the 6th Baron Hawke (born 1860). The *Sketch* was still running this item in 1933, when it tantalizingly noted that Viscount Duncannon, the son and heir of the earl of Bessborough, had 'inherited his father's enthusiasm for the stage'.[33] Likewise, although the *Globe* had started life as a radical paper in 1804, in 1893 it began to run regular Society items, often recounting nothing but the remarkably humdrum. In a regular column on 'movements', for instance, it reported on 8 June 1912 that the marquess of Anglesey and Viscountess Ingestre were off to Anglesey, the earl of Sefton was going to Croxteth Hall, and the countess of Dartrey and Lady Mary Dawson were going to Peterborough. The aristocracy seems to have delighted in this peculiarly ephemeral publicity and actively courted it. The duchess of Marlborough was happy for everyone to know that she was holding an 'At Home' at Sunderland House in aid of 'a self-governing community for boys and girls in Dorset', and Lady Doughty almost certainly notified the *Globe* in person that the countesses of Yarborough and Ancaster, Lord and Lady Tenterden, Lady Edmund Talbot and Lord and Lady Heneage had accepted an invitation to her 'At Home' at 3 Great Cumberland Place on Friday, 7 June 1912.[34] It was all part of being a prominent member of Society. Yet with publicity came scrutiny. As *The Times* put it, 'the shop girl and the schoolboy not only know that the Countess of X brought her daughter to some fashionable reception and that Lady Y looked pretty in grey and silver at the racecourse, but they may actually behold these personages taken in unguarded moments in their habits where they live'.[35] In putting all the ephemera of their lives on show, the aristocrats were inviting criticism. As the number of journals carrying Society news proliferated, their wills, their charitable donations (or lack of them), their entertainments and their holidays were all exposed to public view for the first time.

They still felt they were special, though. As G. S. Street put it in 1910, 'it was a large family, this small community, mostly related and mutually known. You were either in it or outside it.'[36] Most of those who had been added to the peerage in the previous seventy years had been public servants of some kind or other, but the growing army of financiers and industrialists who had found their way into the Lords were looked on with a mixture of envy and disdain by those who considered themselves to be of older, and by implication better, stock. When the first Victorian industrialist to be ennobled, Edward Strutt, was made Baron Belper in 1856, the *Manchester Examiner* imperiously commented: 'It is something for those who claim to be regarded as the descendants of the mailed barons of England to admit into their order a man who not only has made but is making his fortune by spindles and looms.'[37] Belper might have been gratified to know that such snobbery rarely lasted more than a couple of wealthy generations – his great-granddaughter married the duke of Norfolk – but the journalist and constitutional historian Walter Bagehot was not convinced by the admission of such men into the aristocracy. He maintained that merchants and manufacturers 'have no bond of union, no habit of intercourse; their wives, if they care for society, want to see not the wives of other rich men, but "better people", as they say – the wives of men certainly with land, and, if Heaven help, with the titles'.[38] Salisbury, however, assiduously courted wealthy supporters of the Conservative party with the offer of peerages, starting with the brewer and MP Henry Allsopp, who was made Baron Hindlip in 1886 (thereby commencing the tradition of the 'beerage' that included the new Barons Ardilaun and Burton and the earl of Iveagh), and following up with the newspaper barons Glenesk, Burnham, de Reuter, Northcliffe, Rothermere and Beaverbrook. These party political appointments attracted much open derision – and a deal of snobbery. When James Williamson, who may well have bought his title, was made Baron Ashton in Rosebery's resignation list in 1895, he was nicknamed 'Lord Linoleum'; and when two wealthy financier cousins, Sidney and Herbert Stern, were respectively made Lord Wandsworth in 1895 and Lord Michelham in 1905, the *Saturday Review* bugled its protest: 'Do Lord Wandsworth and Sir Herbert Stern answer that description of aristocrats? Obviously not: then why have they been made peers? The answer is, Money.' This was no more than standard aristocratic disdain for new money, but the paper revealed deeper prejudices in its further comments: 'The Zionists looking for a Jewish homeland beyond the seas would be glad to abandon their dreams if the furious ennoblement of mere financiers continued: the House of Lords would have superior attractions.'[39]

In return, many of the wealthy industrialists who came to the fore and occasionally secured peerages looked down on their older peers for their failure to adapt to the modern world. Thus the satirical magazine *Truth* made the point in 1901 that titled millionaires selfishly spent their money on themselves, while every instance of modern philanthropy came from men 'who have sprung from the people'.[40] *Truth* had a point.

Only two titled estates between 1881 and 1914 left more than £100,000 to charity: in 1893 Mary, Lady Forester, left more than £250,000 to establish and endow a cottage hospital and convalescent home in Much Wenlock in honour of her late husband; and two years later the 14th earl of Moray left £170,000 to the Edinburgh Royal Infirmary, the National Lifeboat Association and three churches. But these were exceptions. Neither had children and their wealth was not entailed. By contrast, the 15th earl of Moray left just £1,700 in such legacies in 1901, and the 16th and 17th earls left only private bequests. The American self-made multi-millionaire and philanthropist Andrew Carnegie, who gave away roughly 90 per cent of his wealth, saw it in stark terms: 'Rich Englishmen do not leave their fortunes for uses of this kind as often as Americans do. The ambition to found a family, and the maintenance of an aristocratic class by means of primogeniture and entail, tend to divert fortunes from this nobler path into the meaner end of elevating a name on the social scale.'[41] He was shocked by the public parsimony of the British aristocracy – but not as much as by the persistence of antiquated attitudes revealed by Matthew Arnold, who told him: 'A duke is always a personage with us, always a personage, independent of brains or conduct. We are all snobs. Hundreds of years have made us so, all snobs. We can't help it. It is in the blood.'[42]

✠

Then came the 'Great War'. In common with much of the public, the aristocracy in general nurtured the expectation that it would all be over in a trice. Many relished the whole affair. In the weeks after the declaration of war the *Sketch* even marvelled that 'society' went off to Scotland for the grouse shooting when there was so much 'excitement', but then nonchalantly noted that 'London is the last place to get excited about a war'.[43] Young nobles felt they had a special role to play. If the aristocracy could no longer lead the nation in parliament, it could at least do so on the battlefield. They rushed to sign up. Viscount Castlereagh, the son and heir of the 6th marquess of Londonderry, had served in the Royal Horse Guards before being elected as a Unionist MP in 1906, but now, fearful that he might completely miss the war, he sailed for France to be ADC to the utterly unremarkable General Pulteney the moment hostilities were declared. After succeeding his father as marquess the following year he rejoined his regiment and served with it at Ypres, the Somme and Arras, witnessing gas attacks and the mass slaughter of horses and men, including his own best man. Likewise Lionel Tennyson, the cricketing grandson of the ennobled poet laureate who would later inherit the barony in 1928, wrote in his autobiography that he dressed and packed 'in feverish haste, so anxious was I not to run any chance of missing the war'.[44] Later he boasted: 'I have never liked travelling light and so, though the amount of kit I arrived with may, in fact have aroused a certain amount of astonishment, I was quickly forgiven by my commanding officer as well as by everyone else, when they found out that it included, among other things, a case of champagne.'[45] We can only imagine what his men thought of this, but being patriotically gung-ho was very much the patrician order of the day.

Aristocratic women were keen to play their part, too. According to the *Sketch* of 26 August 1914, Alice, countess of Derby, was 'equipping and accompanying a voluntary field hospital for the front' and Mary, the philanthropic anti-vivisectionist 13th duchess of Hamilton, who had supplied a photograph of herself in uniform, 'will go to the Front in the ranks of the Red Cross'. The most obvious way to help, though, was to offer their large houses as hospitals and convalescent homes. So Mary, 11th duchess of Bedford, turned Woburn Abbey into one of the best hospitals in the country with an operating theatre, X-ray room and 160 beds, all at her husband's expense, and started receiving injured soldiers from the British Expeditionary Force on 24 November 1914, working from 5.30 a.m. every day of the war and keeping meticulous details of every patient in person. Likewise the first soldiers – a group of fifteen refugee Belgian officers – arrived at Burghley House in Lincolnshire in October 1914, and by 24 November Myra, the 5th marchioness of Exeter, had transformed the orangery into a twenty-bed convalescent ward. So too Violet, duchess of Rutland, converted 16 Arlington Street and Belvoir Castle into military hospitals, and the duchess of Sutherland set up a hospital in each of the family seats. All this activity brought a dramatic social change to the stately homes. Just as young peers were thrown into daily contact with Tommies in the trenches, so their wives and daughters had their homes invaded by doctors, nurses, orderlies and patients, strangers all, who owed them some gratitude but showed little deference.

As for the men's experience, since the officer class of the British army still consisted almost entirely of the gentry and aristocracy (the purchase of officer commissions had only been abolished in 1871), the young nobility found themselves in a position of extraordinary authority and responsibility, which they met with considerable fortitude, rarely asking others to perform acts of bravery that they would not perform themselves. Such leadership brought phenomenal personal risks, as the casualty lists show. Overall British casualty numbers were shocking – roughly 12 per cent of all men who enlisted never returned – but they were even worse for officers: 19 per cent of peers and their sons who served were killed. The list seemed endless. The first to die was the 23-year-old Lieutenant Robert Maude, 6th Viscount Hawarden, in the first battle of Ypres. Soon he was joined in foreign fields by Lieutenant Henry Parnell, 5th Baron Congleton (24), Major Lord Bernard Gordon-Lennox, the third son of the 7th duke of Richmond (36) and Lieutenant Regy 'Sinbad' Wyndham (38), the younger brother of the 3rd Baron Leconfield of Petworth House and nephew of the earl of Rosebery. In 1914 alone six peers and fifty sons of peers died, leaving the houses of Abercorn, Ancaster, Annesley, Atholl, Cadogan, Devonshire, Downe, Durham, Glasgow, Granard, Hardinge, Kinnaird, Lansdowne, Saltoun, Tweeddale, Wellington and Westminster bereft. By the end of the war one marquess (of Conyngham), eleven earls, eleven barons and one viscount had laid down their lives, along with 239 sons and grandsons of peers. Death seemed to encircle the aristocracy. The 2nd earl of Kimberley, the 10th Baron Middleton and the 9th earl of Denbigh each lost two sons; five of the ten grandsons of the 3rd marquess of Salisbury were killed; and Arthur French, who had become the 5th Baron de Freyne when his estranged father died in 1913 (they had fallen out over his marriage to the divorced daughter of a Scottish innkeeper), died alongside his half-brother George in 1915, two years before another half-brother, Ernest, died of wounds sustained in battle and three years before a third half-brother, Edward, died as a prisoner of war. A few titles were ultimately extinguished on the battlefield, too. There were to be no more marquesses of Lincolnshire; the barony of Ribblesdale died with the 4th Baron in 1925, as his two sons had died in action in different wars; and when John Rolls, 2nd Baron Llangattock, died unmarried on 31 October 1916 his two younger brothers were already in the grave.

We are so used to accounts of the needless slaughter in what is still termed the 'Great War' that it is easy to forget how exceptionally brutal this war was for the aristocracy. One study shows that whereas 46 per cent of male members of ducal families born between 1330 and 1479 died violently including in war, that fate befell 48 per cent of those born between 1880 and 1939.[46] As David Cannadine put it in his *Decline and Fall of the British Aristocracy*: 'Not since the Wars of the Roses had so many patricians died so suddenly and so violently.'[47] Some thought that this great effort would redound to the aristocracy's glory and re-establish their commanding place in society. The Scottish Liberal MP Alexander Murray, known as the Master of Elibank before his ennoblement in 1912, predicted as much in November 1906 when he argued that 'the position of the Lords in this country will be much stronger, generally on account of the gallantry and losses on the battlefield of the peerage families'.[48] That was before the war. Afterwards, there was no sense of the nation bowing its knee in gratitude for their sacrifice. Far from it. If anything, Britain blamed the officer class for the endless bloodshed; now it turned its attention to righting the wrongs of an inequitable society. All men, even those with no property, would now be allowed to vote, as would women.

✠

The Liberal MP Charles Masterman wrote in 1922 that 'the British aristocracy perished . . . in courage and high effort, and an epic of heroic sacrifice, which will be remembered so long as England endures', adding that 'the Feudal System vanished in blood and fire, and the landed classes were consumed'.[49] He was right. Nothing was quite the same for the nobility after the war. The country houses, which had relied on platoons of servants, found it difficult to hire staff, as so many men had perished and those who survived sought any career other than domestic service. The war had been costly, too: death duties were almost doubled to 40 per cent and interest rates rose from 3.5 per cent to 6 per cent, leaving many estates struggling to make ends meet. The obvious choice was to sell up, liquidate assets, find more profitable investments and – if strictly necessary – downsize.

Lord Ailesbury had plaintively said in 1911 that 'a man does not like to go down to posterity as the alienator of old family possessions',[50] but it had been happening for years. The great sell-off of land in Ireland had been assisted by legislation and state grants, so that by 1909 1.5 million acres had been sold by the likes of the marquesses of Bath and Waterford and the dukes of Abercorn and Leinster. In Wales, the duke of Beaufort had sold his 26,000-acre Monmouthshire estate, including Tintern Abbey; he was followed by Lord Harlech, Lord Wimborne, the duke of Westminster, Lord Glanusk, and the earls of Ashburnham, Denbigh and Winchilsea. In Scotland, partly thanks to a compulsory 30 per cent cut in crofters' rents, the dukes of Sutherland, Argyll and Fife, the marquesses of Tweeddale and Queensferry, and the earls of Perth and Kintore had all disposed of major estates by the time the war broke out. And in England some 900,000 acres had been offloaded by 1909, when Balfour (himself the owner of the neo-classical mansion Whittingehame in East Lothian) claimed that 'the bulk of the great fortunes are now in a highly liquid state . . . They do not consist of huge landed estates, vast parks and castles, and all the rest of it.'[51]

The pace of disposals quickened after the war, as peers increasingly felt the lash of the Chancellor. Some peers cut down the *number* of their homes. The duke of Northumberland sold Stanwick Park but kept Alnwick and four other houses; the 15th earl of Pembroke sold 8,400 acres of the Wilton estate in 1918 and 1919, and his successor followed up with more houses, villas and estates in 1928, but they kept Wilton; the duke of Norfolk sold Glossop Hall in 1925 and gave Bungay Castle to the town in 1987, but kept Carlton Towers and Arundel Castle; and although the duke of Bedford sold Thorney and much of Covent Garden, he kept Woburn. Others cut down the *size* of their properties. In 1927 the 14th earl of Strathmore partially demolished one of his four homes,

Streatlam Castle in county Durham (not long after his daughter Elizabeth had married the future George VI), and in 1930 the self-centred 11th duke of Leeds demolished all bar one wing of Hornby Castle and disappeared to the French Riviera as a tax exile.

A few stately homes were sold but survived in other guises. Stowe became a boarding school, as did Westonbirt, which the 4th earl of Morley sold in 1928. The earl of Dudley turned part of his castle into a zoo, Castle Bromwich Hall became council offices, Whittingehame became a school for Jewish refugees, Hewell Grange became a borstal and then a Category D open prison, Coworth House became a convent school and then a luxury hotel, and Lord Brocket's home Bramshill became the National Police College.

Other properties were abandoned or demolished for salvage. In 1907 the 4th duke of Sutherland offered Trentham Hall near Stafford, which Barry had reconstructed for the 2nd duke and duchess, with a grand semicircular single-storey arcaded entrance, two carriage porches, a clock tower and a sculpture gallery, to the local council. When they refused to take it on, he abandoned it for five years in a fit of pique and then dismantled most of it, leaving a derelict shell. And when Strangways Castle, the Dorset seat of the earls of Ilchester, which overlooked Chesil Beach, suffered a major fire on 13 February 1913, the earl had it rebuilt but never moved back in – and in 1935 he had it demolished. Beaudesert, one of several homes of the earls of Anglesey, was refurbished by the 6th earl after a fire in 1909, but in 1919 the contents were sold and in 1935 the building was sold to a development company, who never got round to rebuilding. The 13th duke of Hamilton never moved back into Hamilton Palace after the war, and in 1921 he demolished it and moved to the smaller castle of Dungavel, which he sold to the National Coal Board in 1947. (It is now an immigration detention centre scheduled to close.) In 1922 Adèle, the dowager countess of Essex, put Cassiobury House and its contents up for sale after her husband had been run over by a taxi, and when no buyers were forthcoming for the house, her son the 8th earl demolished it for salvage in 1927 (ten thousand Tudor bricks were said to have made it across the Atlantic to Bedford, New York). Between 1925 and 1929, Agecroft Hall,

Wollaston Hall and Warwick Priory, each of which had fallen into ruin, were shipped across the Atlantic, lock, stock and mullioned window. Sometimes decades passed before properties were finally taken down. In 1909 the 4th earl of Bradford, who also owned Castle Bromwich Hall and Weston Park, sold the contents of the abandoned, dilapidated and leaking Tong Castle, which had formerly enjoyed every gothic adornment slave money could buy, including 130 oil paintings and six carriages; in 1911 a fire rendered the building unstable; and when the eventual decision was taken to pull it down in 1954, large crowds gathered as the earl's son and heir, Gerald Bridgeman, Viscount Newport, fired the charges on 136lb of plastic explosive and 75lb of amatol in 208 boreholes placed around the building.

As with the country houses, so with the London palaces. In 1919 the 4th marquess of Salisbury sold the Cecils' home in Arlington Street and the 9th duke of Devonshire sold his mansion on Piccadilly. Over the next fifteen years the Harewoods, Curzons, Sunderlands, Rutlands, Derbys, Crewes and Norfolks all followed suit. The same fate came to three mansions on Park Lane that had been requisitioned by the government during the war – the duke of Westminster's Grosvenor House, with its collection of paintings by Gainsborough and Velazquez; Dorchester House, which had been leased to the American ambassador; and Londonderry House, with its rococo chandeliers, gilt mirrors and sculptures by Canova. All three were returned to their owners after the war, but Grosvenor House and Dorchester House were sold and demolished in 1927 and 1928 respectively; the Londonderrys held on until 1962. In October 1929, when Lansdowne House was about to be demolished and a great hole had opened up where Dorchester House had once been, the 27th earl of Crawford wrote in his diary: 'I remember so many London palaces disappearing, in fact one can count on one hand those which survive and soon they must be doomed before long.' He added that Lansdowne had told him he was delighted to leave the old palace and take up residence in a small comfortable house in Brook Street, as 'for the first time in his life he realised what real comfort was – the ease of being within easy reach of a bell, of a table, of a book, and not being obliged to take a walk if he wanted to reach anything'.[52] The bell, of course, was to summon staff.

It was not just houses but their contents that went under the hammer. In the late nineteenth century the duke of Marlborough sold enamels, a Raphael *Madonna* and Van Dyck's equestrian portrait of Charles I; the earl of Ashburnham sold a vast collection of manuscripts; the earl of Dudley sold Fra Angelico's *Last Judgment* (it is now in the Gemäldegalerie in Berlin) and Raphael's *Three Graces* (Musée Condé, Chantilly); the marquess of Exeter parted with a *Madonna* by Petrus Christus (Kaiser Friedrich Museum, Berlin); and the earl of Radnor sold three paintings from Longford Castle by Holbein (*The Ambassadors*), Moroni and Velazquez. When Lady Desborough inherited two *Madonna*s by Raphael in 1913, she immediately sold the smaller one for $565,000 (the larger went for £875,000 in 1928). After the war the sales continued unabated. The duke of Westminster sold Gainsborough's *The Blue Boy* and *Mrs Siddons as the Tragic Muse* by Joshua Reynolds in 1921; in 1928 the 4th Baron Sackville sold George Stubbs' painting of his ancestor the 3rd duke of Dorset's hunter with a groom and a pet dog from Knole; in 1930 the 11th duke of Leeds disposed of the contents of Hornby Castle, and the 10th earl of Egmont sold the contents of Avon Castle which he had recently and unexpectedly inherited; in 1937 the library and the other contents of Clumber went for £130,000, and the executors of Georgiana, widow of the 7th earl of Buckinghamshire, sold Camperdown House and its contents; in 1938 the trustees for the twelve-year-old 3rd Baron Savile decided to sell the contents of Rufford Abbey, followed by the house itself, and the duke of Norfolk made £10,000 from the contents of Norfolk House (the *Sphere* noted that the pictures 'are not particularly notable' apart from a portrait by Rubens[53]); and in 1953 Lady Desborough's executors sold Panshanger to a demolition contractor and dispersed its contents, including Titian's *Holy Conversation* (which was sold again in 2011 for $16.9 million).

This spate of destruction and dispersal did not go unnoticed by the wider public. Sutherland's demolition of Trentham was much commented on, not least because so many of the salvage items had gone unsold thanks to 'a dearth of buyers',[54] and the turned stone roof balustrade and the mirrors from the duchess's private apartments sold 'for a tithe of their cost'.[55] The *Times* reports – and the rampant criticism of the sale and dismemberment of Tattershall Castle before it was rescued by Lord Curzon – prompted the duke of Rutland to ride to the defence of his noble compatriots. 'Fancy my not being allowed to make a necessary alteration to Haddon,' he imperiously declaimed as he denounced the impudence of the conservation movement, 'without first obtaining the leave of some inspector.'[56]

Some thought the selling off of the family silver distasteful, especially when works that had been part of the national patrimony went overseas to those with deep pockets. Ninety thousand people visited the National Gallery to see *The Blue Boy*, by any account a quintessentially British work, before it left for America, and the director of the gallery, Sir Charles Holmes, hopefully inscribed 'Au revoir' on its back. Likewise, when the marquess of Lansdowne sold Rembrandt's *The Mill* to the Philadelphian P. A. B. Widener for £100,000 in 1911 (it is now in the National Gallery of Art, Washington DC) the *New York Times* commented: 'So great has the drain on the art treasures of the United Kingdom owing to the immense sums Americans are willing to pay recently become, that a law similar to that of Italy forbidding the exportation of important art objects has been urged from various quarters.'[57] It was some time before the British themselves took the hint.

The families themselves blamed the decay in their fortunes on 'rank socialism' and the sustained legislative assault on their interests made by Gladstone and Lloyd George. In particular, they blamed income tax and death duties (which rose to 65 per cent in 1940 to pay for another war). But the truth was that many of them had failed to diversify, had racked up debts that could never be repaid, had relied on a deferential and cheap workforce and had lived beyond their means for far too long. The American-born Conservative MP Henry 'Chips' Channon, who spent much of his career unsuccessfully pursuing a ministerial post or a peerage while flitting around London Society, claimed that 'it is the aristocracy that rules England, although nobody wants to believe it',[58] but he was engaging in desperate wishful thinking. The tight knot of land, money, status and power that had lasted for centuries was unravelling. One comment summarizes the poignancy of it all. In common with many peers who acted as posh salvage merchants, when Devonshire House was demolished, Dorothy Cavendish, the daughter of the 9th duke of Devonshire, made sure that a couple of the fireplaces made their way to Birch Grove, the marital home she shared with Harold Macmillan, and much of the furniture made its way to Chatsworth. Deborah, duchess of Devonshire, later recalled: 'Piled high in the kitchen-maids' bedroom were silk curtains, cushions, tassels and braids. Chimney pieces lay on their backs in the forge by the stables, while in the granary loft above were stored the London state harnesses of the carriage horses, extravagantly carved and painted pelmets, gilded fillets, and other grubby and tattered remains of old glory.'[59]

Such elegiac comments implore pity, but Henry Forster was right when he pointed out in his annotated catalogue of the Stowe sale of 1848 that 'persons who occupy a rank and station greatly above the "common lot" seldom excite the sympathy of their inferiors'.[60]

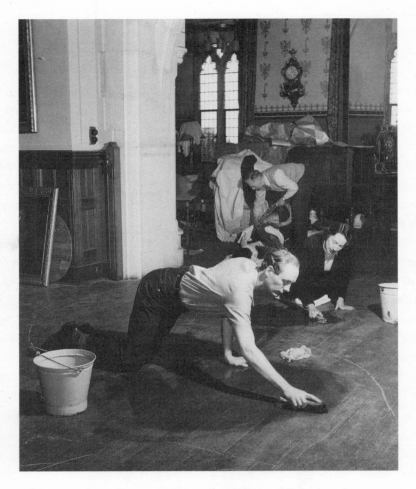

The aristocracy have made much of their political and financial travails, regularly pleading noble poverty and playing hard-done-by for the cameras, as in this photograph of Lord Montagu of Beaulieu getting down on his hands and knees before the opening of his house to the public in 1952. Thanks to state handouts, tax avoidance measures and the intervention of the National Trust, many have been able to sustain their grand lifestyles.

CHAPTER 15

LIVING IN A KIND OF TWILIGHT

A T FOUR-THIRTY ON THE afternoon of 9 May 1940, four men met in the Cabinet Room at No. 10 Downing Street: the Prime Minister, Neville Chamberlain; his chief whip, David Margesson; the First Lord of the Admiralty, Winston Churchill; and the Foreign Secretary, Edward Wood, the 3rd Viscount Halifax. Chamberlain had won a vote of no confidence the night before, but so many Conservative MPs had abstained or voted against him that he knew his premiership was doomed. The question was, who should succeed him – Churchill or Halifax? Both were aristocrats: the former a scion of the dukes of Marlborough who had been born at Blenheim Palace; the latter a baron, a viscount and a grandson of the earl of Devon who had been born at Powderham Castle, had grown up between Hickleton Hall and the 13,500-acre Garrowby estate, and had also inherited No. 88 Eaton Square and Temple Newsam, a Jacobean pile near Leeds. Accounts of the meeting vary, but it seems Halifax made the decision for the rest, saying that since he was not in the Commons, he would 'speedily become a more or less honorary Prime Minister, living in a kind of twilight just outside the things that really mattered'. So it had to be Winston. It was a moment of personal self-denial, but also of collective aristocratic self-doubt, as it seemed wrong for a peer of the realm to take the helm 'at this particular juncture'.[1]

The tide of aristocratic self-assurance had been ebbing for some time. Eustace Percy had a theory about this. As the seventh son of the 7th duke of Northumberland and nephew of the 9th duke of Argyll, he was about as patrician as they came. After Eton and Oxford, he served as a

Conservative President of the Board of Education from 1924 to 1929, he was given a peerage of his own, and he devoted much of his autobiography to accounts of polo matches at the Hurlingham Club, killing wild boar in France and pursuing larger game in Africa. Yet he believed that although 'large private responsibilities do tend to form in their possessors a certain talent for public affairs', that talent was 'one that is apt to be restricted in its range'. The problem, as he saw it, was that a landed aristocrat 'could manage men with whom he could talk, but he was uncertain in judging public opinion or in conducting public debate'.[2]

He was right. Regular cack-handed political interventions by the aristocracy in the twentieth century made them look like a very amateurish second eleven. A prime example came in 1917. The 5th marquess of Lansdowne had been sacked from the Cabinet by Lloyd George in 1916 and was feeling resentful. He was, after all, a former Viceroy of India and leader of the Conservative and Unionists in the Lords. Increasingly convinced that the war would lead to the complete destruction of civilization, he drafted a paper arguing that the government should sue for peace and circulated it round his old colleagues in the Cabinet. When they politely demurred, he tried to get the editor of *The Times* to publish a lengthy letter; and when this was declined, he sent it to the *Daily Telegraph*, who carried it on 29 November 1917. In it he claimed that the 'wanton prolongation' of the war would 'spell ruin for the civilised world, and an infinite addition to the load of human suffering', and he called on Britain 'to end the war honourably'. However valid the call for peace might have been, Lansdowne was immediately condemned for capitulation. The Conservatives disowned him, MPs demanded that he be prosecuted under the Defence of the Realm regulations for encouraging the enemy, and H. G. Wells said it was 'the letter of a peer who fears revolution more than national dishonour'.[3]

The aristocracy showed no greater grasp of world affairs in the 1920s and 1930s. A succession of aristocrats joined avowedly fascist organizations in the 1920s, including the 8th duke of Northumberland, who set up the Boswell Press in 1921 so as to expose the 'hidden hand' of the German–Jewish–Bolshevik plot against the British empire; Lord

Ernest Hamilton, the evangelical seventh son of the duke of Abercorn, who in 1912 poured his anti-semitism into a complex theological tome on Jesus and the Jewish national character, entitled *Involution*; the 5th Earl Temple of Stowe, who with his countess hosted a grand mid-Lenten ball for the British fascists at the Hotel Cecil in March 1926; George Clarke, Baron Sydenham of Combe, who secretly financed the fascist activities of Adrien Arcand, self-declared Führer of Canada; Patrick Boyle, the 8th earl of Glasgow, who angrily denounced communism, socialism and taxation from tax exile in France and successively joined General Blakeney's Loyalists in the General Strike, the January Club and the British Union of Fascists; and Dorothy, Viscountess Downe, a lady-in-waiting to Queen Mary, who regularly spoke at fascist meetings, joined Mosley's British Union of Fascists and narrowly avoided internment in the war.

Such ultra-right tendencies became even stronger with the rise of Hitler. There were plenty of sane people who argued that the Versailles Treaty had been too harsh on Germany. One such was Rufus Isaacs, the inaugural President of the Anglo-German Association in 1928, who had been Lord Chief Justice of England for eight years and Viceroy of India for five, and would serve as Foreign Secretary for two and a half months in 1931. He had risen from MP to peer and scaled the aristocratic ladder, becoming marquess of Reading in 1926. When Hitler banned all Jews from public office in 1933 Reading, who was Jewish, resigned from the association, declaring: 'The attack at this moment ... [is] upon the professors at the universities, the judges and the lawyers, and the men of the medical profession who happen to be members of the Jewish community, and it is made solely because they are members of the Jewish community.'[4] One might have expected other British peers to follow Reading's lead, but his successor as president of the association, General Sir Ian Hamilton, grandson of the 3rd Viscount Gort, described himself as an admirer of the 'great' Adolf Hitler and complained that it was 'extremely dangerous for anyone to displease the Jews as they are so enormously powerful in the press that they can usually manage to ruin their enemies in the long run'.[5] Hamilton's anti-semitism and his determination to strengthen the 'blood tie' with the Germans grew. In

1936 he backed Hitler's illicit remilitarization of the Rhineland, in 1938 he spent the weekend with the German Chancellor at Berchtesgaden and in January 1939 he drafted a letter for the *Evening Standard* supposedly 'correcting' two mistakes: '(1) that the Jews – the men – look much the same as other people; (2) that the Jews act in much the same way as other people.' He elaborated: 'Several Jews holding high positions in British society have asked me whether they were recognizable as Jews evidently thinking that they were not. Always my answer has been in the affirmative ... As to their character and actions, they have a very distinctive trait which is not bad in itself but does not make for popularity – they want to run the show.'[6] The published version omitted an even less savoury part of the draft: 'As you walk Eastwards from Marble Arch to Tottenham Court Road the number of Jews increases block by block until at Holborn they become something like 1 in 4.'[7]

Hamilton was not alone in these views. Gerard Wallop, Viscount Lymington, was the son and heir to the earl of Portsmouth. He had been born in Chicago but brought up in England, and sat as a Conservative MP from 1929 to 1934, when he suddenly resigned out of frustration with democratic politics. A keen occultist, monarchist, agriculturalist and eugenicist, he interviewed Hitler favourably in 1931 (and wrote to thank him afterwards), met Mussolini in 1932, founded the fascist organization English Array in 1936, attended Nazi rallies from 1935 to 1939, established the British Council Against European Commitments with the Nazi apologist William Joyce (Lord Haw-Haw), published the fascist journal *New Pioneer*, wrote for the Nazi journal *Odal* and met Hitler again in 1939. Lymington wanted to ban inter-racial marriage, claiming that 'we did not regard ourselves as Herrenvolk but we wanted our revival to be Anglo-Saxon . . . [because] we felt that outside influences were corrupting our standards and national purpose',[8] and he was so convinced that the Czechoslovakian coup in March 1939 was 'counterproductive' that he wondered 'whether one of [Hitler's] Lieutenants is not either in the service of the Jesuits or the Jews'.[9] Lymington had plenty of aristocratic allies, including Hastings Russell, the evangelical, vegetarian, teetotal marquess of Tavistock, who founded the British People's Party and the British Council for a Christian

Settlement in Europe in 1939. Tavistock succeeded his father as 12th duke of Bedford in August 1940 and two years later had a Lansdowne moment. Having repeatedly written to Halifax in praise of Hitler and worked behind the scenes to try to broach a peace accord with Germany, he started berating the House of Lords about the futility of war. 'Politicians would do well to remember,' he said, 'that there is nothing heroic about talk of fighting in the "last ditch" if they themselves do not intend to occupy that most unpleasant cavity.' As if it was not enough to charge his fellows with cowardice, he added that he was 'literally appalled . . . by the extent to which many of your lordships seem to be living in a cloud-cuckoo-land of complete unreality . . . with regard to the character of foreign statesmen.'[10] It was only when the eighty-year-old Lord Gainford moved that Bedford 'be no longer heard' that he resumed his seat, and even after the war he denounced the Nuremberg trials and argued that the claim that six million Jews had died in the Holocaust was grossly exaggerated. The file MI5 compiled on him stated that 'in the event of the Duke falling into the hands of the enemy he would be likely to be set up as a gauleiter or the head of a puppet British government'.[11] Eventually he took his own life – because, his son thought, 'all his political, social and religious notions had led him nowhere, causing only derision and antipathy . . . and towards the end he was a lonely and rather desolate man'.[12]

Were the nobility especially extreme or gullible? Something in the Nazi lexicon was attractive to them. The emphasis on a pure bloodline was close to the aristocracy's determination to marry within the close circle of family relations and its fascination with thoroughbreds. Some liked the obsession with ancient myths and warrior leaders. The hierarchical society they believed in relied on a strong sense of order for its coherence. And many landowning families distrusted and disliked the rise of wealthy Jewish banking and industrial families. The strongest impetus for appeasement, though, came from the experience of the Great War. Men like Charley, the snobbish 7th marquess of Londonderry, had seen horrors in the trenches and would do anything to prevent their repetition. A Cabinet minister from 1931 to 1935, his reputation suffered as he argued against cuts to the air budget on patriotic grounds in 1932 and 1933 and then against rearmament in 1934 and 1935, so he found himself with few friends in high places when his wife Edith's friend Ramsay Macdonald resigned as Prime Minister and Stanley Baldwin reshuffled him into the largely ceremonial role of Lord Privy Seal and then out of government entirely. Delighted that Germany had become a bulwark against the evils of communism, Londonderry campaigned for an accommodation with Hitler and repeatedly visited Germany. In 1936 Hermann Goering hosted him and Edith on a seven-week tour of Germany which included a stay at the fashionable Adlon Hotel in Berlin, a visit to the Winter Olympics and a dinner at the Chancellery with Hitler. Lady Londonderry was particularly impressed, writing for the *Sunday Sun* on their return: 'I beheld a man of arresting personality, a man with wonderful, far-seeing eyes. I felt I was in the presence of someone truly great. He is simple, dignified, humble. He is a leader of men.'[13] That Whitsun the Londonderrys invited the German ambassador, Joachim von Ribbentrop, to Mount Stewart for a weekend at which the entertainment included an aerobatic display by the famous aviator the marquess of Clydesdale (from 1940 the 14th duke of Hamilton). The following year Londonderry visited Goering again, and in March 1938 he defended the Anschluss, claiming that 'it was only a question of time when this change in the situation would take place' and adding: 'We can see by the enthusiasm with which Herr Hitler is received in Austria that his advent is welcomed by the great majority of the population.'[14]

There was another factor in play. The Nazis deliberately courted the British aristocracy via the odious social climber von Ribbentrop, a former champagne salesman who had purchased his 'von' and was ambassador in London from 1936 to 1938 (and then Hitler's foreign minister until his capture in 1945; he was executed at Nuremberg in 1946). He saw to it that private trips were organized for senior British figures to meet the Führer, and a whole bevy of susceptibly right-wing lords and MPs were invited to the Nuremberg rallies. In 1936 he invited a score of sympathetic politicians to Berlin for the controversial Summer Olympics. The marquess of Clydesdale flew his own plane there and joined the press barons Rothermere and Beaverbrook, the former Conservative chief whip Viscount Monsell, and another wealthy

Conservative aviator, Loel Guinness (who was married to the daughter of the duke of Rutland), at a dinner with Rudolph Hess. Chips Channon, who attended with his wife Lady Honor Guinness, commented on meeting Hitler: 'I was more excited than when I met Mussolini in 1926 in Perugia, and more stimulated, I am sorry to say, than when I was blessed by the Pope in 1920.'[15] Ribbentrop never let up with this lobbying of the British aristocracy. On the collapse of the Anglo-German Association, he assisted Colonel Wilfrid Ashley, a grandson of the 7th earl of Shaftesbury who was made Baron Mount Temple in 1933, in founding the more pro-Nazi Anglo-German Fellowship (it claimed that 'membership does not *necessarily* imply approval of National Socialism'),[16] along with Lords Londonderry, Glasgow and Lothian and Lord and Lady Redesdale, and ensured Mount Temple met Hitler in 1937.

This wooing of the British nobility paid dividends. Philip Kerr, the 11th marquess of Lothian, who had been Lloyd George's parliamentary private secretary during the Versailles negotiations, visited Hitler in 1935 and 1937 and repeatedly supported Germany's right to reassert itself. He urged Britain to make no commitments of mutual solidarity to other European countries, and he praised Neville Chamberlain after Munich for refusing to accept that 'the Nazis were incorrigible'.[17] Lothian changed his mind in 1939, but other aristocrats remained on the far-right end of the spectrum. Captain Archibald Ramsay, great-nephew of the 12th earl of Dalhousie and son-in-law of Viscount Gormanston, sat as the Conservative MP for Peebles and South Midlothian from 1931 to 1945 (after Eton, Sandhurst and the Coldstream Guards). He overtly supported Franco in the Spanish Civil War, he accused 'revolutionary Jews' of being the inspiration behind communism, he called for the Sudetenland to be handed to Hitler, and in May 1939 he set up the Right Club (under the chairmanship of the 5th duke of Wellington) with the declared aim of ridding the Conservative party of Jewish influences. Even when war was declared he distributed leaflets claiming that 'the stark truth is that this war was plotted and engineered by the Jews for world-power and vengeance'.[18] On the very eve of war, Hugh Grosvenor, 2nd duke of Westminster, told the anti-appeasement MP Duff Cooper that Hitler knew that he could count on England as one of his best friends. Cooper exploded with rage; the next day, Westminster phoned a friend to say that the war would be entirely the fault of the Jews and Duff Cooper. Since Westminster called his dog 'Jew' and hounded his brother-in-law out of Society for his homosexuality, he was probably happy to consider himself Hitler's friend.

Another British peer sympathetic to the Nazis in the 1930s who visited Germany for the Olympics was David Freeman-Mitford. Although he was only the 2nd Baron Redesdale, his pretensions hinged on his family's long history of landed wealth in Northumberland, Gloucestershire and Oxfordshire. A particularly stupid man (he failed the entrance exam at Sandhurst and maintained he had only ever read one book, Jack London's *White Fang*), he inherited his far cleverer father's title in 1916 after his elder brother was killed in action. Invalided, he worked sporadically for his father-in-law managing *The Lady*, but largely devoted himself to unaffordable building projects. Prone to terrible rages and harbouring a deep hatred of foreigners, especially Jews and the French, he sided with his daughter Diana when she eloped with Sir Oswald Mosley and with another daughter, Unity, when she moved to Germany to be closer to her beloved Adolf, whom she met at least 140 times. He attended the Nuremberg rallies, spoke in favour of the Anschluss in the Lords, and turned against 'the Hun' Hitler only when war was declared. Thereafter he lived a sad and lonely life, estranged from his wife (whose Nazi sympathies were more robust) and from his communist daughter Jessica. He was distraught when Unity shot herself in the head on the declaration of war and died of related meningitis in 1948, and when his only son Tom was killed in Burma, where he had been stationed after refusing to fight Hitler in Europe. He spent his last days a virtual recluse and died in 1958.

Is it fair to criticize the aristocracy for far-right inclinations? After all, most of the nation supported appeasement even after the Munich crisis, and anti-appeasement voices were crying in the wilderness for most of the 1930s. Plenty of aristocrats fought in the war. Clydesdale and Hamilton both used their civil aviation skills in the battle of Britain, the 6th Viscount Gort led the British Expeditionary Force in 1940, the 15th Lord Lovat commanded the 1st Special Service Brigade during

Operation Overlord, thirty-five peers were killed – four dukes, two marquesses, seven earls, four viscounts and eighteen barons – and twenty-nine peers lost their first sons.* Yet it is striking that so few aristocrats raised objections in the run-up to the war. Churchill was a rare exception among his class.

The social effects of the war were far-reaching. The Blitz delivered direct hits on Bridgewater, Dudley and Spencer Houses, and when peers fled to their country estates and closed their London palaces a pall of melancholic fatalism descended. As the dust-sheets were cast over the furniture, Chips Channon fretted that there would never be another ball at Holland House and that 'the houses of the great will never again open their hospitable doors'.[19] He was right to be disconsolate. Portman and Holland Houses were so badly damaged that they had to be demolished, and once the annual cycle of Society balls had been broken by the war, it proved difficult to reinstate them. Even the royal set-piece at the start of 'the Season', the presentation parties at which young upper-class debutantes made their first double curtsies before the monarch and officially launched themselves into Society – and on to the marriage market – came under fire. John Grigg, the 2nd Baron Altrincham, a Tory of a very liberal stamp, took direct aim at the fustiness of the royal court in 1957, complaining that the quaint, socially lopsided debutante ritual should have been 'quietly discontinued in 1945' because it gave the appearance of the queen 'standing at the apex of an aristocratic and plutocratic pyramid'.[20] For breaking rank in this way, Grigg was attacked in print by the archbishop of Canterbury and physically by a member of the League of Empire Loyalists. Others looking down the telescope from the opposite end claimed that the presentations had been degraded, as virtually anyone could now secure an invitation from the Lord Chamberlain and, as Princess Margaret put it, 'every tart in London was getting in'.[21] Since *The Times* carried advertisements saying 'peeress

---

*The House of Lords includes Alistair Windsor, the 2nd duke of Connaught, in its roll of honour, even though he was reckoned to be incompetent by his regiment and died of hypothermia when he fell out of a window, drunk, in Ottawa. The inclusion of Josiah, Baron Stamp, and his wife and son, who were killed when their house was bombed in the Blitz, is even more curious as Stamp was a founder member of the Anglo-German Fellowship who visited Hitler.

would chaperone a debutante',[22] and the countess of Clancarty and Lady St John of Bletso openly charged £2,000 to 'bring a girl out', it is not surprising that the ritual seemed both outdated and sullied. So in November 1957 the Lord Chamberlain announced that the 1958 Season would see the last presentation parties. Many of the key events of the Season would endure – including Royal Ascot, Henley Royal Regatta, Goodwood and Cowes – but one of the last regiment of 1,441 'debs', Fiona MacCarthy, the granddaughter of the French diplomat Baron de Belabre and great-granddaughter of Sir Robert McAlpine, reckoned that 'even the most inwardly ambitious girls were claiming to be doing the Season on sufferance by 1958'.[23] Henceforth occasions like Queen Charlotte's Birthday Ball, which dates back to the days of George III and continues today, would see wealthy and ambitious young women in search of a suitable husband curtsey before the Queen Charlotte cake rather than the monarch.

✠

The aristocracy continued to take hits from the Exchequer. In order to pay for the all-out war, the governing coalition abolished an exemption from death duties for private estate companies and increased the top rates of death duties and income tax to 65 per cent and 19s 6d in the pound respectively. The post-war Labour government further increased the top rate of death duties to 75 per cent and tightened the loophole whereby one could avoid duty by gifting an estate to one's heir. Such gifts now had to be made a full five years before death rather than three; so more estates were caught before they could slip through. Year by year, the round of aristocratic retrenchments continued. The 3rd earl of Plymouth sold Hewell Grange in 1946; the following year the 7th and last earl of Sefton dispensed with his Kirkby estate and the 4th marquess of Bute gave Cardiff Castle to the city; in 1948 Sotheby's auctioned off the contents of Wentworth-Woodhouse for the 8th Earl Fitzwilliam; in 1949 the 8th Viscount Portman handed over 3,777 acres in Dorset. In 1951 the Calthorpe family sold Gray's Inn Road in London, in 1952 the 2nd duke of Westminster sold Pimlico, in 1954 the 13th duke of Bedford split up his Chenies and Tavistock estates, and by 1963 the 18th earl of

Derby had done away with thirty of the seventy bedrooms at Rudding Park, taken down much of Knowsley Hall and moved into a smaller house in the grounds before turning the old house into a police headquarters.

Why the continual disaggregation of landed estates? They claimed it was all down to death duties, but the truth was more complex. It is true that some families were hit particularly badly when heirs died in swift succession. Dukes of Bedford died in 1940 and 1953; dukes of Wellington in 1934, 1941 and 1943; dukes of Devonshire in 1939, 1944 and 1952; marquesses of Lansdowne in 1927, 1934 and 1944; Earls Fitzwilliam in 1943, 1948 and 1952; and earls of Derby in 1939, 1948 and 1950. Such concertina-squeezing of generations, with the concomitant rapid succession of death duties, made it difficult for noble families to restore their finances in the intervening years. By contrast, the dukes of Norfolk got off relatively lightly, as the 15th and 16th dukes both inherited young and lived long, enjoying their titles for fifty-seven and fifty-eight years respectively; and the dukes of Sutherland had to face death duties only twice in the twentieth century, in 1913 and 1963. But the Exchequer was not the only, or in many cases even the primary, cause of the abandonment of the aristocracy's historic role as landed magnates. For decades, wily estate managers and accountants had been advising their masters to diversify, to invest in stocks and shares, to take on company directorships. After all, they were fully aware that, as one duke of Bedford put it, 'the proverbial danger of carrying all the eggs in one basket was now increased by the possibility that the bottom of the basket might fall out. Experience of a quarter of a century of adversity had shown the precarious nature of an income derived entirely or mainly from an agricultural estate.'[24] Moreover, vast houses were magnificent if you wanted to impress your neighbours or entertain in the grand style, but they were wholly impractical in an era where the typical household was much smaller and attended by a tiny staff. That was certainly Cecil Blathwayt's reason for handing Dyrham Park, which had been in his family since the seventeenth century, over to the National Trust in 1961; as he wrote to Lord Methuen, 'we love it – it's a person – but an exacting one'.[25]

Yet for many upper-class families this abandonment of a historic house felt like a humiliation, and they resented the policies that they insisted were making it necessary. Almost the moment the war was over they started pleading poverty, arguing that their stately homes were a vital part of the national heritage that needed protecting. If they were to be starved of cash, so they argued, the nation would have to step in. They might have expected the wealthy Labour Chancellor Sir Stafford Cripps to lend them a sympathetic ear, as his ancestral home at Parmoor became a convent in 1947, and they were not entirely disappointed. Cripps commissioned a report on the problem from Sir Ernest Gowers, who waxed lyrical about the English country house as 'the greatest contribution made by England to the visual arts . . . which is irreplaceable, and has seldom if ever, been equalled in the history of civilisation'.[26] Gowers also made exorbitant demands for an extensive new regime of tax exemptions and grants to be paid directly to the owners of the largest houses in the land. Labour understandably balked at this. Cripps pointed out to his Cabinet colleagues that it amounted to 'creating 2,000 pensioner families in perpetuity',[27] and Hugh Dalton argued that 'one of the most important of all the causes of great inequality of income is the inheritance of great fortunes by a small minority'.[28] But the Tories, returned to power in 1951, were even more dismissive of any such large-scale plan. The Minister for Works, David Eccles, wrote in 1953 that 'the fact must be faced that the mode of life for which these notable houses stood was doomed . . . All that the Government could hope to do . . . would be to preserve . . . a small selection of these houses as symbols of a former civilisation.'[29] The *Daily Express* agreed. 'The British people', it opined, 'are only interested in preserving a few historic houses. They have no interests in preserving the owners.'[30]

Nevertheless, the post-war years saw the stately home nobility make a remarkable financial comeback, thanks to rocketing rental incomes and land values. So pronounced was this resurgence, indeed, that even the impeccable pen portraitist of the upper classes Evelyn Waugh admitted in 1959 that his elegiac novel *Brideshead Revisited* (which had first been published in 1944) was 'a panegyric preached over an empty coffin . . . [as] the English aristocracy has maintained its identity to a degree that then seemed impossible'.[31] What is more surprising is that, despite the political consensus that there was little sympathy for the landed aristocracy, they secured major financial concessions from successive governments. Labour provided a 45 per cent abatement from death duties for agricultural land and endowed a National Land Fund with £50 million to enable executors to hand land and buildings over to the nation in lieu of death duties; and in 1953 the Tories set up the Historic Buildings Council (HBC) with an annual budget rising in stages from £250,000 to £400,000 and started doling out grants to supposedly indigent landowners. More than a hundred of them received over £10,000 apiece, and George Howard, the grandson of the 9th earl of Carlisle, who owned Castle Howard, got £100,000.

The beneficiaries took these grants with remarkably ill grace. The marquess of Hertford was so incensed when he was offered only £30,000 for repairs at Ragley Hall that he complained vociferously and threatened to pull the whole thing down – and was rewarded with an increase to £100,000. When George, the polo- and tennis-playing 5th marquess of Cholmondeley, was informed that a condition of the HBC grant he sought for Houghton Hall was that he would have to open the house one day a week during the summer, he imperiously tore up the agreement. Since he was one of the wealthiest men in the land, thanks to his marriage to Sybil Sassoon, it is difficult to see why he applied in the first place, other than through sheer greed and a sense that the public owed him something. Robert, the 9th Baron Walpole, took a similar attitude. He had inherited Wolterton Hall, the old home of the earls of Orford, from a distant cousin in 1931, and in 1950 opened it to the public on an occasional basis, charging half a crown to see its six state rooms, but he was hardly a congenial host. He rather pointedly told visitors in 1952 that 'this is a comfortable house to *live* in', immediately impressing upon them that they were his guests and not his equals. No doubt he would have been pleased with the comment of a local reporter: 'Nothing smacks of commerce here. It is not a bit like being a "customer" – despite the half-crown admission and the peaches for sale in the porch.'[32] Yet when the HBC provided a grant following a fire that gutted a whole floor that December and insisted that the house be reopened in June 1955, Walpole's response was first to close it again after barely two months, pleading dry rot, and then to open only on Thursday afternoons, without any publicity. To his great delight just forty-six visitors appeared in the whole of 1966. Likewise Major Le Gendre Horton-Fawkes, a distant descendant of Guy Fawkes, whose family had owned Farnley Hall near Otley since the Middle Ages, and had hosted J. M. W. Turner so often that the house contained hundreds of his drawings, told the Gowers Committee in 1949 that while his family held 'a sense of Trusteeship' about Farnley, his idea of opening the house was to allow art societies to visit by appointment and to allow 'individuals with whom I am acquainted to bring two or three friends'. Above all, he forcibly asserted, 'it is essential to rule out parties and individuals who just want a day out and can "tick off" Farnley Hall as "Visited" (not seen and felt, and little appreciated'.[33]

Similar scruples inspired the 16th duke of Norfolk to call for a special personal exemption in 1957. As hereditary Earl Marshal he had organized the coronations of George VI and Elizabeth II and the funerals of George VI and Winston Churchill, yet his estate was bound by a strict parliamentary entail from 1627 and he feared death duties would leave his successor in an invidious position. He therefore tried to get a private Bill through parliament that would end the entail and exempt Arundel Castle from death duties on the grounds that it was the official residence of the Earl Marshal. In exchange, he would give the castle to the nation with a £250,000 endowment. He probably thought he was being generous, and indeed the Lords, heartily applauding his magnanimity, let the Bill pass unscathed. It was given short shrift when it appeared in the Commons, though. MPs pointed out that he could easily hand Arundel over to the National Trust if things were really that bad, and by the time they had finished it was a one-clause Bill simply repealing the 1627 entail.

The role of the National Trust in this era of burgeoning state subventions for the peerage is fascinating. Founded by Octavia Hill in 1892 as the National Trust for Places of Historic Interest or Natural Beauty, it had been incorporated in statute law in 1907. In 1934, though, the 11th marquess of Lothian called for a tax exemption for country houses gifted by their owners to the National Trust so long as they came with sufficient other endowments to prevent them becoming a drain on the Trust. In 1937 this provision was enshrined in the National Trust Act, which allowed the Trust to preserve properties and ensure public access to them on a semi-commercial basis. The well-bred idea, wherever possible, was to keep the house, the family and the contents together as a living entity, albeit under new management and open to the public. When Lothian died in 1940 and duly left Blickling Hall, its contents, a hundred houses and cottages and 4,700 acres of woodland to the Trust, he was starting a trend. In 1947 the 3rd Baron Leconfield, who had put the Trust in charge of Scafell Pike in 1919, handed over Petworth House and its 735-acre estate, followed a few years later by its contents. In 1956 the 2nd Baron Faringdon and the 5th marquess of Bristol followed suit with Buscot Park and Ickworth House; in 1957 the duke of Devonshire surrendered Hardwick and half a dozen items from Chatsworth, and the earl of Morley opened Saltram House in Plympton to the public under the National Trust flag; and in 1958 the countess of Chesterfield's executors gifted Beningborough Hall in North Yorkshire. Not everyone approved. The 13th duke of Bedford felt that 'if Woburn was sold or otherwise disposed of to the National Trust or some institution, something would have gone out of the family, and indeed the history of England'.[34]

The Trust's officials were assiduous, scouring the countryside for potential properties, and by 1960 it had opened seventy-five country houses, up from forty-two in 1950. This was not always a simple process. Some families claimed such poverty that they sought to hand over their house without any endowment. Others refused to hand over a cash dowry because they wanted to part with the house, its leaking roof and its peeling wallpaper, but were determined to retain the money-spinning agricultural estate. The Trust, however, had learned that lesson back in 1907, when it accepted the virtually derelict Tudor manor house Barrington Court in Somerset and only managed to bring it back to life thanks to Colonel Lyle of the Tate & Lyle sugar company, who took a sudden interest in it – and a 99-year repair lease. So, as the first secretary of the Trust's Country House Committee, James Lees-Milne, traipsed round the dilapidated long galleries and walled gardens of England, he tried to put together financial packages that both kept owners in residence and minimized the financial risks to the Trust. It was a very polite form of nationalization and the compensation was generous. As Simon Jenkins put it in *The Times*, 'the great houses of England were brought into public ownership by confident delegation, by mild nepotism . . . by leaning on the great and the good. This was the old-boy network's finest hour . . . the noblest nationalisation. The aristocracy of England yielded up its finest possessions . . . into the care of like-minded guardians . . . They shared assumptions, friends, even families.'[35] Jenkins was right about their interconnectedness. Lees-Milne wrote a discreet biography of his friend Harold Nicolson, and his wife had an affair with Nicolson's wife Vita Sackville-West, who was born at Knole and created the garden at Sissinghurst Castle, both of which came to the Trust. When Lees-Milne visited Knole, which then belonged to Vita's cousin, the 3rd Baron Sackville, he found 'piles of dust under the chairs from worm borings. The gesso furniture too is in a terrible state. All the picture labels want renewing; the silver furniture cleaning; the window mullions mending.'[36] He eventually persuaded a very reluctant owner to hand Knole over; and the reports back from the early seasons suggested that Sackville had appointed tour guides who 'still feel, and sometimes show, that they are doing the public a great favour in admitting them to My Lord's house at all'.[37]

Sackville's simmering disgruntlement was commonplace and found open expression in 1974, when the fiercest defender of the stately home faith, Sir Roy Strong, was appointed director of the Victoria and Albert Museum. Even before Strong arrived in post he started planning a polemical exhibition on the fate of the hundreds of English stately homes that had already been lost. He was open about his intentions. The Labour government was threatening to introduce a capital transfer tax, which would apply whenever assets were transferred, whether in life or after death, and would therefore close off all means of avoiding death duties. Strong wildly predicted 'the end of a thousand years of English history and culture, as pell-mell the contents are unloaded into the saleroom, the houses handed over to the Government or demolished', and warned about 'the horrors looming unless one fights and intrigues at every level behind the scenes'.[38] He designed the 'Destruction' exhibition as propaganda pure and simple. In the main hall there were photographs of dozens of lost houses along with pictures of impoverished peers; alongside them, a panel explained that 'above all, they have gone because the nation as a whole was asleep to their beauty'. Another stated baldly: 'In modern times no other country has been party to such artistic destruction in a period of peace.' The exhibition/campaign had its effect. By the time of the next budget the new tax had evaporated.

Another twist in the tale came in 1977. Ever since his father's death three years earlier, the 7th earl of Rosebery had been trying to sell the elaborate (and to many minds ugly) Buckinghamshire mansion Mentmore Towers to the nation for £2 million in part settlement of his father's death duties. Prime Minister Jim Callaghan had refused to countenance the idea, so Rosebery decided to put the house and contents up for auction. There was a national outcry, of sorts. A 'Save Mentmore for the Nation' campaign was launched. Christopher Booker wrote in the *Spectator* that 'even in the crudest economic terms, the . . . case that Mentmore should be bought for the nation is unanswerable'.[39] Lees-Milne wrote to *The Times* to claim in spectacularly snobbish and exaggerated terms that 'in the eyes of discerning people, [it] constitutes one of the glories of Britain's peak of greatness',[40] and Strong weighed in to try to get the government to change its mind. But Callaghan stood firm – upon which Rosebery carted some of his favourite pieces off to his Scottish home, Dalmeny Castle, and sold the rest of the collection (including works by Gainsborough, Reynolds and Chippendale) for about £6.5 million. The house itself took a little longer but was eventually bought by the Maharishi Foundation for a mere £220,000.

The Mentmore saga sparked a national mania for the conservation and preservation of country houses, which bore fruit in the Thatcher government's decision to replace the National Land Fund with the National Heritage Memorial Fund (NHMF) in 1980. Its first grant, to the tune of £1.5 million from the taxpayer, was made to the National Trust to rescue and endow the dilapidated Elizabethan manor house of Canons Ashby in Northamptonshire. Although many of the NHMF's subsequent grants were for specific items, such as the purchase of

Antonio Canova's *The Three Graces* from the duke of Bedford for £3 million in 1994, it has also endowed several landed properties, including Hopetoun House, the home of the 4th marquess of Linlithgow and his son the earl of Hopetoun, which received £4 million in 1995. One such grant was particularly contentious. The Curzons had lived at Kedleston since the thirteenth century and Nathaniel Curzon, the 1st Baron Scarsdale, had commissioned the beautiful Palladian mansion Kedleston Hall in 1759, but when Richard Curzon, the 2nd Viscount Scarsdale, died in 1977, his cousin and heir Francis began lengthy negotiations with a view to selling it on the open market or handing it over to the National Trust. With his son demanding 10 per cent of any sale, the state requiring £2.5 million in death duties and the Trust initially reckoning the house needed £2.5 million for immediate repairs and another £6 million as a long-term endowment, it took a decade to reach a deal; and when the bargain was finally struck, it entailed the NHMF giving the Trust a whopping £13.5 million from the taxpayer and the viscount handing over a set of the keys in exchange for a guarantee that he and his family could remain in a 23-room wing with two flats for servants and the run of the grouse moors in perpetuity.

Many peers turned their noses up at even such generous state subventions and found another route to financial salvation. Spotting a commercial opportunity, many kept the stately home business in-house. Longleat and Woburn gained safari parks and Beaulieu a motor museum. Alton Towers, once the seat of the earls of Shrewsbury, became a theme park with a Corkscrew rollercoaster and Log Flume. By 1966 Lord Montagu of Beaulieu reckoned that nine houses each had at least a hundred thousand visitors a year. Castle Howard became the star of Granada's adaptation of *Brideshead Revisited*, Wrotham Park and Syon House featured in *Gosford Park*, Alnwick Castle became Harry Potter's school Hogwarts and Highclere became the fictitious earl of Grantham's home in *Downton Abbey*. The inexorable roll-out of the stately-home business has continued into new territory, too, as peers have taken advantage of the growing trend for civil weddings. In 2009 the 11th Earl De La Warr started renting out the library and drawing room at Buckhurst Park for weddings, and you can now get married in Warwick

Castle, Castle Howard, Haddon Hall, Hatfield, Chatsworth or Burghley, not to mention the Great Hall, Saloon or Long Library at Blenheim (with dancing in the Water Terraces).

A few peers seemed to enjoy playing up to this new role. Lord Montagu of Beaulieu delighted television audiences by singing (badly) Noël Coward's song 'The Stately Homes of England'. Raine, Countess Spencer, used to stand at the exit from the tour at Althorp House signing postcards for a fiver. And when the 13th duke of Bedford succeeded to his title in 1953, he seemed ready to do anything to get the family fortunes back in the black or get his face in the press. Facing a £5 million bill for death duties with few pictures left to sell after his father had disposed of much of the Woburn collection, he opened the house in 1954, invited Marilyn Monroe to sleep in Queen Victoria's bed, allowed a nudist convention to use the premises, and in 1958 appeared on the American panel show *To Tell the Truth* for an undisclosed fee alongside two impostor dukes (to his chagrin, only one of the four panellists correctly identified him). In 1959 Pathé filmed him getting dressed from his underpants to his tie in ninety seconds thanks to custom-made walk-in wardrobe fittings. The newsreel ended with the question: 'Why not turn *your* bedroom upside down? But preferably not when the little woman's at home.' Since the duke had more than four dozen pairs of shoes on show and had pleaded 'ducal poverty' in another Pathé newsreel in 1957, men as well as women might have wanted to take him to task for being quite so out of touch. In 1963 the duke even filmed an advert in which two women mopped the floor at Woburn with Flash and with another cleaner. As they finished, the duke turned to camera to say: 'Well, that certainly showed how Flash saved work and time. After that impressive result I'd say it was the best cleaner for any home.' The pay-off line was not exactly ducal, but then that was precisely what the advertisers had paid for.

Nobody could be in any doubt that the aristocracy had become part of the luxury entertainment and hospitality business. Its consolation prize was its titles, its wealth and its remembrance of things past.

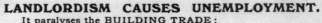

LANDLORDISM CAUSES UNEMPLOYMENT.

It paralyses the BUILDING TRADE;
It Pauperises the Peasantry;
12 Landlords "own" (?) London, taking £20,000,000 a year;
500 Peers "own" (?) an entire one-third of England;
4,000 Landlords "own" (?) an entire half of England;
The Land Octopus Sucks the Lifeblood of the People.

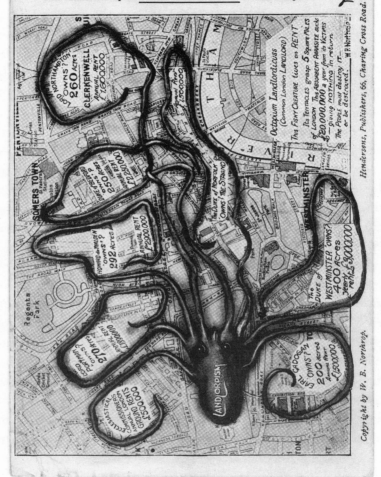

Although the twentieth century saw many aristocratic stately homes sold, converted or demolished, and many aristocrats relinquished substantial parts of their extensive landholdings, the map of London landlordism has not changed much since this one was produced in 1909; the Cadogan, Westminster, Bedford, de Walden and Portman estates still incorporate much of the most valuable property in the world.

CHAPTER 16

WE'RE ALL TAX DODGERS, AREN'T WE?

O N I I JANUARY 2017 Charlie, the genial 3rd Baron Lyell, died aged seventy-seven at Ninemills Hospital in Dundee after a short illness. He had inherited his title and the 10,000-acre Kinnordy estate when he was just four; after Eton, Christ Church and the Scots Guards, he spent nearly forty-seven years in the Lords, serving as a Conservative minister from 1979 to 1989. He never married and his title died with him, but under the byzantine rules drawn up when the majority of hereditary peers were excluded from the Lords in 1999, his seat was contested in a by-election in which twenty-seven hereditary peers stood. In the short statement required of them, most of the candidates emphasized their career and credentials, but Hugh Crossley, the 45-year-old 4th Baron Somerleyton, went straight for the ideological jugular: 'I think the hereditary peerage worth preserving and its principle creates a sense of innate commitment to the welfare of the nation,' he wrote. It is not difficult to understand why he would think that way. He was born in, owns, lives in and runs Somerleyton Hall near Lowestoft, which was bought by his carpet-manufacturer ancestor Sir Francis Crossley in 1863. It is palatial, with elaborate Italianate features, a maze, an aviary, a pergola 300 feet long, a marina, a 12-acre garden and a 5,000-acre estate. His own publicity material claims that 'a trip to Somerleyton is an experience of historical opulence'. Of course he believes in the hereditary principle and his own entitlement.

Yet for most of the twentieth century the aristocracy showed itself remarkably indifferent to 'the welfare of the nation', if attendance in the upper house is any indication. Debates in the Lords were cursory and poorly attended. Peers had a short week – rarely sitting on a Monday or Friday – and short days, starting at 3.45 or 4.15 p.m. In July 1931, for instance, while the Labour government was imploding, the Lords only sat once past 8 p.m. On 3 July they sat for just two minutes. It was the same in April 1934. The Commons sat on seventeen days that month, but the Lords managed just nine, averaging two and a half hours with one day lasting only thirty minutes. Numbers attending fell dramatically, too. In the two divisions in April 1934 only 63 out of 748 voted on one Bill and 66 on another, and when it came to the Protection of Animals Bill, a traditional preoccupation of their lordships, just thirty-seven peers voted. Even as war loomed, attendances were low and divisions rare. On 17 July 1939 the earl of Lucan told the House that he wanted it to sit early the following day, at 3 p.m., 'as there is a great deal of business on the Paper', but they still finished three minutes before six.[1] Hardly ever did they sit past the dinner hour. During the Second World War there were rarely more than two dozen peers in attendance, and in the post-war years the trend was accentuated: the average attendance in the 1953/4 session was ninety-seven, and on one occasion slipped as low as twenty-two. The overwhelming majority of the 847 peers regularly or permanently absented themselves; and yet they retained extraordinary power if and when they chose to exercise it. This became evident in 1956 when the Commons carried a private member's Bill to abolish the death penalty and the Lords voted it down by a resounding 238 votes to 95. The tedious business of daily attendance no longer interested their lordships, but when their personal interest was at stake or their reactionary hackles were raised, they would turn up in force. Lord Redesdale's daughter Nancy Mitford wrote in 1955 that the aristocracy still had 'real political power through the House of Lords',[2] but it flexed that particular muscle rarely and capriciously.

They had lost political potency as well, as a Commons by-election in 1944 made clear. The Cavendish family had dominated the West Derbyshire seat almost since it was formed. Apart from five short years when it had fallen into the hands of a Liberal, Charles White, it had been represented from 1891 to 1938 by three future peers, who became in due course the 9th duke of Devonshire, the 6th marquess of Lansdowne (brother of the 9th duke) and the 10th duke. The pattern was set to continue, as the 10th duke's brother-in-law Henry Hunloke succeeded him in 1938, and when Hunloke decided to make a swift exit from the political stage on the collapse of his marriage in 1944, the duke chaired the selection meeting at which it was agreed that his son the marquess of Hartington should stand. This should have been a formality, not least as the wartime convention was that the parties would not contest by-elections. But when White's son put his name forward as an 'Independent Labour' candidate, the campaign turned sour. Hartington got so exasperated at being asked at every meeting whether he had ever milked a cow that he challenged White to shovel muck at a local farm. This played into White's hands, as he told a meeting: 'The Marquess's interest in farming is limited to the rent roll. Last year I reared 50 pigs [and] maintained three cows.'[3] The Tories condemned this as 'filthy and reprehensible conduct',[4] but voters objected to Hartington's apparent sense of entitlement and White won. One paper concluded that 'to be the heir of a duke is now as much of a handicap to a political candidate as it once was an advantage'.[5]

Whether it was due to aristocratic laziness, self-doubt or umbrage, the fact that the Lords had become an institutional *Mary Celeste* gave successive governments a headache, as the functioning of the house required several dozen members on either side. This was evident enough when the Liberals were in government, but it became even more obvious when Labour came to power in 1945, as Clement Attlee had only fifteen supportive peers. Both sides gave ground simultaneously. Despite Labour's abhorrence of the hereditary principle, Attlee created forty-four hereditary peers to staff his own front bench and keep the Lords operating; and despite being a proud scion of the hereditary peerage, the Conservative leader in the Lords, the 5th marquess of Salisbury, volunteered a self-denying ordinance whereby they would not vote down a measure that had been promised in a manifesto. Despite this seeming magnanimity, it felt as if the Lords were just going through the motions, for form's sake.

It was a patrician Conservative government that attempted to sort out this unbalanced equation and enacted the biggest changes to the hereditary house. Harold Macmillan, the subtle, gentlemanly heir to a publishing fortune, was married to Dorothy Cavendish, a daughter of the 9th duke of Devonshire, and included in his extended family the duke of Leeds, the marquess of Salisbury, the earls of Crawford, Iveagh, Bradford and Dunmore, and a whole precinct of other lords – and his ministry included a duke, three marquesses, twelve earls, three viscounts and eight barons. Yet in 1957 he introduced a Bill that dismantled the historic meaning of a peerage and rescued the House of Lords from oblivion. In presenting the Bill, the Leader of the Lords, Alec Douglas-Home, the 14th earl of Home, argued that the House was 'perilously near a breakdown in its machinery', because there were not enough Labour peers 'to present to the world a picture of an efficient and informed House'. The only answer therefore was to offer life peerages 'to those persons who feel, for various good reasons, that they cannot accept hereditary peerages to-day'.[6]

The *Illustrated London News* called this 'a milestone in the history of the House of Lords',[7] but the idea of life peerages had been in the air for a century. Palmerston's government had been caught on the horns of a similar dilemma in the 1850s. Keen to appoint senior judges to the Lords to preside over the growing number of cases that were being brought to it as the highest court of appeal, but reluctant to burden the house with yet more permanent members or to provide the fortune deemed appropriate for a new hereditary dignity, Palmerston cast his eyes over the history books and found that although nearly all peerages had been heritable, a smattering had been granted without any remainder, most notably to eighteen royal mistresses and natural daughters, including Charles II's lover Louise de Kérouaille, George I's mistress Madame de Schulenberg and their natural daughter Petronella Melusina. Palmerston's plan was to start creating life peers again. So in 1856 Sir James Parke, a distinguished though gouty judge, was created Baron Wensleydale 'for and during the term of his natural life'. The government argued that the crown, the 'fount of all honour', had always enjoyed this right – but then snobbery kicked in, when the former Conservative Lord Chancellor Lord Lyndhurst, himself a new creation, objected to Wensleydale's letters patent, insisted that they did not entitle him to sit in the Lords and argued that the 'ancient hereditary character of this House [should not be] broken in upon and remodelled to the extent and according to the discretion and interest of the Minister for the time being'.[8] Gladstone's close friend the 2nd Earl Glanville, who was Lord President of the Council, replied by wryly asking: 'if the Crown could ... make Peeresses for life of an unpopular King's foreign mistresses, how can the right of the Crown in Baron Parke's instance be disputed?'[9] It was a good debating point, but the government lost the vote; so new letters patent were issued giving Parke the title of Baron Wensleydale of Walton with the usual remainder to heirs male. Since he was seventy-four and had no sons, the end result was the same, but the Lords had effectively exercised a veto on life peerages. This lasted until 1876, when the Appellate Jurisdiction Act allowed two senior judges to sit in the Lords as Lords of Appeal in Ordinary; a further development came in 1887 when these judges were allowed to remain members of the Lords after their retirement.

Like the law lords, the life peers announced under the new Act in 1958 were not especially wealthy. They were useful as 'working peers', an oxymoron that would have been anathema to the old leisured class, whose claim to independence was based on the fact that they had no vested interest because they did not need to work. Macmillan's Act was crafty. It restocked the Lords without diminishing the status of more ancient titles, and it left the hereditary peerage exactly where it wanted to be: entitled to sit and vote in the legislature but not required or even expected to attend. Yet further evidence of the aristocracy's political self-doubt came two years later. Medieval kings had used Acts of Attainder to deprive rebellious peers and their heirs of their titles and possessions, but no peer had willingly surrendered his title, which was considered as indelible as baptism. The honour was in the blood. But in 1960 a Labour peer, William Wedgwood Benn, Viscount Stansgate, died and, since his eldest son Michael had predeceased him in the war, the succession passed to his surviving son Anthony, who abhorred the hereditary system, refused to sit in the Lords and fought a legal battle not to be barred from his seat in the Commons. Conveniently for him, two Conservative hereditary peers, Alec Douglas-Home and Quintin Hogg, the 2nd

Viscount Hailsham, harboured ambitions to succeed Macmillan as Prime Minister. Both had served in the Commons before inheriting their fathers' titles but were convinced that the country would not countenance a Prime Minister who sat in the Lords. So in 1963 Macmillan introduced a Bill to allow peers to disclaim their titles, and when he resigned as Prime Minister that October, both Hailsham and Home availed themselves of its provisions while carefully securing themselves Commons seats. Once they had surfeited on politics, they both subsequently returned to the Lords with new life peerages.

When the Life Peerages Bill was introduced Attlee, now an earl, complained that it did 'nothing to correct excessive numbers'.[10] He had no idea what was coming, though. Aristocratic jealousy and public snobbery had made prime ministers think twice about appointing hereditary peers. Heavy criticism had been aimed at premiers for cheapening the honour. Lloyd George had unfairly taken most of the opprobrium for the sale of titles to inappropriate wealthy industrialists during his coalition government, but the Conservatives' strategy of promoting their donors proceeded apace throughout the century. With the insistence that a peer be wealthy enough to maintain their dignity now forgotten, all that held prime ministers back was the sense that every additional hereditary award increased the size of the house in perpetuity – and undermined the exclusivity of the peerage. With life peerages, though, there was no such restraint. So the numbers grew exponentially. Macmillan and his successor Home added 46 and 16 peers respectively, and when the next Labour occupant of No. 10, Harold Wilson, arrived in Downing Street in 1964 he set about evening up the score, appointing 122 peers in his first term and 80 in his second, an average of 25 a year. Heath, Callaghan, Thatcher and Major each doled out roughly 20 peerages a year between 1970 and 1997 as the expectation grew that retiring archbishops, chiefs of the defence staff, governors of the Bank of England and Cabinet members – all 'useful' men and women – were entitled to seats in the Lords. Much criticism was levelled at Wilson for his 'lavender list' of resignation honours, and every member of the Labour Cabinet of 1979 – apart from Michael Foot, Tony Benn and Albert Booth – accepted a peerage after leaving the Commons; but these elevations paled by comparison with those handed out by Tony Blair and David Cameron, who between them created 599 peers, among them diary secretaries, party apparatchiks and an assortment of the preternaturally loyal and financially generous.

The advent of a battalion of former MPs and party loyalists as life peers had a cultural effect on the Lords. Increasingly it became a place of partisan political business. As the battle over racial and sexual equality raged around them in the 1960s the very presence of the hereditary peers in the legislature, let alone their numerical predominance, became an evident anachronism. In 1968 Harold Wilson made a brave attempt at reform. Thanks to the quiescent support of Douglas-Home, who accepted that the Lords was becoming dysfunctional by virtue of its 'overwhelming built-in Conservative majority',[11] Wilson published a white paper calling for the phased abolition of sitting and voting rights for 'peers of succession' and tabled motions supporting it in both Houses. The Commons backed Wilson on 20 November 1968 by 270 votes to 159, but support in the Lords the following night was surprisingly even more emphatic – 251 to 56. In a significant display of self-denial twenty-six earls, including those of Glasgow, Malmesbury, Essex, Listowel, Buckinghamshire, De La Warr and Bathurst, along with Lloyd George's grandson the 3rd Earl Lloyd-George of Dyfor, voted for the white paper, as did the 8th marquess of Lansdowne and the archbishop of Canterbury. Even the 5th marquess of Salisbury admitted that 'few people in the world to-day ... would still attempt to maintain the view that the fact that a man is the son of his father could of itself justify a claim to be a Member of this House'.[12] Wilson must have thought success was assured. Yet when a Bill was presented in the Commons it was savaged by the vituperative wit and delaying tactics of Michael Foot and other Labour members on the grounds that a purely appointed house would give too much power to the government of the day – and it never got to the Lords, as Wilson decided to withdraw the proposal.

No further government attempt at reform was made until 1997, when Tony Blair included a commitment in the Labour manifesto to remove all the hereditary peers. The mood in the Lords had changed substantially since 1968. The Conservative governments of Thatcher and Major had suffered 241 defeats in the Lords in the course of eighteen years – roughly thirteen a year – while Wilson and Callaghan had been overturned 240 times between 1975 and 1979 alone. Fearful of the landslide Labour majority in the Commons and conscious of the corresponding value of the Conservative majority in their own house, the Lords issued dire warnings that such tinkering with the constitution would lead to constant obstructionism. A single lord could, as the 7th earl of Onslow pointed out, insist on a vote on each clause of every government Bill and endlessly tie the house up in procedural rows. William Hague attacked Blair's plan as an attempt to create a house of cronies – quietly ignoring the fact that he was relying on Conservative cronies to see off any Labour measure he disliked. The Conservative party chairman Brian Mawhinney (later a peer) claimed that reform of the Lords was 'driven by class envy'. Ever the pragmatist, by the time the Bill got its third reading in the Commons, Blair had struck a deal with the Conservative leader in the Lords, the latest Viscount Cranborne, who would urge his allies to sit on their hands on the condition that a royal commission be set up to consider wider reform of the Lords and that ninety-two hereditary peers, including the ceremonial posts of Lord Great Chamberlain and Earl Marshal, were allowed to survive until fuller reform was possible. When the Bill arrived in the Lords there was a great deal of huffing and puffing, and highly tendentious amendments were tabled and debated at length, but on 26 October it was carried by 221 votes to 81, with 6 earls supporting the government against 16 earls and 8 viscounts opposing the measure (including the 3rd Earl Lloyd-George, who had changed his mind since 1968, and the 11th Earl De La Warr, who evidently disagreed with his grandfather). The following March the cull occurred. The Lords now had 669 members instead of 1,330, and elections were held for the ninety hereditary seats.

Some might think this a fall from grace, but the aristocracy clung on to power long after the battles of 1911, and overturned the Commons (especially a Labour-led Commons) time and again. The very fact that ninety-two hereditaries were to remain (a larger number than had attended most debates over the previous eight decades) was a victory that proved their enduring strength. They had not just delayed but prevented democratic reform of the Lords, and they had entrenched their reactionary presence. And as late as 13 April 1999 they called in their troops, including the duke of Montrose, 3 marquesses, 21 earls and 17 viscounts, many of whom had barely darkened parliament's door in years, to vote down the equalization of the age of consent which had been carried in the Commons, forcing the government to use the Parliament Acts to overturn them.

Politics had become a minority interest for the aristocracy, yet for those who chose to exercise their parliamentary rights, the Lords gave them safe passage into government. In the 1990s John Major appointed a string of hereditary peers to his government. The Leader of the House of Lords was Viscount Cranborne, heir to the 6th marquess of Salisbury, and among the ministers were seven earls (7th Earl Howe, 9th Earl of Arran, 9th Earl of Courtown, 13th Earl Ferrers, 16th Earl of Lindsay, 18th earl of Strathmore and 20th Earl of Caithness), four viscounts (Ullswater, St Davids, Goschen and Astor) and five hereditary barons (8th Baron Henley, 2nd Baron Strathclyde, 2nd Baron Inglewood, 12th Baron Lucas, 6th Baron Chesham).[13] In addition, the National Heritage Memorial Fund and the Arts Council were both chaired by hereditary peers, Lord Rothschild and the Earl Gowrie (who had left the Cabinet in 1985 to be chairman of Sotheby's, saying he couldn't live in London on a ministerial salary). Even the administration formed by Theresa May in June 2017 included the 7th Earl Howe, the 4th Baron Ashton of Hyde, the 8th Baron Henley (who also holds the title of 6th Baron Northington), the 5th Viscount Younger and George Young, now Baron Young of Cookham, although his only hereditary title is his baronetcy.

When the horse-breeding owner of Highclere, the 7th earl of Carnarvon, argued against the exclusion of the hereditary peers in 1995, he claimed that 'one of the things which has distinguished our society has been the continuity of institutions encouraging those who are born with advantages to use those advantages in public life'.[14] Yet the modern aristocracy has shown remarkably little interest in public life. Very few peers have disclaimed their titles in order to sit in the Commons and the dukes, marquesses and earls have performed a great disappearing trick, absconding from the national stage to manage their private fortunes.

One aspect of the historic aristocracy has not changed, though. For all the tales of noble poverty and leaking ancestral homes, their private wealth remains phenomenal. According to a 2010 report for *Country Life*, a third of Britain's land still belongs to the aristocracy, and the Country Land and Business Association's 36,000 members own half the nation's rural land. Notwithstanding the extinction of some titles (such as the duke of Portland) and the sales of land early in the twentieth century, the lists of major aristocratic landowners in 1872 and in 2001 remain remarkably similar. Some of the oldest families have survived in the rudest financial health. In one analysis, the aristocratic descendants of the Plantagenet kings were worth £4 billion in 2001, owning 700,000 acres, and forty-two of them were members of the Lords up to 1999, including the dukes of Northumberland, Bedford, Beaufort and Norfolk. The figures for Scotland are even more striking. Nearly half the land is in the hands of 432 private individuals and companies. More than a quarter of all Scottish estates of more than 5,000 acres are held by a list of aristocratic families headed by the dukes of Buccleuch, Westminster and Atholl, the countess of Sutherland, the earls of Seafield and Moray, the Earl Granville, the Viscount Astor and the Baroness Willoughby de Eresby. In total they hold some 2.24 million acres, largely in the Lowlands. The table opposite offers a quick rundown.

Many noble landholdings are among the most prestigious and valuable in the world. In addition to his 96,000-acre Reay Forest, the 23,500-acre Abbeystead estate in Lancashire and the 11,500-acre Eaton estate in Cheshire, the duke of Westminster owns large chunks of Mayfair and Belgravia, Earl Cadogan owns parts of Cadogan Square, Sloane Street and the Kings Road, the marquess of Northampton owns 260 acres in Clerkenwell and Canonbury, the duke of Bedford retains twenty acres in Bloomsbury, the Baroness Howard de Walden (successor to the Portland estates) holds most of Harley Street and Marylebone High Street, and Viscount Portman owns 110 acres in Marylebone. Even the duke of Norfolk's four acres on Arundel Street off the Aldwych (in addition to his other 46,000 or so acres elsewhere) are particularly valuable. These attract some of the highest rental values in the world, a situation little changed since 1925, when W. B. Northrop published a

The greatest titled landowners in 1872 and 2001

Peer	Acres held in 1872	Peer	Acres held in 2001
Duke of Sutherland	1,358,545	Duke of Buccleuch and Queensbury	270,700
Duke of Buccleuch and Queensbury	460,108	Duke of Atholl	148,000
		Duke of Northumberland	132,200
Earl of Breadalbane	438,358	Duke of Westminster	129,300
Earl of Seafield	305,930	Earl of Seafield	101,000
Duke of Richmond and Gordon	286,411	Viscount Cowdray	93,600
		Countess of Sutherland	83,239
Earl of Fife	249,220	Baroness de Eresby	78,200
Duke of Atholl	201,640	Duke of Devonshire	73,000
Duke of Devonshire	198,572	Earl of Lonsdale	70,000
Duke of Northumberland	186,000	Duke of Roxburghe	65,600
Duke of Portland	183,199	Earl Granville	62,200
Lord Lovat	181,791	Duke of Argyll	60,800
Duke of Argyll	175,144		
Marquess of Conyngham	166,710		

Source: Kevin Cahill, *Who Owns Britain*, Edinburgh, Canongate, 2001.

postcard portraying the octopus of landlordism with its tentacles spread across London, charging the aristocracy with pauperizing the peasantry, paralysing the building trade and sucking the lifeblood of the people. One legal provision unique to England and Wales has been of particular importance to these aristocratic landlords, as over the centuries they built many millions of houses, mansion blocks and flats, which they sold on a leasehold rather than freehold basis. This meant, and still means, that purchasers are not buying the property outright, but merely a time-limited interest in it, so even the 'owners' of multi-million-pound residences have to pay 'ground rent' to the owner of the freehold, to whom the property reverts when their leases (which in some areas of central London are for no more than thirty-five years) run out. This is unearned income *par excellence*.

Built property aside, land ownership itself is still the source of exorbitant wealth, as agricultural land has increased in value. According to the 2016 '*Sunday Times* Rich List', thirty peers are each worth £100 million or more:

Top 30 richest peers, 2016: wealth in £ millions

Duke of Westminster 8,560	Lord Iliffe 235
Earl Cadogan 4,800	Marquess of Bath 210
Baroness Howard de Walden 3,230	Viscount Astor 200
Viscount Portman 1,720	Duke of Buccleuch 198
Lord Grantchester 1,200	Duke of Beaufort 145
Viscount Rothermere 1,000	Earl of Pembroke 145
Duke of Devonshire 850	Duke of Rutland 140
Earl of Iveagh 850	Duke of Roxburghe 125
Lord Vestey 700	Earl Spencer 125
Duke of Bedford 680	Earl of Rosebery 120
Duke of Sutherland 580	Earl of Stockton 120
Lord Rothschild 485	Marquess of Bute 117
Duke of Northumberland 350	Duke of Marlborough 110
Marquess of Salisbury 320	Marquess of Northampton 110
Viscount Cowdray 250	Earl of Halifax 100

Many aspects of their lives have barely changed. Edward William Fitzalan Howard, the 18th duke of Norfolk, is still the premier duke of England, the Earl Marshal, the Hereditary Marshal of England, a member of the Lords and the holder of nine other titles. His landholdings are obscure, but as he (under-)stated in his maiden (and only) speech in the Lords, 'I farm in West Sussex and own moorland in North Yorkshire,'[15] and he still lives at Arundel Castle, while his younger brother occupies Alton Towers. Many of those who have ceded their homes to the National Trust or to a charitable trust of their own devising (with all the concomitant tax advantages) still occupy their ancestral pads with the added benefit of modern plumbing and wiring. The dowager countess of Cawdor still lives in her former husband's castle thanks to a tax exemption, the marquess of Curzon still lives and shoots at Kedleston thanks to the NHMF and the duke of Marlborough seemingly still dines in the saloon at Blenheim courtesy of the £24.90 a head entry fee for visitors.

The country-house business is in fine fettle. True, the owners of lesser homes face significant challenges and a few peers have decided to downsize. In 2005 Lord Hesketh sold Easton Neston – designed by Nicholas Hawksmoor – in Northamptonshire (but kept Towcester racecourse). The 7th marquess of Bute offered Dumfries House to the National Trust for Scotland, and when they refused it Prince Charles stepped in with a consortium that found £45 million to purchase the house and its contents in 2007 and endow it for the future (it got £7 million from the NHMF). Michael Pearson, the 4th Viscount Cowdray, tried to find a partner to run Cowdray Park House as a hotel, and when that failed he sold the contents in 2011 for £7.9 million. But the grand homes like Chatsworth, Woburn and Longleat attract many thousands of visitors, the stately homes that survived in private hands up until 1960 are virtually all still in the same private hands today, and many peers continue their annual peregrination from one well-appointed palace to another. The Buccleuchs, for instance, have the rose-coloured sandstone palace of Drumlanrig as their main home, but they spend winter months at the much-enlarged hunting lodge, Bowhill, in the borders and at Boughton in Northamptonshire, an 11,000-acre estate that includes five villages and a stately home which hosts forty sketches by Van Dyck, *The Adoration of the Shepherds* by El Greco and a portrait of Mary Montagu by Thomas Gainsborough. When the previous duke made this journey he used to be accompanied by Leonardo da Vinci's *Madonna of the Yarnwinder* – the only Leonardo in private hands – until it was stolen. Among the hereditary peers in the Lords, the Earl Howe still lives at Penn House, the earl of Glasgow has covered his home Kelburn Castle in colourful graffiti, Viscount Thurso still lives in Thurso Castle, the duke of Montrose still lives on his ancestral estates at Auchmar near Loch Lomond, the duke of Somerset still holds Bradley House in Wiltshire and Berry Pomeroy Castle in Devon, and the duke of Wellington flits between Stratfield Saye in Hampshire and Apsley House on Hyde Park Corner.

Habits and obsessions have barely changed. Of today's twenty-four non-royal dukes, half went to Eton. Twenty-first-century aristocrats still belong to the same clubs their ancestors frequented: Brooks's, Boodle's, Pratt's and White's. Like Nancy Mitford in 1955, they entertain themselves distinguishing between 'non-u' ('serviettes', 'dentures', 'glasses' and 'greens') and 'u' terms (napkins, false teeth, spectacles and vegetables).[16] They play polo and love guns, horses and hounds. The 12th duke of Devonshire has been the queen's representative at Ascot Senior Steward of the Jockey Club and a prominent buyer and seller of fine art (in 2012 he sold a Raphael for £29.7 million). The 10th duke of Roxburghe describes the Floors Stud, which his father started in 1947, as his 'passion'; his horses Huntlaw, Twitch and Myopic won several races in 2016. The 10th duke of Beaufort was master of his eponymous hunt for sixty years and the hunt still meets regularly at Badminton. Emma, duchess of Rutland, hostess of the Belvoir Hunt and countless shooting parties, is so committed to making shooting a central attraction at Belvoir that she toured all the best shoots in the land and published her rhapsody to hunting in *Shooting: A Season of Discovery*. Likewise, the duke of Devonshire's 30,000-acre Bolton Abbey estate is reckoned to be one of the best for shooting pheasant and grouse, the marquess of Cholmondeley's estate at Houghton Hall in Norfolk has 'plenty of wild grey partridges on its rolling acres',[17] and the 8th Baron Brabourne's Hampshire estate at Broadlands with its Capability Brown park and ancestral home is said to excel for fishing brown and sea trout and salmon and for shooting snipe and duck.

How have the aristocracy achieved such a remarkable recovery of their fortunes?

First, in common with their ancestors, they have systematically, repeatedly and successfully sought to avoid tax. The eighteenth-century

WE'RE ALL TAX DODGERS, AREN'T WE?

satirist Charles Churchill wrote words that might have been the common motto of the aristocracy:

What is't to us, if taxes rise or fall,
Thanks to our fortune, we pay none at all.[18]

Thus, when the 2nd duke of Westminster deliberately paid his gardeners in a way that obviated any tax liability and was challenged in court, the judge Lord Tomlin ruled in 1936 that: 'Every man is entitled if he can to order his affairs so that the tax attracted under the appropriate act is less than it otherwise would be. If he succeeds in ordering them so as to secure this result, then, however unappreciative the commissioners of Inland Revenue or his fellow taxpayers may be of his ingenuity, he cannot be compelled to pay an increased tax.'[19] His fellow peers took this principle to heart. William and Edmund Vestey, the meat-packing businessmen who bought themselves a peerage and a baronetcy from Lloyd George for £20,000, regularly begged to be excused income tax, went into tax exile in Argentina and settled their finances in a trust based in Paris whose accounts were filed in Uruguay that saved the family £88 million in tax. When the 4th duke of Westminster died of cancer in 1967 his brother, the 5th duke, sought to exploit a loophole whereby anyone who had died in the service of their country was exempt from death duties. He improbably argued for twelve years that the cancer derived from a war wound from 18 July 1944 received while commanding his regiment – and, even more improbably, the courts agreed. He then exploited every other loophole going, so that on inheriting the family fortune in 2016, the 7th duke paid barely a penny of inheritance tax. In 1974 the 12th duke of Bedford went into tax exile in Monaco. In 1980 Samuel, the 3rd Baron Vestey, and his cousin Edmund were found to have paid just £10 in tax on the family business's £2.3 million profit; when they were challenged, Edmund shrugged his shoulders and said 'Let's face it. Nobody pays more tax than they have to. We're all tax dodgers, aren't we?'[20] Lord Thorneycroft added: 'Good luck to them.'[21] When the trustees of Castle Howard sold Joshua Reynolds's painting *Omai* for £9.7 million to pay for the castle's aristocratic occupant Simon Howard's divorce in 2001, they argued they should not have to pay capital gains tax on it as it was part of the fabric of the castle and therefore a 'wasting asset' which was exempt. Extraordinarily, in 2014 the Court of Appeal agreed. Dozens more, including the 8th earl of Glasgow and Viscount Rothermere, have left the country as tax exiles, returning for less than ninety days a year.

The primary means of squirrelling away substantial assets so as to preserve them intact and deliver a healthy income for aristocratic descendants without bothering the taxman is the trust. Countless peers with major landholdings and stately homes have put all their assets into discretionary trusts, thereby avoiding both public scrutiny and inheritance tax. This is what the duke of Westminster has done with the Grosvenor estates, whose trustees, chaired by the duke, dole out benefits and payments to members of the family while keeping the assets separate from any individual's estate. Her Majesty's Revenue and Customs is entitled to a percentage of the value of the trust fund every tenth anniversary of its creation, but after exemptions for farms and businesses have been taken into consideration, the Revenue is left virtually empty-handed. Income is subject to tax, but the patrimonial asset remains intact. There are countless examples: take the 6,750-acre Angmering Park Estate, which dates back to the Norman Conquest and includes farming, racing, shooting, fishing and forestry; it is owned not by the duke of Norfolk, but by the trustees of the 16th duke for the benefit of his daughters and other family members. Likewise the 9th duke of Buccleuch complained in 1995 that the 'Sunday Times Rich List' had overestimated his worth at £200 million, as he owned 'no shares in Buccleuch Estates Ltd'.[22] Legally, he was quite correct. Despite being a parent company for a string of valuable joint ventures and property holdings, the company is vested in four Edinburgh shareholder lawyers at a total value of £4. Since today's directors are the 10th duke, the duchess, their heir the earl of Dalkeith, and the duke's two brothers John and Damian, it is difficult not to conclude that the Buccleuchs are in reality the beneficial owners. Dozens of the old nobility have done the same, meaning that the family trust can quietly provide a house, an income, a lifestyle (and if required a divorce settlement) to any number of beneficiaries without fearing inheritance tax or the prying eyes of the public.

Inheritance tax has not been entirely escaped, but the 'acceptance in lieu' scheme has helped aristocratic collections stay together. George Howard, grandson of the 9th earl of Carlisle and son-in-law of the 8th duke of Grafton, died in 1984 having been given a life peerage as Baron Howard of Henderskelfe. He inherited the magnificent Castle Howard, opened it to the public (and to Granada television for *Brideshead Revisited*), and put it and its contents into trust. In 2016 the government accepted one of Castle Howard's paintings, Joshua Reynolds' portrait of the 5th earl of Carlisle, in lieu of £4.7 million in inheritance tax – and promptly put it back in Castle Howard. The scheme has helped many other paintings into public collections – also in 2016, the duke of Northumberland surrendered a Van Dyck to the Bowes Museum in Barnard Castle in lieu of £2.8 million inheritance tax – but the tax regime means that the item being offered is worth 17 per cent more to the owner than if they had sold it at auction. In addition, large amounts of the contents of stately homes are exempted from inheritance and capital gains tax if they are deemed sufficiently important to the national heritage and the owner gives an undertaking (however loose) to make them accessible to the public. Thus Burghley House, the beautiful Elizabethan home of the 6th marquess of Exeter, which is held in trust, has 289 items of artwork, furniture and jewellery deemed exempt, and the earl of Ilchester estates inherited by Charlotte Townshend have 497 items at Melbury House which are available for viewing – but only by appointment. The 12th duke and duchess of Grafton have twenty-seven such exempt items at Euston Hall, including three paintings by Reynolds, three by Stubbs, two by Lely, a Van Dyck and a Daniel Mytens; they are viewable in 2017 for the bare legal minimum of twenty-eight days (and then only from 10 a.m. to 1 p.m.). Even more bizarrely, although nearly all of Scotland has been opened up to 'responsible access' under Scottish law since 2003, the earl of Airlie still gets a tax exemption for allowing 'pre-arranged access ... for groups arranged by recognised wildlife organisations for up to 25 days each year'.[23] None of this feels as if the aristocracy are entering into the spirit of the law.

Second, they may not like paying tax, but they don't object to taking handouts from the taxpayer. The landed aristocracy have benefited to an extraordinary degree from payments under the EU's Common Agricultural Policy. The figures are staggering. At least one in five of the UK's top one hundred single-payment recipients in 2015/16 was aristocratic. The 8th earl of Yarborough, who owns the 27,000-acre Brocklesby estate and lives at Brocklesby Park with what he terms the oldest private pack of foxhounds in the country, received £654,204. The 4th earl of Iveagh, whose company Elveden Farms is owned through an offshore trust based in Jersey, received £980,774 through the single-payment scheme, and £1,285,419 overall. The Vestey family, who own the 17,000-acre Thurlow Estate, received £1,024,918. John Fellowes, 4th baron de Ramsey, whose family home is Abbots Ripton Hall, with an 8-acre park, 10-acre lake and 5,700-acre farm, received £639,766. The 3rd Baron Iliffe chairs the Yattendon Group, which includes a marina development company, a property development company in British Columbia and his 9,000-acre Christmas-tree-producing Yattendon estate. The group posted pre-tax profits of £29.6 million and received £527,291 from the EU. The Buckminster estates, which were put into trust in 1915 for the Tollemache family, the earls of Dysart, received £1,048,906. The richest have carried off the most. The duke of Westminster's Grosvenor Farms estate received £913,517, the duke of Northumberland's Percy Farms took £1,010,672, the duke of Marlborough's Blenheim Farms got £823,055 and Lord Rothschild's Waddesdon estates received £708,919. This is all in a single year. Multiplied across the years, the payments from the EU have benefited the British aristocracy to the tune of many millions of pounds. One of the wealthiest is Charlotte Townshend, whose parents were the 9th Viscount Galway and a daughter of the 7th earl of Ilchester. Charlotte inherited both her parents' family estates (but not their titles, which went to cousins), leaving her with 20 acres in Holland Park, 15,000 acres at Evershot in Dorset and the Ilchester home, Melbury House. She is reckoned to be worth £342 million and is a director of sixteen companies including two building firms, Ilchester Estates, Moorcrest Solutions Ltd (which is registered in the British Virgin Islands) and Evershot Farms, which received £803,994 from the CAP.[24]

Legally exploiting the system is second nature to the landowning class. The 11th duke and duchess of Beaufort, the owners of Badminton

House, have benefited handsomely from their property rights. Their company Swangrove Estates Ltd, whose directors are the duke and duchess, their son the marquess of Worcester and grandson the earl of Glamorgan, received £456,810 from the CAP in 2014/15, and in 2009 it was discovered that the duke had exercised his ancestral rights over the riverbed in Swansea by charging the council £281,341 to build a bridge across the river from a shopping centre to the Liberty stadium. With the help of the taxpayer – and no little ingenuity of his own – the duke has secured a fortune reckoned to be in the region of £145 million.

The EU is not their only source of financial assistance. Charles Chetwynd-Talbot, 22nd earl of Shrewsbury, who lives at the seventeenth-century manor house of Wanfield Hall in Shropshire and is president of the Gun Trade Association, has auctioned off a number of feudal titles, including that of High Steward of Ireland, a practice which has helped keep several other peers (including the earl of Shannon, the lord de Freyne, Viscount Gormanston and Lord Inchiquin) in the style to which their families had become accustomed. In April 2015 the earl put the lordship of Whitchurch up for sale, in 1996 Earl Spencer sold the lordship of the manor of Wimbledon for $250,000, and at the time of writing Manorial Auctioneers Ltd claim to be auctioning lordships of the manor, a seignory in Jersey and a feudal barony in Ireland on the instructions of 'members of the aristocracy'. Attendance in the House of Lords brings in an income too, although peers are keen to state that it is not a salary. When life peerages were introduced, the marquess of Salisbury was quick to point out that the three guineas a day they were paid did not represent 'any additional remuneration; it is merely repayment for expenditure which has already been incurred by noble Lords in the performance of their duties'.[25] So too today peers may claim £300 a day if the Lords records show that they attended a sitting of the house that day, or £150 a day if they undertook qualifying work away from Westminster. In March 2016, when the Lords sat for fifteen days, sixteen earls were paid £52,650 between them in tax-free attendance allowance, plus travel costs, and thirteen viscounts received £43,050. The duke of Somerset claimed £3,600 and the duke of Montrose was paid £2,750 plus £1,570 in travel costs: £76 for the use of his car, £258 for train tickets, £1,087 for air tickets and £149 for taxis and parking costs. The noble duke spoke in debate or in Grand Committee just twice in the whole parliamentary session, and not at all that March.

✠

The secret to the survival of the old aristocracy through the centuries was the mystique of grandeur that they cultivated. They dressed, decorated and built to impress, so that nobody dared question their right to rule. The secret of their modern existence is their sheer invisibility. As the *Daily Mail* commented when the *Tatler* gathered a table of ten dukes together in 2009: 'Once, the holders of these titles would have been the A-list celebrities of their time. Today, most people would be pushed to name a single one of them.'[26] That is no accident. British laws on land tenure, inheritance tax, corporate governance and discretionary trusts still make it easy to hide wealth from public view. Land is subsidized, and taxed more lightly than residential property. Unearned income bears less of a burden than earned income. All this quiet underpinning maintains the aristocracy, wrapped in the old aura of entitlement, counting its blessings and hoping that nobody notices. Curiously enough, that sceptical daughter of the ignorant and preposterously right-wing 2nd Baron Redesdale, Nancy Mitford, was probably right: 'It may well be that he who, for a thousand years has weathered so many a storm, religious, dynastic and political, is taking cover in order to weather yet one more.'[27]

So could you always spot an aristocrat? Not if you came up against Rhodri Philipps, who in July 2017 was sentenced to twelve weeks' imprisonment for offering £5,000 to anyone who would 'accidentally' run over the pro-EU campaigner Gina Miller, suggesting that she was a 'bloody troublesome first generation immigrant' and that 'if this is what we should expect from immigrants, [we should] send them back to their stinking jungles'.[28] Such is the supposedly indelible status of the aristocracy that despite his malice and racism he proudly retains his titles as 4th Viscount St Davids, 17th Baron Strange, 24th Baron de Moleyns and 25th Baron Hungerford – and that is the ignoble iniquity of today's entitled class.

NOTES

Abbreviations

CJ   *House of Commons Journal*
CSP   *Calendar of State Papers*
HC   *Hansard's Parliamentary Debates, Commons*
HL   *Hansard's Parliamentary Debates, Lords*
HMC   Historical Manuscripts Commission
LJ   *House of Lords Journal*
SRO   Scottish Record Office (National Archive of Scotland)
TNA   The National Archives

Introduction

1 *Stamford Mercury*, Friday, 21 April 1837, p. 4.
2 Nancy Mitford, *The Stanleys of Alderley*, London, Hamish Hamilton, 1939, p. 186.
3 Pamela Horn, *Ladies of the Manor*, Stroud, Amberley, 2012, pp. 19–20.
4 *HL*, 8 May 1934, vol. 92, col. 85.
5 Mary Hervey, *The Life, Correspondence and Collections of Thomas Howard, Earl of Arundel*, Cambridge, Cambridge University Press, 1921, p. 191.
6 *Spectator*, 5 Nov. 1831, p. 15.
7 *Tatler*, 25 June 1902.
8 *Tatler*, 20 Aug. 1902.

Chapter 1: Not of some meaner sort, but of some quality

1 A. M. Sellar, ed., *Bede's Ecclesiastical History of England*, London, George Bell, 1907, p. 269.
2 Thomas Alan Shippey, ed., *Poems of Wisdom and Learning in Old English*, Cambridge, Brewer, 1976, pp. 66–7.
3 Sellar, ed., *Bede's Ecclesiastical History*, p. 117.
4 *The Battle of Maldon*, trans. R. M. Liuzza, in Joseph Black, ed., *The Broadview Anthology of British Literature*, Peterborough, Ont., Broadview, 2009, p. 104.
5 Ibid.
6 Michael Alexander, trans., *Beowulf*, London, Penguin, 1973, p. 142.
7 Benjamin Thorpe, ed., *Ancient Laws and Institutes of England*, London, Commissioners of Public Records, 1840, vol. 1, pp. 191–2.
8 Agnes Robertson, ed., *The Laws of the Kings of England from Edmund to Henry I*, Oxford, Oxford University Press, 1925, pp. 32–3.
9 K. H. Jackson, ed. and trans., *The Gaelic Notes in the Book of Deer*, Cambridge, Cambridge University Press, 1972, p. 31.

10 Dorothy Whitelock, ed., *English Historical Documents*, 2nd edn, vol. 1, London, Eyre & Spottiswoode, 1979, p. 542.

11 Mercedes Salvador-Bello's translation, in Donald Scragg, ed., *Edgar, King of the English*, Woodbridge, Boydell, 2008, p. 265.

12 Joseph Stevenson, ed. and trans., *The Church Historians of England*, vol. 2, pt 1, London, Seeleys, 1853, p. 90.

13 R. R. Darlington and P. McGurk, eds; J. Bray and P. McGurk, trans., *The Chronicle of John of Worcester*, Oxford, Clarendon Press, 1995, pp. 504–5.

14 J. A. Giles, ed., *Roger of Wendover's Flowers of History*, London, Henry Bohn, 1849, vol. 1, pp. 276–7.

15 J. A. Giles, ed., *William of Malmesbury's Chronicle of the Kings of England*, London, Henry Bohn, 1847, p. 169.

16 W. D. Macray, *Chronicon Abbatiae de Ramsey*, London, Rolls Series, 1886, p. 80.

17 Michael Swanton, ed. and trans., *The Anglo-Saxon Chronicle*, London, Dent, 1996, pp. 160–1.

18 Darlington et al., eds and trans, *The Chronicle of John of Worcester*, vol. 2, p. 532.

19 Swanton, ed. and trans., *The Anglo-Saxon Chronicle*, p. 182.

20 Peter Sawyer, ed., *Anglo-Saxon Charters: an Annotated List and Bibliography*, London, Royal Historical Society, 1963, no. S39, available online at www.esawyer.org.uk.

21 Ibid., no. S315.

22 Cited in Stephen David Baxter, ed., *Early Medieval Studies in Honour of Patrick Wormald*, Farnham, Ashgate, 2009, p. 351.

23 Dorothy Whitelock, ed. and trans., *Anglo-Saxon Wills*, Cambridge, Cambridge University Press, 1930, pp. 11–13.

24 Darlington et al., eds and trans, *The Chronicle of John of Worcester*, vol. 2, pp. 582–3.

25 Alistair Campbell and Simon Keynes, eds, *Encomium Emmae Reginae*, Cambridge, Cambridge University Press, 1998, p. xxxii.

Chapter 2: Get it they must

1 Nora Kershaw Chadwick, ed. and trans., *Anglo-Saxon and Norse Poems*, Cambridge, Cambridge University Press, 1922, p. 51.

2 Marjorie Chibnall, ed. and trans., *The Ecclesiastical History of Orderic Vitalis*, Oxford, Oxford University Press, 1969, vol. 2, pp. 214, 216–19.

3 Joseph Stevenson, ed. and trans., *The Historical Works of Simeon of Durham*, vol. 3, part 2 of *The Church Historians of England*, London, Seeleys, 1855, p. 686.

4 J. A. Giles, ed., *William of Malmesbury's Chronicle of the Kings of England*, London, Henry Bohn, 1847, p. 286.

5 Chibnall, ed. and trans., *The Ecclesiastical History of Orderic Vitalis*, pp. 231, 233.

6 Giles, ed., *William of Malmesbury's Chronicle of the Kings of England*, p. 286.

7 Jacob Langebek, ed., *Scriptorum Rerum Danicorum*, Copenhagen, 1774, vol. 3, pp. 346–7, cited by Ann Williams, *The English and the Norman Conquest*, Woodbridge, Boydell & Brewer, 1996, p. 81.

8 David Douglas and George Greenaway, eds, *English Historical Documents, 1042–1189*, London, Routledge, 1981, p. 1125.
9 Chibnall, ed. and trans., *The Ecclesiastical History of Orderic Vitalis*, vol. 2, p. 190.
10 Ibid., p. 267.
11 Thomas Arnold, ed., *Memorials of St Edmund's Abbey*, London, Eyre & Spottiswoode, 1890, vol. 1, p. 58.
12 Catherine Morton and Hope Muntz, eds, *The Carmen de Hastingi Proelio of Guy, bishop of Amiens*, Oxford, Clarendon Press, 1972, pp. 22–3.
13 Thomas Forester, ed. and trans., *The Chronicle of Henry of Huntingdon*, London, Henry Bohn, 1853, p. 215.
14 Diana E. Greenway, ed., *Charters of the Honour of Mowbray 1107–1191*, Oxford, Oxford University Press, 1972, p. 7.
15 Forester, ed. and trans., *The Chronicle of Henry of Huntingdon*, p. 216.
16 Robert Fleming, *Domesday Book and the Law*, Cambridge, Cambridge University Press, 1998, p. 259.
17 Thomas Forester, ed. and trans., *Orderic Vitalis, The Ecclesiastical History of England and Normandy*, London, Henry Bohn, 1854, vol. 2, book 8, p. 432.
18 L. J. Downer, ed., *Leges Henrici Primi*, Oxford, Clarendon Press, 1972, p. 224.
19 Richard Howlett, ed., *Chronicles of the Reigns of Stephen, Henry II and Richard I*, Cambridge, Cambridge University Press, 2012, vol. 3, p. 73.
20 *Tractatus de legibus et consuetudinibus regni Angliae vocatur Glanvilla*, trans. John Beames, Washington DC, 1812.
21 Ernest-Joseph Tardif, ed., *Coutumiers de Normandie*, Paris, A. Picard, 1903, vol. 1, part 2, p. 6.
22 Chibnall, ed. and trans., *The Ecclesiastical History of Orderic Vitalis*, vol. 4, p. 134.
23 Ibid., vol. 2, p. 262.
24 Alexander Bell, ed., *L'Estoir des Engleis by Geffrei Gaimar*, Oxford, Oxford University Press, 1960, Gaimar, lines 5881–2.
25 Forester, ed. and trans., *The Chronicle of Henry of Huntingdon*, pp. 216–17.

Chapter 3: Give me my father's inheritance

1 Jan M. Ziolkowski, ed. and trans., *The Cambridge Songs*, Tempe, AZ, Medieval and Renaissance Texts and Studies, 1998, p. 25.
2 James Daley, ed., *Great Inaugural Addresses*, Mineola, NY, Dover, 2012, p. 74.
3 Charles Johnson, ed., *Dialogus de Scaccario*, Oxford, Clarendon Press, 1983, pp. 64–5.
4 J. A. Giles, ed., *The Anglo-Saxon Chronicle*, London, G. Bell, 1914, pp. 200–1.
5 John Beames, ed. and trans., *A Translation of Glanville*, London, W. Reed, 1812, p. 232.
6 Ernest-Joseph Tardif, ed., *Coutumiers de Normandie*, Paris, A. Picard, 1903, vol. 1, part 2, p. 9.
7 A. J. Robertson, ed. and trans., *The Laws of the Kings of England from Edmund to Henry I*, Cambridge, Cambridge University Press, 1925, p. 286.
8 Thomas Hearne, ed., *Liber Niger Scaccarii*, Oxford, 1728, vol. 1, p. 384.

9 Anthony J. Holden and David Crouch, eds; Stewart Gregory, trans., *History of William Marshal*, Oxford, Anglo-Norman Text Society, 2002–6, vol. 2, lines 1367–74.

10 Henry T. Riley, ed., *Gesta Abbatum Monasterii Sancti Albani, a Thoma Walsingham*, London, Rolls Series 28 (1867–9), vol. 1, p. 227.

11 Francisque Michel, ed., *Histoire des ducs de Normandie et des rois d'Angleterre*, Paris, Jules Renouard, 1840, pp. 117–18.

12 Ibid., p. 105.

13 J. A. Giles, ed. and trans., *Roger of Wendover's Flowers of History*, London, Henry Bohn, 1849, vol. 2, p. 303.

14 J. A. Giles, ed. and trans., *Matthew Paris's English History*, London, Henry Bohn, 1854, vol. 3, p. 327.

15 J. R. Maddicott, *Simon de Montfort*, Cambridge, Cambridge University Press, 1994, p. 341.

16 H. Ellis, ed., *Chronica Johannis de Oxenedes*, Rolls Series 13, London, Longmans et al., 1859, p. 229.

17 Giles, ed. and trans., *Matthew Paris's English History*, p. 354.

18 William Stubbs, ed., *Gesta Regis Henrici*, London, Longmans, Green, Reader & Dyer, 1867, vol. 1, pp. 143–4

19 Maddicott, *Simon de Montfort*, p. 1.

Chapter 4: They could not transport all the spoils

1 From the charter to William de Clinton, appointing him earl of Huntingdon, in *Reports from the Lords Committee Touching the Dignity of a Peer of the Realm*, London, House of Lords, 1829, vol. 5, pp. 28–9.

2 Ibid., vol. 5, p. 320.

3 Edward Maunde Thompson, ed., *Adæ Murimuth Continuatio Chronicarum*, London, Rolls Series, 1889, p. 232.

4 R. Barber, *Life and Campaigns of the Black Prince*, Woodbridge, Boydell & Brewer, 1986, pp. 33–4.

5 M. K. Pope and E. C. Lodge, *The Chandos Herald's Life of the Black Prince*, Oxford, Oxford University Press, 1910, vol. 2, pp. 1395–7.

6 Richard Colt Hoare, *Heytesbury Hundred*, London, John Bowyer Nichols, 1824, p. 29.

7 Ibid., p. 101.

8 Thomas Rymer, *Foedera*, London, Joannem Neulme, 1739, vol. 1, part 1, p. 297.

9 Quoted in A. Harding, *Medieval Law and the Foundation of the State*, Oxford, Oxford University Press, 2002, p. 214.

10 *Reports . . . Touching the Dignity of a Peer*, vol. 5, p. 321.

11 Thompson, ed., *Adæ Murimuth Continuatio Chronicarum*, p. 273 (emphasis added).

12 George James Aungier, ed., *Chroniques de London*, London, Camden Society, 1844, pp. 89–90.

13 15 Edward III, st. 1, sec. 2 (emphasis added).

14 *Reports . . . Touching the Dignity of a Peer*, vol. 5, p. 81.

15 *Calendar of Patent Rolls 1441–6*, London, HMSO, 1908, p. 51.

16 *Rotuli Parliamentorum*, London, 1832, vol. 3, p. 343.

17 N. H. Nicholas, ed., *Proceedings and Ordinances of the Privy Council of England*, London, Commissioner of Public Records, 1834, vol. 2, pp. 104–5.

18 Jacob, Baron Hastings, ed., *An Account of the Controversy between Lord Grey of Ruthyn and Edward Hastings in the Court of Chivalry*, London, College of Arms, 1841, pp. xiii–xiv.

19 John Raithby, ed., *Statutes of the Realm*, London, Eyre & Spottiswoode, 1870, vol. 1, p. 304.

20 J. S. Hamilton, *Piers Gaveston*, Detroit, MI, Wayne State University Press, 1988, p. 50.

21 Francis Blomefield and Charles Parkin, *An Essay towards a Topographical History of the County of Norfolk*, London, William Miller, 1806, vol. 4, pp. 87–8.

22 James Raine, ed., *Testamenta Eboracensia*, London, J. B. Nichols, 1836, vol. 1, pp. 236–7.

Chapter 5: To make my fame endure

1 Edmund Lodge, ed., *Portraits of Illustrious Personages*, London, Harding & Lepard, 1835, vol. 3, p. 8.

2 Joseph Robertson, ed., *The Works of Algernon Sidney*, London, W. Strahan, 1772, p. 213.

3 D. Dean, 'Elizabethan government and politics', in R. Tittler and N. Jones, eds, *A Companion to Tudor England*, Oxford, Oxford University Press, 2004, p. 48.

4 John Roche Dasent, ed., *Acts of the Privy Council*, vol. 8, London, HMSO, 1894, pp. 203–6.

5 James Gairdner, ed., *Letters and Papers Foreign and Domestic, Henry VIII*, vol. 8, London, HMSO, 1885, p. 56.

6 James Gairdner, ed., *Letters and Papers Foreign and Domestic, Henry VIII*, vol. 12, London, 1891, part 2, p. 205.

7 James Gairdner and R. H. Brodie, eds, *Letters and Papers Foreign and Domestic, Henry VIII*, vol. 17, London, 1900, no. 304.

8 *Account of Kett's Rebellion*, Norwich Record Office, COL/9/117, fo. 1.

9 Ralph Holinshed, *Chronicles of England, Scotland and Ireland*, London, J. Johnson, 1807, vol. 3, p. 990.

10 Nicolas Harris, ed., *Memoirs of the Life and Times of Sir Christopher Hatton*, London, Richard Bentley, 1847, p. 126.

11 John Stow, *Annales or A General Chronicle of England*, London, 1603, pp. 808–9.

12 Cited in Barbara Harris, *Edward Stafford, Third Duke of Buckingham, 1478–1521*, Stanford, CA, Stanford University Press, 1986, p. 80. I am indebted to Ms Harris for her account of Thornbury.

13 Henry Ellis, ed., *Hall's Chronicle*, London, J. Johnson et al., 1809, p. 832.

14 Norman Egbert McClure, ed., *The Epigrams of Sir John Harington*, Philadelphia, University of Pennsylvania Press, 1926, p. 364.

15 Shakespeare, *Romeo and Juliet*, Act 2, scene 4.

16 D. M. Brodie, ed., *The Tree of Commonwealth: A Treatise Written by Edmund Dudley*, Cambridge, Cambridge University Press, 1948, p. 19.

17 Henry Herbert Croft, ed., *The Book Named The Governor*, London, Dent, 1880, vol. 1, p. 99.
18 *The Arte of English Poesie*, in E. Arber, ed., *English Reprints*, London, Alexander Murray, 1869, p. 74.
19 George Gilfillan, ed., *The Poetical Works of Edmund Spenser*, Edinburgh, James Nichol, 1849, vol. 5, p. 32.
20 Croft, ed., *The Book Named The Governor*, vol. 1, pp. 3–4.
21 *Sermons and Homilies Appointed to be Read in Churches*, London, Prayer Book and Homily Society, 1840, p. 103
22 Gilfillan, ed., *The Poetical Works of Edmund Spenser*, vol. 5, p. 32.
23 College of Arms MS, L. 12.
24 Lucy Toulmin Smith, ed., *Leland's Itinerary in England and Wales*, London, George Bell, 1907, vol. 3, p. 53.
25 Thomas Allen, ed., *A New and Completed History of the County of York*, London, I. T. Hinton, 1831, vol. 3, p. 398.
26 Barbara J. Harris, *English Aristocratic Women, 1450–1550*, Oxford, Oxford University Press, 2002, p. 25.
27 Ibid.
28 See Lawrence Stone, *The Family, Sex and Marriage in England, 1500–1800*, London, Weidenfeld & Nicolson, 1977.
29 Harris, *English Aristocratic Women*, p. 20.
30 Muriel St Clare Byrne, *The Lisle Letters*, Chicago, University of Chicago Press, 1981, vol. 4, p. 74.
31 Emrys Jones, ed., *Henry Howard, Earl of Surrey: Poems*, Oxford, Oxford University Press, 1964, p. 44, line 12.
32 Sir William Segar, *Honor, Military and Civil*, Delmar, NY, Scholar's Facsimiles and Reprints, 1975, p. 253.

Chapter 6: We will not that persons of place should be so neglected

1 HMC, *The Manuscripts of His Grace the Duke of Portland, preserved at Welbeck Abbey* (HMC Portland), vol. 9, p. 113.
2 Cited in Roger Lockyer, *Buckingham: The Life and Career of George Villiers, First Duke of Buckingham*, London, Longman, 1981, p. 43.
3 Yale University Library, Manuscripts and Archives, Osborn FB240.
4 Arundel Castle MS T9, Newman, 'A Draft Will of the Earl of Arundel', pp. 692–6.
5 Henry E. Huntingdon Library, San Marino, CA, Bridgewater MSS 6560, 17 Aug. 1640, cited in Linda Levy Peck, *Consuming Splendor*, Cambridge, Cambridge University Press, 2005, p. 209.
6 The numbers are taken from the *Catalogue of the Curious Collection of Pictures of George Villiers*, London, Brian Fairfax, 1758.
7 J. S. Brewer, ed., *Bishop Geoffrey Goodman's* The Court of King James the First, London, 1839, vol. 2, pp. 369–70.
8 John Pye, *Patronage of British Art*, London, Longman, Brown, Green & Longmans, 1845, p. 31.

9 Anon., *Secret Memoirs of Robert Dudley, Earl of Leicester*, London, Sam Briscoe, 1706, p. 82.
10 Norman Egbert McClure, ed., *The Letters of John Chamberlain*, Philadelphia, American Philosophical Society, 1939, vol. 2, p. 630.
11 *CSP Venetian 1625–26*, London, HMSO, 1913, pp. 12, 21.
12 William Huse Dunham, 'William Camden's commonplace book', *Yale University Library Gazette*, vol. 43, 1969, pp. 151–2.
13 John Rushworth, ed., *Historical Collections of Private Passages of State*, London, D. Browne, 1721, vol. 1, p. 335.
14 Ibid., vol. 1, p. 338.
15 TNA, SP 16/191/6.
16 TNA, SO1/2, fos 162–3.
17 TNA, SP 16/363/82.
18 HMC, *Report on the Manuscripts of the Marquess of Downshire, preserved at Easthampstead Park, Berks*, vol. 4, p. 202.
19 Annibale Romei, *The Courtiers Academie*, trans. John Keper, London, 1598, pp. 105–6.

Chapter 7: Stone-dead hath no fellow

1 *The Parliament-kite*, London, 1648, no. 8, pp. 44–5.
2 *Mercurius Britannicus*, no. 9, 11 July 1648, p. 70.
3 *A Speech made in the House of Peers by the Right Honourable the Earle of Monmouth*, London, I. Benson, 1642.
4 C. Hibbard, 'Theatre of destiny', in R. M. Smuts, ed., *The Stuart Court and Europe*, Cambridge, Cambridge University Press, 1996, p. 161.
5 Ben Jonson, *The Works*, London, Thomas Hodgkin, 1692, p. 289.
6 TNA, SO1/3, fos 114–15.
7 T. B. Howell, ed., *A Complete Collection of State Trials*, London, Hansard, 1816, vol. 2, col. 787.
8 Edward Hyde, earl of Clarendon, *The History of the Rebellion*, Oxford, Clarendon Press, 1826, vol. 1, p. 202.
9 *LJ*, 5 May 1641.
10 BL, Harleian MS 6424, fo. 58, cited in Richard Cust, *Charles I and the Aristocracy, 1625–1642*, Cambridge, Cambridge University Press, 2013.
11 Hyde, *History of the Rebellion*, vol. 1, p. 426.
12 *His Majestie's Declaration Made the 13th of June 1642*, London, Robert Young, 1642, p. 2.
13 Hyde, *History of the Rebellion*, vol. 4, p. 255.
14 Ibid., vol. 3, p. 285n.
15 Centre for Kentish Studies, uncatalogued Cranfield MSS, Dorset to the countess of Middlesex, Aug. 1642, fos 1–1, 3.
16 G. N. Godwin, *The Civil War in Hampshire*, Southampton, Henry March Gilbert, 1904, p. 112.
17 Alison Plowden, *Women All On Fire*, Stroud, Sutton, 1998, p. 37.
18 *A Journal of the Siege of Lathom House*, London, Harding, Mavor & Lepard, 1823, pp. 46–7.

19 T. C. Pease, *The Leveller Movement*, Washington DC, American Historical Association, 1916, p. 146.
20 S. R. Gardiner, *History of the Great Civil War*, London, Longmans, Green, 1901, vol. 4, p. 285.
21 *CJ*, vol. 2, p. 808, 14 Oct. 1642.
22 *CJ*, vol. 2, p. 953, 2 Feb. 1643.
23 Mary Anne Everett Green, ed., *Calendar, Committee for Compounding*, London, HMSO, 1890, vol. 2, p. 1479.
24 *LJ*, 3 May 1660.

Chapter 8: There is respect due to a lord

1 *LJ*, 25 April 1660.
2 *Archaeologica Cambrensis*, 4th ser., vol. 13, no. 52, Oct. 1882, p. 273, 24 July 1660.
3 *LJ*, 6 June 1660.
4 William A. Shaw, ed., *Calendar of Treasury Books*, London, 1904, vol. 1, p. 534, 9 March 1667.
5 Ibid., vol. 1, p. 735, 13 July 1663.
6 *LJ*, 23 Nov. 1678.
7 To be precise, the earls of Devonshire, Danby and Shrewsbury and Richard, Baron Lumley, together with Edward Russell, the brother of the 5th earl of Bedford, the alcoholic former MP Henry Sidney, and Henry Compton, the bishop of London.
8 William A. Shaw, ed., *Calendar of Treasury Books*, London, 1904, vol. 2, p. 512.
9 James Joel Cartwright, ed., *The Wentworth Papers, 1705–39*, London, Wyman, 1883, p. 347.
10 HMC Portland, vol. 7, p. 160, William Stratford to Robert Harley.
11 *Articles of Impeachment of High Treason and Misdemeanors against Robert Earl of Oxford and Earl Mortimer*, London, J. Roberts, A. Dodd, E. Nott, 1727, pp. 87–8.
12 Christ Church, Oxford, Wake MSS, 21, fo. 107, W. Wotton to Wake, 7 March 1718.
13 Gilbert Burnet, ed., *Bishop Burnet's History*, London, Samuel Bagster, 1815, vol. 6, p. 14.
14 Ibid., vol. 6, p. 15.
15 C. H. Firth, ed., *Macaulay's History of England*, London, Macmillan, 1914, vol. 2, p. 918.
16 George Lillie Craik, *Romance of the Peerage*, London, Chapman & Hall, 1849, vol. 4, pp. 342, 351.
17 HMC, *14th Report*, appendix IX, p. 459.
18 Peter Cunningham, ed., *The Letters of Horace Walpole, Earl of Orford*, London, Richard Bentley, 1857, vol. 3, p. 47.
19 Ibid., vol. 6, p. 357.
20 Warwickshire Record Office, Denbigh Letter Books, CR2017, C244, fo. 481.
21 BL, Add. MSS 51725, Egremont to Holland, 21 Jan. 1795.
22 H. B. Wheatley, ed., *The Historical and the Posthumous Memoirs of Sir Nathaniel William Wraxall, 1772–1784*, London, Bickers, 1884, vol. 2, pp. 174–5.

23 *The Parliamentary Register*, London, John Stockdale, 1802, vol. 17, p. 153.
24 H. T. Dickinson, ed., *The Political Works of Thomas Spence*, London, Avero, 1982, p. 77.
25 *Newcastle Journal*, 21 March 1767.
26 Cited in Michael McCahill and Ellis Archer Wasson, 'The new peerage: recruitment to the House of Lords, 1704–1847', *Historical Journal*, vol. 46, no. 1, March 2003, p. 15.
27 *A Candid and Impartial Account of the Behaviour of Simon Lord Lovat*, London, J. Newbery, 1747, p. 23.
28 *The Trials of William Earl of Kilmarnock*, London, R. Walker, 1746, p. 37.
29 *LJ*, 7 Feb. 1782.
30 *Gentleman's Magazine*, Oct. 1799, p. 903.
31 *LJ*, 18 Feb. 1782.
32 A. Olson, *The Radical Duke*, Oxford, Oxford University Press, 1961, p. 12.
33 Bowood MSS, Bowood House, 9 Dec. 1783.
34 William Coombe, *An Heroic Epistle to the Right Honourable the Lord Craven*, London, John Wheble, 1775, p. 5.

Chapter 9: What is a woman without gold or fee simple?

1 Mary Astell, *Some Reflections upon Marriage*, London, John Nutt, 1700, p. 13.
2 Ibid., p. 4.
3 Huntington Library, CA, MO 4716, 12 Dec. 1740, cited in Rosemary Baird, *Mistress of the House: Great Ladies and Grand Houses, 1670–1830*, London, Weidenfeld & Nicolson, 2003, pp. 172–3.
4 Matthew Montagu, ed., *The Letters of Mrs Elizabeth Montagu*, Boston, Wells & Lilly, 1825, vol. 1, p. 54.
5 James A. Home, ed., *Lady Louisa Stuart, Selections from her Manuscripts*, Edinburgh, David Douglas, 1899, p. 158.
6 Montagu, ed., *The Letters of Mrs Elizabeth Montagu*, p. 240.
7 Elaine Chalus, *Elite Women in English Political Life*, Oxford, Clarendon Press, 2005, p. 21.
8 Douglas J. Hamilton, ed., *Jacobitism, Enlightenment and Empire*, Abingdon, Routledge, 2016, p. 32.
9 SRO, Dalguise Muniments, GD406/1/6675.
10 Blair Castle, duke of Atholl MS, 45.(2).114.
11 Brian Fitzgerald, ed., *Correspondence of Emily Duchess of Leinster*, vol. 1, Dublin, Irish Manuscripts Commission, 1949, p. 92.
12 Cited in Catherine MacLeod and Julia Alexander, *Painted Ladies: Women at the Court of Charles II*, London, National Portrait Gallery, 2001, p. 180.
13 I am grateful to John Cannon for his work in *Aristocratic Century: The Peerage of Eighteenth Century England*, Cambridge, Cambridge University Press, 1984, for these figures.
14 John Bailey, ed., *The Diary of Lady Frederick Cavendish*, New York, Stokes, 1927, vol. 1, p. 266.
15 Anon., *A Master-Key to the Rich Ladies Treasury*, London, J. Roberts, 1742, p. iv.

16 Gerard Edward Jensen, ed., *The Covent Garden Journal*, Oxford, Oxford University Press, 1915, vol. 2, p. 41.

17 Lord Ilchester, ed., *Letters to Henry Fox, Lord Holland*, London, Roxburghe Club, 1915, p. 280, Selwyn to Holland, 29 Aug. 1767.

18 H. B. Wheatley, ed., *The Historical and the Posthumous Memoirs of Sir Nathaniel William Wraxall, 1772–1784*, London, Bickers, 1884, vol. 4, p. 66.

19 H. Reeve, ed., *The Greville Memoirs*, London, Longmans, Green, 1899, vol. 3, p. 20.

20 Castalia, Countess Granville [C. R. Leveson-Gower], ed., *Lord Granville Leveson Gower: Private Correspondence, 1781–1821*, London, John Murray, 1916, vol. 2, p. 20.

21 Sir Nathaniel Wraxall, *Posthumous Memoirs of His Own Time*, London, Richard Bentley, 1836, vol. 2, p. 299.

22 Cited in Edward Walford, 'Mayfair', *Old and New London*, London, Cassell, Petter & Galpin, 1878, vol. 4, p. 346.

23 *Daily Post*, 20 July 1744.

24 BL, Add. MSS, Egerton 1719, fo. 34.

25 HMC, *Manuscripts of the Earl of Egmont* (HMC Egmont), vol. 3, p. 308.

26 *The Parliamentary History of England from the Earliest Period to the Year 1803*, London, T. C. Hansard, 1813, vol. 15, col. 3.

27 Ibid., cols 14–15.

28 *Reformation Necessary to Prevent Our Ruine: A Sermon Preached to the Societies for Reformation of Manners, at St Mary-le-Bow, on Wednesday, January 10th, 1727*, London, Joseph Downing, 1728, p. 2.

29 George Edward Cockayne, ed., *The Complete Peerage*, London, George Bell, 1889, vol. 2, p. 334.

30 John Croker Wilson, ed., *Letters to and from Henrietta, Countess of Suffolk*, London, John Murray, 1824, vol. 1, p. 97.

31 Romney Sedgwick, ed., *Lord Hervey's Memoirs*, London, William Kimber, 1952, p. 40.

32 Bonamy Dobree, ed., *The Letters of Philip Dormer Stanhope, 4th Earl of Chesterfield*, London, Eyre & Spottiswoode, 1932, vol. 5, p. 1931.

33 Cited in Fergus Linnane, *The Lives of the English Rakes*, London, Portrait, 2006, p. 171.

34 Oliver Goldsmith, *The Life of Henry St John, Lord Viscount Bolingbroke*, London, T. Davies, 1770, p. 8.

35 HMC Egmont, vol. 2, p. 299.

36 Francis Hare, *A Sermon Preached to the Societies for Reformation of Manners*, London, 1731, pp. 23–4.

37 Georges Lamoine, ed., *Charges to the Grand Jury, 1689–1803*, Camden Society, 4th ser., vol. 43, London, Royal Historical Society, 1992, p. 396.

38 Anchitell Grey, ed., *Debates of the House of Commons*, London, D. Henry & R. Cave, 1763, vol. 1, p. 251.

39 Ibid.

40 Ibid., p. 253.

41 Ibid.

42 Edward Thompson, ed., *The Works of Andrew Marvell*, London, Henry Baldwin, 1776, vol. 2, p. 559.

42 Edward Thompson, ed., *The Works of Andrew Marvell*, London, Henry Baldwin, 1776, vol. 2, p. 559.
43 Lord Dover and J. Wright, eds, *The Letters of Horace Walpole, Earl of Orford*, London, Richard Bentley, 1840, vol. 1, p. 99.
44 John Harris, ed., *Trials for Adultery*, London, S. Bladon, 1780, vol. 2, p. 14.
45 *Gentleman's Magazine*, 1st ser., vol. 69, no. 1 (1799), p. 169.
46 Thomas Moore, ed., *The Life of Lord Byron*, London, John Murray, 1844, p. 677.

Chapter 10: Negroes, and gold and silver on the same footing

1 Cecil Carr, ed., *Select Charters of Trading Companies*, London, Selden Society, 1913, pp. 173, 177.
2 Ibid., p. 180.
3 Cited in Douglas Bradburn and John C. Coombs, eds, *Early Modern Virginia: Reconsidering the Old Dominion*, Charlottesville, University of Virginia Press, 2011, p. 41.
4 Carr, ed., *Select Charters of Trading Companies*, p. 180.
5 BL, Add. MSS 25495, Royal African Company to John Clark, 14 Aug. 1713, T 70/52, fo. 332.
6 Anthony Collins, ed., *A Collection of Several Pieces of Mr John Locke*, London, R. Francklin, 1739, pp. 13, 15.
7 *Proceedings and Acts of the General Assembly of Maryland*, Sept. 1664, Maryland State Archive, Liber WH & L, pp. 28–9.
8 Anthony S. Parent, *Foul Means: The Formation of a Slave Society in Virginia, 1660–1740*, Chapel Hill, NC, Omohundro Institute of Early American History and Culture, University of North Carolina, 2003.
9 *Gentleman's Magazine*, vol. 71, 1792, p. 10.
10 Edmund Heward, *Lord Mansfield: A Biography of William Murray 1st Earl of Mansfield 1705–1793, Lord Chief Justice for 32 years*, Chichester, Barry Rose, 1979, p. 141.
11 Lascelles Slavery Archive, York University, 3/58, 14 Nov. 1825.
12 Cited in James LoGerfo, 'Sir William Dolben and "the cause of humanity": the passage of the Slave Trade Regulation Act of 1788', *Eighteenth-Century Studies*, vol. 6, no. 4, 1973, p. 447.
13 William Cobbett, *Parliamentary History of England*, 35 vols, London, T. C. Hansard, 1806–20, vol. 27, col. 643.
14 Ibid., vol. 34, col. 1109.
15 Ibid., vol. 34, col. 1139.
16 *HL*, 5 Feb. 1807, vol. 8, col. 665.
17 Ibid., col. 670.
18 *Papers Presented to the House of Commons on the 7th May 1804 Respecting the Slave Trade*, London, 1804, p. 45.
19 *HL*, 5 Feb. 1807, vol. 8, col. 667.
20 *HL*, 25 June 1833, vol. 18, cols 1226–7.
21 *The Debates in Parliament on the Resolutions and Bill for the Abolition of Slavery*, London, Maurice, 1834, p. 904.

22 Ibid., pp. 904–5.
23 Ibid., p. 307.
24 Ibid., p. 308.
25 Ibid., p. 812.
26 Ibid., p. 11.
27 Ibid., p. 909.
28 Ibid., p. 910.
29 Ibid., p. 905.
30 Cobbett, *Parliamentary History*, vol. 4, col. 198.
31 Edward Pearse, *Pitt the Elder, Man of War*, London, Pimlico, 2011, p. 58.
32 Ibid., p. 218.
33 Sir John Fortescue, ed., *The Correspondence of King George the Third*, London, Macmillan, 1927, vol. 4, p. 433, George III to earl of Sandwich, 13 Sept. 1779.

Chapter 11: The influence of property fairly exercised

1 Beatrice Cary Davenport, ed., *A Diary of the French Revolution by Gouverneur Morris 1752–1816*, Boston, Houghton Mifflin, 1939, vol. 1, p. 134.
2 Edna Hindie Lemay, ed., *Dictionnaire des Constituents, 1789–91*, Paris, Universitas, 1991, vol. 1, p. 418.
3 Cited in William Doyle, *Aristocracy and its Enemies in the Age of Revolution*, Oxford, Oxford University Press, 2009, p. 5.
4 Anne Cary Morris, ed., *The Diary and Letters of Gouverneur Morris*, New York, Charles Scribner, 1888, vol. 1, p. 14.
5 William Cobbett, *Parliamentary History of England*, 35 vols, London, T. C. Hansard, 1806–20, vol. 29, col. 1513.
6 Treasonable and Seditious Practices Act 1795 (36 George III, c. 7), sec. 2.
7 Cited in Brigid Clesham, 'Lord Altamont's letters to Lord Lucan about the Act of Union 1800', *Journal of the Galway Archaeological and Historical Society*, vol. 54, 2002, p. 27.
8 *HL*, 24 Feb. 1817, vol. 35, col. 554.
9 John Wade, *The Black Book, or Corruption Unmasked!*, London, John Fairburn, 1820, vol. 1, p. 389.
10 John Wade, *The Black Book, or Corruption Unmasked!*, London, Effingham Wilson, 1835, p. 258.
11 Ibid., p. 260.
12 John Cartwright, *Letter to Mr Lambton*, London, T. Dolby, 1820, p. 20.
13 Louis J. Jennings, ed., *Correspondence and Diaries of the Late Rt Hon. John Wilson Croker*, London, John Murray, 1885, vol. 1, p. 369.
14 Wade, *The Black Book*, 1835 edn, p. 257.
15 Lionel Robinson, ed., *Letters of Dorothea, Princess Lieven*, London, Longmans, Green, 1902, pp. 278–9.
16 Herbert Maxwell, ed., *The Creevey Papers*, London, John Murray, 1904, vol. 2, p. 32.
17 *Mirror of Parliament*, 22 Nov. 1830, cols 310–11.
18 *HL*, 3 Oct. 1831, vol. 7, col. 946.

19 Ibid.
20 *HL*, 3 Oct. 1831, vol. 7, col. 1018.
21 *HL*, 4 Oct. 1831, cols 1188–9, 1200, 1202.
22 Charles C. F. Greville, *A Journal of the Reigns of King George IV and King William IV*, London, Longmans Green, 1874, vol. 2, p. 213.
23 *HL*, 3 Oct. 1831, vol. 7, col. 983.
24 Ibid., col. 984.
25 Hon. F. Leveson Gower, ed., *Letters of Harriet, Countess Granville*, London, Longmans, Green, 1894, vol. 1, p. 114.
26 *HL*, 3 Oct. 1831, vol. 7, cols 994–5.

Chapter 12: This Lord loves nothing but horses

1 John Wright, ed., *The Letters of Horace Walpole, Earl of Orford*, Philadelphia, Lea & Blanchard, 1842, vol. 2, p. 336.
2 Mike Huggins, *Flat Racing and British Society*, Abingdon, Routledge, 2013, p. 44.
3 Henry Reeve, ed., *The Greville Memoirs*, London, Longmans, Green, 1899, vol. 6, p. 411.
4 'The late Earl of Derby', *Baily's Magazine*, Nov. 1869, pp. 234–5 (emphasis in original).
5 Huggins, *Flat Racing and British Society*, p. 42.
6 Rees Howell Gronow, *Celebrities of London and Paris*, London, Smith, Elder, 1865, p. 138.
7 Ibid., p. 139.
8 James Greig, ed., *The Farington Diary*, London, Hutchinson, 1926, vol. 6, p. 236.
9 Francis Bamford and the duke of Wellington, eds, *The Journal of Mrs Arbuthnot, 1820–32*, London, Macmillan, 1950, vol. 1, pp. 252–3.
10 *Spectator*, 11 Dec. 1897, p. 3.
11 Joseph Osborne, ed., *The Horse-Breeder's Handbook*, London, Edmund Seale, 1898, p. xciv.
12 *Baily's Magazine*, Sept. 1872, p. 187.
13 Ibid., p. 188.
14 1671, 22 & 23 Charles II, c. 25.
15 William Blackstone, *Commentaries on the Laws of England*, Oxford, Clarendon Press, 1765, vol. 4, p. 409.
16 Vicesimus Knox, *Essays Moral and Literary*, Dublin, 1783, vol. 2, p. 154.
17 Joseph Arch, *Ploughtail to Parliament*, London, Norman Willis & Alun Howkins, 1986, pp. 159–61.
18 Richard MacKenzie Bacon, *A Memoir of the Life of Edward, Third Baron Suffield*, Norwich, Bacon, Kinnebrook & Bacon, 1838, pp. 184–5.
19 *The Annual Biography and Obituary*, London, Longman, Rees et al., 1836, vol. 20, p. 181.
20 George Montagu, *The Sportsman's Dictionary*, London, G. G. J. and J. Robinson, 1792, p. 98.
21 *Sporting Magazine*, May 1828, p. 45.

22 George Thomas, earl of Albemarle, *Fifty Years of My Life*, London, Macmillan, 1876, vol. 2, p. 40.
23 P. B. Munsche, *Poachers and Gentlemen: The English Game Laws, 1671–1831*, Cambridge, Cambridge University Press, 1981, p. 48.
24 Ibid., p. 49.
25 David Wetzel, *A Duel of Giants*, Madison, University of Wisconsin Press, 2001, p. 217.
26 *Sporting Magazine*, Jan. 1822, p. 194.
27 Peter Beckford, *Thoughts upon Hunting*, Sarum, E. Easton, 1781, p. 187.
28 Harry Hieover (pseud. Charles Brindley), *The Hunting-Field*, London, Longman, Brown, 1850, p. 28.
29 'Fox-hunting ladies', *The Times*, 22 Sept. 1836.
30 *Sportsman*, May–June 1838, p. 315.
31 Munsche, *Poachers and Gentlemen*, p. 50.
32 H. B. Wheatley, ed., *The Historical and the Posthumous Memoirs of Sir Nathaniel William Wraxall, 1772–1784*, London, Bickers, 1884, vol. 5, p. 107.
33 William Woodfall, ed., *Parliamentary Reports*, London, T. Chapman, 1796, vol. 4, p. 328.

Chapter 13: Leave us still our old nobility

1 *Monthly Epitome*, June 1801, p. 329.
2 *Blackwood's Magazine*, Jan. 1844, p. 775.
3 *Gentleman's Magazine*, vol. 69, Jan. 1799, part 1, p. 74.
4 Rosemary Baird, *Mistress of the House: Great Ladies and Grand Houses, 1670–1830*, London, Weidenfeld & Nicolson, 2003, p. 233.
5 *Correspondence of Elizabeth Duchess of Rutland with Sir Frederick Trench*, vol. 1, no. 58, 20 Nov. 1824, cited in Baird, *Mistress of the House*, p. 251.
6 Ibid., p. 252.
7 Francis Bamford and the duke of Wellington, eds, *The Journal of Mrs Arbuthnot, 1820–1832*, London, Macmillan, 1850, vol. 2, p. 230.
8 Helena Gleichen, *Contacts and Contrasts*, London, John Murray, 1940, p. 19.
9 *The Times*, 3 July 1897.
10 Consuelo Vanderbilt Balsan, *The Glitter and the Gold*, London, William Heinemann, 1953, p. 96.
11 Ibid., p. 107.
12 Henry James, *English Hours*, London, Heinemann, 1905, p. 188.
13 Peter Mandler, *The Rise and Fall of the Stately Home*, New Haven, CT, Yale University Press, 1998, p. 77.
14 *Murray's Handbook for Shropshire, Cheshire and Lancashire*, London, John Murray, 1870, p. 138.
15 Nikolaus Pevsner and Edward Hubbard, *Buildings of England: Cheshire*, London, Penguin, 1971, p. 208.
16 Susan Oldfield, *Some Records of the Later Life of Harriet, Countess Granville*, London, Longmans, Green, 1901, p. 161.
17 Mandler, *The Fall and Rise of the Stately Home*, p. 80.
18 *Daily Telegraph*, 22 Dec. 1871, p. 5.

19 *Daily Telegraph*, 23 Dec. 1871, pp. 4–5.
20 *The Times*, 21 Dec. 1871.
21 William Howitt, *Visits to Remarkable Places*, London, Longman, Orme, Brown et al., 1840, p. 37.
22 Ibid, p. 48.
23 *Penny Magazine*, 16 Feb. 1839, pp. 58–9.
24 Lord John Manners, *England's Trust and Other Poems*, London, Rivington, 1841, p. 89.
25 Ibid., p. 24.
26 *Derbyshire Courier*, 26 Aug. 1848, p. 3.
27 HC, 10 Feb. 1847, vol. 89, col. 1119.
28 HC, 11 April 1842, vol. 62, col. 213.
29 E. A. Smythe, Viscountess Strangford, ed., *Angela Pisani*, London, Richard Bentley, 1875, vol. 1, p. xxix.
30 Nikolaus Pevsner, *Buildings of England: Derbyshire*, London, Penguin, 1978, p. 221.
31 *The Trial of James Thomas, Earl of Cardigan*, London, William Brodie, 1841, frontispiece.
32 Ibid., p. 4.
33 Ibid., pp. 10–11.
34 Ibid., p. 123.
35 Donald McLeod, *Gloomy Memories in the Highlands of Scotland*, Glasgow, Archibald Sinclair, 1892, p. 17.
36 Janet Hilderley, *Mrs Catherine Gladstone*, Eastbourne, Alpha, 2012, p. 191.
37 McLeod, *Gloomy Memories*, p. 92.
38 *The Times*, 29 Nov. 1852, p. 8.
39 K. D. Reynolds, *Aristocratic Women and Political Society in Victorian Britain*, Oxford, Clarendon Press, 1998, p. 127.
40 *The Times*, 2 Dec. 1852, p. 6.
41 *People's Paper*, 12 March 1852, p. 5.
42 *The Times*, 1 Dec. 1852, p. 8.

Chapter 14: Tattered remains of old glory

1 J. V. Beckett, *The Rise and Fall of the Grenvilles*, Manchester, Manchester University Press, 1994, p. 212.
2 P. Wilson, *The Greville Diary*, London, Heinemann, 1927, vol. 2, p. 176.
3 *The Times*, 14 Aug. 1848.
4 F. M. L. Thompson, 'The end of a great estate', *Economic History Review*, 2nd ser., vol. 8, 1955–6, p. 48.
5 Other estimates such as that by W. D. Rubinstein in *Men of Property: The Very Wealthy in Britain since the Industrial Revolution* (London, Croom Helm, 1981) have taken other sources of income into consideration and arrived at even higher figures but the same conclusion, namely that, pound for pound, the landed aristocracy still far outranked the plutocrats of the City.
6 Thomas Carlyle, *Past and Present*, London, Chapman & Hall, 1843, p. 150.
7 *Chelmsford Chronicle*, 17 Oct. 1879, p. 2.

8 Duke of Bedford, *The Story of a Great Agricultural Estate*, London, John Murray, 1897, p. 181.
9 Charles W. Boyd, ed., *Mr Chamberlain's Speeches*, London, Constable, 1914, vol. 1, p. 147.
10 Charles Milne Gaskell, 'The Country Gentleman', *Nineteenth Century*, Sept. 1882.
11 *HL*, 3rd ser., 29 June 1868, vol. 193, col. 88.
12 Duke of Argyll, 'The new Irish Land Bill', *Nineteenth Century*, vol. 9, 1881, p. 883.
13 Boyd, ed., *Mr Chamberlain's Speeches*, vol. 1, p. 131.
14 Lord Randolph Churchill, *Speeches*, London, Longmans, Green, 1889, vol. 1, p. 259.
15 *HC*, 6 Nov. 1884, vol. 293, col. 1164.
16 Cited in John Charmley, *A History of Conservative Politics since 1830*, London, Macmillan, 2008, p. 64.
17 *Hampshire Chronicle*, 9 Feb. 1889.
18 *Maidstone and Kentish Journal*, 5 Feb. 1889.
19 *HC*, 1 March 1894, vol. 21, col. 1151.
20 Thomas Coates, ed., *Lord Rosebery, His Life and Speeches*, London, Hutchinson, 1900, vol. 2, p. 716.
21 Ibid.
22 George Earle Buckle, ed., *The Letters of Queen Victoria*, 3rd ser., London, John Murray, 1931, vol. 2, p. 415.
23 Cited in Roy Douglas, *Land, People and Politics*, London, St Martin's, 1976, p. 160.
24 Herbert du Parcq, ed., *Life of David Lloyd George*, vol. 4: *Speeches*, London, Caxton, 1912, pp. 627–8.
25 *HC*, 29 April 1909, vol. 4, col. 548.
26 Ibid., col. 536.
27 *Belfast Telegraph*, 30 Nov. 1909.
28 *London Daily News*, 20 Sept. 1909, p. 5.
29 *North Devon Journal*, 8 June 1911, p. 6.
30 George Dangerfield, *The Strange Death of Liberal England*, London, Transaction, 2011, p. 52.
31 *HC*, 3 Nov. 1909, vol. 12, col. 1868.
32 W. Forbes Gray, ed., *Comments and Characters by John Buchan*, London, Thomas Nelson, 1940, p. 31, 22 Oct. 1907.
33 *Sketch*, 8 March 1933, p. 5.
34 *Globe*, 7 June 1912.
35 *The Times*, 4 Jan. 1912.
36 G. S. Street, *People and Questions*, London, Martin Secker, 1910, pp. 186–7.
37 Cited in Jamie Camplin, *The Rise of the Plutocrats*, London, Constable, 1978, p. 25.
38 Walter Bagehot, *The English Constitution*, London, Fontana, 1963, pp. 173–4.
39 *Saturday Review*, 16 Dec. 1905.
40 *Truth*, 5 Sept. 1901.

41 Andrew Carnegie, *An American Four-in-Hand in Britain*, New York, Charles Scribner's Sons, 1887, p. 222.
42 Andrew Carnegie, *Autobiography*, London, Constable, 1920, p. 301.
43 *Sketch*, 19 Aug. 1914.
44 Lionel, Lord Tennyson, *From Verse to Worse*, London, Cassell, 1933, p. 7.
45 Ibid.
46 T. H. Hollingsworth, 'A demographic study of the British ducal families', *Population Studies*, vol. 11, no. 1, 1957, pp. 4–26.
47 David Cannadine, *The Decline and Fall of the British Aristocracy*, London, Macmillan, 1992, p. 83.
48 Lady Algernon Gordon-Lennox, *Diary of Lord Bertie of Thame*, London and New York, George H. Doran, 1924, vol. 2, p. 67.
49 C. F. G. Masterman, *England after War*, London, Hodder & Stoughton, 1922, pp. 31–3.
50 *Estates Gazette*, 11 Nov. 1911.
51 Cannadine, *The Decline and Fall*, p. 91.
52 John Vincent, ed., *The Journal of David Lindsay, 27th Earl of Crawford*, Manchester, Manchester University Press, 1984, p. 529.
53 *Sphere*, 5 Feb. 1938.
54 *The Times*, 22 Sept. 1911.
55 *The Times*, 23 Sept. 1911.
56 *The Times*, 12 Oct. 1911.
57 *New York Times*, 28 Feb. 1911.
58 Robert Rhodes James, *Chips: The Diaries of Sir Henry Channon*, London, Weidenfeld & Nicolson, 1967, p. 130.
59 Deborah Devonshire, *Home to Roost, and Other Peckings*, London, John Murray, 2009, p. 73.
60 Henry Rumsey Forster, *The Stowe Catalogue, Priced and Annotated*, London, David Bogue, 1848, p. xiii.

Chapter 15: Living in a kind of twilight

1 Andrew Roberts, *The Holy Fox*, London, Weidenfeld & Nicolson, 1991, p. 205.
2 Eustace Percy, *Some Memories*, London, Eyre & Spottiswoode, 1958, p. 15.
3 H. G. Wells, *The Works*, London, T. Fisher Unwin, 1924, vol. 21, p. 349.
4 *HL*, 30 March 1933, vol. 87, col. 211.
5 Cited in Ian Kershaw, *Making Friends with Hitler: Lord Londonderry and Britain's Road to War*, London, Penguin, 2004, p. 55.
6 *Evening Standard*, 27 Jan. 1939
7 King's College London, Hamilton papers.
8 Earl of Portsmouth, *A Knot of Roots*, London, Geoffrey Bles, 1965, pp. 129, 127.
9 Hampshire Record Office, 15M84/F189, Wallop to Norman Hay, 23 March 1939, cited in Philip Conford, 'Organic society: agriculture and radical politics in the career of Gerard Wallop, Earl of Portsmouth (1898–1984), *Agricultural History Review*, vol. 52, no. 1, 2004, pp. 78–96 at p. 93.
10 *HL*, 21 July 1942, vol. 123, col. 971.
11 *Daily Telegraph*, 12 Oct. 2004.

12 John, duke of Bedford, *A Silver-Plated Spoon*, London, Cassell, 1959, p. 188.
13 *Sunday Sun*, 17 May 1936, cited in David Clay Large, *Nazi Games: The Olympics of 1936*, New York, Norton, 2007, p. 138.
14 *HL*, 16 March 1938, vol. 108, col. 140.
15 Robert Rhodes James, ed., *Chips: The Diaries of Sir Henry Channon*, London, Weidenfeld & Nicolson, 1967, diary entry for 6 Aug. 1936.
16 University of Southampton MSS, Mount Temple papers, BR81/1 (emphasis added).
17 J. R. M. Butler, *Lord Lothian, Philip Kerr, 1882–1940*, London, St Martin's, 1960, p. 262.
18 TNA, PRO HO 144/22454/109.
19 Rhodes James, ed., *Chips*, p. 224.
20 John Grigg, '"Crawfie", Sir Henry Marten', *National and English Review*, Aug. 1957, p. 64.
21 *Guardian*, 3 Sept. 2011.
22 One example on 3 July 1936 was followed by: 'Titled lady having had clothes made for abroad is unable to go and must dispose of her whole wardrobe.'
23 Fiona MacCarthy, *Last Curtsey: The End of the Debutantes*, London, Faber, 2007, p. 36.
24 Lord Ernle, *Whippingham to Westminster*, London, John Murray, 1938, pp. 213–14.
25 Corsham Court MSS D(59)m, 18 Nov. 1954.
26 HM Treasury, *Report of the Committee on Homes of Outstanding Historic or Architectural Interest*, London, HMSO, 23 June 1950, p. vii.
27 TNA, PRO T 218/86, Stafford Cripps, 29 April 1950.
28 Ben Pimlott, *Hugh Dalton*, London, Jonathan Cape, 1985, p. 455.
29 TNA, PRO T 218/13, Cabinet, Historic Buildings Committee, minutes of a meeting, 6 March 1953.
30 *Daily Express*, 19 June 1953.
31 Evelyn Waugh, *Brideshead Revisited*, Boston, Little, Brown, 1977 (first publ. 1944), p. 8.
32 *Thetford and Watton Times and People's Weekly Journal*, 8 Aug. 1952, p. 4.
33 TNA, PRO T 219/178, cited in Peter Mandler, *The Fall and Rise of the Stately Home*, New Haven, CT, Yale University Press, 1997, pp. 377–8.
34 John, duke of Bedford, *A Silver-Plated Spoon*, p. 193.
35 *The Times*, 23 Oct. 1992.
36 Cited in Robert Sackville-West, *Inheritance: The Story of Knole and the Sackvilles*, London, Bloomsbury, 2010, p. 248.
37 James Lees-Milne, *People and Places*, London, John Murray, 1992, p. 182.
38 Roy Strong, *The Story of Britain: A People's History*, London, 1996, p. 141.
39 *Spectator*, 12 Feb. 1977, p. 12.
40 *The Times*, 8 Feb. 1977.

Chapter 16: We're all tax dodgers, aren't we?

1 *HL*, 17 July 1939, vol. 114, col. 254.
2 Nancy Mitford, 'The English aristocracy', *Encounter*, Sept. 1955, p. 5.

3 *Derby Daily Telegraph*, 17 Feb. 1944.
4 *Birmingham Daily Gazette*, 19 Feb. 1944, p. 1.
5 *Dundee Evening Telegraph*, 11 Feb. 1944.
6 HL, 3 Dec. 1957, vol. 206, col. 610.
7 *Illustrated London News*, 2 Aug. 1958.
8 HL, 7 Feb. 1856, vol. 140, col. 264.
9 HL, 7 Feb. 1856, vol. 140, cols 285-6.
10 HL, 5 Dec. 1957, vol. 206, col. 866.
11 HC, 3 Feb. 1969, vol. 777, col. 149.
12 HL, 19 Nov. 1968, vol. 297, col. 674.
13 Other scions of the hereditary nobility in the ministry included Sir George Young, Bart; William Waldegrave, the younger son of the 12th Earl Waldegrave; Douglas Hogg, who later succeeded his father as 3rd Viscount Hailsham; Mark Lennox-Boyd, the son of another Viscount Boyd of Merton; Tom Sackville, the younger son of the 10th Earl De La Warr; Archie Hamilton, younger son of the 3rd Baron Hamilton of Dalzell; Michael Ancram, heir to the Marquess of Lothian; James Douglas-Stuart, heir to the earl of Selkirk; and Richard Needham, whose title as 6th Earl of Kilmorey did not exclude him from the Commons.
14 Privately printed paper, cited in Andrew Adonis and Stephen Pollard, *A Class Act*, London, Hamish Hamilton, 1997.
15 HL, 11 June 2003, vol. 649, col. 224.
16 Mitford, 'The English aristocracy', p. 10.
17 *Field*, 7 Sept. 2015.
18 Alexander Chalmers, ed., *The Works of the English Poets*, London, J. Johnson, 1810, vol. 14, p. 286.
19 *The Commissioners of Inland Revenue v. The Duke of Westminster* (1936), A.C. 1 19 TC 490.
20 *Spectator*, 31 July 1981, p. 20.
21 *Guardian*, 11 Aug. 1999, p. 5.
22 Andy Wightman, *The Poor Had No Lawyers*, Edinburgh, Birlinn, 2010, p. 271.
23 The HMRC list of tax-exempt heritage assets is available at www.hmrc.gov.uk/heritage/.
24 All figures from the DEFRA CAP payments website for 2014/15: www.cap-payments.defra.gov.uk.
25 HL, 5 Dec. 1957, vol. 579, col. 843.
26 *Daily Mail*, 7 Oct. 2009.
27 Mitford, 'The English aristocracy', p. 12.
28 BBC News, 13 July 2017, http://www.bbc.co.uk/news/uk-40599992.

GLOSSARY

advowson The right to make an appointment of a cleric to a vacant office as rector, vicar or priest of a parish.

allodium The family patrimonial holding.

amber A medieval measure of varying size, derived from the Latin *amphora*.

Angevin Of or pertaining to Anjou.

banneret A knight banneret fought under his own square-shaped banner, unlike an ordinary knight who carried a tapering standard.

baron The lowest order of nobility. Barons derived their title as tenants-in-chief who held their lands from the Norman kings 'per baroniam'. The more significant barons were subsequently summoned to parliament. All life peers since have been created as barons.

baroness A life peer, the female equivalent of a baron and not the wife of a baron.

baronet A hereditary knighthood, often abbreviated as Bart or Bt, as in Sir — — Bart, to distinguish a baronet from a knight.

book-land In the pre-Norman era, land that had been awarded by charter.

burh-gate seat A seat at the town gate where a court was held to try cases between tenants

burnie A shirt of mail, forming part of Anglo-Saxon armour.

cadet (branch) Branch of a noble family descended from a younger son of the founding father.

capriole A dressage move in which the horse leaps from the ground without moving forward and kicks out with its hind legs.

caput From the Latin *caput* meaning head, the central seat of an English or Scottish barony or multiple estate.

castellan The governor of a castle.

ceorl The lowest rank of freeman in Anglo-Saxon England.

chaldron A measure of coal by volume that was used from medieval times until 1835. A Newcastle chaldron was fixed in 1678 at 5,880lb and increased to 5,940lb in 1694.

GLOSSARY

Clerk of the Crown and Hanaper in Ireland A Chancery official in the British administration of Ireland charged with issuing letters patent for sheriffs, nobles and grants of land, and all injunctions, writs and crown appointments.

coat of arms An arrangement of heraldic emblems on an escutcheon, shield, surcoat or tabard used to distinguish a warrior, family, corporation or country. All rights to bear a coat of arms, together with crests, badges, standards and supporters, are granted by the senior herald, the Garter King of Arms.

collateral heir A successor to property who is not directly descended from the deceased but comes from another part of the family: for example, a brother, sister, uncle, aunt, nephew, niece or cousin.

countess Although there have been some *suo jure* countesses, such as Mary and Anne Scott, who successively inherited their father's title as the 3rd and 4th countess of Buccleuch in 1651 and 1661, a countess is normally the wife of an earl.

Court of Chivalry Formally the High Court of Chivalry, it has existed as the Earl Marshal's court since the fourteenth century and has jurisdiction over all matters of noble precedence, heraldry and coats of arms. It was last convened in 1954. It has a single judge, the hereditary Earl Marshal.

courtesy title A title that has no legal import, but is used as a courtesy, for instance in denoting a person's noble parentage. Thus the son and heir of the duke of Leeds is known by the duke's subsidiary title of marquess of Carmarthen, although this does not grant him a seat in the Lords, and the duke's other children are styled 'Lord' and 'Lady'.

creation money An annuity paid to peers according to their rank, supposedly to maintain them in their dignity.

cumb A medieval measure of liquid.

drugget A coarse floor covering.

duchess Normally the wife of a duke, although Cecilia Underwood was made duchess of Inverness in her own right by Queen Victoria in 1840.

duke From the Latin word *dux* meaning 'leader': the highest aristocratic title, ranking below the monarch, first used in England in 1337 when Edward, the Black Prince, was made duke of Cornwall.

ealdorman An Anglo-Saxon regional territorial noble with extensive semi-regal powers. Cnut replaced the title with that of 'earl'.

earl The oldest English aristocratic title, equivalent to a French *comte*, formerly entitled to the 'third penny' in his county.

Earl Marshal The eighth most senior officer of state, ranking below the Lord High Constable, with responsibility for state ceremonies such as the coronation and for the Royal College of Arms. The Howard family has held the post in hereditary succession since 1672 and the 18th duke of Norfolk has held the post since 2002. The post still entitles its holder to a seat in the Lords.

entail A means of restricting the disposal of inherited property over a number of generations so that ownership remains within the family.

fee An estate of land held in the Norman era and thereafter on condition of military service.

fee simple Permanent and absolute land tenure which entitles the holder to sell, mortgage or bequeath it at will.

fee tail A form of trust that prevents an estate from being sold or alienated at will and ensures it passes automatically to the predetermined heir.

fyrd The Anglo-Saxon army, raised to defend the shire or participate in a royal expeditionary force.

Groom of the Stool Also 'Groom of the Close Stole'. One of the most intimate roles in the royal household, charged with assisting the monarch in his or her ablutions. The post was especially important during the Tudor and early Stuart period but was abolished on the accession of Edward VII in 1901.

heriot From the Old English for 'war-gear': a form of early death duty paid by a lord to the king out of the deceased's military equipment including horses, swords and helmets.

hide The amount of land considered necessary to provision a free family – roughly 120 acres.

high-reeve A senior local magistrate.

hundred A division of an English county for military and judicial purposes.

jointure An estate or annuity settled on a wife for the rest of her life after the death of her husband.

lathe An administrative and military subdivision in Kent.

letters patent A written order from the monarch granting a title, honour, monopoly or status to a person or a corporation.

letus Fur from the winter coat of the weasel.

levade A dressage move in which the horse bends both its hind legs simultaneously and raises its front legs from the ground to take its whole weight on its hindquarters.

lord of the manor A title attached to a specific landholding granting specified rights which might be held direct from the crown as a tenant-in-chief or from a senior lord who would himself be tenant-in-chief. The lord of the manor would hold all of the land, live in the great house or manor, enjoy rights over the parks and forests, and extract rent from his tenants.

marchioness The wife of a marquess, with only one exception: Anne Boleyn, who was made marchioness of Pembroke before her marriage to Henry VIII in 1532.

marquess Sometimes rendered as marquis: the second highest noble title, ranking below a duke. First used for Robert de Vere, 9th earl of Oxford, who was made marquess of Dublin in 1385.

Master of the Horse The third most senior dignitary of the royal court, with responsibility for the stables, stud and mews. Until 1782 the post-holder, who was always a peer, was a member of the Cabinet.

miniver White fur from the winter coat of an ermine or red squirrel.

miscegenation Interracial marriage or breeding.

mormaer A high steward (mor-maer) of one of the ancient provinces of Scotland, whose title eventually became earl.

palfrey A horse trained to be particularly docile.

privilege of peerage A provision by which, from 1547, a peer who had been convicted of a crime, including manslaughter (but not murder or treason), as a first offence could avoid punishment.

rape An administrative and military subdivision in Sussex.

reeve A local magistrate or official. A reeve appointed for a whole shire was a 'shire-reeve' or 'sheriff'.

relief An early form of death duty paid by a lord to the monarch (or a tenant to his lord) before he could assume his inherited title and estates.

reversion The right to assume an estate after the death of the holder.

sake and soke This alliterative term, derived from the Old English words for 'to contend' and 'to seek', was used to denote a variety of Anglo-Norman jurisdictional rights, including those of holding court and receiving fines.

sarsenet A particularly fine form of silk fabric often used for lining.

scutage Money paid by a vassal to his lord (or by the lord to the monarch) in lieu of military service.

serf A labourer bound to work on his lord's estate in return for protection and justice in the lord's court.

suo jure Latin, 'in her own right': a *suo jure* peeress held a title in her own right, though until 1963 it did not entitle her to a seat in the Lords.

tenant-in-chief Because after the Norman Conquest all land was officially owned by the monarch, and landholders merely enjoyed rights to use the land granted to them by the crown, the major aristocrats were 'tenants-in-chief', holding their lands directly from the king.

thane After the eleventh-century Anglicization of the Scottish court, a thane was a royal official, often the hereditary chieftain of a clan, who held land from the king and exercised authority over a shire. Thanes eventually became Scottish lords. The current 7th earl of Cawdor is also the 26th thane of Cawdor.

thegn From the Old English word meaning 'servant' or 'retainer', a thegn was a minor hereditary Anglo-Saxon noble, ranking below an ealdorman or a royal atheling but above a ceorl or common freeman. Some English thegns were termed 'king's thegns' and were considered a superior class.

third penny The third of revenues from their territories – especially fines – to which earls from at least the Norman Conquest were entitled.

trial by peers From 1341 to 1948 peers (and from 1442 peeresses) could be tried for a felony only by their peers, either in the full House of Lords or in a specially convened court of the Lord High Steward.

tun A medieval measure of liquid equal to 216 gallons.

viscount The fourth rank of peer, above a baron. The oldest extant viscountcy, which dates from 1550, is held by Robin Devereux, the 19th Viscount Hereford.

viscountess Normally the wife of a viscount, although Anne Murray was made Viscountess Bayning in her own right and for life in 1674.

wapentake A subdivision of the English counties of Yorkshire, Derbyshire, Leicestershire, Northamptonshire, Nottinghamshire, Rutland and Lincolnshire.

wardship If a tenant-in-chief died while his son and heir was still a minor the estate reverted to the monarch, who brought the heir up as a royal ward while exploiting the estate. The monarch could arrange a marriage for a royal ward and could sell this right to others.

wergild Compensation payable on the killing of a person to the deceased's family, the sum being commensurate with the social rank of the victim.

writ of acceleration Formally a 'writ in acceleration', which summoned the eldest son and heir apparent of a peer with several titles to attend the Lords using one of his father's subsidiary titles. In the most recent instance Robert Gascoyne-Cecil, whose courtesy title was Viscount Cranborne, was summoned to the Lords in the title of his father, the marquess of Salisbury, as Baron Cecil of Essendon in 1992.

BIBLIOGRAPHY

Periodicals

Annual Biography and Obituary
Archaeologica Cambrensis
Baily's Magazine
Belfast Telegraph
Birmingham Daily Gazette
Blackwood's Magazine
Chelmsford Chronicle
Daily Mail
Daily Post
Daily Telegraph
Derby Daily Telegraph
Derbyshire Courier
Dundee Evening Telegraph
Economic History Review
Encounter
Estates Gazette
Evening Standard
Field
Gentleman's Magazine
Globe
Guardian
Hampshire Chronicle
Historical Journal
House of Commons Journal
House of Lords Journal
Illustrated London News
London Daily News

Maidstone and Kentish Journal
Mercurius Britannicus
Mirror of Parliament
Monthly Epitome
National and English Review
New York Times
Newcastle Journal
Nineteenth Century
North Devon Journal
Parliamentary Register
Parliament-kite
Penny Magazine
People's Paper
Saturday Review
Sketch
Spectator
Sphere
Sporting Magazine
Sportsman
Stamford Mercury
Sunday Sun
The Tatler
The Times
Thetford and Watton Times and People's
Weekly Journal
Truth
Yale University Library Gazette

Archives, manuscripts and online resources

Arundel Castle MSS
Blair Castle, duke of Atholl MSS
Bowood House, Bowood MSS

380

British Library, Additional MSS
Centre for Kentish Studies, Cranfield MSS
Christ Church, Oxford, Wake MSS
College of Arms MSS
Corsham Court MSS
Historic Manuscripts Commission
      Portland MSS
      Downshire MSS
      Egmont MSS
King's College London, Hamilton papers
Maryland State Archive
National Archives of Scotland
Norwich Record Office, *Account of Kett's Rebellion*
University of Southampton MSS, Mount Temple papers
Warwickshire Record Office, Denbigh Letter Books
Yale University Library Manuscripts and Archives
York University, Lascelles Slavery Archive

Published works

A Candid and Impartial Account of the Behaviour of Simon Lord Lovat, London,
J. Newbery, 1747

*A List of the Earls and Lords that were present in the House of Peers, on Friday,
April the 27th 1660*, London, Isaac Pridmore, 1660

*A Speech made in the House of Peers by the Right Honourable the Earle of
Monmouth*, London, I. Benson, 1642

Albemarle, George Thomas, earl of, *Fifty Years of My Life*, London, Macmillan, 1876

Alexander, Michael, trans., *Beowulf*, London, Penguin, 1973

Allen, Thomas, ed., *A New and Completed History of the County of York*,
London, I. T. Hinton, 1831

Anon., *A Master-Key to the Rich Ladies Treasury*, London, J. Roberts, 1742

Anon., *Secret Memoirs of Robert Dudley, Earl of Leicester*, London, Sam Briscoe,
1706

Arber, E., ed., *English Reprints*, London, Alexander Murray, 1869

Arch, Joseph, *Ploughtail to Parliament*, London, Norman Willis & Alun Howkins,
1986

Argyll, duke of, 'The new Irish Land Bill', *Nineteenth Century*, vol. 9, 1881

Arnold, Thomas, ed., *Memorials of St Edmund's Abbey*, London, Eyre &
Spottiswoode, 1890

Articles of Impeachment of High Treason and Misdemeanors against Robert Earl of Oxford and Earl Mortimer, London, J. Roberts, A. Dodd, E. Nott, 1727

Aslet, Clive, *The Edwardian Country House*, London, Frances Lincoln, 2012

— *The Last Country Houses*, New Haven, CT, Yale University Press, 1983

Astell, Mary, *Some Reflections upon Marriage*, London, John Nutt, 1700

Aungier, George James, ed., *Chroniques de London*, London, Camden Society, 1844

Ayton, Andrew, *Knights and Warhorses: Military Service and the English Aristocracy under Edward III*, Woodbridge, Boydell, 1994

Bacon, Richard MacKenzie, *A Memoir of the Life of Edward, Third Baron Suffield*, Norwich, Bacon, Kinnebrook & Bacon, 1838

Badeau, Adam, *Aristocracy in England*, London, Harper & Bros, 1886

Bagehot, Walter, *The English Constitution*, London, Fontana, 1963

Bailey, John, ed., *The Diary of Lady Frederick Cavendish*, New York, Stokes, 1927

Baird, Rosemary, *Mistress of the House: Great Ladies and Grand Houses, 1670–1830*, London, Weidenfeld & Nicolson, 2003

Bamford, Francis, and Wellington, duke of, eds, *The Journal of Mrs Arbuthnot, 1820–32*, London, Macmillan, 1950

Barber, R., *Life and Campaigns of the Black Prince*, Woodbridge, Boydell & Brewer, 1986

Baxter, Stephen David, ed., *Early Medieval Studies in Honour of Patrick Wormald*, Farnham, Ashgate, 2009

Beale, Catherine, *Champagne and Shambles: The Arkwrights and the Country House in Crisis*, Stroud, History Press, 2009

Beames, John, ed. and trans., *A Translation of Glanville*, London, W. Reed, 1812

Bean, John Malcolm William, *From Lord to Patron: Lordship in Late Medieval England*, Manchester, Manchester University Press, 1989

Beckett, J. V., *The Aristocracy in England 1660–1914*, Oxford, Blackwell, 1986

— *The Rise and Fall of the Grenvilles*, Manchester, Manchester University Press, 1994

Beckford, Peter, *Thoughts upon Hunting*, Sarum, E. Easton, 1781

Bedford, duke of, *The Story of a Great Agricultural Estate*, London, John Murray, 1897

Bedford, John, duke of, *A Silver-Plated Spoon*, London, Cassell, 1959

Bell, Alexander, ed., *L'Estoir des Engleis by Geffrei Gaimar*, Oxford, Oxford University Press, 1960

Bence-Jones, Mark, and Montgomery-Massingberd, Hugh, *The British Aristocracy*, London, Constable, 1979

Bentinck, Ruth Cavendish, *The Point of Honour: A Correspondence on Aristocracy and Socialism*, London, Fabian Society, 1910

Bernard, G. W., *The Power of the Early Tudor Nobility: A Study of the Fourth and Fifth Earls of Shrewsbury*, Totowa, NJ, Barnes & Noble, 1985

Black Book of the British Aristocracy, London, Wm. Strange, 1848

Black, Joseph, ed., *The Broadview Anthology of British Literature*, Peterborough, Ont., Broadview, 2009

Blackstone, William, *Commentaries on the Laws of England*, Oxford, Clarendon Press, 1765

Blomefield, Francis, and Parkin, Charles, *An Essay towards a Topographical History of the County of Norfolk*, London, William Miller, 1806

Boyd, Charles W., ed., *Mr Chamberlain's Speeches*, London, Constable, 1914

Bradburn, Douglas, and Coombs, John C., eds, *Early Modern Virginia: Reconsidering the Old Dominion*, Charlottesville, University of Virginia Press, 2011

Brewer, J. S., ed., *Bishop Geoffrey Goodman's* The Court of King James the First, London, 1839

Brodie, D. M., ed., *The Tree of Commonwealth: A Treatise Written by Edmund Dudley*, Cambridge, Cambridge University Press, 1948

Bromhead, P. A., *The House of Lords and Contemporary Politics, 1911–1957*, London, 1958

Brown, D., 'The industrial revolution, political economy and the British aristocracy: the second Viscount Dudley and Ward as an eighteenth century canal promoter', *Journal of Transport History*, vol. 27, no. 1, 2006, pp. 1–24

Buckle, George Earle, ed., *The Letters of Queen Victoria*, 3rd ser., London, John Murray, 1931

Burnet, Gilbert, ed., *Bishop Burnet's History*, London, Samuel Bagster, 1815

Bush, M. L., *Noble Privilege*, Manchester, Manchester University Press, 1983

— *The English Aristocracy: A Comparative Synthesis*, Manchester, Manchester University Press, 1984

— *The Government Policy of Protector Somerset*, London, Edward Arnold, 1975

Butler, J. R. M., *Lord Lothian, Philip Kerr, 1882–1940*, London, St Martin's, 1960

Byrne, Muriel St Clare, *The Lisle Letters*, Chicago, University of Chicago Press, 1981

Cahill, Kevin, *Who Owns Britain*, Edinburgh, Canongate, 2001

Calendar of Patent Rolls 1441–6, London, HMSO, 1908

Calendar of State Papers Relating to English Affairs in the Archives of Venice, vol. 19, 1625–1626, London, HMSO, 1913

Cam, Helen M., 'The decline and fall of English feudalism', *History*, vol. 25, no. 99, 1940, pp. 216–33

— *Liberties and Communities in Medieval England*, Cambridge, Cambridge University Press, 1944

Campbell, Alistair, and Keynes, Simon, eds, *Encomium Emmae Reginae*, Cambridge, Cambridge University Press, 1998

Camplin, Jamie, *The Rise of the Plutocrats*, London, Constable, 1978

Cannadine, David, 'Aristocratic indebtedness in the nineteenth century: the case reopened', *Economic History Review*, 2nd ser., vol. 30, no. 4, 1977, pp. 624–50

— *Aspects of Aristocracy: Grandeur and Decline in Modern Britain*, New Haven, CT, Yale University Press, 1994

— *The Decline and Fall of the British Aristocracy*, New Haven, CT, Yale University Press, 1990; London, Macmillan, 1992

— *Lords and Landlords, the Aristocracy and the Towns, 1774–1967*, Leicester, Leicester University Press, 1980

Cannon, John, *Aristocratic Century: The Peerage of Eighteenth Century England*, Cambridge, Cambridge University Press, 1984

— *Parliamentary Reform, 1640–1832*, Cambridge, Cambridge University Press, 1972

— *The Whig Ascendancy: Colloquies on Hanoverian England*, London, Edward Arnold, 1981

Carlyle, Thomas, *Past and Present*, London, Chapman & Hall, 1843

Carnegie, Andrew, *An American Four-in-Hand in Britain*, New York, Charles Scribner's Sons, 1887

— *Autobiography*, London, Constable, 1920

Carpenter, Edward, *British Aristocracy and the House of Lords*, London, A. C. Field, 1908

Carr, Cecil, ed., *Select Charters of Trading Companies*, London, Selden Society, 1913

Cartwright, James Joel, ed., *The Wentworth Papers, 1705–39*, London, Wyman, 1883

Cartwright, John, *Letter to Mr Lambton*, London, T. Dolby, 1820

Catalogue of the Curious Collection of Pictures of George Villiers, London, Brian Fairfax, 1758

Chadwick, Nora Kershaw, ed. and trans., *Anglo-Saxon and Norse Poems*, Cambridge, Cambridge University Press, 1922

Chalmers, Alexander, ed., *The Works of the English Poets*, London, J. Johnson, 1810

Chalus, Elaine, *Elite Women in English Political Life*, Oxford, Clarendon Press, 2005

Charmley, John, *A History of Conservative Politics since 1830*, London, Macmillan, 2008

Chibnall, Marjorie, ed. and trans., *The Ecclesiastical History of Orderic Vitalis*, Oxford, Oxford University Press, 1969

Chrimes, S. B., ed., *Fifteenth Century England, 1399–1509*, Manchester, Manchester University Press, 1972

Christie, Christopher, *The British Country House in the 18th Century*, Manchester, Manchester University Press, 1999

Churchill, Lord Randolph, *Speeches*, London, Longmans, Green, 1889

Clemenson, H. A., *English Country Houses and Landed Estates*, London, Croom Helm, 1982

Clesham, Brigid, 'Lord Altamont's letters to Lord Lucan about the Act of Union 1800', *Journal of the Galway Archaeological and Historical Society*, vol. 54, 2002, pp. 25–34.

Coates, Thomas, ed., *Lord Rosebery, His Life and Speeches*, London, Hutchinson, 1900

Cobbett, William, *Parliamentary History of England*, 35 vols, London, T. C. Hansard, 1806–20

Cockayne, George Edward, ed., *The Complete Peerage*, London, George Bell, 1889

Colley, L., *In Defiance of Oligarchy: The Tory Party 1714–1760*, Cambridge, Cambridge University Press, 1982

Collins, Anthony, ed., *A Collection of Several Pieces of Mr John Locke*, London, R. Francklin, 1739

Conford, Philip, 'Organic society: agriculture and radical politics in the career of Gerard Wallop, Earl of Portsmouth (1898–1984), *Agricultural History Review*, vol. 52, no. 1, 2004

Coombe, William, *An Heroic Epistle to the Right Honourable the Lord Craven*, London, John Wheble, 1775

Coward, B., *The Stanleys, 1395–1672*, Manchester, Manchester University Press, 1982

Cowell, Andrew, *The Medieval Warrior Aristocracy: Gifts, Violence, Performance, and the Sacred*, Woodbridge, Brewer, 2007

Craik, George Lillie, *Romance of the Peerage*, London, Chapman & Hall, 1849

Croft, Henry Herbert, ed., *The Book Named The Governor*, London, Dent, 1880

Crouch, David, *The Birth of Nobility: Constructing Aristocracy in England and France, 900–1300*, Harlow, Longman, 2005

— *The English Aristocracy, 1070–1272: a social transformation*, New Haven, CT, Yale University Press, 2011

Cunningham, Peter, ed., *The Letters of Horace Walpole, Earl of Orford*, London, Richard Bentley, 1857

Cust, Richard, *Charles I and the Aristocracy, 1625–1642*, Cambridge, Cambridge University Press, 2013

Daley, James, ed., *Great Inaugural Addresses*, Mineola, NY, Dover, 2012

Dangerfield, George, *The Strange Death of Liberal England*, London, Transaction, 2011

Darlington, R. R., and McGurk, P., eds; J. Bray and P. McGurk, trans., *The Chronicle of John of Worcester*, Oxford, Clarendon Press, 1995

Dasent, John Roche, ed., *Acts of the Privy Council*, vol. 8, London, HMSO, 1894

Davenport, Beatrice Cary, ed., *A Diary of the French Revolution by Gouverneur Morris 1752–1816*, Boston, Houghton Mifflin, 1939

Dean, D., 'Elizabethan government and politics', in R. Tittler and N. Jones, eds, *A Companion to Tudor England*, Oxford, Oxford University Press, 2004

BIBLIOGRAPHY

The Debates in Parliament on the Resolutions and Bill for the Abolition of Slavery, London, Maurice, 1834

Devonshire, Deborah, *Home to Roost, and Other Peckings*, London, John Murray, 2009

Dickinson, H. T., ed., *The Political Works of Thomas Spence*, London, Avero, 1982

Dobree, Bonamy, ed., *The Letters of Philip Dormer Stanhope, 4th Earl of Chesterfield*, London, Eyre & Spottiswoode, 1932

Douglas, David, and Greenaway, George, eds, *English Historical Documents, 1042–1189*, London, Routledge, 1981

Douglas, Roy, *Land, People and Politics*, London, St Martin's, 1976

Dover, Lord, and Wright, J., eds, *The Letters of Horace Walpole, Earl of Orford*, London, Richard Bentley, 1840

Downer, L. J., ed., *Leges Henrici Primi*, Oxford, Clarendon Press, 1972

Doyle, William, *Aristocracy and its Enemies in the Age of Revolution*, Oxford, Oxford University Press, 2009

— *Aristocracy: A Very Short Introduction*, Oxford, Oxford University Press, 2010

Dunham, William Huse, 'William Camden's commonplace book', *Yale University Library Gazette*, vol. 43, 1969

Dunn, Alastair, *The Politics of Magnate Power in England and Wales, 1389–1413*, Oxford, Clarendon Press, 2003

du Parcq, Herbert, ed., *Life of David Lloyd George*, vol. 4: *Speeches*, London, Caxton, 1912

Ellis, Henry, ed., *Chronica Johannis de Oxenedes*, Rolls Series 13, London, Longmans et al., 1859

— *Hall's Chronicle*, London, J. Johnson et al., 1809

Ernle, Lord, *Whippingham to Westminster*, London, John Murray, 1938

Ferguson, A. B., *The Indian Summer of English Chivalry*, Durham, NC, Duke University Press, 1960

Firth, C. H., *The House of Lords during the Civil War*, London, Methuen, 1974

— ed., *Macaulay's History of England*, London, Macmillan, 1914

Fitzgerald, Brian, ed., *Correspondence of Emily Duchess of Leinster*, 3 vols, Dublin, Irish Manuscripts Commission, 1949–67

Fleming, Robert, *Domesday Book and the Law*, Cambridge, Cambridge University Press, 1998

Forbes Gray, W., ed., *Comments and Characters by John Buchan*, London, Thomas Nelson, 1940

Forester, Thomas, ed. and trans., *The Chronicle of Henry of Huntingdon*, London, Henry Bohn, 1853

— *Orderic Vitalis, The Ecclesiastical History of England and Normandy*, London, Henry Bohn, 1854

Forster, Henry Rumsey, *The Stowe Catalogue, Priced and Annotated*, London, David Bogue, 1848

Fortescue, Sir John, ed., *The Correspondence of King George the Third*, London, Macmillan, 1927

Gairdner, James, ed., *Letters and Papers Foreign and Domestic, Henry VIII*, vol. 8, London, HMSO, 1885

— *Letters and Papers Foreign and Domestic, Henry VIII*, vol. 12, London, 1891

— and Brodie, R. H., eds, *Letters and Papers Foreign and Domestic, Henry VIII*, vol. 17, London, 1900

Gardiner, S. R., *History of the Great Civil War*, London, Longmans, Green, 1901

Gaskell, Charles Milne, 'The Country Gentleman', *Nineteenth Century*, Sept. 1882

Giles, J. A., ed., *The Anglo-Saxon Chronicle*, London, G. Bell, 1914

— *William of Malmesbury's Chronicle of the Kings of England*, London, Henry Bohn, 1847

— and trans., *Matthew Paris's English History*, London, Henry Bohn, 1854

— and trans., *Roger of Wendover's Flowers of History*, London, Henry Bohn, 1849

Gilfillan, George, ed., *The Poetical Works of Edmund Spenser*, Edinburgh, James Nichol, 1849

Given-Wilson, Chris, *The English Nobility in the Late Middle Ages: The Fourteenth Century Political Community*, London, Routledge & Kegan Paul, 1987

— Kettle, Ann, and Scales, Len, eds, *War, Government and Aristocracy in the British Isles, c.1150–1500*, Woodbridge, Boydell, 2008

Gleichen, Helena, *Contacts and Contrasts*, London, John Murray, 1940

Gliddon, Gerald, *The Aristocracy and the Great War*, Norwich, Gliddon, 2002

Godwin, G. N., *The Civil War in Hampshire*, Southampton, Henry March Gilbert, 1904

Goldsmith, Oliver, *The Life of Henry St John, Lord Viscount Bolingbroke*, London, T. Davies, 1770

Goodrich, Amanda, *Debating England's Aristocracy in the 1790s*, Woodbridge, Boydell, 2005

Gordon-Lennox, Lady Algernon, *Diary of Lord Bertie of Thame*, London and New York, George H. Doran, 1924

Granville, Countess, Castalia [C. R. Leveson-Gower], ed., *Lord Granville Leveson Gower: Private Correspondence, 1781–1821*, London, John Murray, 1916

Green, Mary Anne Everett, ed., *Calendar, Committee for Compounding*, London, HMSO, 1890

Greenway, Diana E., ed., *Charters of the Honour of Mowbray 1107–1191*, Oxford, Oxford University Press, 1972

Greig, James, ed., *The Farington Diary*, London, Hutchinson, 1926

Greville, Charles C. F., *A Journal of the Reigns of King George IV and King William IV*, London, Longmans, Green, 1874

Grey, Anchitell, ed., *Debates of the House of Commons*, London, D. Henry & R. Cave, 1763

Grigg, John, '"Crawfie", Sir Henry Marten', *National and English Review*, Aug. 1957

Gronow, Rees Howell, *Celebrities of London and Paris*, London, Smith, Elder, 1865

Habakkuk, H. J., 'The rise and fall of English landed families, 1600–1800', *Transactions of the Royal Historical Society*, 5th series, vol. 29, 1979, pp. 187–208

Hamilton, Douglas J., ed., *Jacobitism, Enlightenment and Empire*, Abingdon, Routledge, 2016

Hamilton, J. S., *Piers Gaveston*, Detroit, MI, Wayne State University Press, 1988

Hampden, John (pseud. William Howitt), *The Aristocracy of England: A History for the People*, London, Chapman Brothers, 1845

Harding, A., *Medieval Law and the Foundation of the State*, Oxford, Oxford University Press, 2002

Hare, Francis, *A Sermon Preached to the Societies for Reformation of Manners*, London, 1731

Harris, Barbara J., *English Aristocratic Women, 1450–1550*, Oxford, Oxford University Press, 2002

— *Edward Stafford, Third Duke of Buckingham, 1478–1521*, Stanford, CA, Stanford University Press, 1986

Harris, John, ed., *Trials for Adultery*, London, S. Bladon, 1780

Harris, Nicolas, ed., *Memoirs of the Life and Times of Sir Christopher Hatton*, London, Richard Bentley, 1847

Hastings, Jacob, Baron, ed., *An Account of the Controversy between Lord Grey of Ruthyn and Edward Hastings in the Court of Chivalry*, London, College of Arms, 1841

Hearne, Thomas, ed., *Liber Niger Scaccarii*, Oxford, 1728

Hervey, Mary, *The Life, Correspondence and Collections of Thomas Howard, Earl of Arundel*, Cambridge, Cambridge University Press, 1921,

Heward, Edmund, *Lord Mansfield: A Biography of William Murray 1st Earl of Mansfield 1705–1793 Lord Chief Justice for 32 years*, Chichester, Barry Rose, 1979

Hibbard, C., 'Theatre of destiny', in R. M. Smuts, ed., *The Stuart Court and Europe*, Cambridge, Cambridge University Press, 1996

Hieover, Harry (pseud. Charles Brindley), *The Hunting-Field*, London, Longman, Brown, 1850

Hilderley, Janet, *Mrs Catherine Gladstone*, Eastbourne, Alpha, 2012

Hill, Christopher, *The World Turned Upside Down*, London, Penguin, 1972

Hoare, Richard Colt, *Heytesbury Hundred*, London, John Bowyer Nichols, 1824

Holden, Anthony J., and Crouch, David, eds; Stewart Gregory, trans., *History of William Marshal*, 2 vols, Oxford, Anglo-Norman Text Society, 2002–6

Holinshed, Ralph, *Chronicles of England, Scotland and Ireland*, London, J. Johnson, 1807

Hollingsworth, T. H., 'A demographic study of the British ducal families', *Population Studies*, vol. 11, no. 1, 1957

Holmes, G. A., *The Estates of the Higher Nobility in Fourteenth Century England*, Cambridge, Cambridge University Press, 1957

Home, James A., ed., *Lady Louisa Stuart, Selections from her Manuscripts*, Edinburgh, David Douglas, 1899

Horn, Pamela, *Ladies of the Manor*, Stroud, Amberley, 2012

Howell, T. B., ed., *A Complete Collection of State Trials*, London, Hansard, 1816

Howitt, William, *Visits to Remarkable Places*, London, Longman, Orme, Brown et al., 1840

Howlett, Richard, ed., *Chronicles of the Reigns of Stephen, Henry II and Richard I*, Cambridge, Cambridge University Press, 2012

Huggins, Mike, *Flat Racing and British Society*, Abingdon, Routledge, 2013

Hyde, Edward, earl of Clarendon, *The History of the Rebellion*, Oxford, Clarendon Press, 1826

Ilchester, Lord, ed., *Letters to Henry Fox, Lord Holland*, London, Roxburghe Club, 1915

Jackson, K. H., ed. and trans., *The Gaelic Notes in the Book of Deer*, Cambridge, Cambridge University Press, 1972

James, Henry, *English Hours*, London, Heinemann, 1905

James, Lawrence, *Aristocrats: Power, Grace and Decadence*, London, Little, Brown, 2009

Jennings, Louis J., ed., *Correspondence and Diaries of the Late Rt Hon. John Wilson Croker*, London, 1885

Jensen, Gerard Edward, ed., *The Covent Garden Journal*, Oxford, Oxford University Press, 1915

Johns, Susan M., *Noblewomen, Aristocracy and Power in the Twelfth-Century Anglo-Norman Realm*, Manchester, Manchester University Press, 2003

Johnson, Charles, ed., *Dialogus de Scaccario*, Oxford, Clarendon Press, 1983

Jones, Emrys, ed., *Henry Howard, Earl of Surrey: Poems*, Oxford, Oxford University Press, 1964

Jonson, Ben, *The Works*, London, Thomas Hodgkin, 1692

A Journal of the Siege of Lathom House, London, Harding, Mavor & Lepard, 1823

Kelch, R. A., *Newcastle: A Duke without Money*, London, Routledge & Kegan Paul, 1974

Kenyon, J. P., *The Nobility and the Revolution of 1688*, Hull, University of Hull Publications, 1963

Kershaw, Ian, *Making Friends with Hitler: Lord Londonderry and Britain's Road to War*, London, Penguin, 2004

Knox, Vicesimus, *Essays Moral and Literary*, Dublin, 1783

Lambert, Angela, *Unquiet Souls: The Indian Summer of the British Aristocracy*, London, Macmillan, 1984

Lamoine, Georges, ed., *Charges to the Grand Jury, 1689–1803*, Camden Society, 4th ser., vol. 43, London, Royal Historical Society, 1992

Lander, J. R., *Crown and Nobility, 1450–1509*, Oxford, Oxford University Press, 1976

Lapidge, Michael, ed., *Byrhtferth of Ramsey, The Lives of Saint Oswald and Saint Ecgwine*, Oxford, Oxford University Press, 2009

Large, David Clay, *Nazi Games: The Olympics of 1936*, New York, Norton, 2007

Lassiter, J. C., 'Defamation of peers: the rise and decline of the action of Scandalum Magnatum, 1497–1773', *American Journal of Legal History*, vol. 22, 1978, pp. 216–36.

Law, Susan Carolyn, *Through the Keyhole: Sex, Scandal and the Secret Life of the Country House*, Stroud, History Press, 2015

Lees-Milne, James, *People and Places*, London, John Murray, 1992

Lemay, Edna Hindie, ed., *Dictionnaire des Constituents, 1789–91*, Paris, Universitas, 1991

Leveson Gower, Hon. F., ed., *Letters of Harriet, Countess Granville*, London, Longmans, Green, 1894

Linnane, Fergus, *The Lives of the English Rakes*, London, Portrait, 2006

Lockyer, Roger, *Buckingham: The Life and Career of George Villiers, First Duke of Buckingham*, London, Longman, 1981

Lodge, Edmund, ed., *Portraits of Illustrious Personages*, London, Harding & Lepard, 1835

LoGerfo, James, 'Sir William Dolben and "the cause of humanity": the passage of the Slave Trade Regulation Act of 1788', *Eighteenth-Century Studies*, vol. 6, no. 4, 1973, pp. 431–51

MacCaffrey, W. T., 'England, the crown and the new aristocracy, 1540–1600', *Past and Present*, vol. 30, no. 1, 1965, pp. 52–64

McCahill, M. W., 'Peerage creations and the changing character of the British nobility, 1750–1830', *English Historical Review*, vol. 96, no. 379, 1981, pp. 259–84

McCahill, Michael, and Archer Wasson, Ellis, 'The new peerage: recruitment to the House of Lords, 1704–1847', *Historical Journal*, vol. 46, no. 1, March 2003

MacCarthy, Fiona, *Last Curtsey: The End of the Debutantes*, London, Faber, 2007

McClure, Norman Egbert, ed., *The Letters of John Chamberlain*, 2 vols, Philadelphia, American Philosophical Society, 1939

— ed., *The Epigrams of Sir John Harington*, Philadelphia, University of Pennsylvania Press, 1926

McFarlane, K. B., *The Nobility of Later Medieval England*, Oxford, Oxford University Press, 1973

MacLeod, Catherine, and Alexander, Julia Marciari, *Painted Ladies: Women at the Court of Charles II*, London, National Portrait Gallery, 2001

McLeod, Donald, *Gloomy Memories in the Highlands of Scotland*, Glasgow, Archibald Sinclair, 1892

Macray, W. D., *Chronicon Abbatiae de Ramsey*, London, Rolls Series, 1886

Maddicott, J. R., *Simon de Montfort*, Cambridge, Cambridge University Press, 1994

— *Thomas of Lancaster, 1307–1322*, Oxford, Oxford University Press, 1970

Mandler, Peter, *The Fall and Rise of the Stately Home*, New Haven, CT, Yale University Press, 1997

Manning, B. S., 'The aristocracy and the downfall of Charles I', in *Politics, Religion and the English Civil War*, London, Edward Arnold, 1973

Martrions, S. W., *A Great Estate at Work: The Holkham Estate and its Inhabitants in the Nineteenth Century*, Cambridge, Cambridge University Press, 1980

Masterman, C. F. G., *England after War*, London, Hodder & Stoughton, 1922

Maxwell, Herbert, ed., *The Creevey Papers*, London, John Murray, 1904

Michel, Francisque, ed., *Histoire des ducs de Normandie et des rois d'Angleterre*, Paris, Jules Renouard, 1840

Miller, E., and Hatcher, J., *Medieval England, 1086–1348*, London, Longmans, 1995

Mingay, G. E., *English Landed Society in the Eighteenth Century*, London, Routledge & Kegan Paul, 1963

Mitford, Nancy, 'The English aristocracy', *Encounter*, Sept. 1955

— *The Stanleys of Alderley*, London, Hamish Hamilton, 1939

Montagu, George, *The Sportsman's Dictionary*, London, G. G. J. and J. Robinson, 1792

Montagu, Matthew, ed., *The Letters of Mrs Elizabeth Montagu*, Boston, Wells & Lilly, 1825

Moore, D. C., *The Politics of Deference*, Hassocks, Harvester, 1976

Moore, Thomas, ed., *The Life of Lord Byron*, London, John Murray, 1844

Morgan, D. H. J., 'The social and educational background of Anglican bishops', *British Journal of Sociology*, vol. 20, no. 3, 1969, pp. 295–310

Morris, Anne Cary, ed., *The Diary and Letters of Gouverneur Morris*, New York, Charles Scribner, 1888

Mortlock, D. P., *Aristocratic Splendour: Money and the World of Thomas Coke Earl of Leicester*, Stroud, Sutton, 2007

Morton, Catherine, and Muntz, Hope, eds, *The Carmen de Hastingi Proelio of Guy, bishop of Amiens*, Oxford, Clarendon Press, 1972

Munsche, P. B., *Poachers and Gentlemen, The English Game Laws, 1671–1831*, Cambridge, Cambridge University Press, 1981

Murland, Jerry, *Aristocrats Go to War: Uncovering the Zillebeke Churchyard Cemetery*, Barnsley, Pen & Sword Military, 2010

Murray's Handbook for Shropshire, Cheshire and Lancashire, London, John Murray, 1870

Naylor, John Francis, ed., *The British Aristocracy and the Peerage Bill of 1719*, Oxford, Oxford University Press, 1968

Newby, H., *Property, Paternalism and Power: Class and Control in Rural England*, London, Hutchinson, 1978

Nicholas, N. H., ed., *Proceedings and Ordinances of the Privy Council of England*, London, Commissioner of Public Records, 1834

Nicolas, Harris, ed., *Memoirs of the Life and Times of Sir Christopher Hatton*, London, Richard Bentley, 1847

North, Dudley (Lord North), *A Forest of Varieties*, London, 1645

Oldfield, Susan, *Some Records of the Later Life of Harriet, Countess Granville*, London, Longmans, Green, 1901

Olson, A., *The Radical Duke*, Oxford, Oxford University Press, 1961

Orme, Nicholas, *From Childhood to Chivalry: The Education of the English Kings and Aristocracy 1066–1530*, London, Methuen, 1984

Osborne, Joseph, ed., *The Horse-Breeder's Handbook*, London, Edmund Seale, 1898

Papers Presented to the House of Commons on the 7th May 1804 Respecting the Slave Trade, London, 1804

Parent, Anthony S., *Foul Means: The Formation of a Slave Society in Virginia, 1660–1740*, Chapel Hill, NC, Omohundro Institute of Early American History and Culture, University of North Carolina, 2003

The Parliamentary History of England from the Earliest Period to the Year 1803, London, T. C. Hansard, 1813

Pearse, Edward, *Pitt the Elder, Man of War*, London, Pimlico, 2011

Pease, T. C., *The Leveller Movement*, Washington DC, American Historical Association, 1916

Peck, Linda Levy, *Consuming Splendor*, Cambridge, Cambridge University Press, 2005

Percy, Eustace, *Some Memories*, London, Eyre & Spottiswoode, 1958

Pevsner, Nikolaus, *Buildings of England: Derbyshire*, London, Penguin, 1978

Pike, L. O., *A Constitutional History of the House of Lords*, London, Macmillan, 1884

Pimlott, Ben, *Hugh Dalton*, London, Jonathan Cape, 1985

Plowden, Alison, *Women All On Fire*, Stroud, Sutton, 1998

Pollard, A. J., ed., *Property and Politics: Essays in Later Medieval English History*, Stroud, Sutton, 1984

Ponsonby, Arthur, *The Decline of Aristocracy*, London, Fisher Unwin, 1912

Pope, M. K., and Lodge, E. C., *The Chandos Herald's Life of the Black Prince*, Oxford, Oxford University Press, 1910

Portsmouth, earl of, *A Knot of Roots*, London, Geoffrey Bles, 1965

Powis, Jonathan, *Aristocracy*, Oxford, Blackwell, 1984

Prestwich, Michael, ed., *Liberties and Identities in the Medieval British Isles*, Woodbridge, Boydell, 2008

Pye, John, *Patronage of British Art*, London, Longman, Brown, Green & Longmans, 1845

Raine, James, ed., *Testamenta Eboracensia*, London, J. B. Nichols, 1836

Raithby, John, ed., *Statutes of the Realm*, London, Eyre & Spottiswoode, 1870

Reeve, H., ed., *The Greville Memoirs*, 8 vols, London, Longmans, Green, 1899

Reformation Necessary to Prevent Our Ruine: A Sermon Preached to the Societies for Reformation of Manners, at St Mary-le-Bow, on Wednesday, January 10th, 1727, London, Joseph Downing, 1728

Reid, R. R., 'Barony and thanage', *English Historical Review*, vol. 35, no. 138, 1920, pp. 161–99

Reports from the Lords Committee Touching the Dignity of a Peer of the Realm, London, House of Lords, 1829

Reynolds, K. D., *Aristocratic Women and Political Society in Victorian Britain*, Oxford, Clarendon, 1998

Rhodes James, Robert, ed., *Chips: The Diaries of Sir Henry Channon*, London, Weidenfeld & Nicolson, 1967

Richards, E., *The Leviathan of Wealth: The Sutherland Fortune in the Industrial Revolution*, London, Routledge, 1973

Riley, Henry T., ed., *Gesta Abbatum Monasterii Sancti Albani, a Thoma Walsingham*, London, Rolls Series 28 (1867–9)

Roberts, Andrew, *The Holy Fox*, London, Weidenfeld & Nicolson, 1991

Robertson, A. J., ed., *Anglo-Saxon Charters*, Cambridge, Cambridge University Press, 1956

— *The Laws of the Kings of England from Edmund to Henry I*, Oxford, Oxford University Press, 1925

Robertson, Joseph, ed., *The Works of Algernon Sidney*, London, W. Strahan, 1772

Robinson, Lionel, ed., *Letters of Dorothea, Princess Lieven*, London, Longmans, Green, 1902

Romei, Annibale, *The Courtiers Academie*, trans. John Keper, London, 1598

Ross, Alan S. C.; Mitford, Nancy; Waugh, Evelyn; 'Strix'; Sykes, Christopher; and Betjeman, John, *Noblesse Oblige: An Enquiry Into the Identifiable Characteristics of the English Aristocracy*, Oxford, Oxford University Press, 2002 (first publ. 1956)

Rotuli Parliamentorum, London, 1832

Royal Commission on Historical Manuscripts, *Fourteenth Report*, London, 1896

Rubinstein, W. D., *Men of Property: The Very Wealthy in Britain since the Industrial Revolution*, London, Croom Helm, 1981

Rushworth, John, ed., *Historical Collections of Private Passages of State*, London, D. Browne, 1721

Rymer, Thomas, *Foedera*, London, Joannem Neulme, 1739

Sackville-West, Robert, *Inheritance: The Story of Knole and the Sackvilles*, London, Bloomsbury, 2010

Sanders, I. J., *English Baronies: A Study of their Origin and Descent, 1086–1327*, Oxford, Oxford University Press, 1960

Sawyer, Peter, ed., *Anglo-Saxon Charters: An Annotated List and Bibliography*, London, Royal Historical Society, 1963

Schutte, Kimberly, *Women, Rank, and Marriage in the British Aristocracy, 1485–2000: An Open Elite?*, Basingstoke, Palgrave Macmillan, 2014

Scragg, Donald, ed., *Edgar, King of the English*, Woodbridge, Boydell, 2008

Sedgwick, Romney, ed., *Lord Hervey's Memoirs*, London, William Kimber, 1952

Segar, Sir William, *Honor, Military and Civil*, Delmar, NY, Scholar's Facsimiles and Reprints, 1975

Sellar, A. M., ed., *Bede's Ecclesiastical History of England*, George Bell, London, 1907

Sermons and Homilies Appointed to be Read in Churches, London, Prayer Book and Homily Society, 1840

Shaw, William A., ed., *Calendar of Treasury Books*, London, 1904

Shippey, Thomas Alan, ed., *Poems of Wisdom and Learning in Old English*, Cambridge, Brewer, 1976

Simpkin, David, *The English Aristocracy at War: From the Welsh Wars of Edward I to the Battle of Bannockburn*, Woodbridge, Boydell & Brewer, 2008

Slater, Victor, *High Life, Low Morals: The Duel that Shook Stuart Society*, London, John Murray, 1999

Smith, E. A., *Whig Principles and Party Politics: Earl Fitzwilliam and the Whig Party, 1718–1833*, Manchester, Manchester University Press, 1975

Smith, Lucy Toulmin, ed., *Leland's Itinerary in England and Wales*, London, George Bell, 1907

Smollett, Tobias, *History of England*, London, R. Scholey, 1810

Smythe, E. A., Viscountess Strangford, ed., *Angela Pisani*, London, Richard Bentley, 1875

Spencer, Andrew, *Nobility and Kingship in Medieval England: The Earls and Edward I, 1272–1307*, Cambridge, Cambridge University Press, 2013

Spring, D., 'Aristocracy, social structure and religion in the early Victorian period', *Victorian Studies*, vol. 6, no. 3, 1963, pp. 263–80

Spring, Eileen, *Law, Land, and Family: Aristocratic Inheritance in England, 1300 to 1800*, Chapel Hill, NC, University of Carolina Press, 1993

Squibb, G. D., *Precedence in England and Wales*, Oxford, Oxford University Press, 1981

Stevenson, John, *Popular Disturbances in England, 1700–1870*, London, Longman, 1979

Stevenson, Joseph, ed. and trans., *The Church Historians of England*, London, Seeleys, 1853–6

Stone, Lawrence, *The Crisis of the Aristocracy, 1558–1641*, Oxford, Oxford University Press, 1965

— *The Family, Sex and Marriage in England, 1500–1800*, London, Weidenfeld & Nicolson, 1977

— 'Social mobility in England, 1500–1700', *Past and Present*, vol. 33, no. 1, 1966, pp. 16–55

Stow, John, *Annales or A General Chronicle of England*, London, 1603

Street, G. S., *People and Questions*, London, Martin Secker, 1910

Strong, Roy, *The Story of Britain: A People's History*, London, Jonathan Cape, 1996

Stubbs, William, ed., *Gesta Regis Henrici*, London, Longmans, Green, Reader and Dyer, 1867

Swanton, Michael, ed. and trans., *The Anglo-Saxon Chronicle*, London, Dent, 1996

Swatland, Andrew, *The House of Lords in the Reign of Charles II*, Cambridge, Cambridge University Press, 1996

Tardif, Ernest-Joseph, ed., *Coutumiers de Normandie*, Paris, A. Picard, 1903

Taylor, Antony, *Lords of Misrule: Hostility to Aristocracy in Late Nineteenth- and Early Twentieth-Century Britain*, Basingstoke, Palgrave Macmillan, 2004

Tennyson, Lionel, Lord, *From Verse to Worse*, London, Cassell, 1933

Thompson, Edward Maunde, ed., *Adæ Murimuth Continuatio Chronicarum*, London, Rolls Series, 1889

Thompson, Edward, ed., *The Works of Andrew Marvell*, London, Henry Baldwin, 1776

Thompson, F. M. L., 'The end of a great estate', *Economic History Review*, 2nd ser., vol. 8, 1955–6

— *English Landed Society in the Nineteenth Century*, London, Routledge & Kegan Paul, 1963

Thorpe, Benjamin, ed., *Ancient Laws and Institutes of England*, London, Commissioners of Public Records, 1840

Tittler, R., and Jones, N., eds, *A Companion to Tudor England*, Oxford, Oxford University Press, 2004

Tomkins, Isaac (pseud.), *Thoughts upon the Aristocracy of England*, London, Henry Hooper, 1835

Tomkins, Lydia (pseud.), *Thoughts on the Ladies of the Aristocracy*, London, Hodgsons, 1835

Tractatus de legibus et consuetudinibus regni Angliae vocatur Glanvilla, trans. John Beames, Washington DC, 1812

Treasury, HM, *Report of the Committee on Homes of Outstanding Historic or Architectural Interest*, London, HMSO, 23 June 1950

The Trial of James Thomas, Earl of Cardigan, London, William Brodie, 1841

The Trials of William Earl of Kilmarnock, London, R. Walker, 1746

Trumbach, Randolph, *The Rise of the Egalitarian Family: Aristocratic Kinship and Domestic Relations in Eighteenth Century England*, London, Academic Press, 1978

Tuck, Anthony, *Crown and Nobility, England 1272–1461*, Oxford, Blackwell, 1999

— *Richard II and the English Nobility*, London, Edward Arnold, 1973

Turbeville, A. S., 'Aristocracy and revolution, the British peerage, 1789–1832', *History*, vol. 26, no. 104, 1942, pp. 240–63

Vanderbilt Balsan, Consuelo, *The Glitter and the Gold*, London, Heinemann, 1953

Van Eerde, K. S., 'The creation of the baronetage in England', *Huntington Library Quarterly*, vol. 22, no. 4, 1959, pp. 313–22

Vincent, John, ed., *The Journal of David Lindsay, 27th Earl of Crawford*, Manchester, Manchester University Press, 1984

Waddy, N., 'Restoration by stages: The debate over the House of Lords during the reign of Richard Cromwell, 1658–59', *Parliaments, Estates and Representation*, vol. 24, no. 1, 2004, pp. 173–91

Wade, John, *The Black Book, or Corruption Unmasked!*, London, John Fairburn, 1820; London, Effingham Wilson, 1835

Walford, Edward, 'Mayfair', *Old and New London*, London, Cassell, Petter & Galpin, 1878

Waugh, Evelyn, *Brideshead Revisited*, Boston, Little, Brown, 1977 (first publ. 1944)

Wells, H. G., *The Works*, London, T. Fisher Unwin, 1924

Wetzel, David, *A Duel of Giants*, Madison, University of Wisconsin Press, 2001

Wheatley, H. B., ed., *The Historical and the Posthumous Memoirs of Sir Nathaniel William Wraxall, 1772–1784*, London, Bickers, 1884

Whitelock, Dorothy, ed. and trans., *Anglo-Saxon Wills*, Cambridge, Cambridge University Press, 1930

— *English Historical Documents*, 2nd edn, vol. 1, London, Eyre & Spottiswoode, 1979

Wightman, Andy, *The Poor Had No Lawyers*, Edinburgh, Birlinn, 2010

Willcox, William, *The Age of Aristocracy 1688 to 1830*, Boston, D. C. Heath, 1966

Williams, Ann, *The English and the Norman Conquest*, Woodbridge, Boydell & Brewer, 1996

Wilson, John Croker, ed., *Letters to and from Henrietta, Countess of Suffolk*, London, John Murray, 1824

Wilson, P., *The Greville Diary*, London, Heinemann, 1927

Woodfall, William, ed., *Parliamentary Reports*, London, T. Chapman, 1796

Worsthorne, Peregrine, *In Defence of Aristocracy*, London, HarperCollins, 2004

Wraxall, Sir Nathaniel, *Posthumous Memoirs of His Own Time*, London, Richard Bentley, 1836

Wright, John, ed., *The Letters of Horace Walpole, Earl of Orford*, Philadelphia, Lea & Blanchard, 1842

Wrightson, K., *English Society, 1580–1680*, London, Hutchinson, 1982

Yass, Marion, *The English Aristocracy*, London, Wayland, 1974

Ziolkowski, Jan M., ed. and trans., *The Cambridge Songs*, Tempe, AZ, Medieval and Renaissance Texts and Studies, 1998

Picture acknowledgements

In-text illustrations

p.xii: The marquess of Waterford. *Punch*, Vol. 1, July 24, 1841; p.12: Battle of Assandun, showing Edmund Ironside (*left*) and Cnut the Great. Master and Fellows of Corpus Christi College, Cambridge; p.36: King William I receives the allegiance of his nephew Alain le Roux, earl of Brittany, and grants him a charter of the Honour of Richmond. © The British Library Board; p.58: Robert Fitzwalter's seal die. © The Trustees of the British Museum; p.82: Drawing of the monument to Thomas de Beauchamp, 11th earl of Warwick and his wife Katherine Mortimer, countess of Warwick, Collegiate Church of St Mary, Warwick; p.106: Audley End, Essex. Engraving by Winstanley, 1688. Chronicle/Alamy Stock Photo; p.134: Portrait of Mervyn Tuchet, 2nd earl of Castlehaven. © The British Library Board; p.156: The Siege of Basing House, 1645, Wenceslaus Hollar. Private Collection/Bridgeman Images; p.174: robes worn by a baron and a duke during a 17th-century creation ceremony, Wenceslas Hollar. University of Toronto Wenceslaus Hollar Digital Collection; p.220: mock playbill reproduced from an original in the Borthwick Institute/Lascelles/Harewood West Indian Papers/Posters, University of York; p.236: Guillotines from the time of the French Revolution. Classic Image/Alamy Stock Photo; p.250: Cavendish performing volte, with Bolsover in the background. After Abraham Jansz van Diepenbeeck. Private Collection/The Stapleton Collection/ Bridgeman Images; p.268: Banqueting Hall, Haddon Hall, Derbyshire. Look and Learn/Bridgeman Images; p.288: Trentham Hall. Arthur Engazung/Deviant Art; p.314: Lord Montagu scrubbing the floors of Palace House, 1952. Motoring Picture Library/Alamy Stock Photo; p.334: Landlordism Causes Unemployment. Cornell University – PJ Mode Collection of Persuasive Cartography

First plate section

p.1: *The Life of King Edward the Confessor*, manuscript *c.*1250-60. Reproduced by kind permission of the Syndics of Cambridge University Library; miniature of Arthur in conversation with his barons. British Library, London, UK/© British Library Board. All Rights Reserved/Bridgeman Images. p.2: Jean Froissart, *Chroniques*. Brussels, KBR, Ms II 88, folio 8v. © Royal Library of Belgium; central illustration from the Black Book of the Garter, *c.*1534. Reproduced by kind permission of the Dean and Canons of Windsor. p.3: tomb of Roesia de Verdun, St John's Church, Belton. Colin Underhill/Alamy Stock Photo; Tewkesbury Abbey. Angelo Hornak/ Alamy Stock Photo. p.4: detail of the Parliamentary procession roll for Henry VII, 1512. British Library, London, UK/© British Library Board. All Rights Reserved/ Bridgeman Images; p.5: Sir Richard Rich, 1st Baron Rich of Leez. Druidic; Leez Priory, Essex. Alf Gris. p.6: George Villiers, 1st duke of Buckingham, attr. William Larkin, 1616. © National Portrait Gallery, London. p.7: *The cole-heavers*, James

Gillray, 1783. © The Trustees of the British Museum; *The Gordon-Knot, or The Bonny Duchess Hunting the Bedford Bull*, James Gillray. Courtesy of the Warden and Scholars of New College, Oxford/Bridgeman Images. **p.8:** *A Negro hung alive by the Ribs to a Gallows,* William Blake/Private Collection/Archives Charmet/Bridgeman Images; portrait of an African, prob. Ignatius Sancho (*c.* 1729–1780), Allan Ramsay. Royal Albert Memorial Museum, Exeter, Devon, UK/Bridgeman Images; Harewood House. Lee Beel/Alamy Stock Photo

Second plate section

p.1: *Emily Marchioness of Salisbury Taking the Field*, James Pollard, 1792–1867. Bequeathed by Mrs F. Ambrose Clark through the British Sporting Art Trust 1982. © Tate, London 2017; Wentworth Castle, design for south front, c.1760, John Platt. Leeds Museums and Galleries (Leeds Art Gallery) UK/Bridgeman Images; George Stubbs, *Whistlejacket.* © The National Gallery, London. Bought with the support of the Heritage Lottery Fund, 1997. **p.2:** Giovanna Francesca Antonia Guiseppe Zanerini, attr. Giovanni Battista Locatelli © National Trust / Jane Mucklow; Elizabeth Manners, duchess of Rutland, 1826, Matthew Cotes Wyatt/Belvoir Castle, Leicestershire, UK/Bridgeman Images. **p.3:** *The Humours of Belvoir Castle, or The Morning After*, Isaac Cruikshank, 1799. The Library of Congress. **p.4:** Chatsworth House. Dave Porter/Alamy Stock Photo; King Edward VII leaves Lismore Castle, c.1905. Hulton Archive/Getty Images; Bolton Abbey. CW Images/Alamy Stock Photo. **p.5:** Louise Frederica Augusta Cavendish, duchess of Devonshire, 1897. © National Portrait Gallery, London; *Lady Warwick and her son*, John Singer Sargent, 1905. Worcester Art Museum, Massachusetts, USA/Bridgeman Images. **p.6:** SAVE Mentmore for the Nation. Reproduced by kind permission of Save Britain's Heritage; Demolition of Devonshire House, Job Nixon, 1925. © The Trustees of the British Museum; dining room of Lansdowne House, 1767–1769, Robert Adam. Heritage Images/Getty Images. **p.7:** Hitler receiving Henry Vane-Tempest Stewart, marquess of Londonderry, on a private visit in Berlin. Ullsteinbild/Getty Images; Philip Kerr, 11th marquess of Lothian, 1940. John Frost Newspapers/Alamy Stock Photo. **p.8:** marquess of Cholmondeley at State Opening of Parliament.1988. Tim Graham/Getty Images; duke of Westminster, 2013. PA Photos/Topfoto; funeral cortege of 11th duke of Marlborough, 2014. Steve Parsons/PA Images; 4th Viscount St Davids, Rhodri Philipps, arriving at Westminster Magistrates' Court, July 2017. David Mirzoeff/PA Images

INDEX

INDEX

INDEX

DINNER of the FOUR IN HA